Shugo Chara!

10

PEACH-PIT

Translated by
Satsuki Yamashita

Lettered by
North Market Street Graphics

KC
KODANSHA
COMICS

A Kodansha Comics Trade Paperback Original.

Shugo Chara! volume 10 copyright © 2009 PEACH-PIT
English translation copyright © 2011 PEACH-PIT

Published in the United States by Kodansha Comics, an imprint of Kodansha USA Publishing, LLC., New York.

Publication rights for this English edition arranged through Kodansha Ltd., Tokyo.

First published in Japan in 2009 by Kodansha Ltd., Tokyo.

ISBN 978-1-935-42993-7

Original cover design by Akiko Omo.

Printed in the United States of America.

www.kodanshacomics.com

9 8 7 6 5 4 3 2 1

Translator: Satsuki Yamashita
Lettering: North Market Street Graphics

Contents

Honorifics Explained

Throughout the Kodansha Comics books, you will find Japanese honorifics left intact in the translations. For those not familiar with how the Japanese use honorifics and, more important, how they differ from American honorifics, we present this brief overview.

Politeness has always been a critical facet of Japanese culture. Ever since the feudal era, when Japan was a highly stratified society, use of honorifics—which can be defined as polite speech that indicates relationship or status—has played an essential role in the Japanese language. When addressing someone in Japanese, an honorific usually takes the form of a suffix attached to one's name (example: "Asuna-san"), is used as a title at the end of one's name, or appears in place of the name itself (example: "Negi-sensei," or simply "Sensei!").

Honorifics can be expressions of respect or endearment. In the context of manga and anime, honorifics give insight into the nature of the relationship between characters. Many English translations leave out these important honorifics and therefore distort the feel of the original Japanese. Because Japanese honorifics contain nuances that English honorifics lack, it is our policy at Kodansha Comics not to translate them. Here, instead, is a guide to some of the honorifics you may encounter in Kodansha Comics books.

-san: This is the most common honorific and is equivalent to Mr., Miss, Ms., or Mrs. It is the all-purpose honorific and can be used in any situation where politeness is required.

-sama: This is one level higher than "-san" and is used to confer great respect.

-dono: This comes from the word "tono," which means "lord." It is an even higher level than "-sama" and confers utmost respect.

-kun: This suffix is used at the end of boys' names to express familiarity or endearment. It is also sometimes used by men among friends, or when addressing someone younger or of a lower station.

-chan:	This is used to express endearment, mostly toward girls. It is also used for little boys, pets, and even among lovers. It gives a sense of childish cuteness.
Bozu:	This is an informal way to refer to a boy, similar to the English terms "kid" and "squirt."
Sempai/ Senpai:	This title suggests that the addressee is one's senior in a group or organization. It is most often used in a school setting, where underclassmen refer to their upperclassmen as "sempai." It can also be used in the workplace, such as when a newer employee addresses an employee who has seniority in the company.
Kohai:	This is the opposite of "sempai" and is used toward underclassmen in school or newcomers in the workplace. It connotes that the addressee is of a lower station.
Sensei:	Literally meaning "one who has come before," this title is used for teachers, doctors, or masters of any profession or art.
-[blank]:	This is usually forgotten in these lists, but it is perhaps the most significant difference between Japanese and English. The lack of honorific means that the speaker has permission to address the person in a very intimate way. Usually, only family, spouses, or very close friends have this kind of permission. Known as *yobisute,* it can be gratifying when someone who has earned the intimacy starts to call one by one's name without an honorific. But when that intimacy hasn't been earned, it can be very insulting.

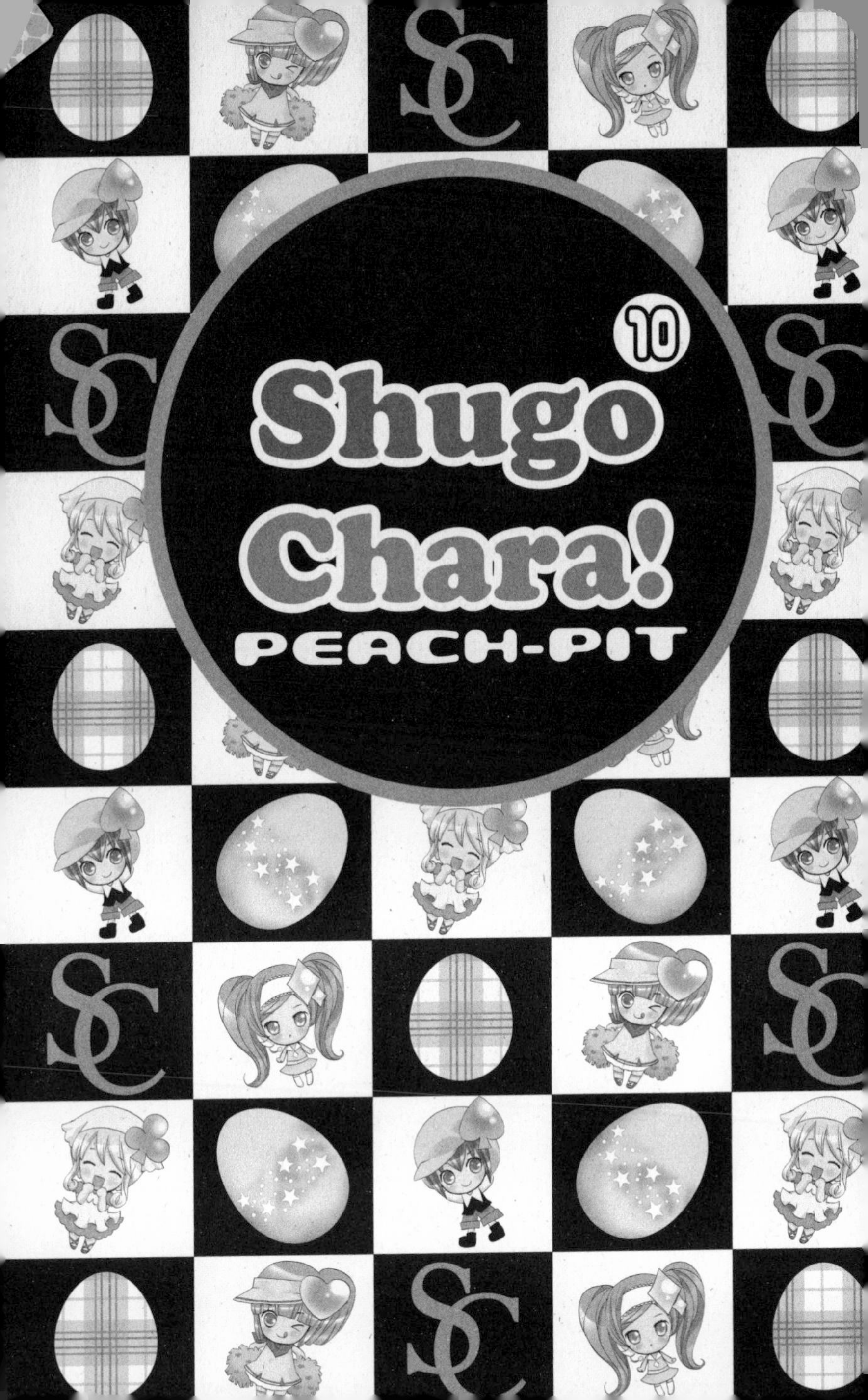
10
Shugo Chara!
PEACH-PIT

Character Introductions

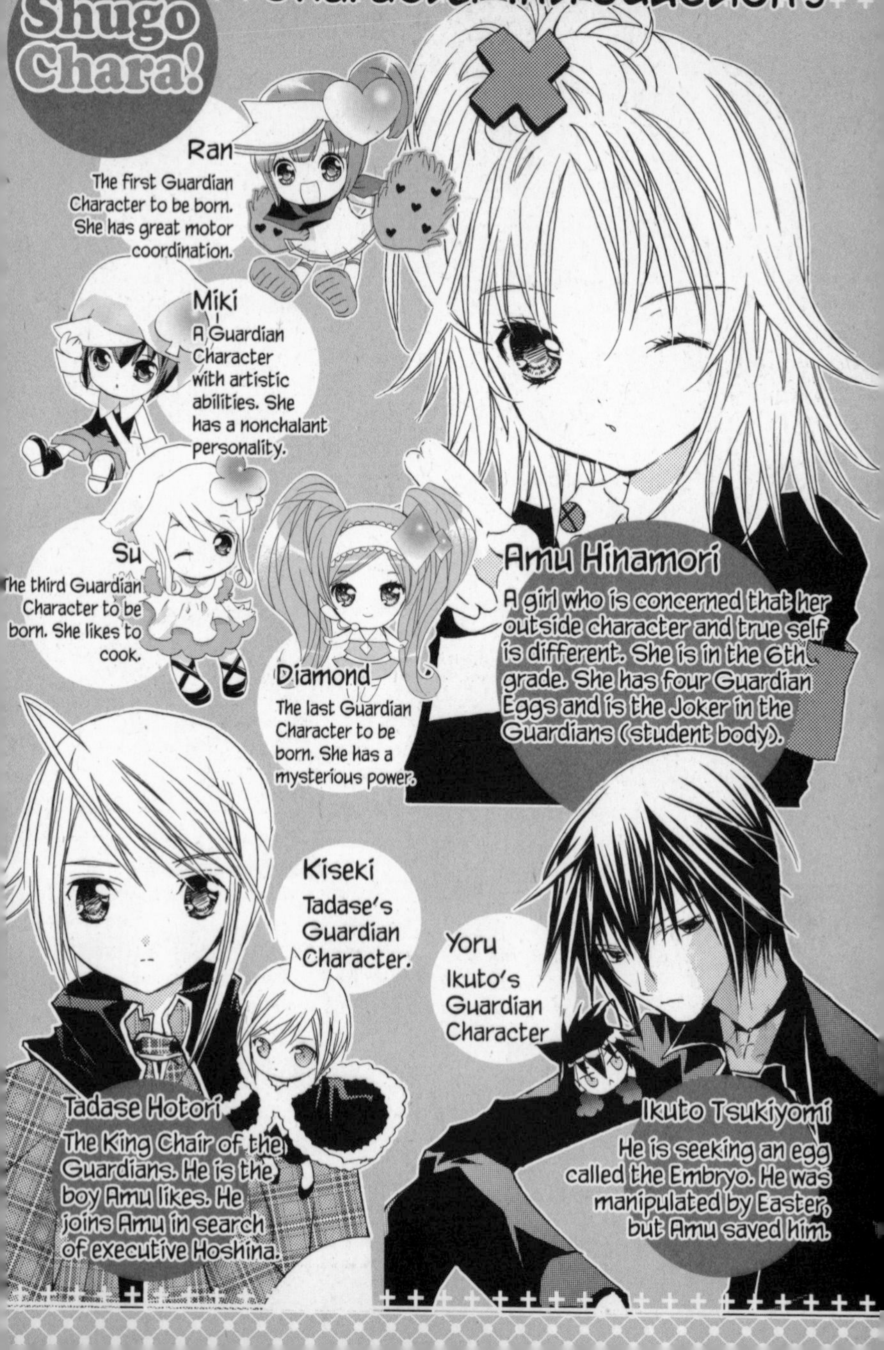
Shugo Chara!
Ran
The first Guardian Character to be born. She has great motor coordination.
Miki
A Guardian Character with artistic abilities. She has a nonchalant personality.
Su
The third Guardian Character to be born. She likes to cook.
Diamond
The last Guardian Character to be born. She has a mysterious power.
Amu Hinamori
A girl who is concerned that her outside character and true self is different. She is in the 6th grade. She has four Guardian Eggs and is the Joker in the Guardians (student body).
Kiseki
Tadase's Guardian Character.
Yoru
Ikuto's Guardian Character
Tadase Hotori
The King Chair of the Guardians. He is the boy Amu likes. He joins Amu in search of executive Hoshina.
Ikuto Tsukiyomi
He is seeking an egg called the Embryo. He was manipulated by Easter, but Amu saved him.

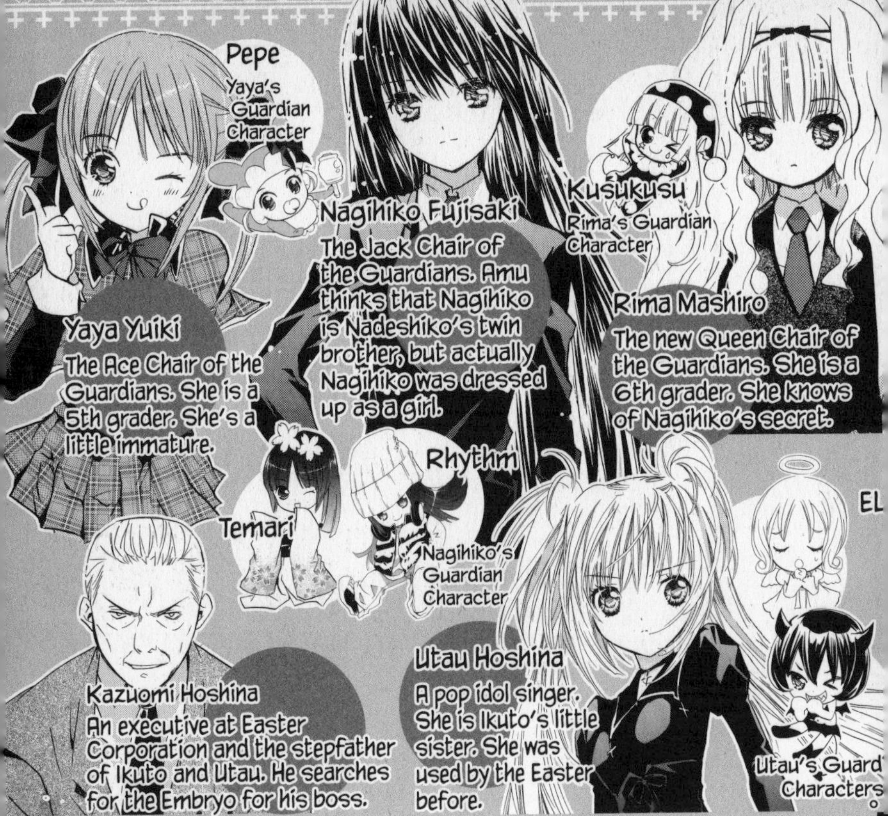

Pepe
Yaya's Guardian Character
Nagihiko Fujisaki
The Jack Chair of the Guardians. Amu thinks that Nagihiko is Nadeshiko's twin brother, but actually Nagihiko was dressed up as a girl.
Kusukusu
Rima's Guardian Character
Rima Mashiro
The new Queen Chair of the Guardians. She is a 6th grader. She knows of Nagihiko's secret.
Yaya Yuiki
The Ace Chair of the Guardians. She is a 5th grader. She's a little immature.
Rhythm
Temari
Nagihiko's Guardian Character
EL
Kazuomi Hoshina
An executive at Easter Corporation and the stepfather of Ikuto and Utau. He searches for the Embryo for his boss.
Utau Hoshina
A pop idol singer. She is Ikuto's little sister. She was used by the Easter before.
Utau's Guard Characters

The Story So Far

- Amu comes across as cool. But that isn't who she really is. Deep inside, she is shy and a little cynical. One day, she wished she could be more true to herself, and the next day she found three eggs in her bed!
- Ran, Miki, and Su each hatched from their eggs. They are Amu's "Guardian Characters." Amu was recruited to become one of the Guardians at Seiyo Academy, and ever since, she's become good friends with other Guardian Character holders.
- As the Joker of the Guardians, Amu's job is to find Heart's Eggs with X's on it and save them. But it seems that the Easter Corporation is looking for an egg known as the Embryo, and collecting countless X Eggs. Amu and the Guardians challenge the corporation in order to save Ikuto!
- In the middle of the battle, Amu found out about Ikuto's sad past. She hugged him and his manipulated heart returned to normal. The two Characters Transformed and purified many X Eggs! Among them was the Embryo!? But it was taken away by executive Hoshina. Now Amu, Ikuto, and Tadase need to get it back before he takes it to the boss!

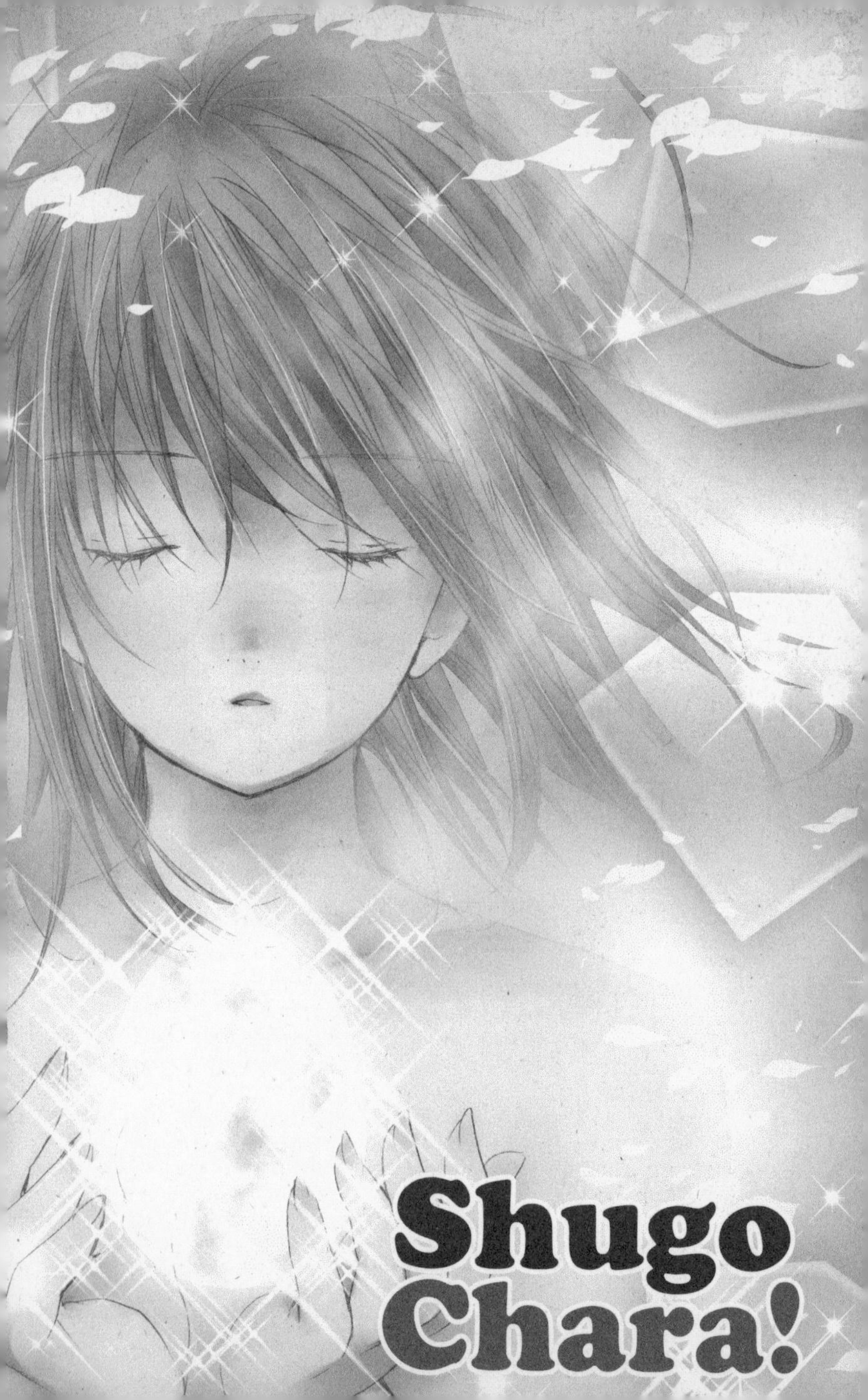
Shugo
Chara!

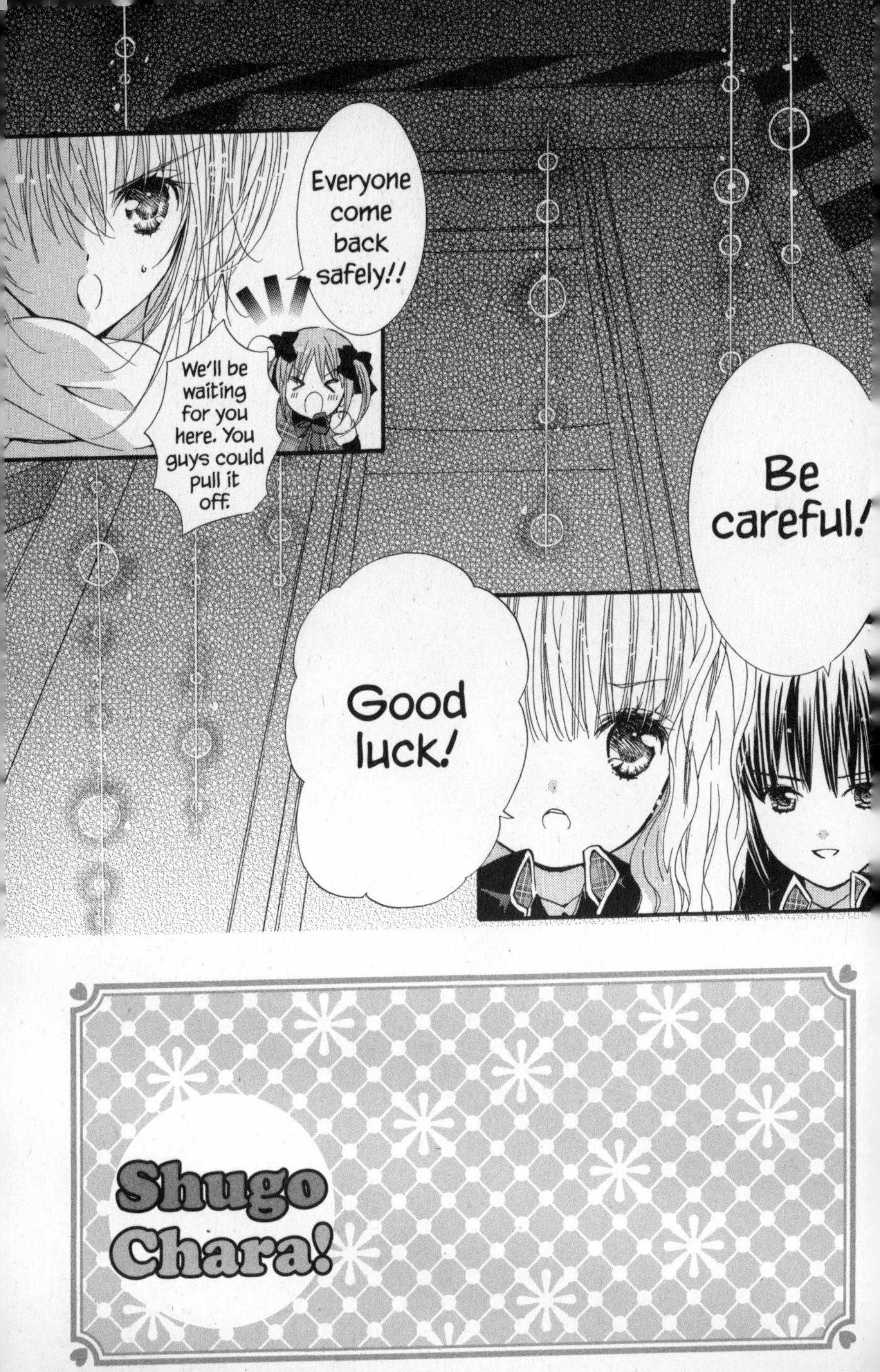
Everyone come back safely!!
We'll be waiting for you here. You guys could pull it off.
Be careful!
Good luck!

Shugo Chara!

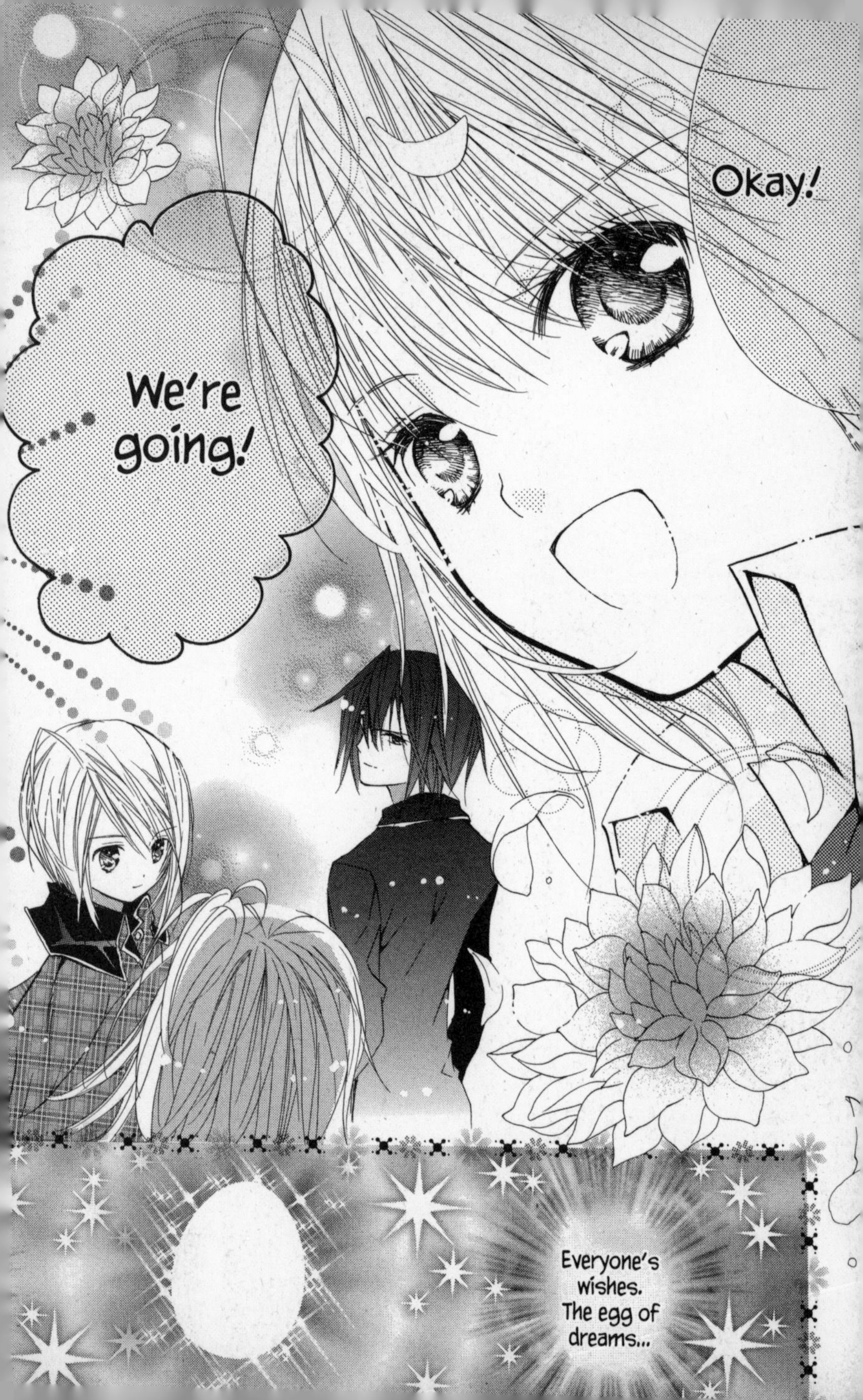
Okay!
We're going!
Everyone's wishes. The egg of dreams...

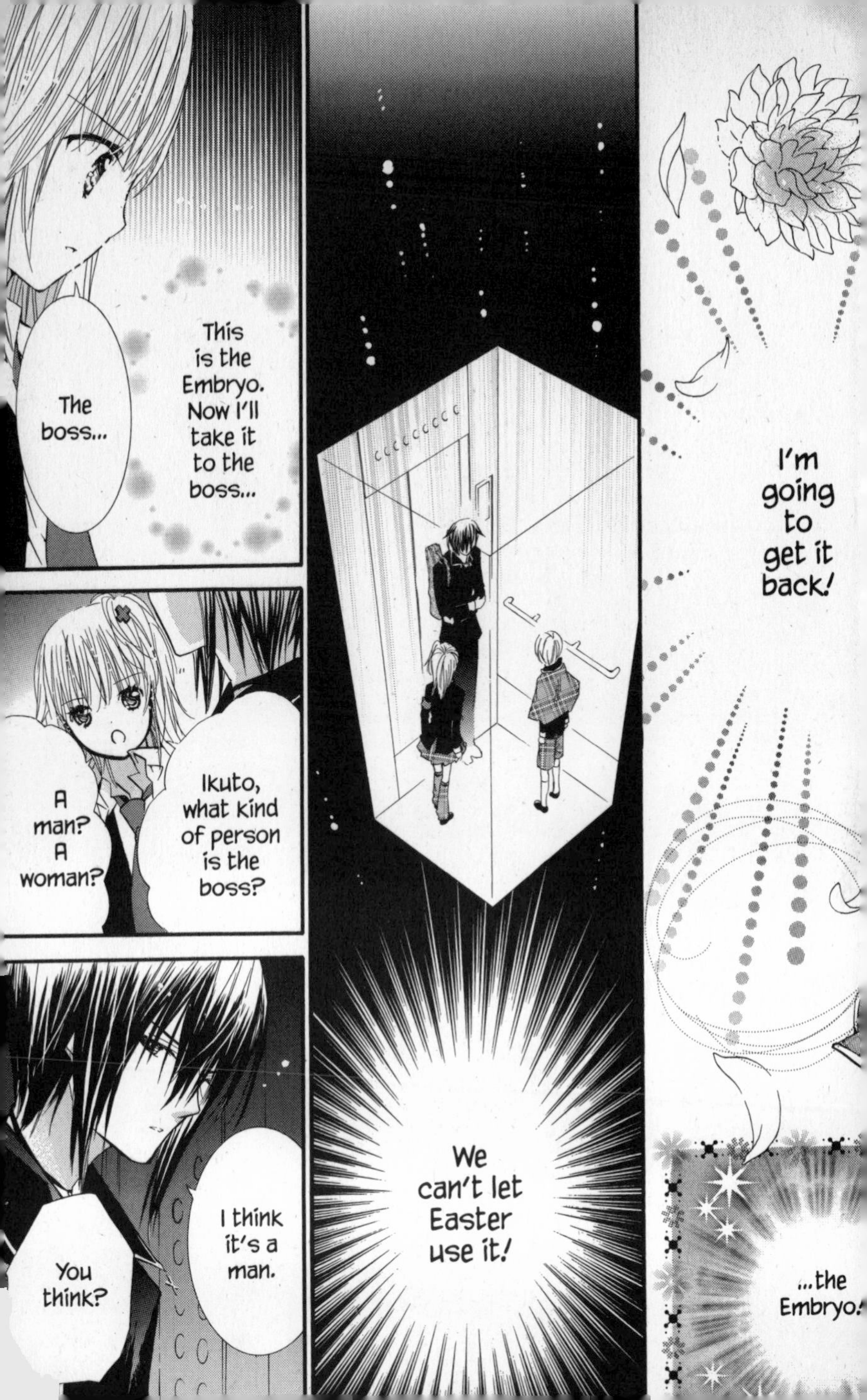
I'm going to get it back!
...the Embryo!
We can't let Easter use it!
This is the Embryo. Now I'll take it to the boss...
The boss...
Ikuto, what kind of person is the boss?
A man? A woman?
I think it's a man.
You think?

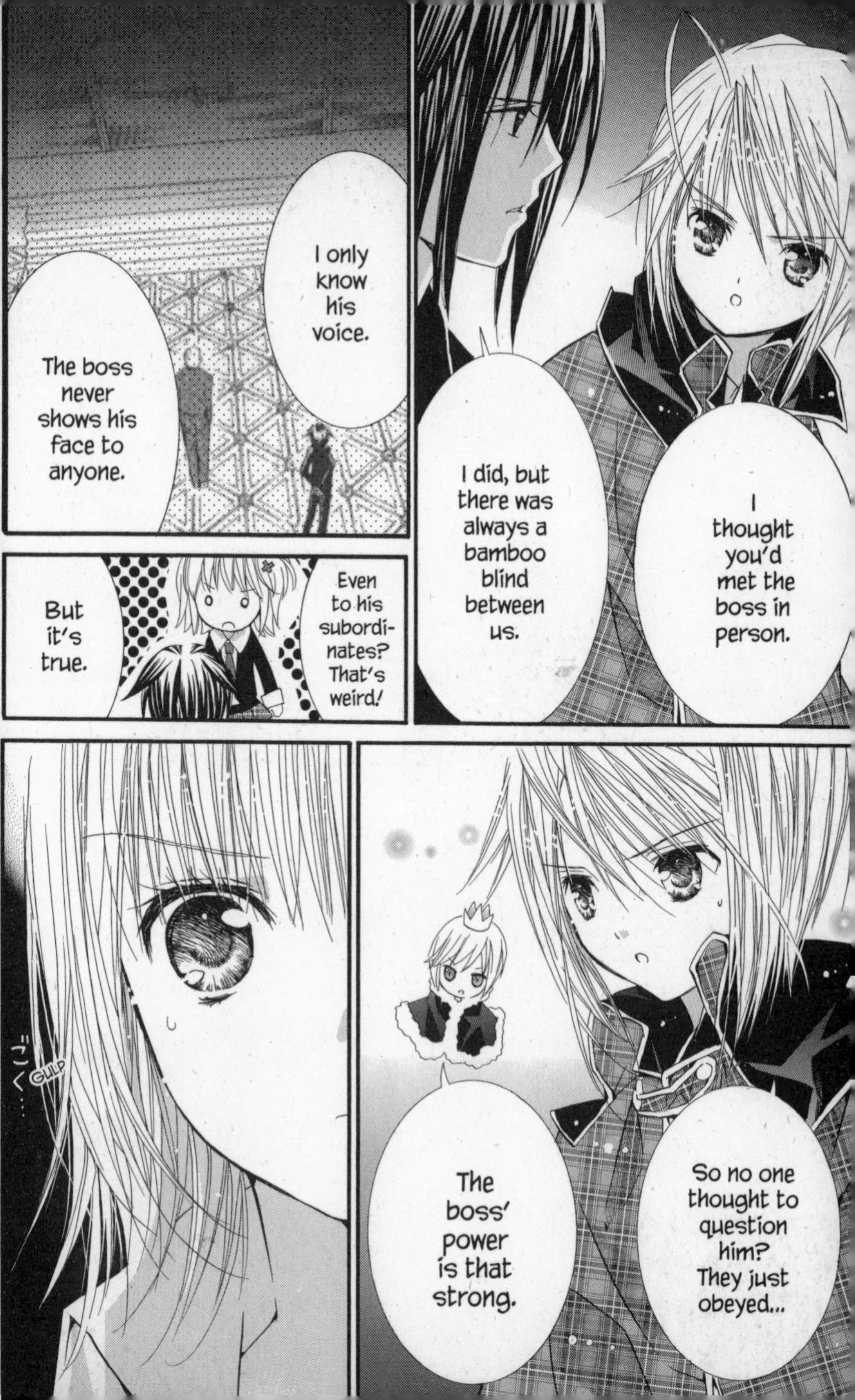

I thought you'd met the boss in person.
I did, but there was always a bamboo blind between us.
I only know his voice.
The boss never shows his face to anyone.
Even to his subordinates? That's weird!
But it's true.
So no one thought to question him? They just obeyed...
The boss' power is that strong.
GULP

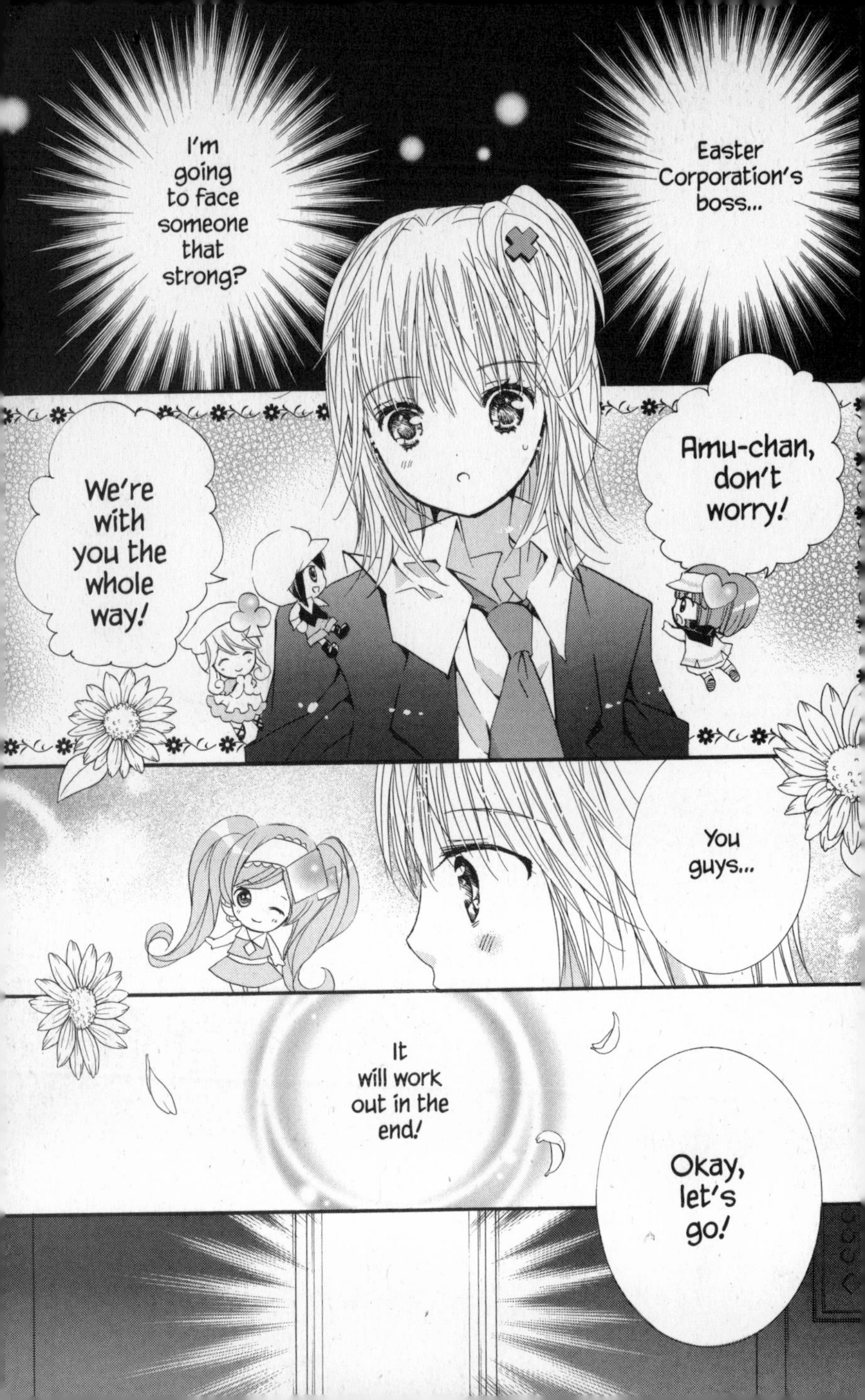
Easter Corporation's boss...
I'm going to face someone that strong?
Amu-chan, don't worry!
We're with you the whole way!
You guys...
It will work out in the end!
Okay, let's go!

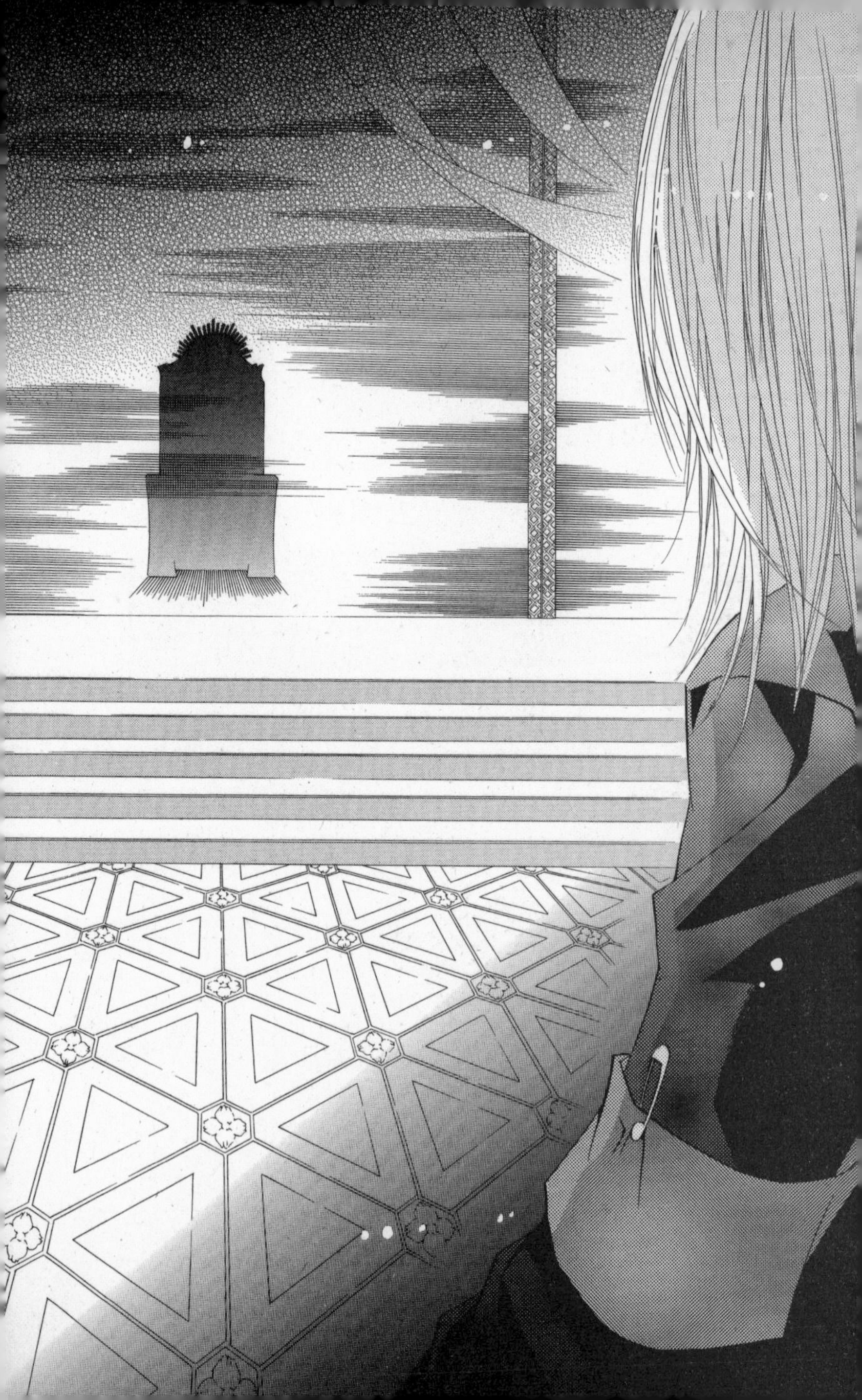

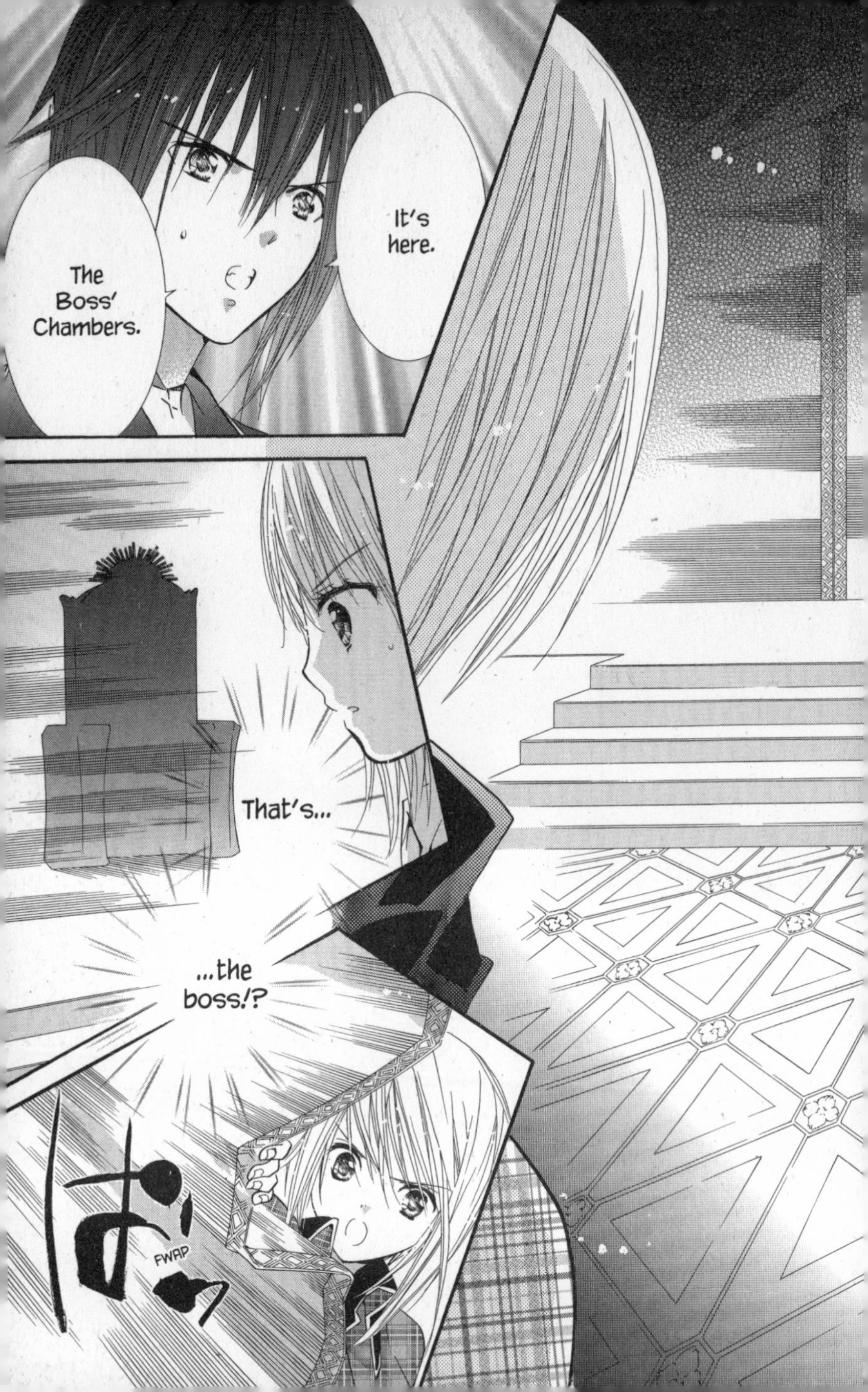
It's here.
The Boss' Chambers.
That's...
...the boss!?
FWAP

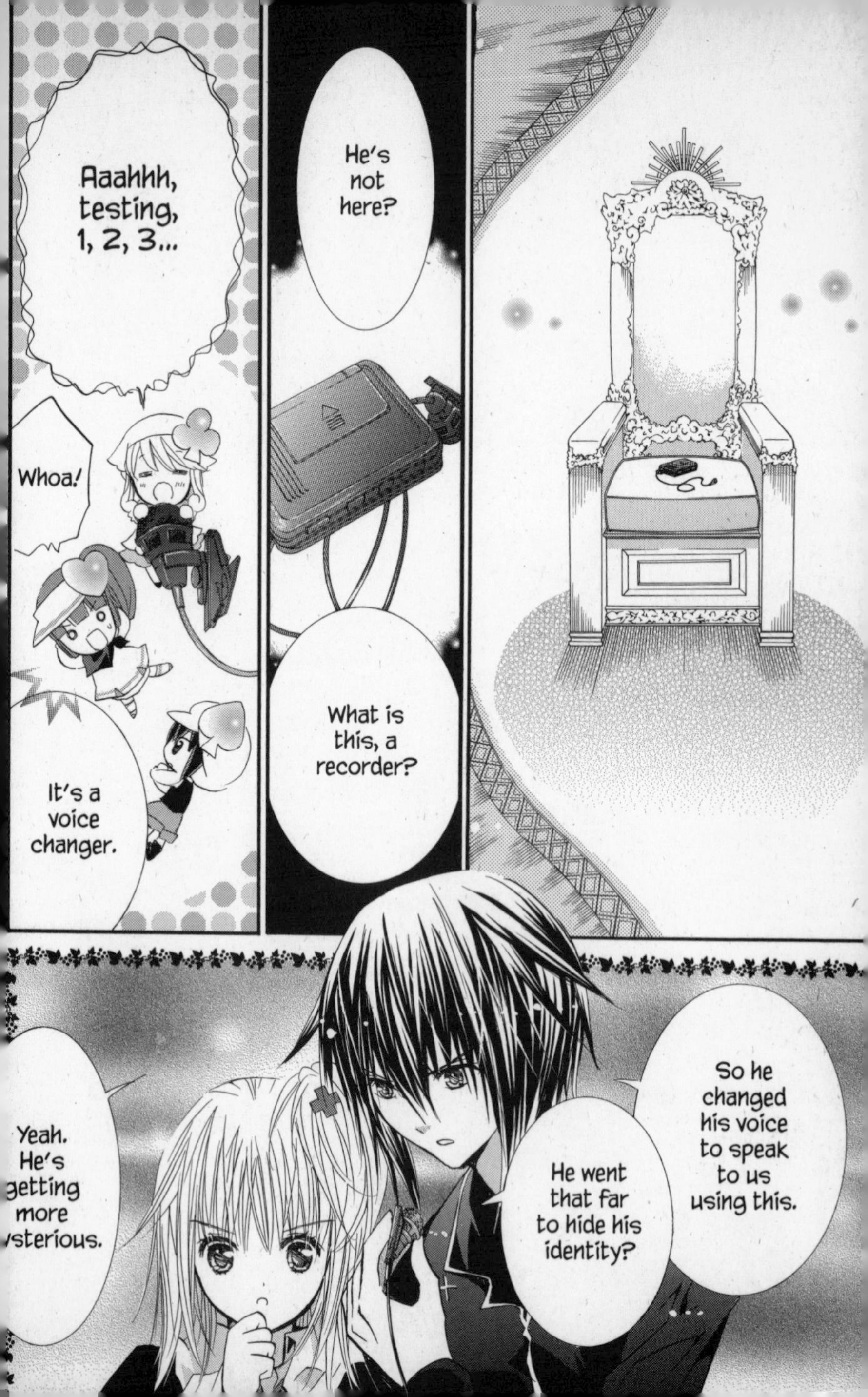
He's not here?
What is this, a recorder?
Aaahhh, testing, 1, 2, 3...
Whoa!
It's a voice changer.
So he changed his voice to speak to us using this.
He went that far to hide his identity?
Yeah. He's getting more ysterious.

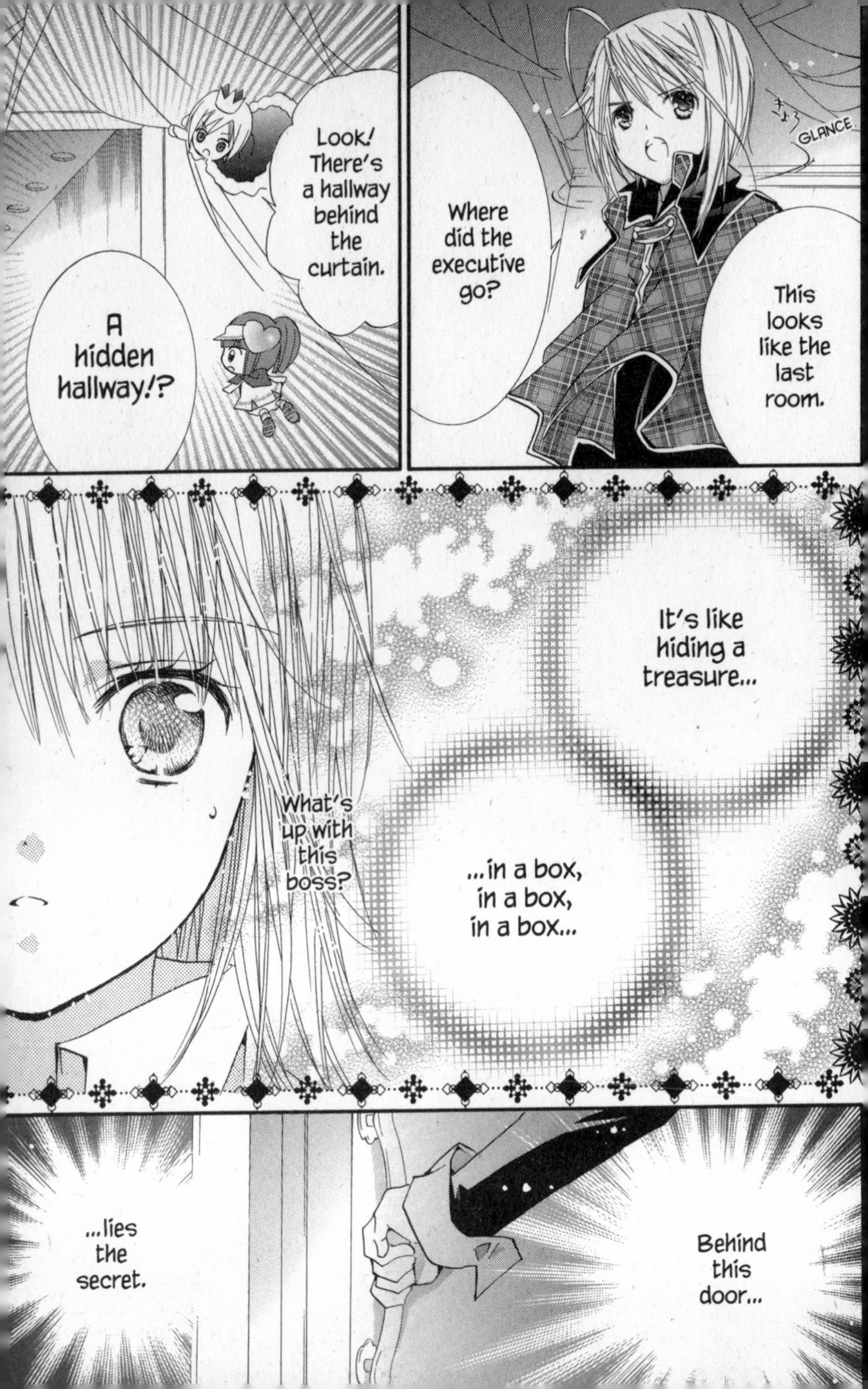
きょろ
GLANCE
This looks like the last room.
Where did the executive go?
Look! There's a hallway behind the curtain.
A hidden hallway!?
It's like hiding a treasure...
...in a box, in a box, in a box...
What's up with this boss?
Behind this door...
...lies the secret.

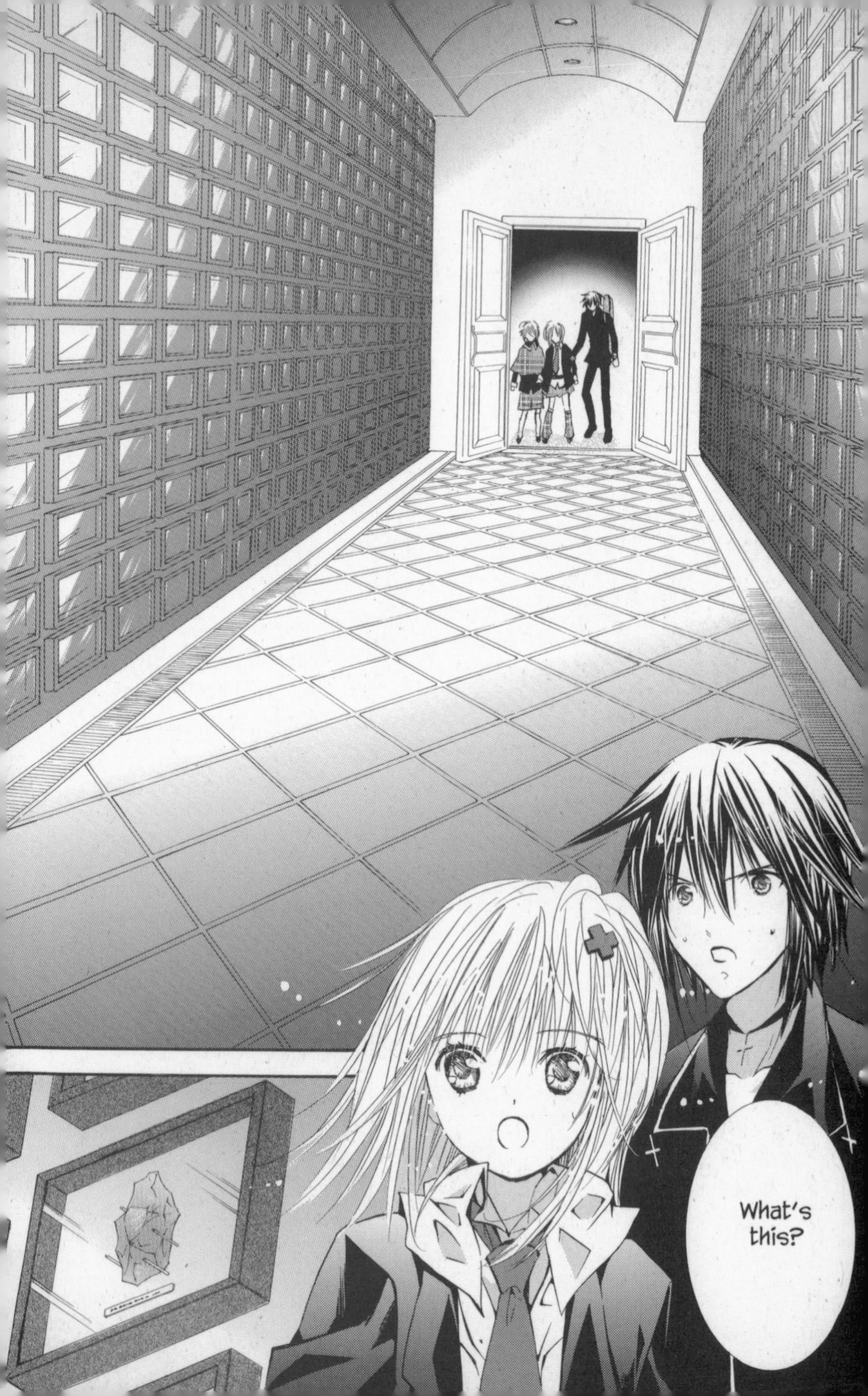
What's this?

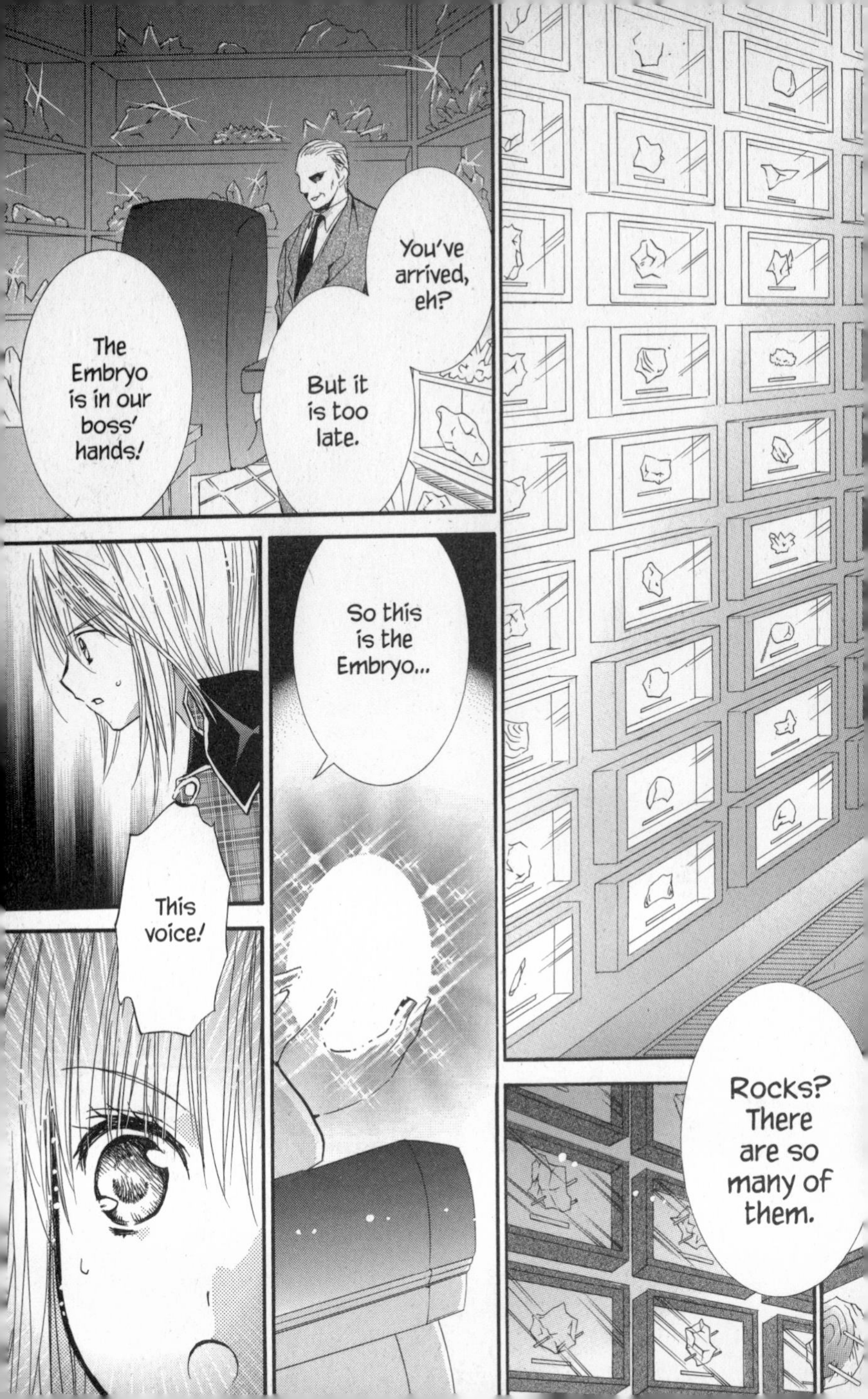
Rocks? There are so many of them.
You've arrived, eh?
But it is too late.
The Embryo is in our boss' hands!
So this is the Embryo...
This voice!

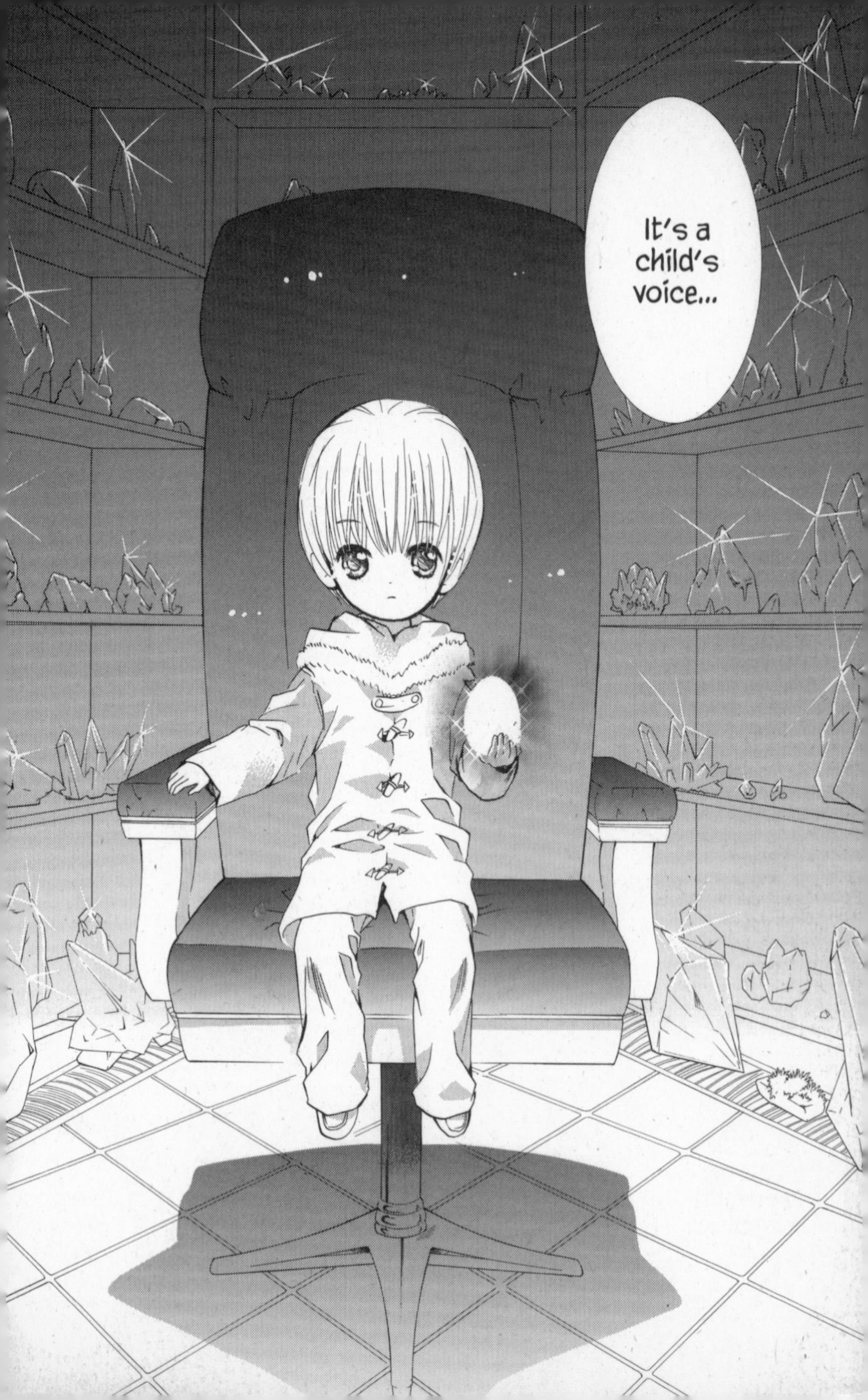
It's a child's voice...

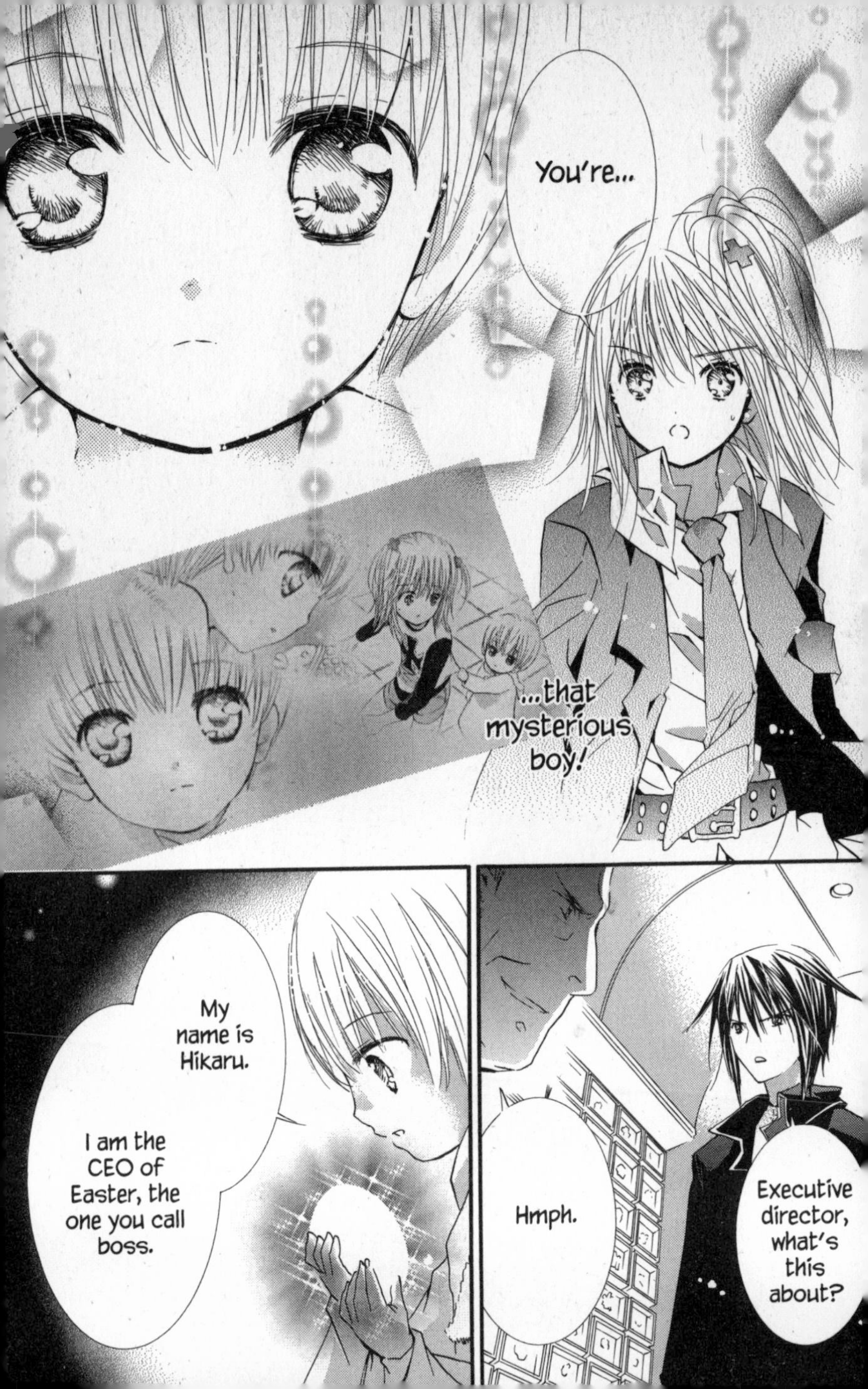
You're...
...that mysterious boy!
Executive director, what's this about?
Hmph.
My name is Hikaru.
I am the CEO of Easter, the one you call boss.

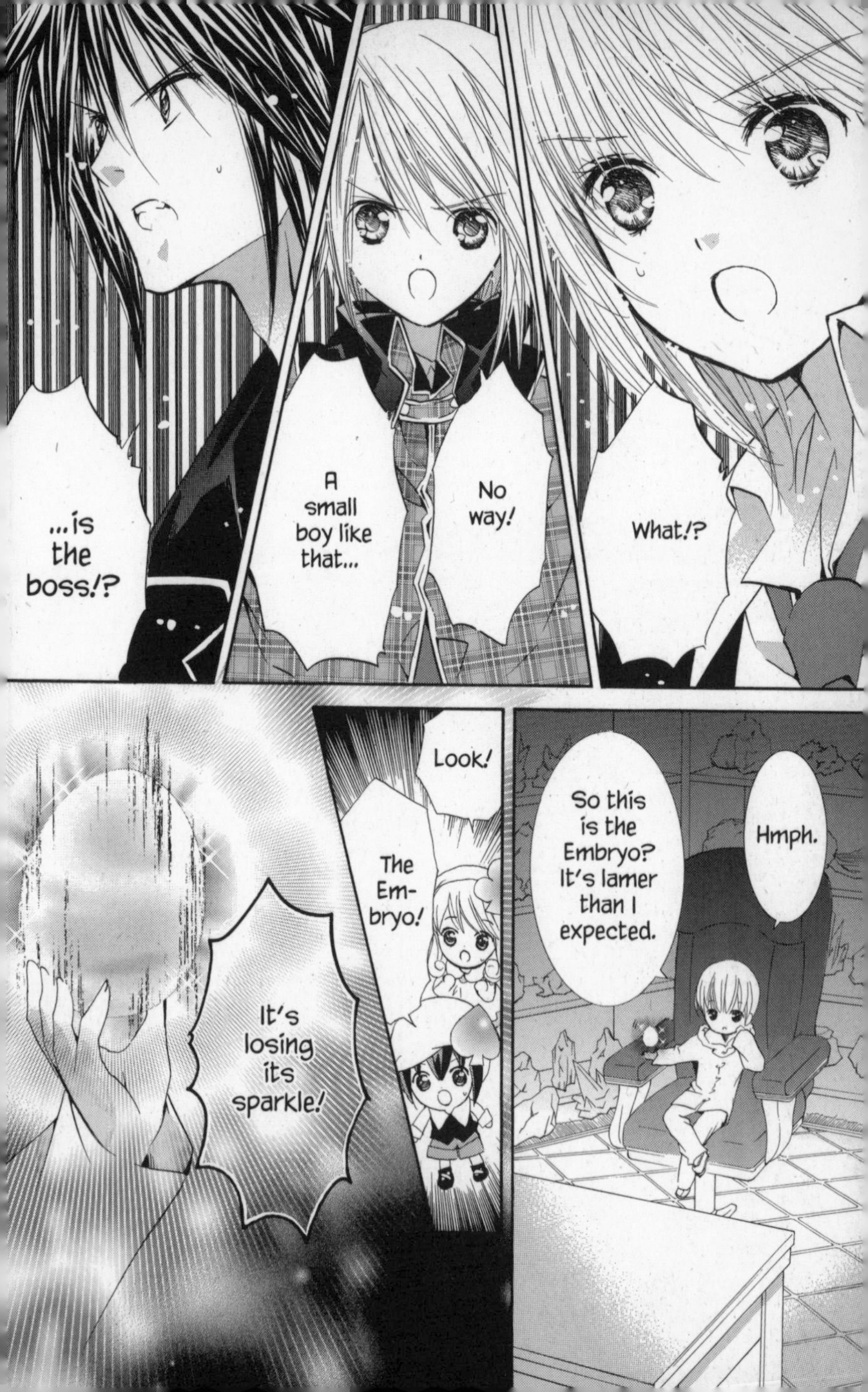
What!?
No way!
A small boy like that...
...is the boss!?
Hmph.
So this is the Embryo? It's lamer than I expected.
Look!
The Em-bryo!
It's losing its sparkle!

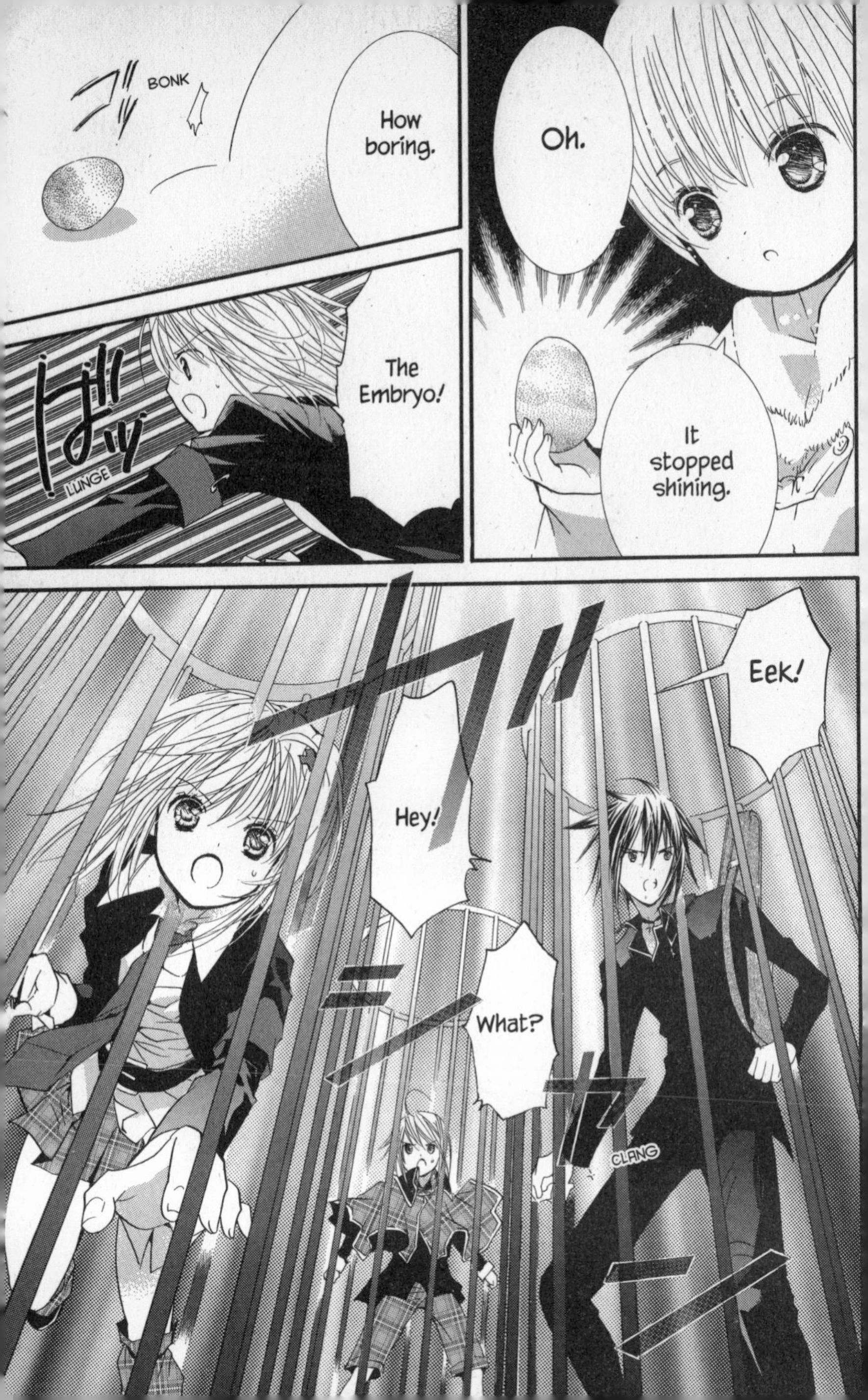
Oh.
It stopped shining.
How boring.
BONK
The Embryo!
LUNGE
Eek!
Hey!
What?
CLANG

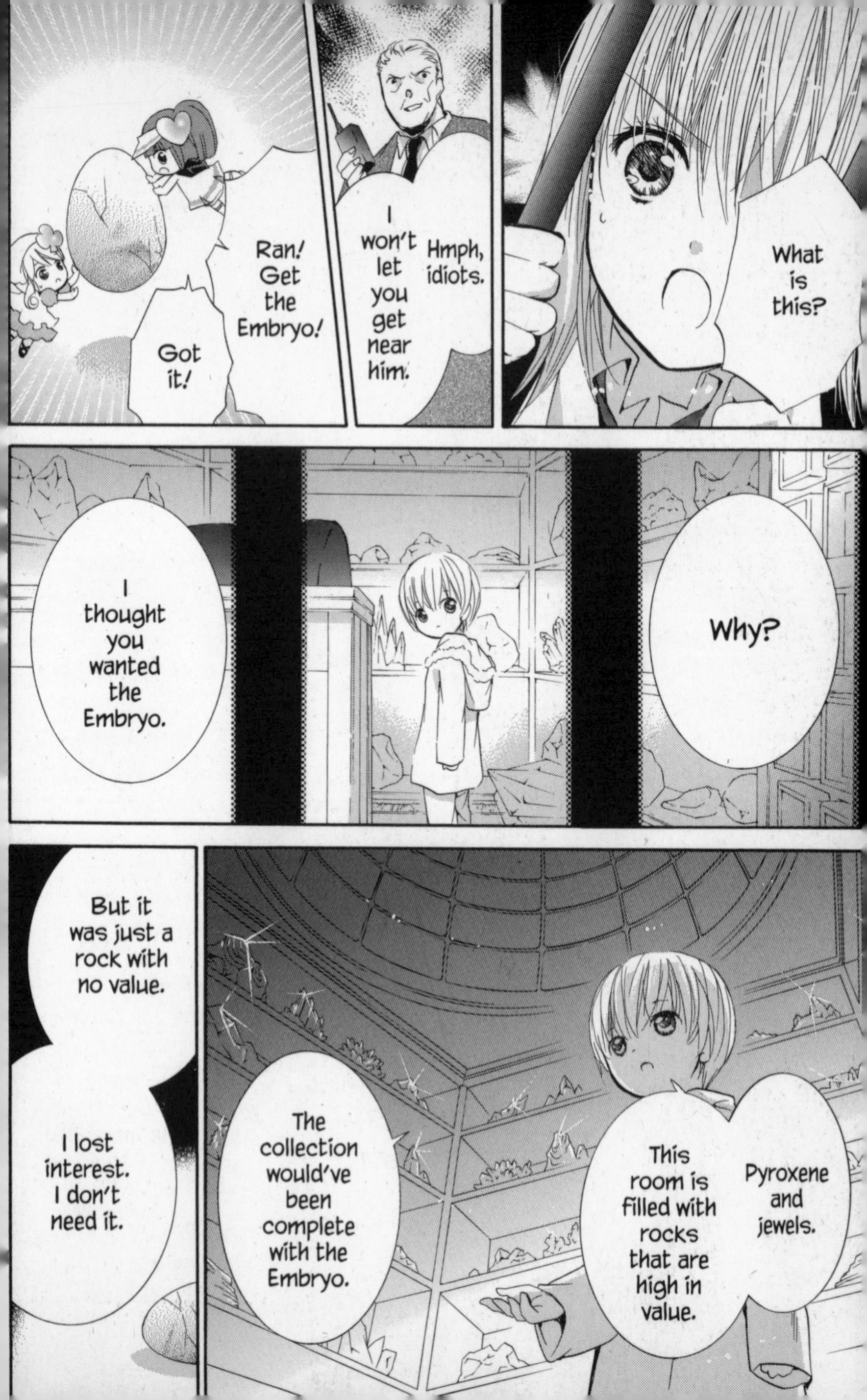
What is this?
Hmph, idiots.
I won't let you get near him.
Ran! Get the Embryo!
Got it!
Why?
I thought you wanted the Embryo.
Pyroxene and jewels.
This room is filled with rocks that are high in value.
The collection would've been complete with the Embryo.
But it was just a rock with no value.
I lost interest. I don't need it.

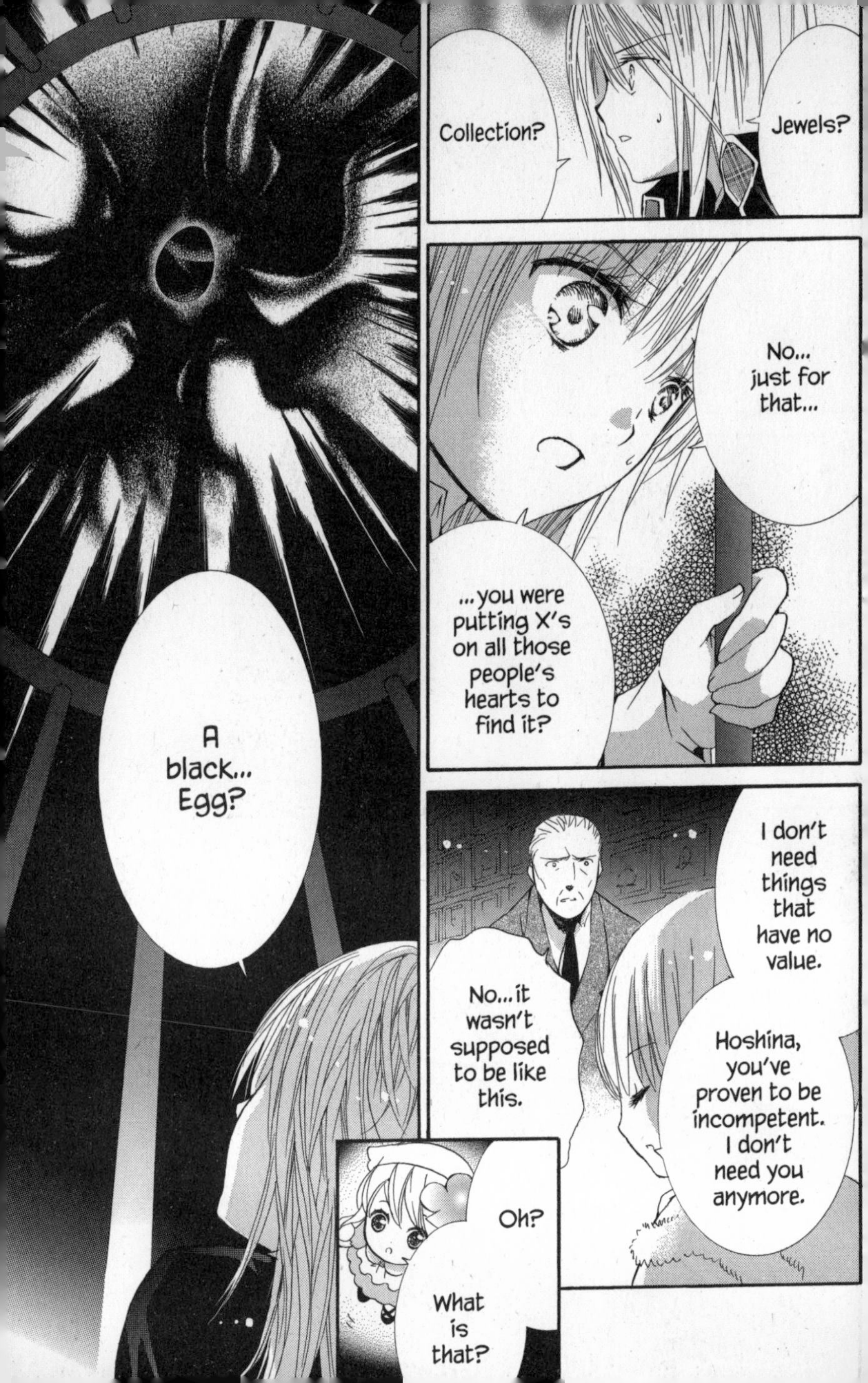
Jewels?
Collection?
No... just for that...
...you were putting X's on all those people's hearts to find it?
I don't need things that have no value.
Hoshina, you've proven to be incompetent. I don't need you anymore.
No...it wasn't supposed to be like this.
Oh?
What is that?
A black... Egg?

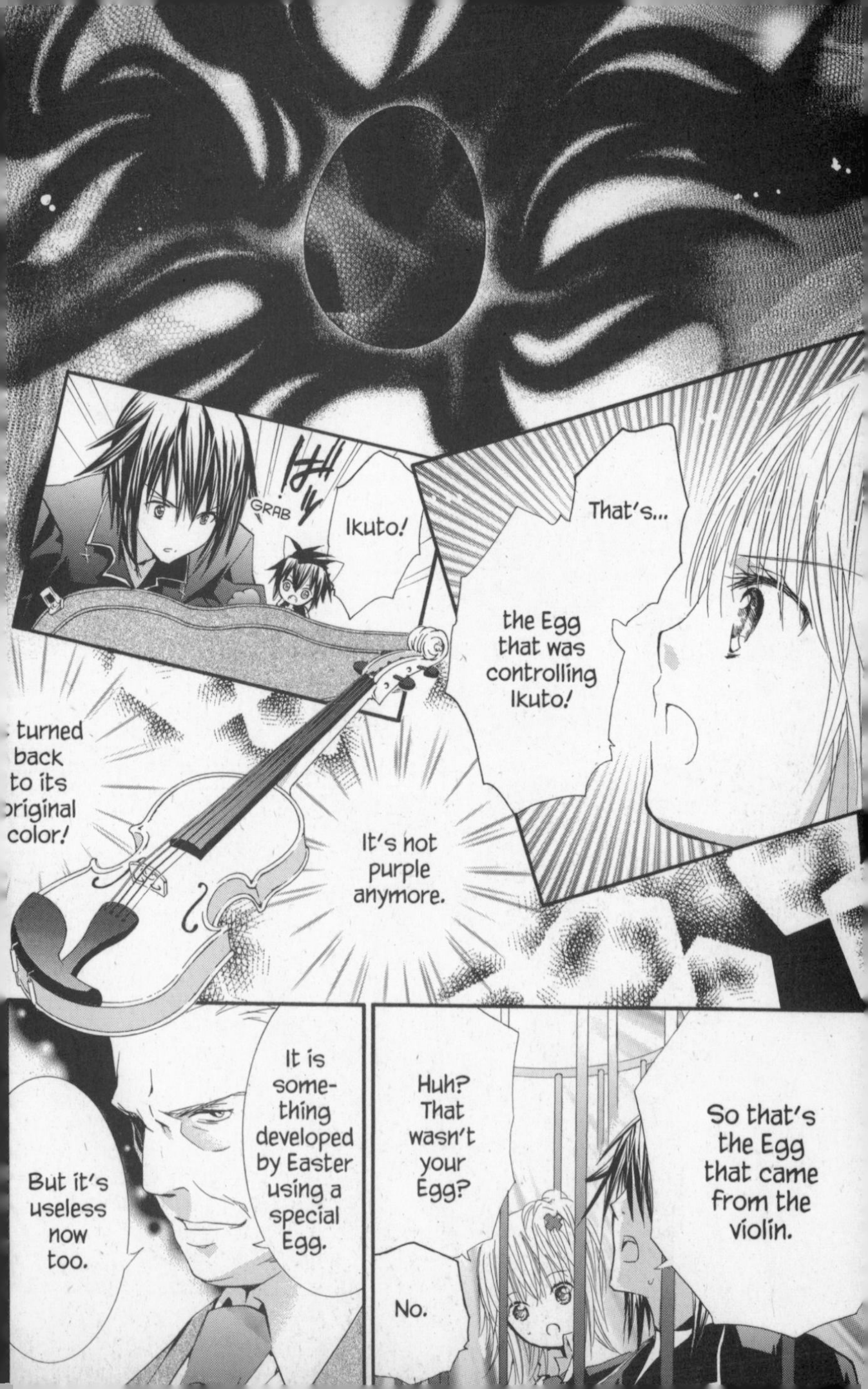
That's...
the Egg that was controlling Ikuto!
Ikuto!
GRAB
It's not purple anymore.
turned back to its riginal color!
So that's the Egg that came from the violin.
Huh? That wasn't your Egg?
No.
It is some-thing developed by Easter using a special Egg.
But it's useless now too.

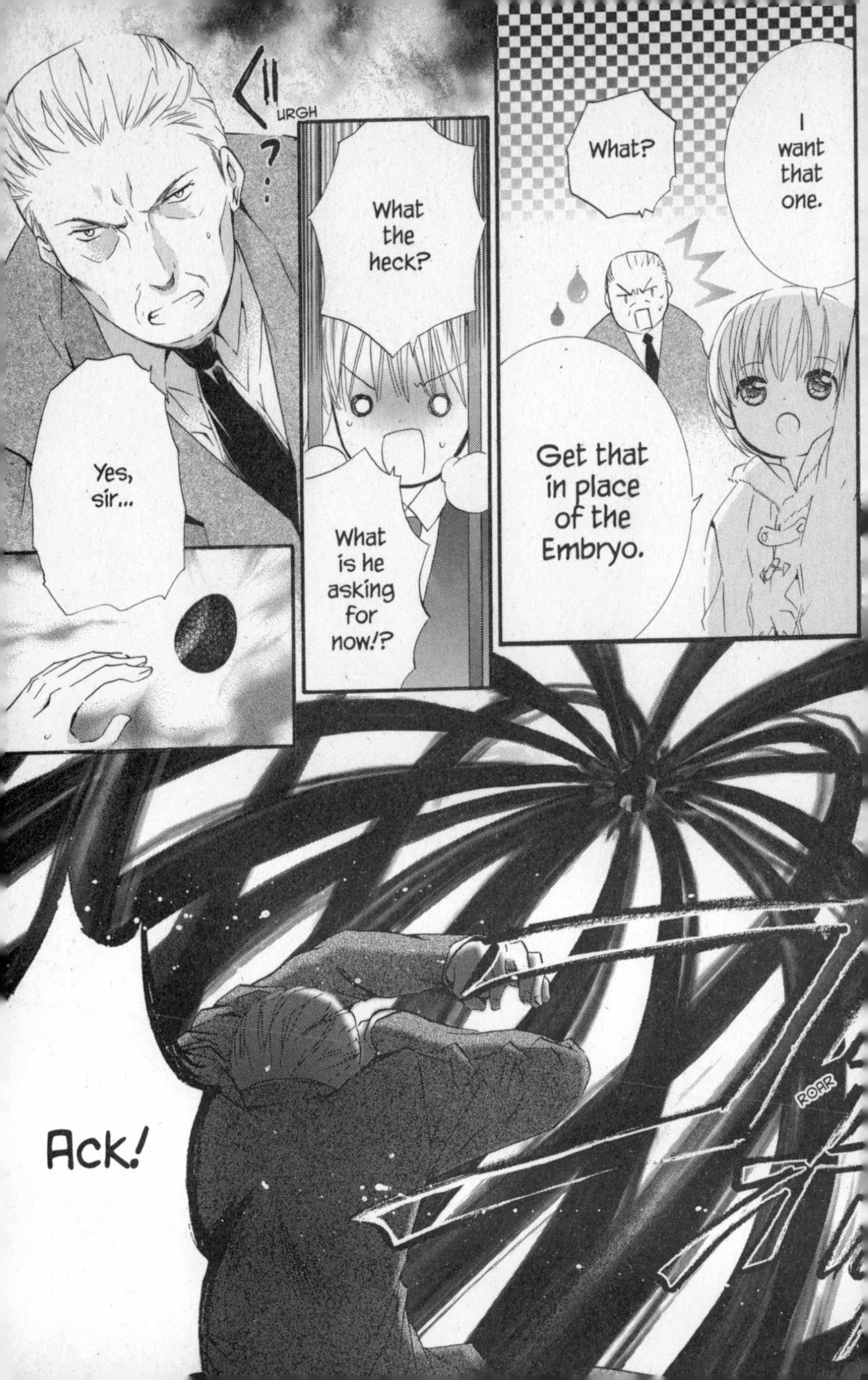
I want that one.
What?
Get that in place of the Embryo.
What the heck?
What is he asking for now!?
URGH
Yes, sir...
ROAR
Ack!

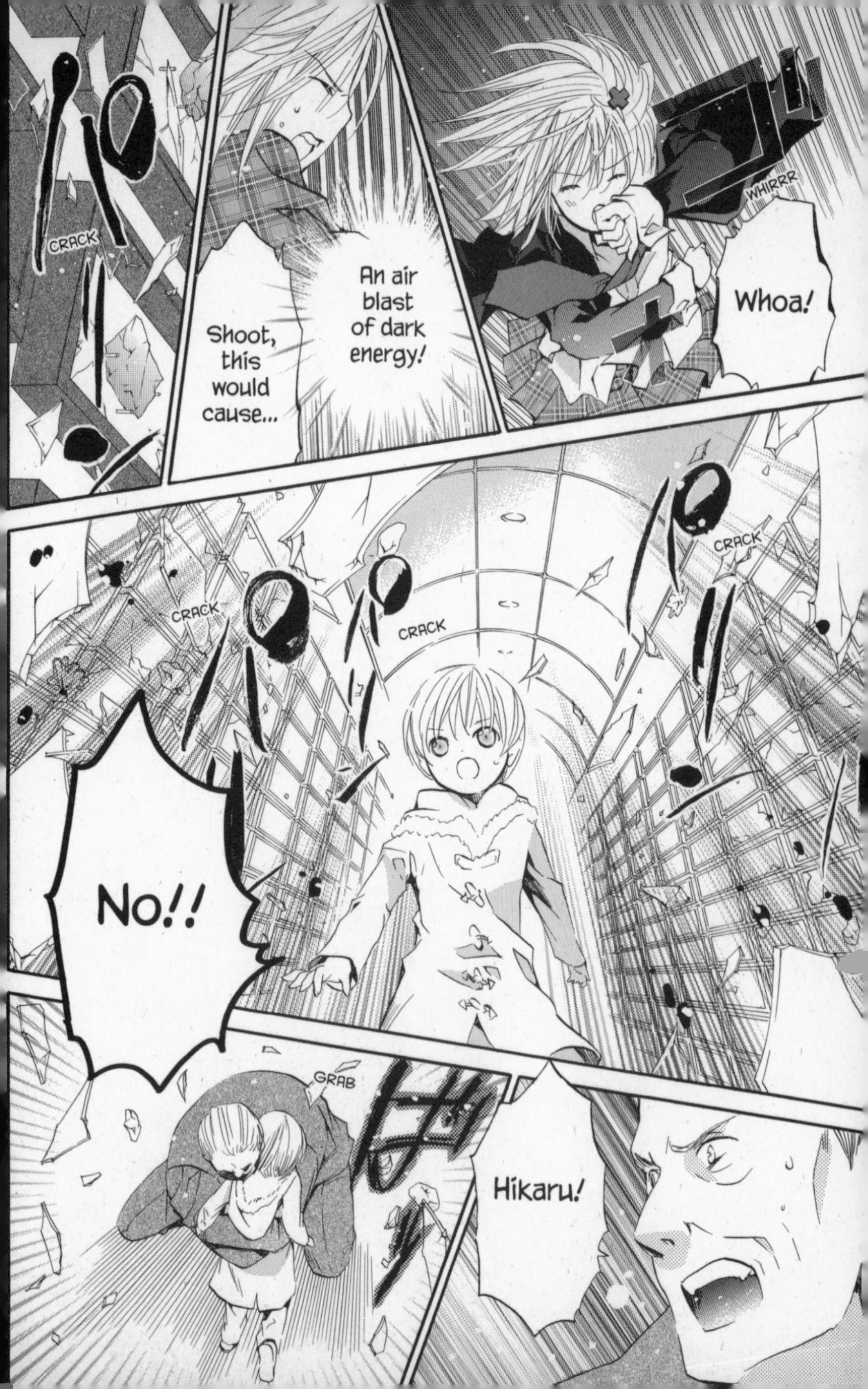
WHIRRR
Whoa!
An air blast of dark energy!
Shoot, this would cause...
CRACK
CRACK
CRACK
CRACK
No!!
Hikaru!
GRAB

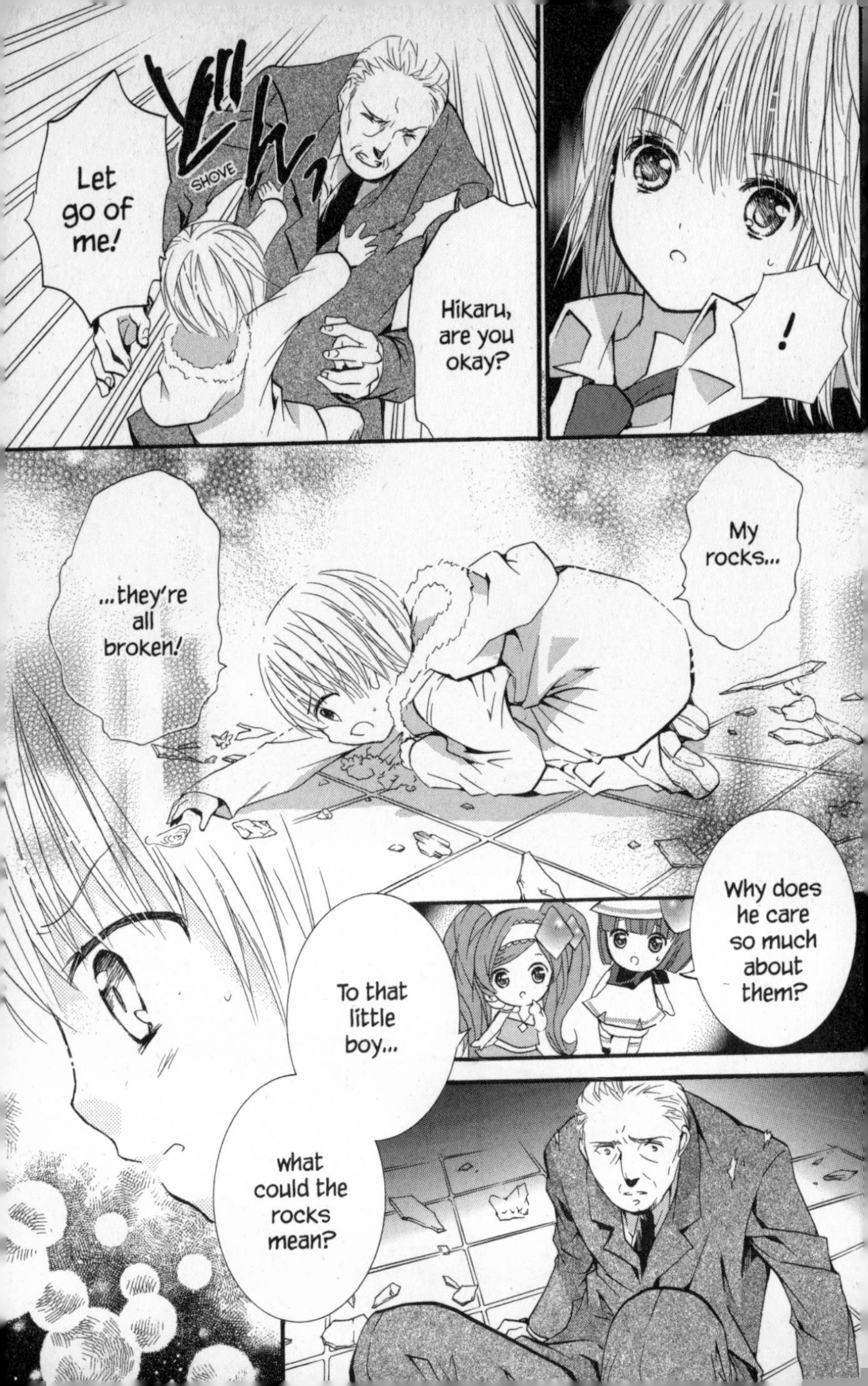
!
Let go of me!
SHOVE
Hikaru, are you okay?
My rocks...
...they're all broken!
Why does he care so much about them?
To that little boy...
what could the rocks mean?

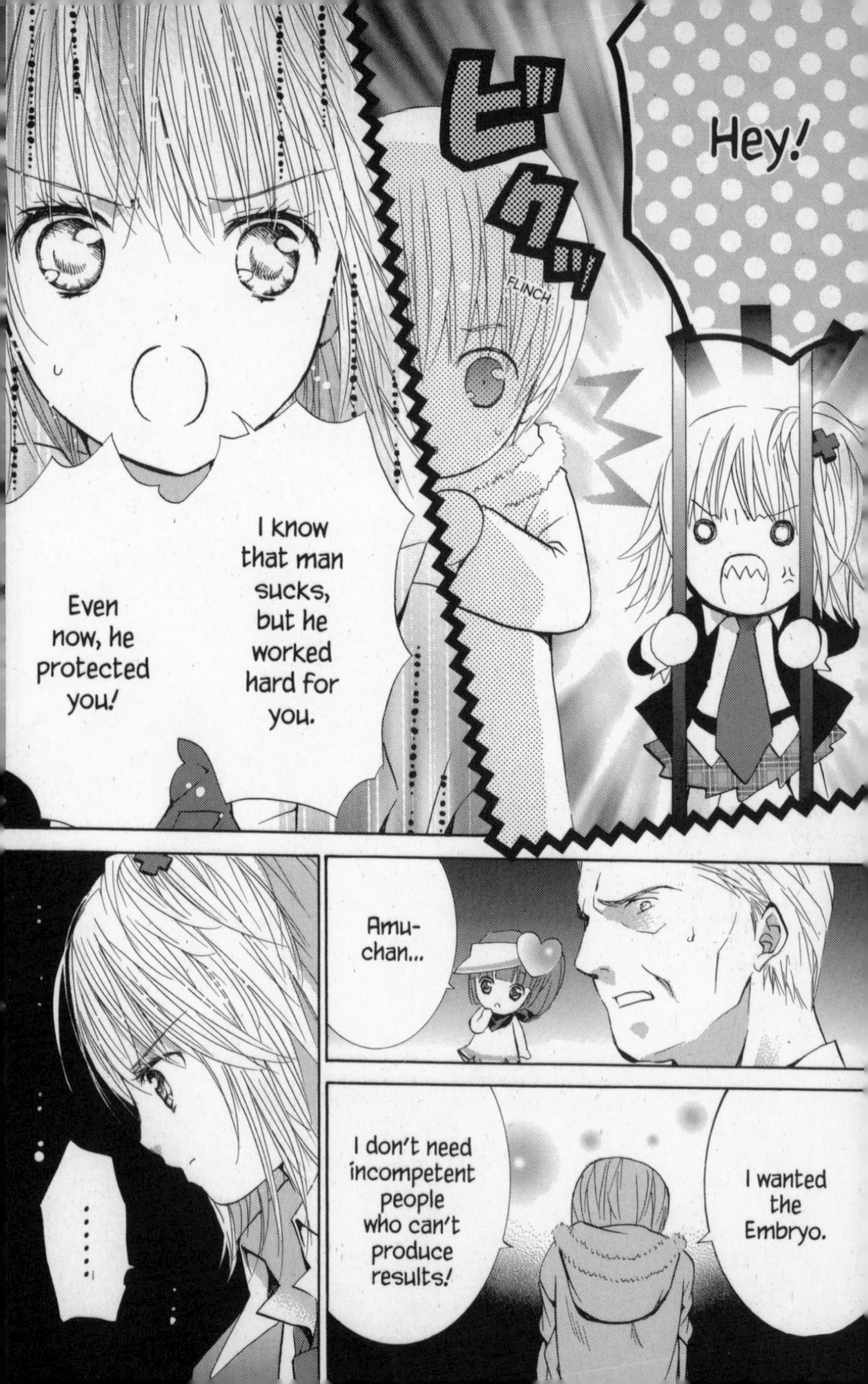
Hey!
ビクッ
FLINCH
I know that man sucks, but he worked hard for you.
Even now, he protected you!
Amu-chan...
I wanted the Embryo.
I don't need incompetent people who can't produce results!
......

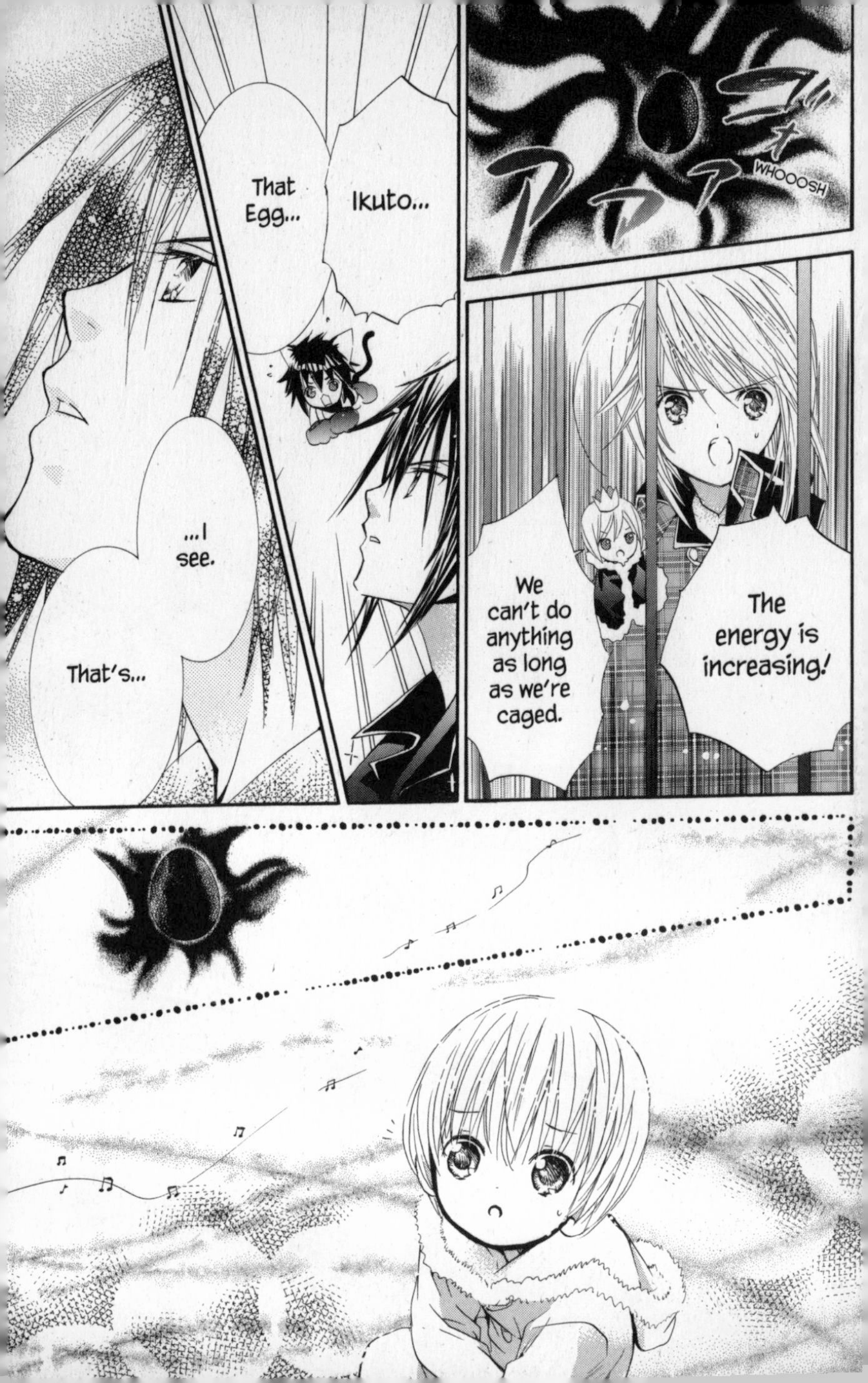
WHOOOSH
The energy is increasing!
We can't do anything as long as we're caged.
Ikuto...
That Egg...
...I see.
That's...

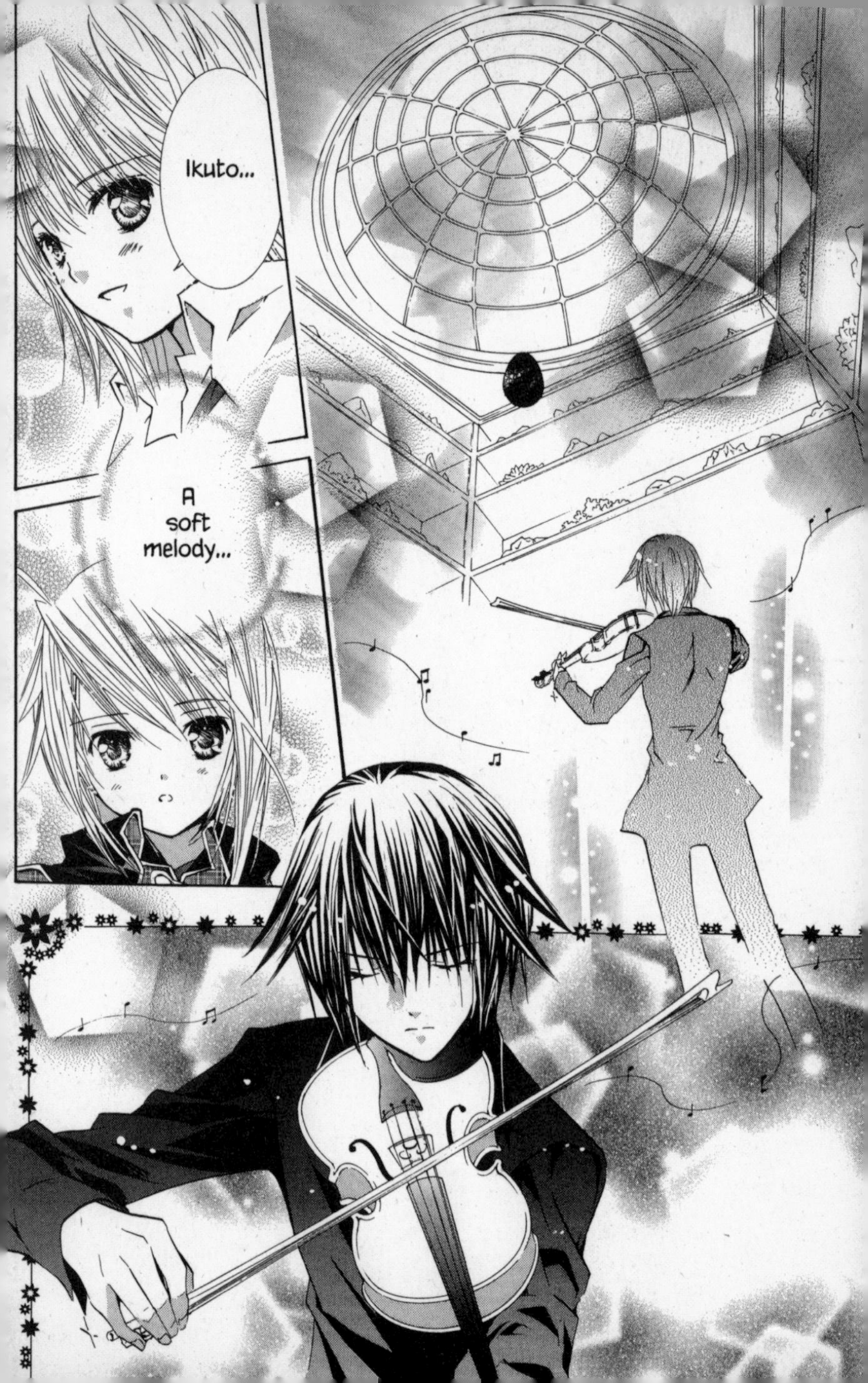
Ikuto...
A soft melody...

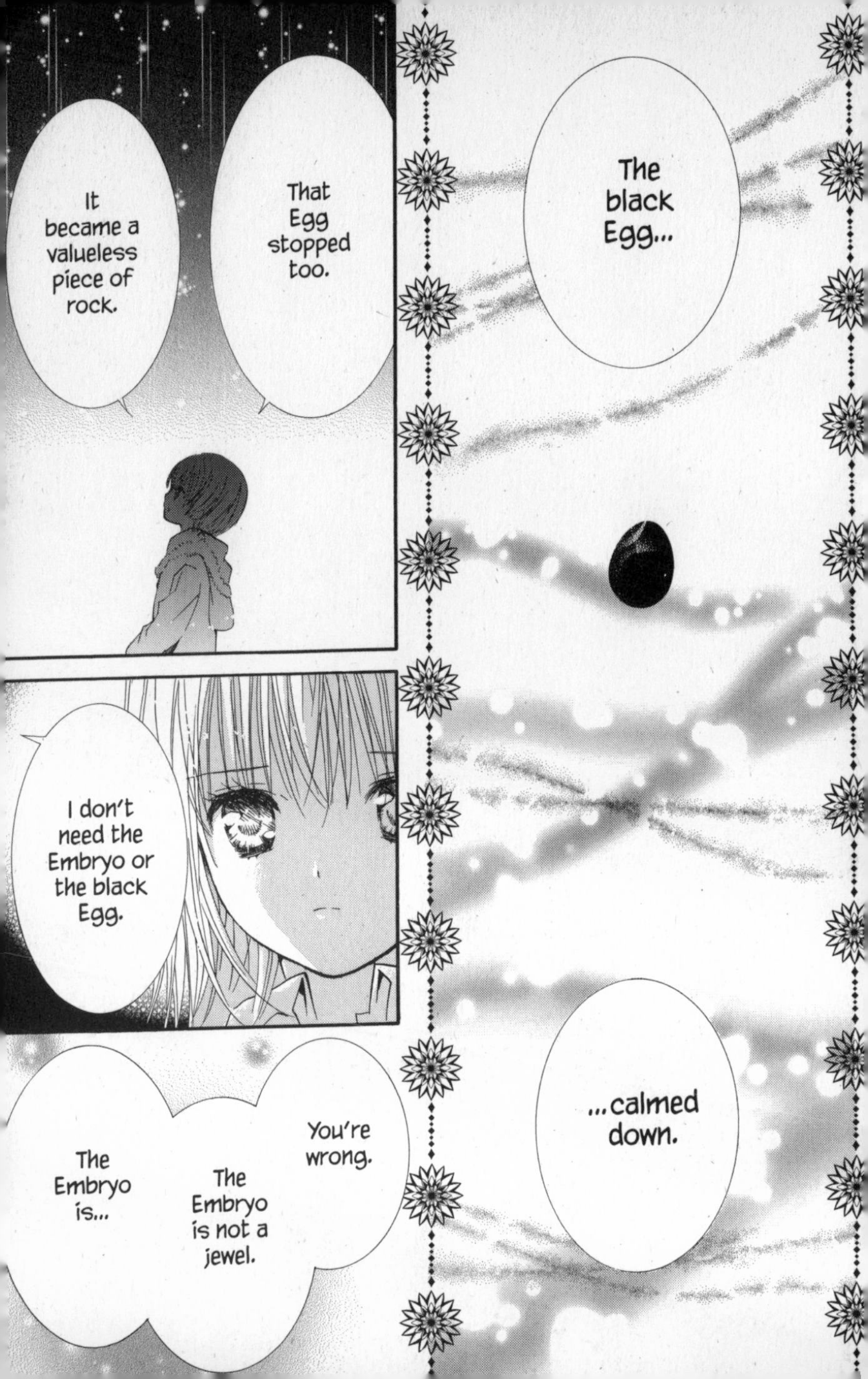
The black Egg...
...calmed down.
That Egg stopped too.
It became a valueless piece of rock.
I don't need the Embryo or the black Egg.
You're wrong.
The Embryo is not a jewel.
The Embryo is...

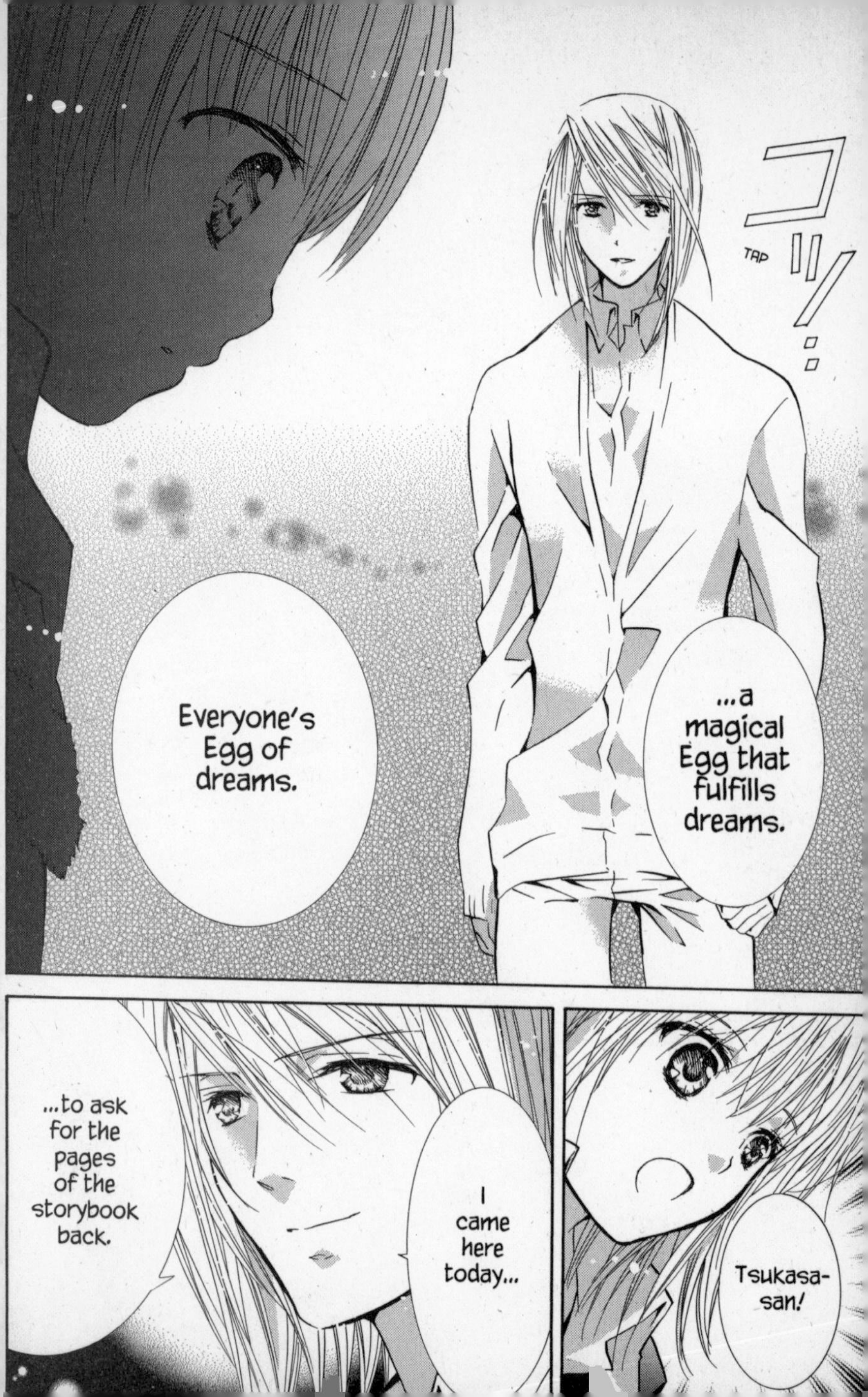
TAP
...a magical Egg that fulfills dreams.
Everyone's Egg of dreams.
Tsukasa-san!
I came here today...
...to ask for the pages of the storybook back.

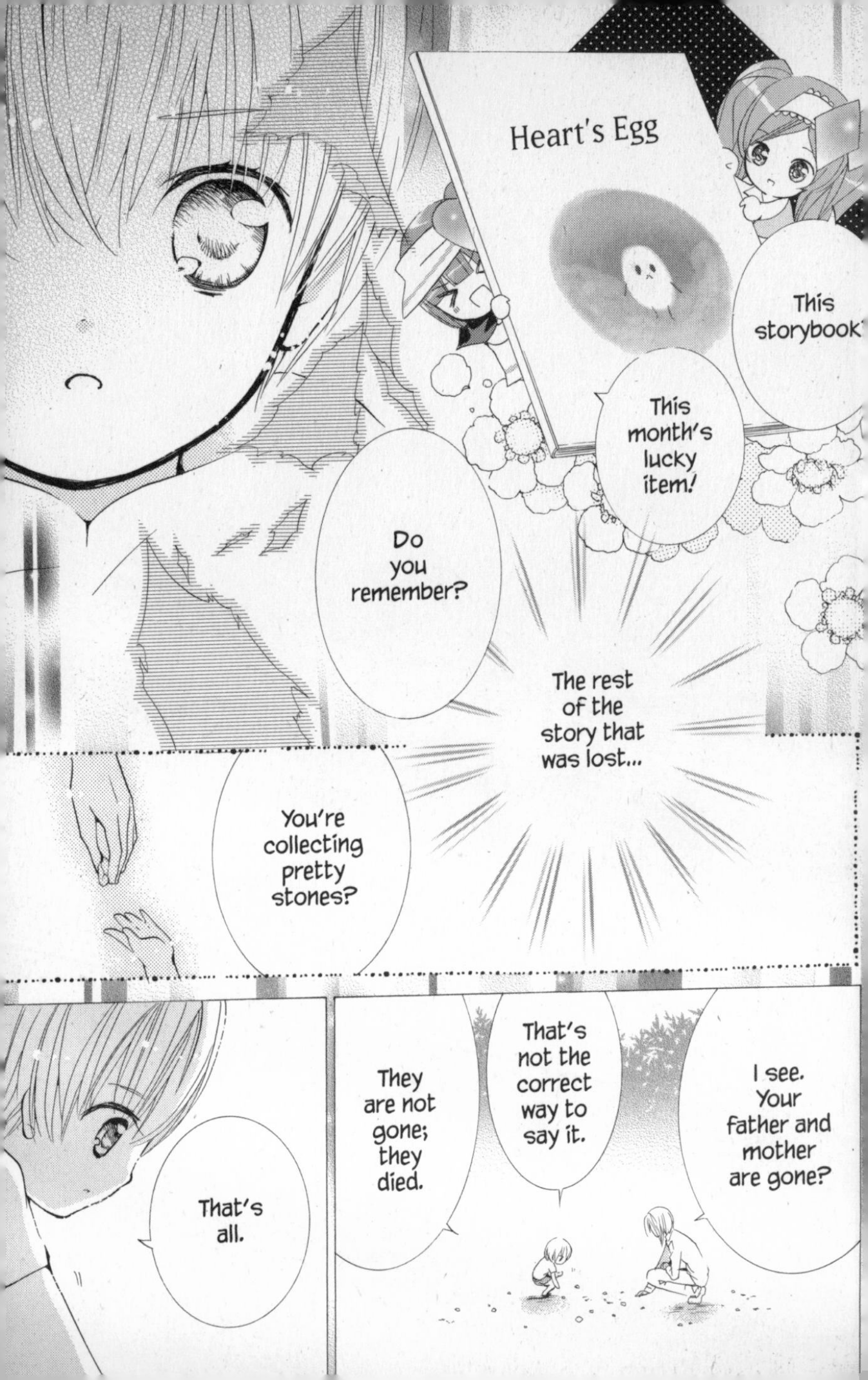

Heart's Egg
This storybook!
This month's lucky item!
Do you remember?
The rest of the story that was lost...
You're collecting pretty stones?
I see. Your father and mother are gone?
That's not the correct way to say it.
They are not gone; they died.
That's all.

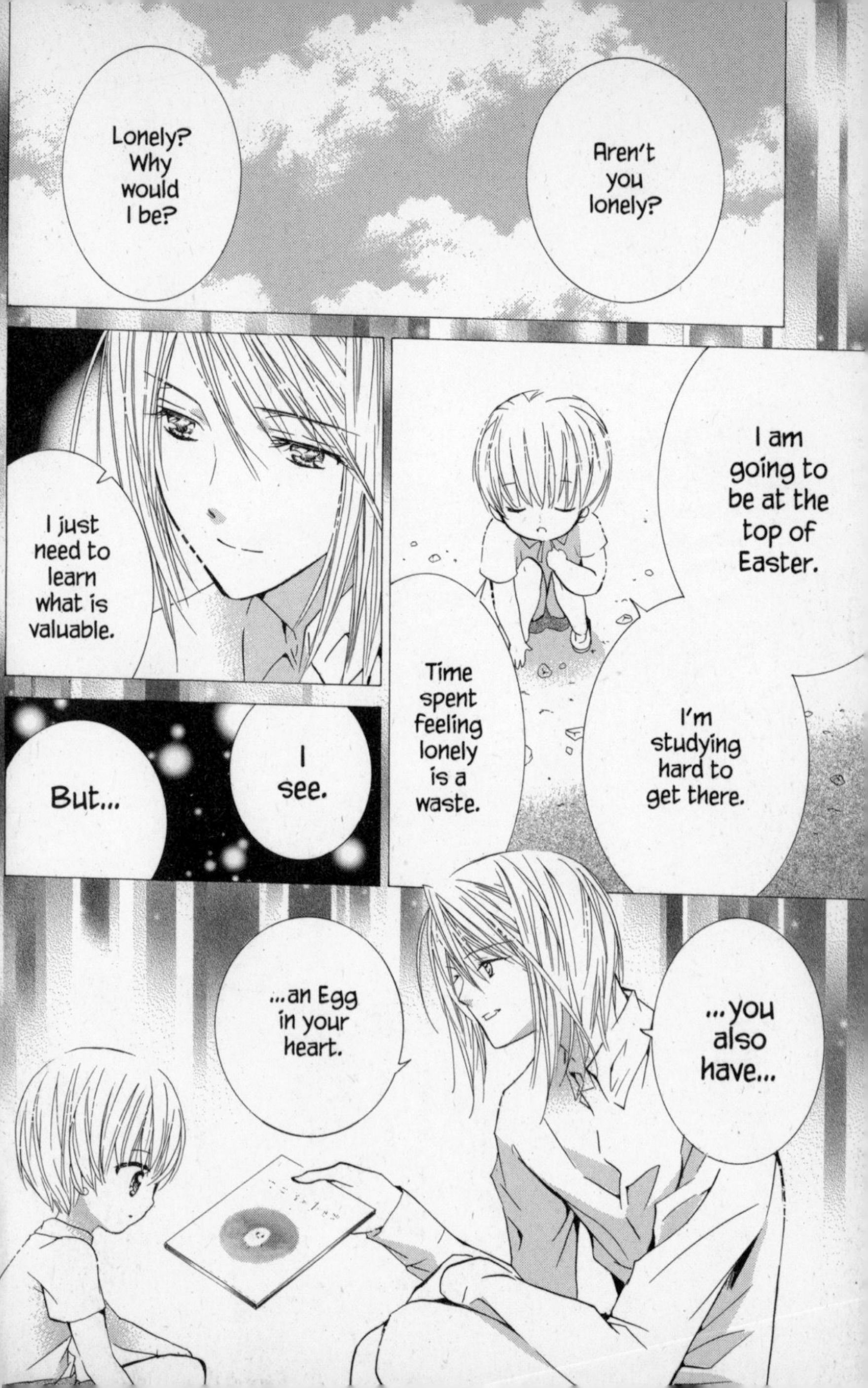
Aren't you lonely?
Lonely? Why would I be?
I am going to be at the top of Easter.
I'm studying hard to get there.
Time spent feeling lonely is a waste.
I just need to learn what is valuable.
I see.
But...
...you also have...
...an Egg in your heart.

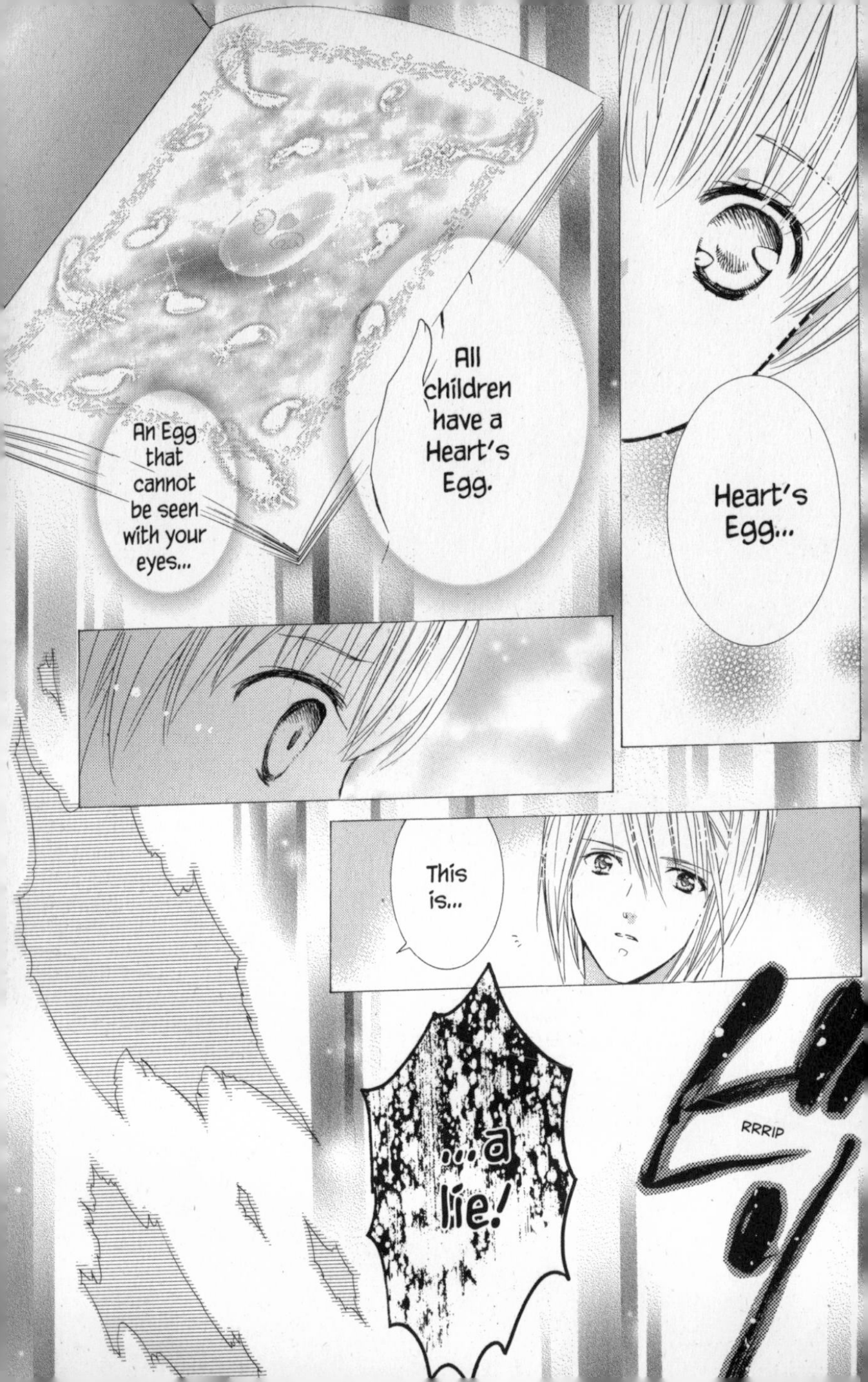
Heart's Egg...
All children have a Heart's Egg.
An Egg that cannot be seen with your eyes...
This is...
RRRIP
...a lie!

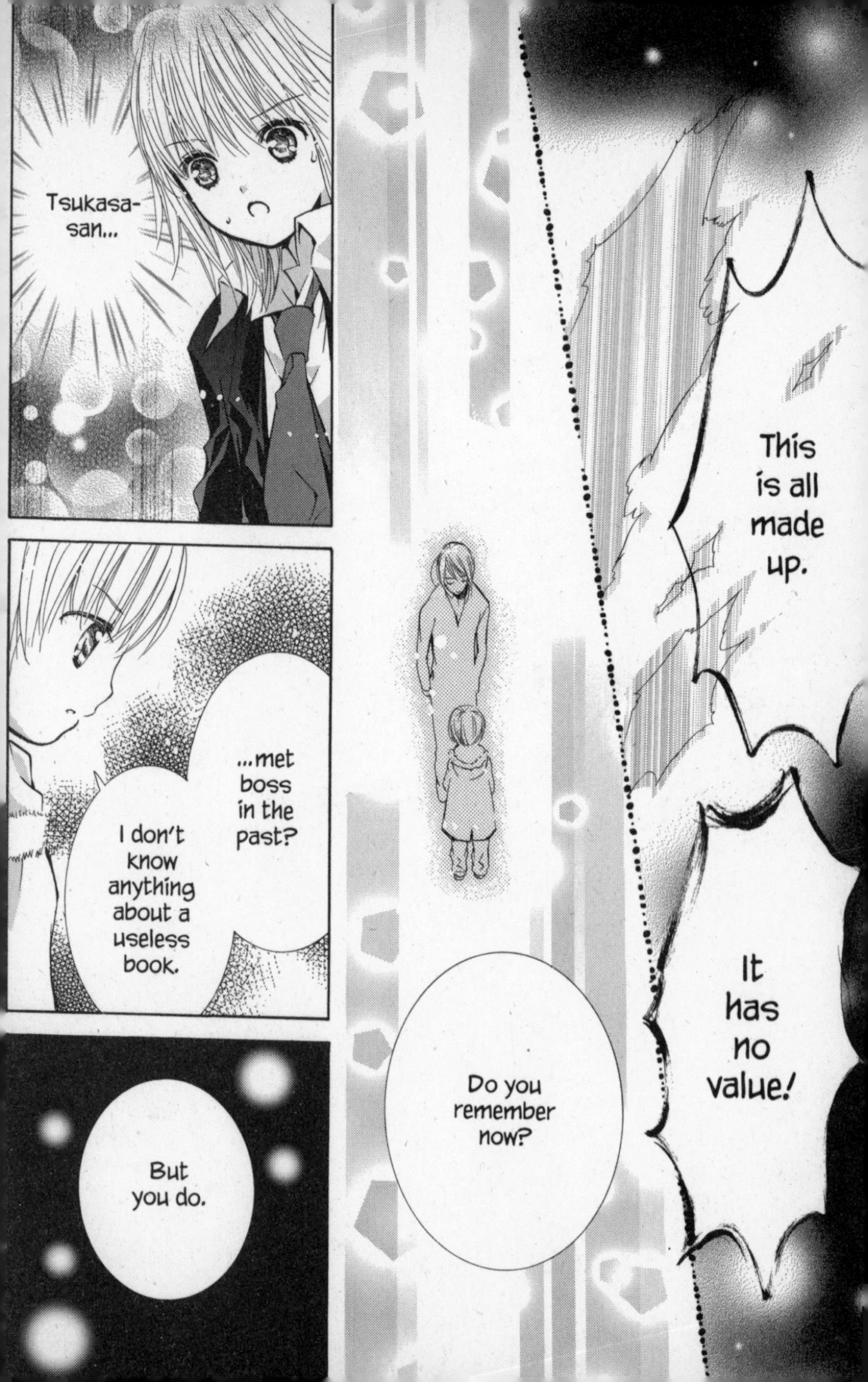
This is all made up.
It has no value!
Do you remember now?
Tsukasa-san...
...met boss in the past?
I don't know anything about a useless book.
But you do.

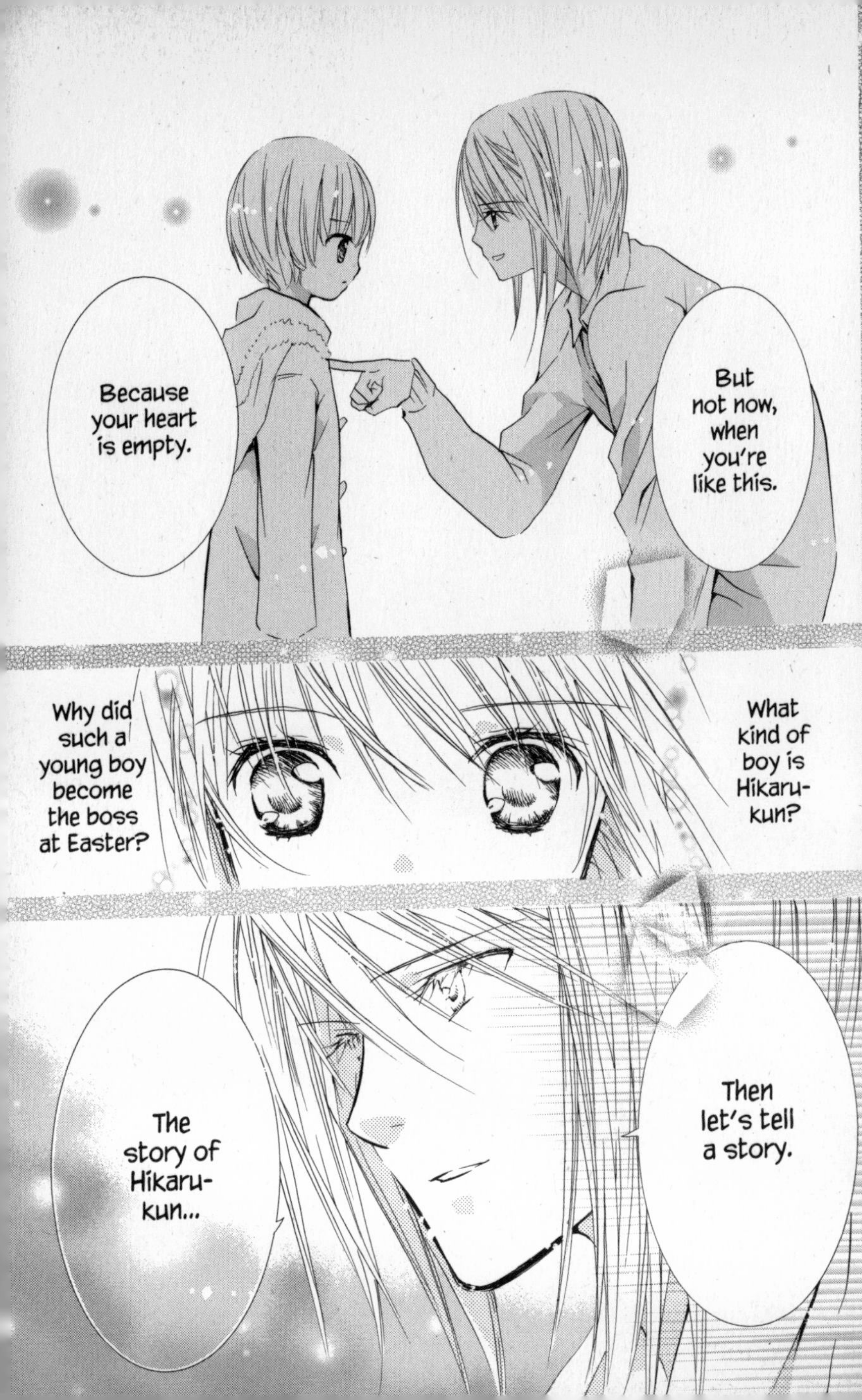
But not now, when you're like this.
Because your heart is empty.
What kind of boy is Hikaru-kun?
Why did such a young boy become the boss at Easter?
Then let's tell a story.
The story of Hikaru-kun...

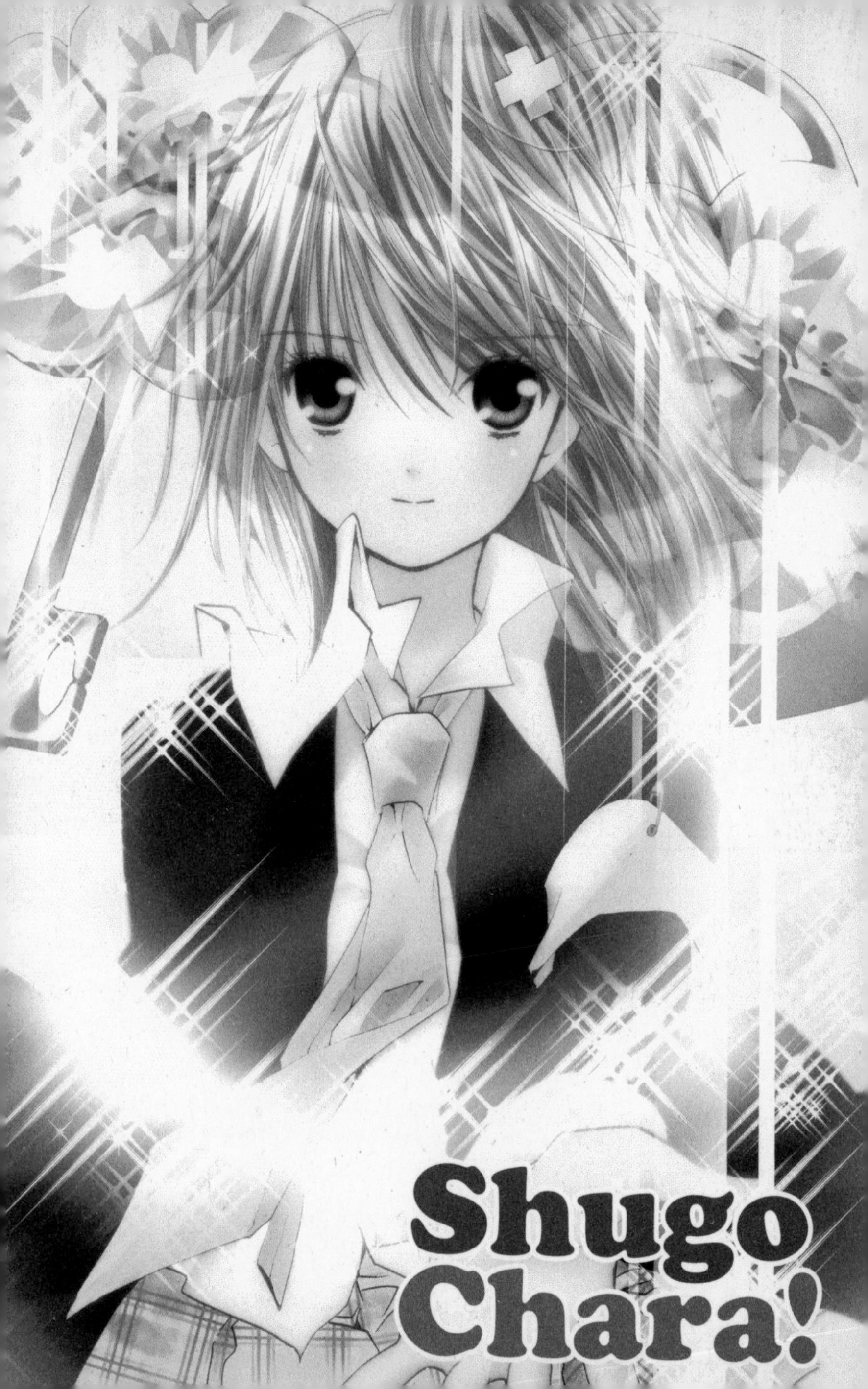
Shugo
Chara!

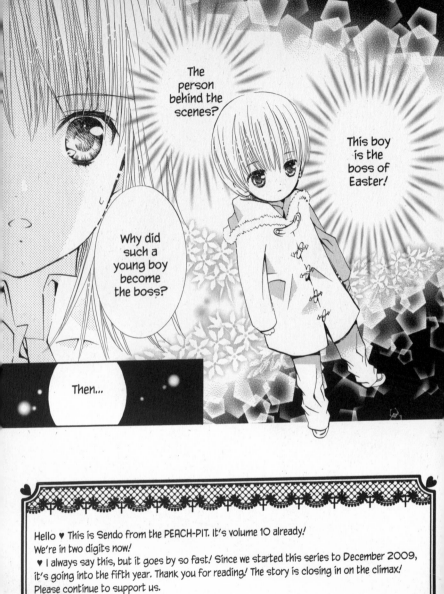

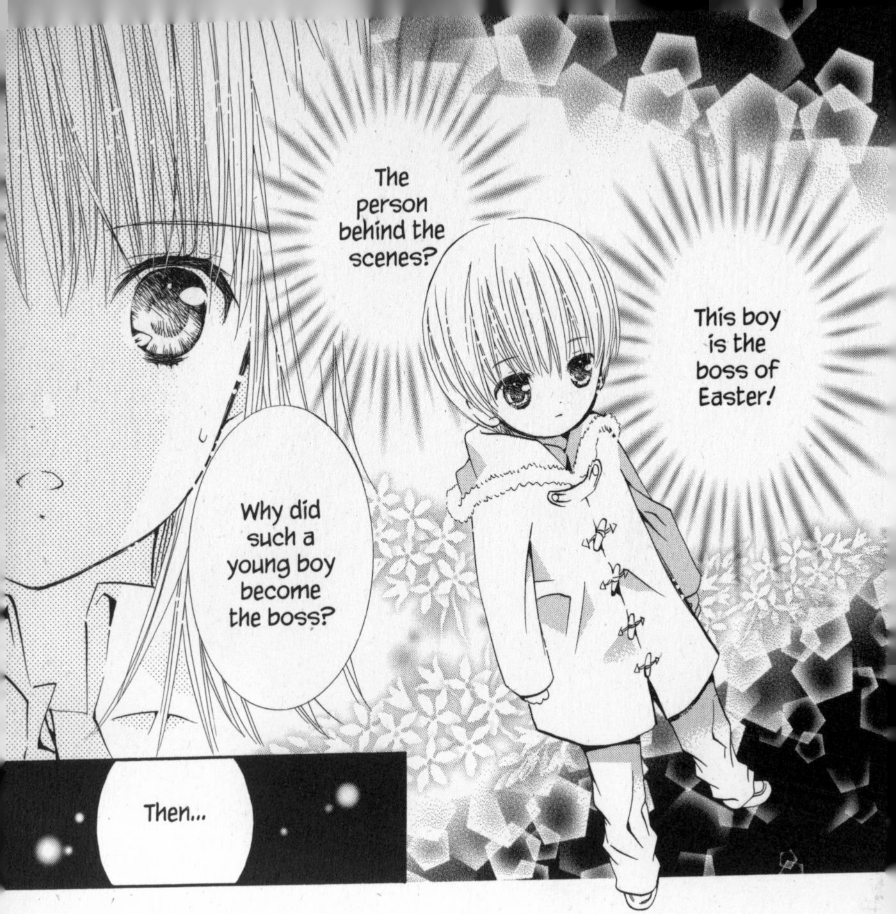
The person behind the scenes?
This boy is the boss of Easter!
Why did such a young boy become the boss?
Then...

Hello ♥ This is Sendo from the PEACH-PIT. It's volume 10 already!
We're in two digits now!
♥ I always say this, but it goes by so fast! Since we started this series to December 2009, it's going into the fifth year. Thank you for reading! The story is closing in on the climax! Please continue to support us.
♥ Now, let's go on to the Q & A!
Q1: At what times do you think of where the story is going to go?

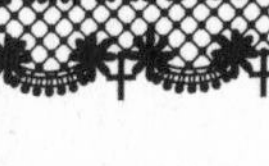
It's going to be continued.

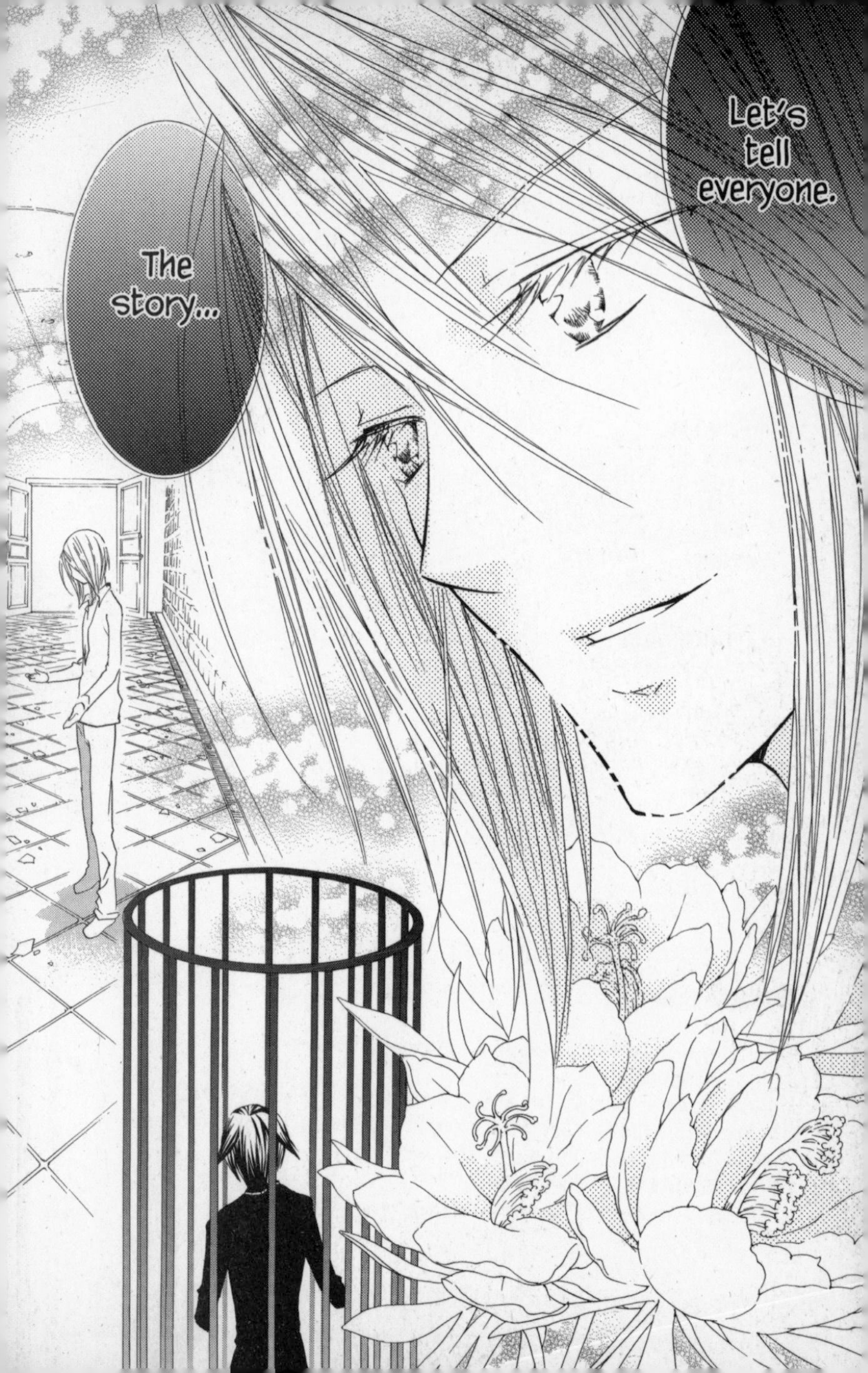
Let's tell everyone.
The story...

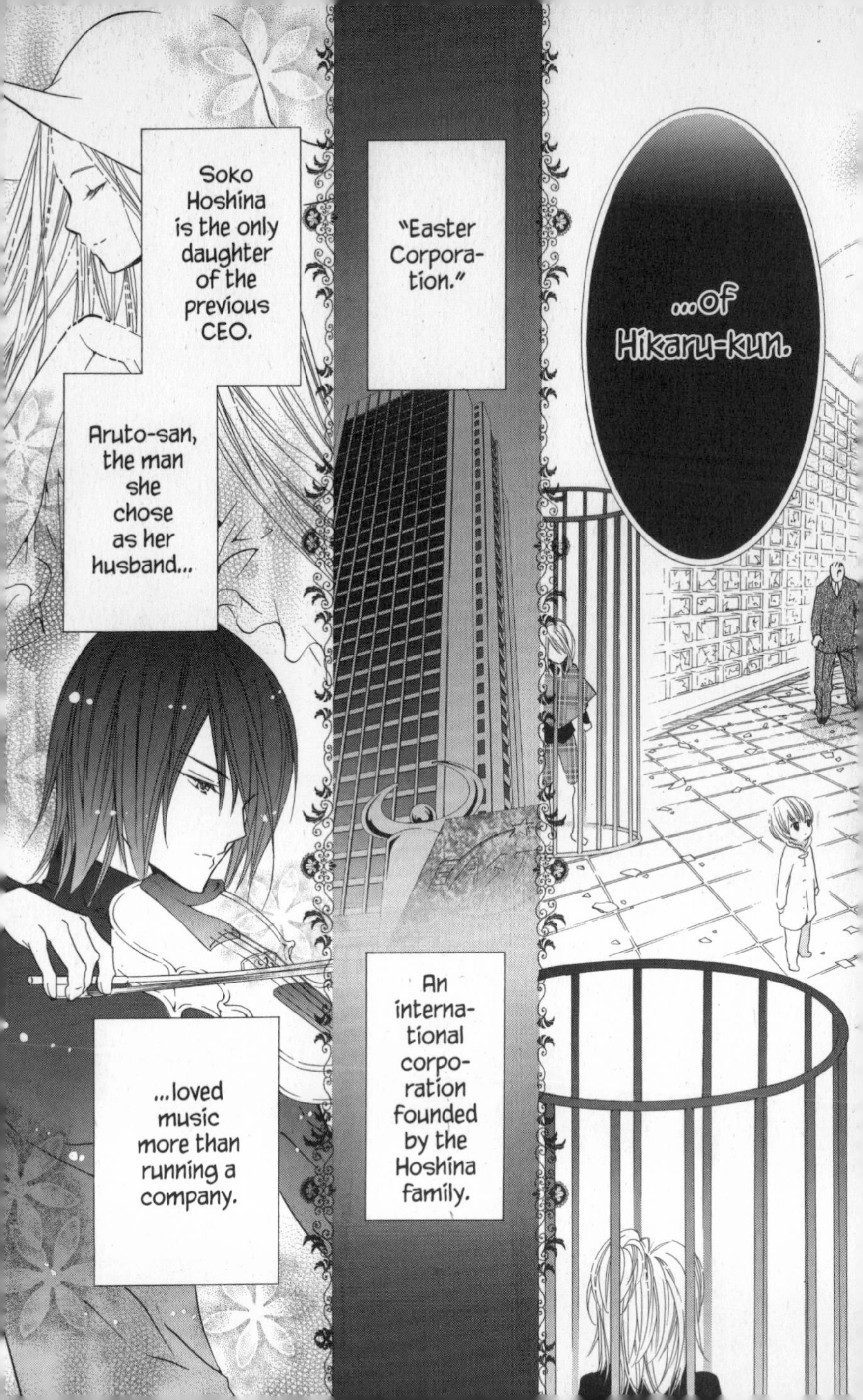
...of Hikaru-kun.
"Easter Corporation."
An international corporation founded by the Hoshina family.
Soko Hoshina is the only daughter of the previous CEO.
Aruto-san, the man she chose as her husband...
...loved music more than running a company.

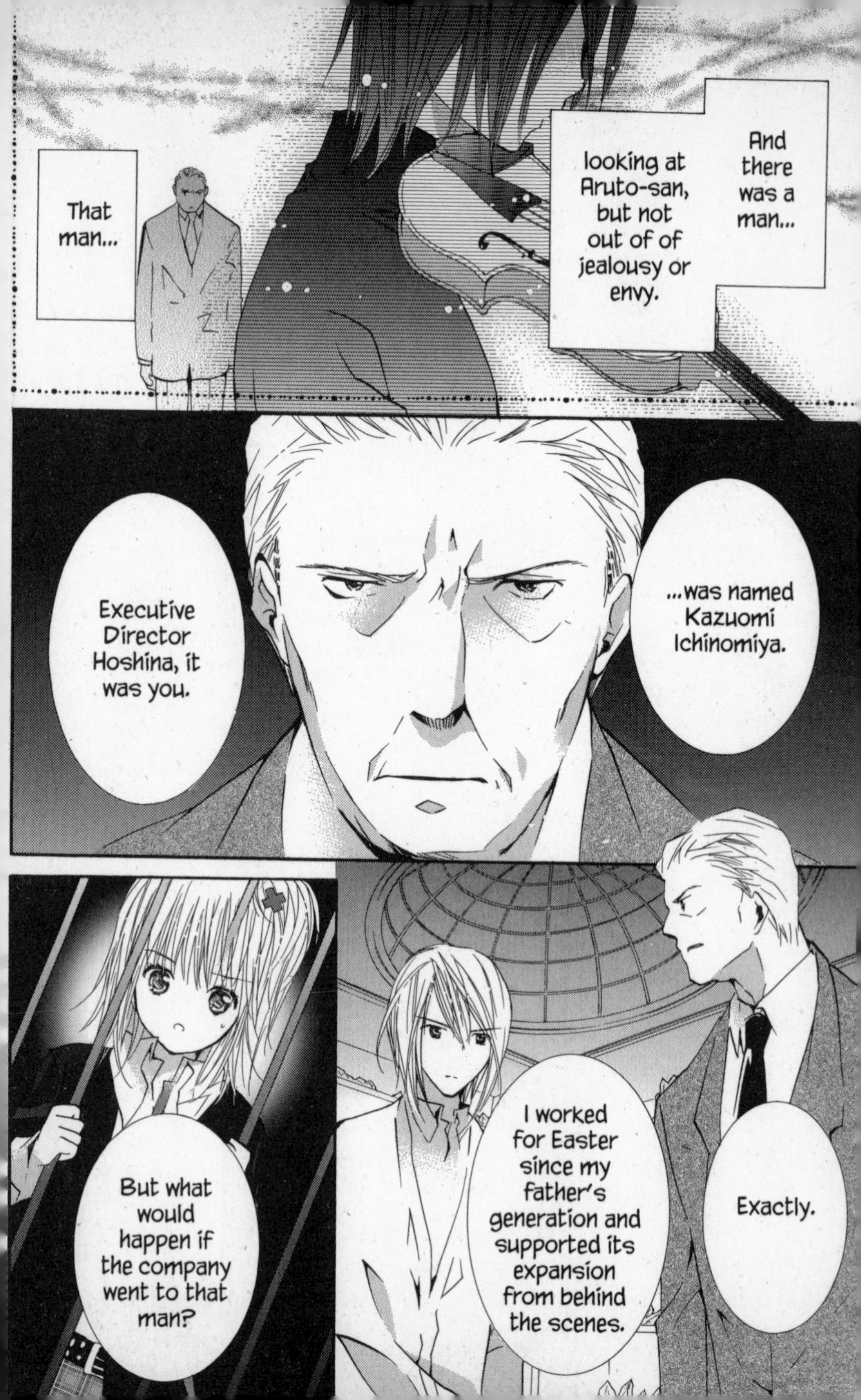
And there was a man...
looking at Aruto-san, but not out of of jealousy or envy.
That man...
...was named Kazuomi Ichinomiya.
Executive Director Hoshina, it was you.
Exactly.
I worked for Easter since my father's generation and supported its expansion from behind the scenes.
But what would happen if the company went to that man?

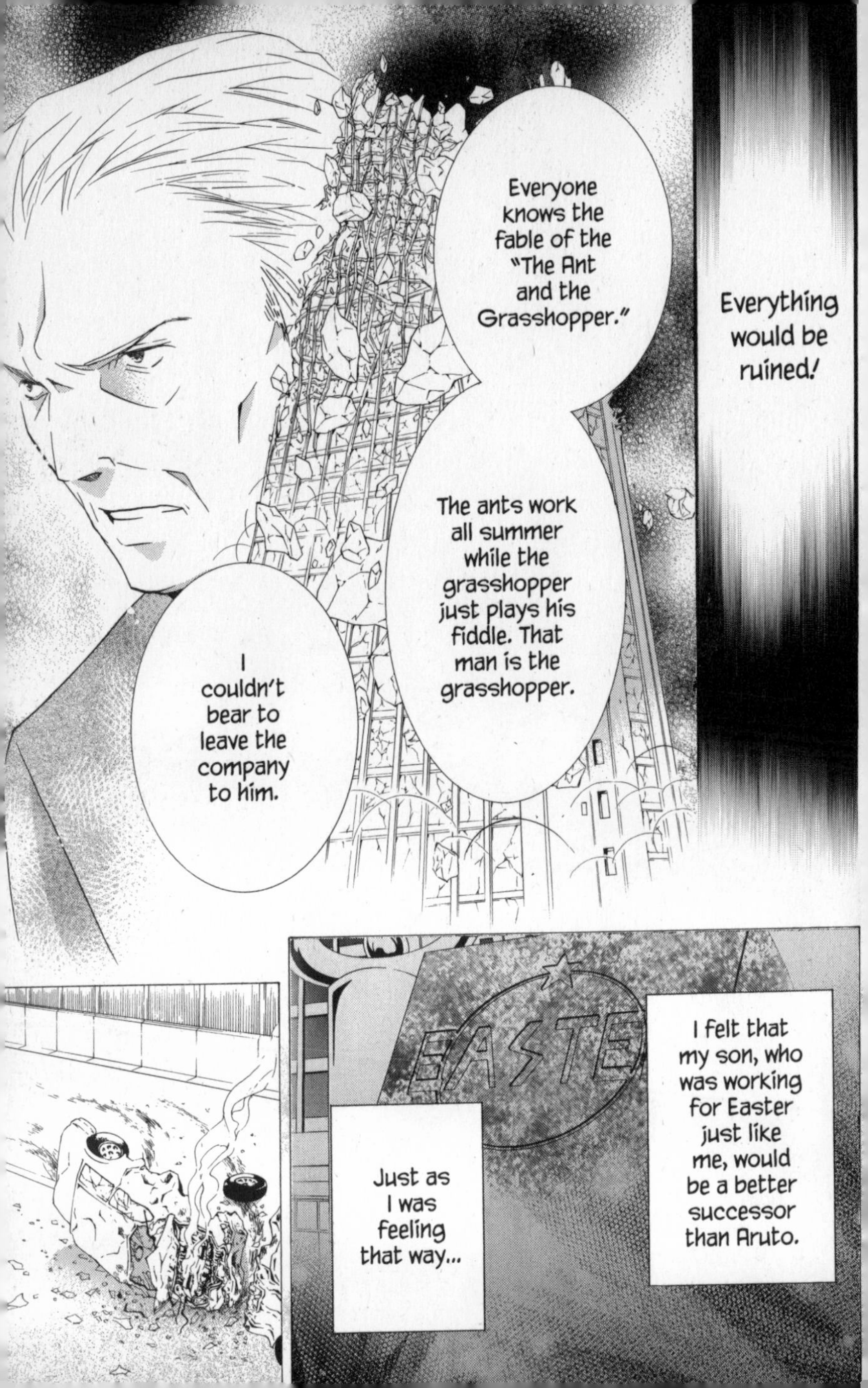
Everything would be ruined!
Everyone knows the fable of the "The Ant and the Grasshopper."
The ants work all summer while the grasshopper just plays his fiddle. That man is the grasshopper.
I couldn't bear to leave the company to him.
I felt that my son, who was working for Easter just like me, would be a better successor than Aruto.
Just as I was feeling that way...
EASTE

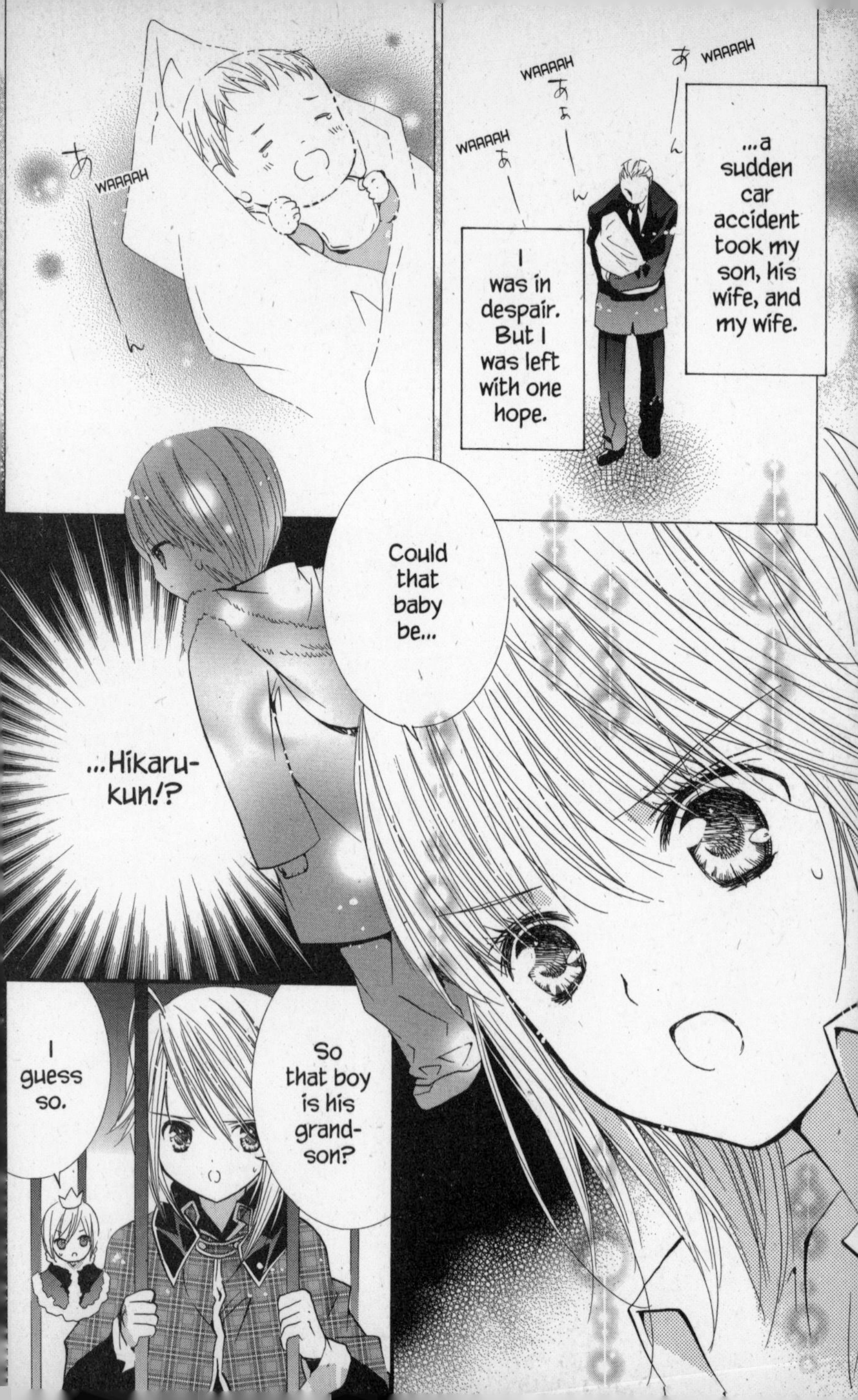
あ WAAAAH
WAAAAH あぁ
WAAAAH あ
...a sudden car accident took my son, his wife, and my wife.
I was in despair. But I was left with one hope.
あ WAAAAH
Could that baby be...
...Hikaru-kun!?
So that boy is his grand-son?
I guess so.

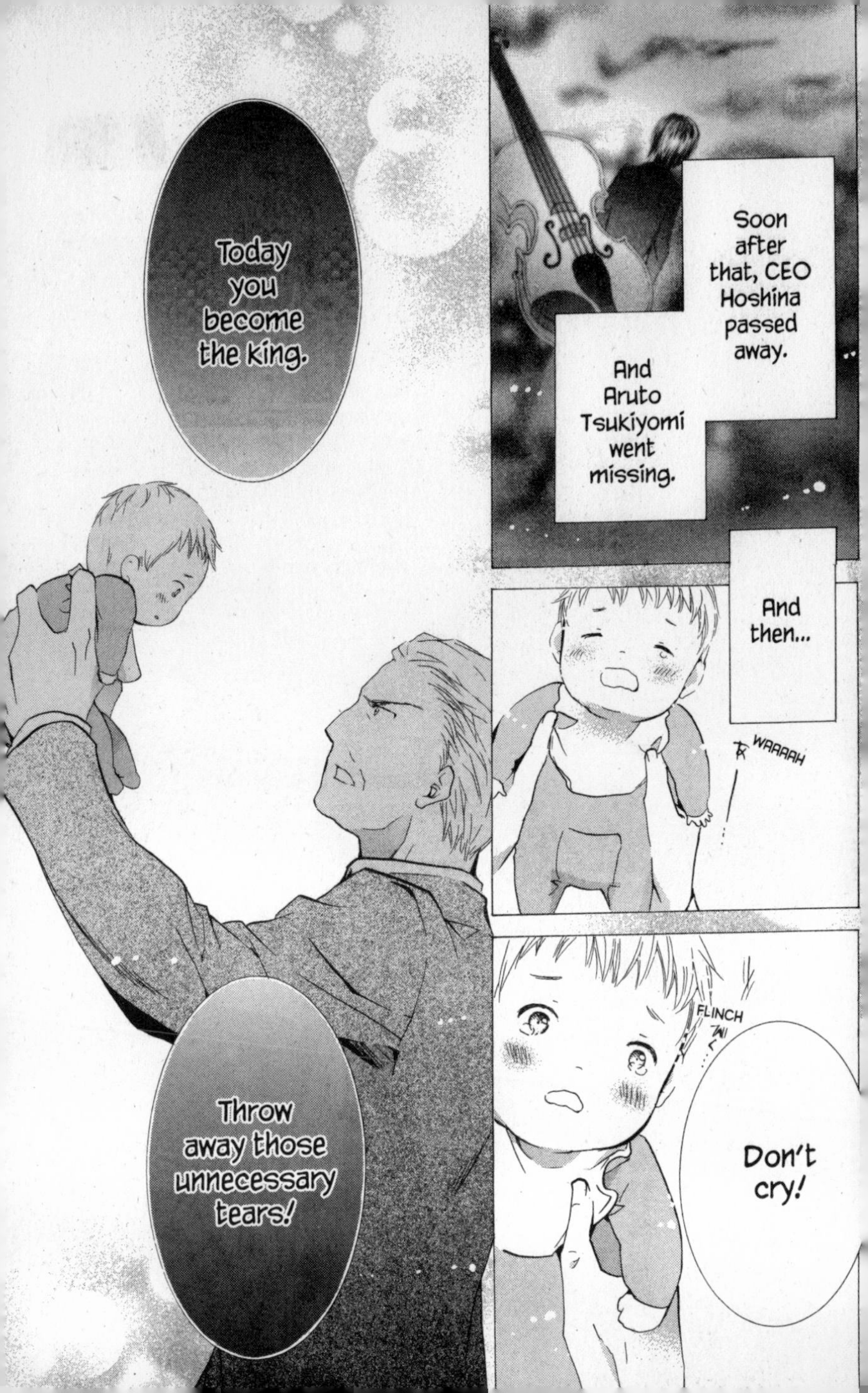
Soon after that, CEO Hoshina passed away.
And Aruto Tsukiyomi went missing.
And then...
WAAAAH
FLINCH
Don't cry!
Today you become the king.
Throw away those unnecessary tears!

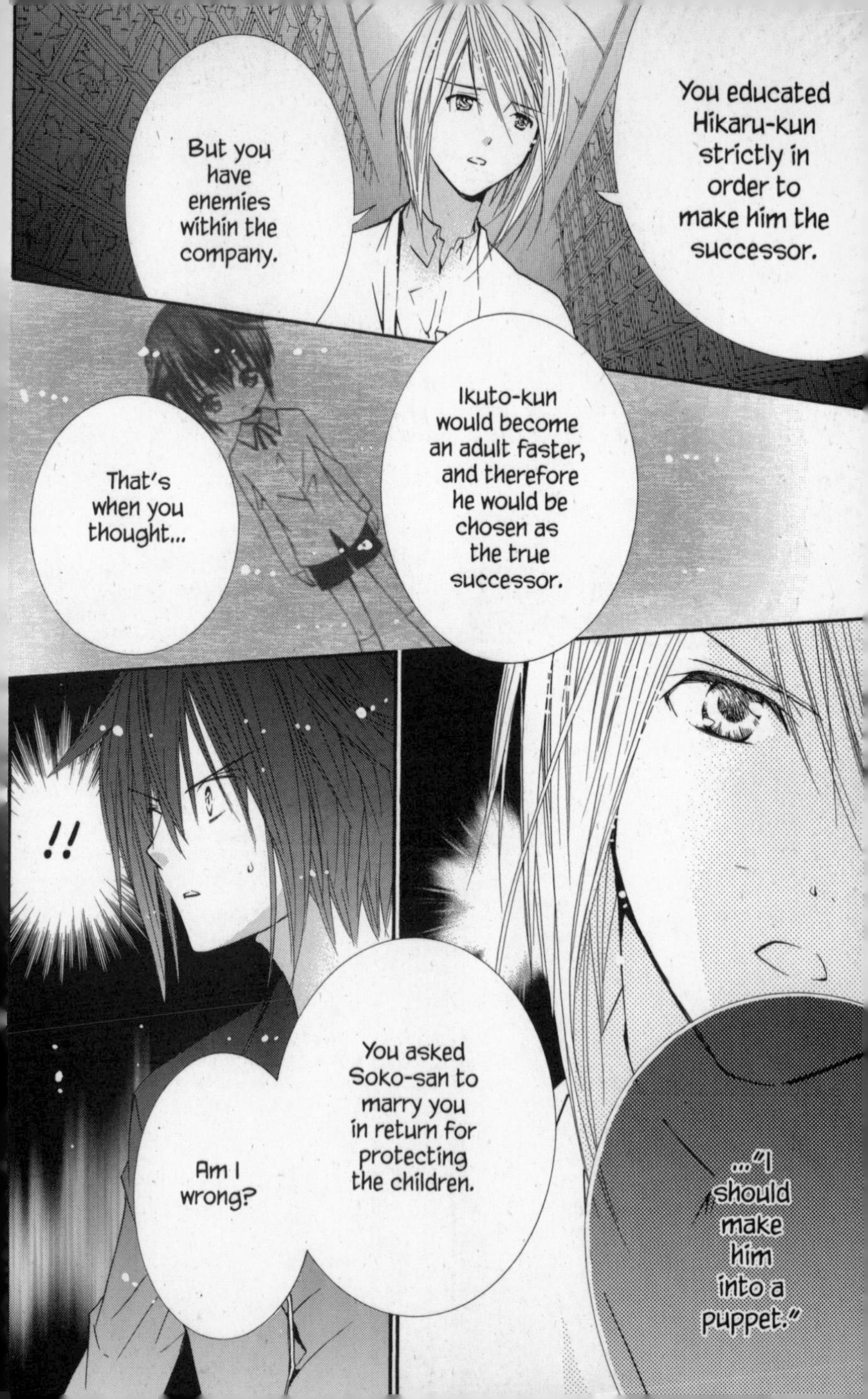

You educated Hikaru-kun strictly in order to make him the successor.
But you have enemies within the company.
Ikuto-kun would become an adult faster, and therefore he would be chosen as the true successor.
That's when you thought...
..."I should make him into a puppet."
You asked Soko-san to marry you in return for protecting the children.
Am I wrong?
!!

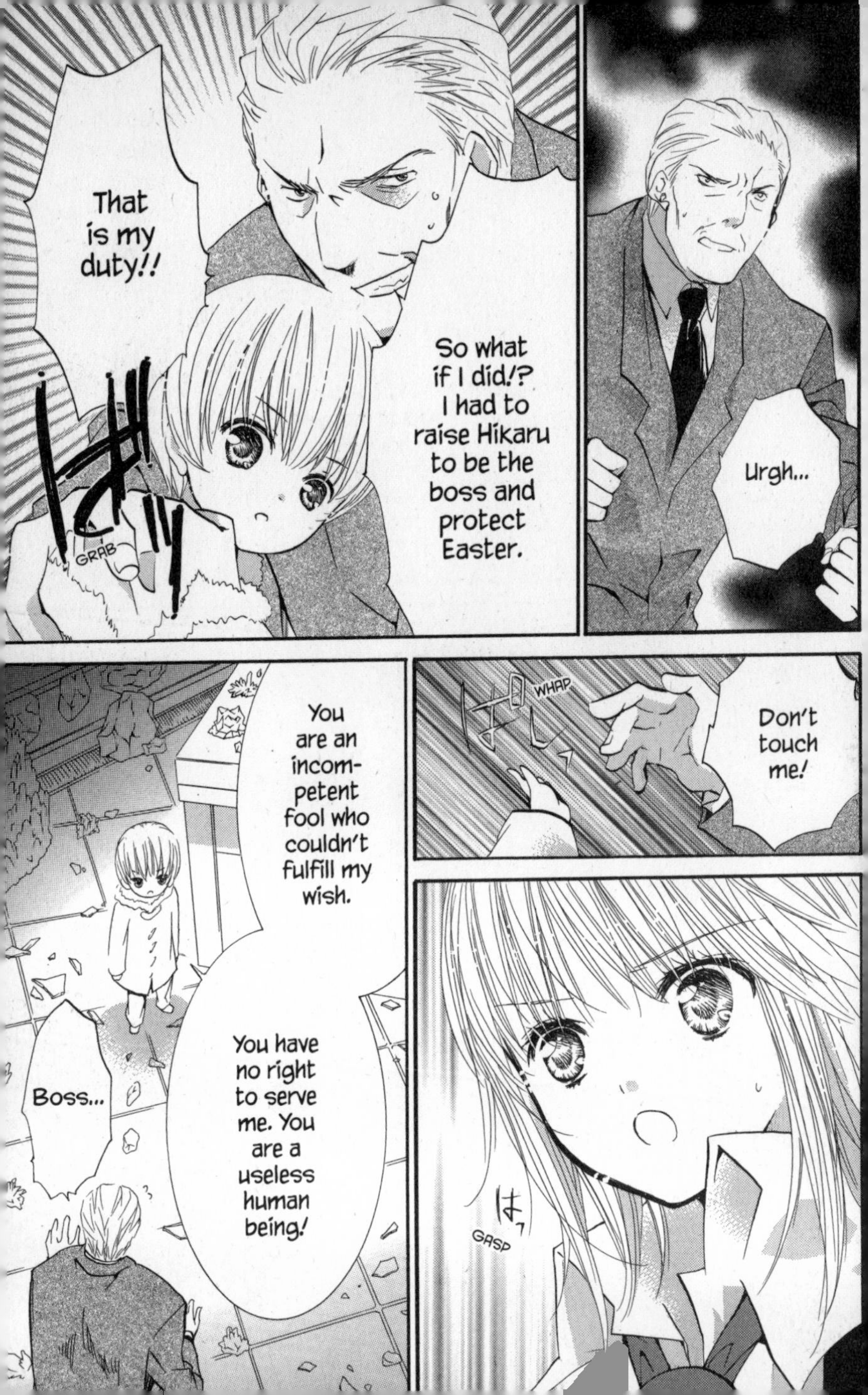
Urgh...
So what if I did!? I had to raise Hikaru to be the boss and protect Easter.
That is my duty!!
GRAB
Don't touch me!
WHAP
GASP
You are an incom-petent fool who couldn't fulfill my wish.
You have no right to serve me. You are a useless human being!
Boss...

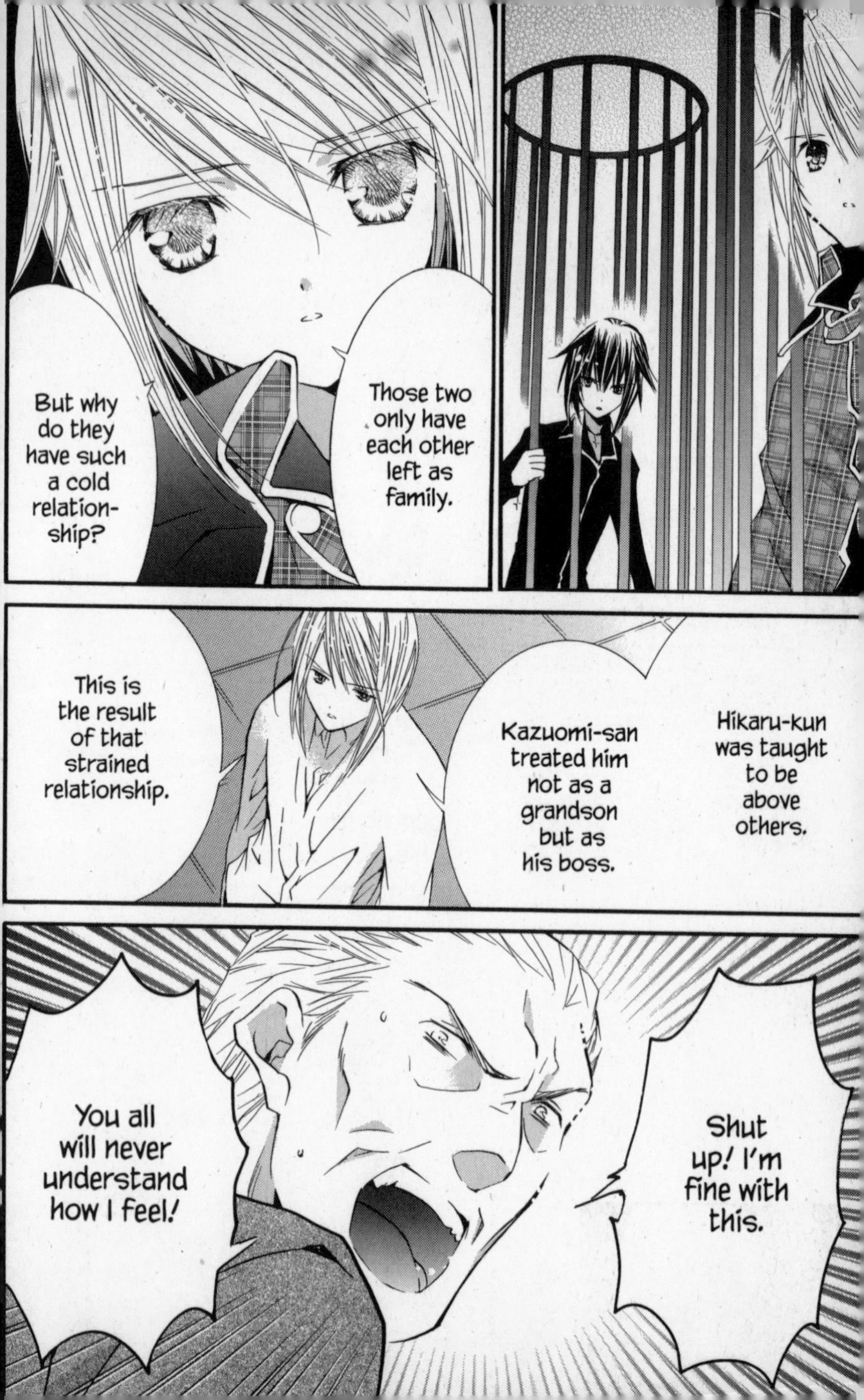
Those two only have each other left as family.
But why do they have such a cold relationship?
Hikaru-kun was taught to be above others.
Kazuomi-san treated him not as a grandson but as his boss.
This is the result of that strained relationship.
Shut up! I'm fine with this.
You all will never understand how I feel!

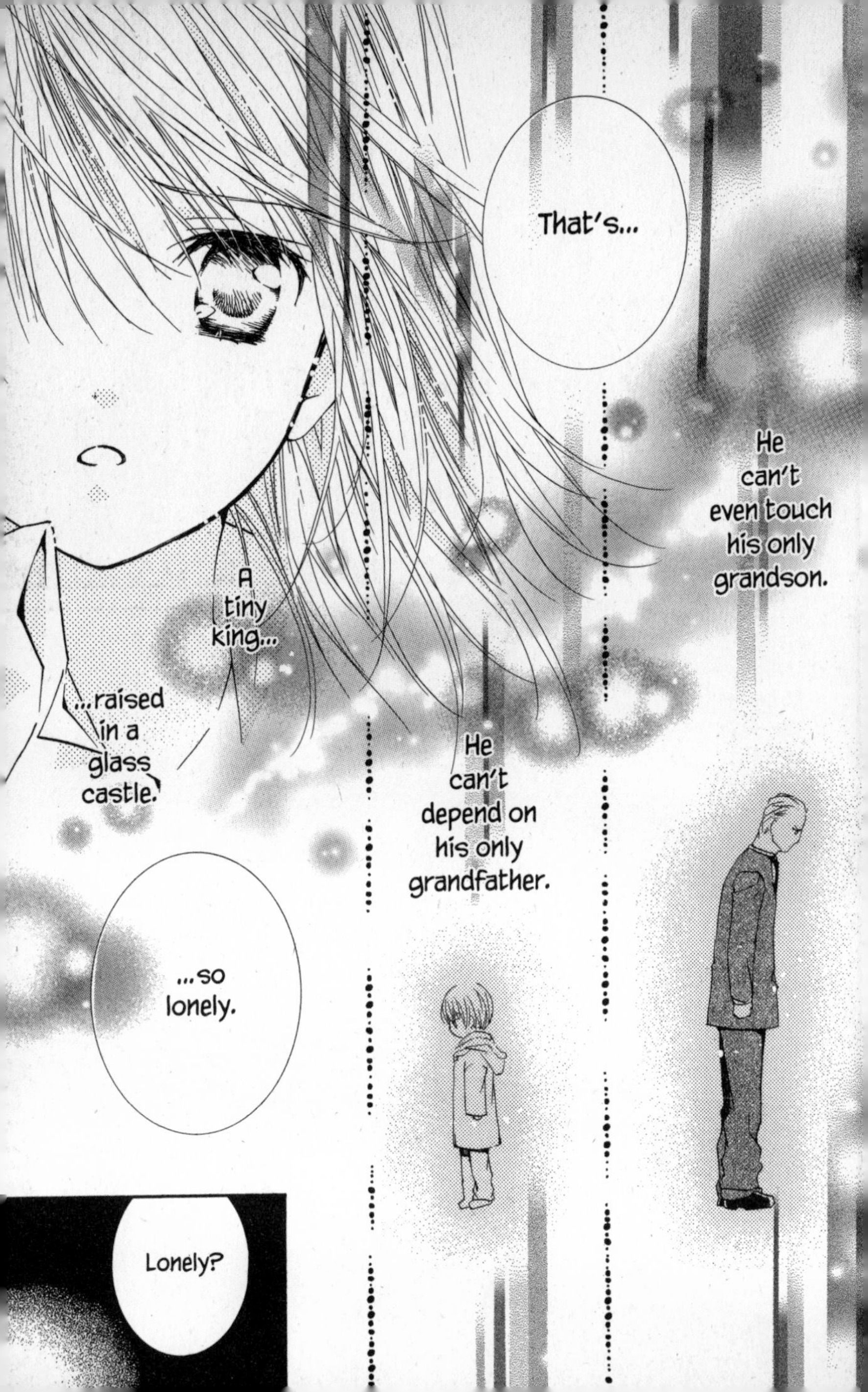
That's...
He can't even touch his only grandson.
He can't depend on his only grandfather.
A tiny king...
...raised in a glass castle.
...so lonely.
Lonely?

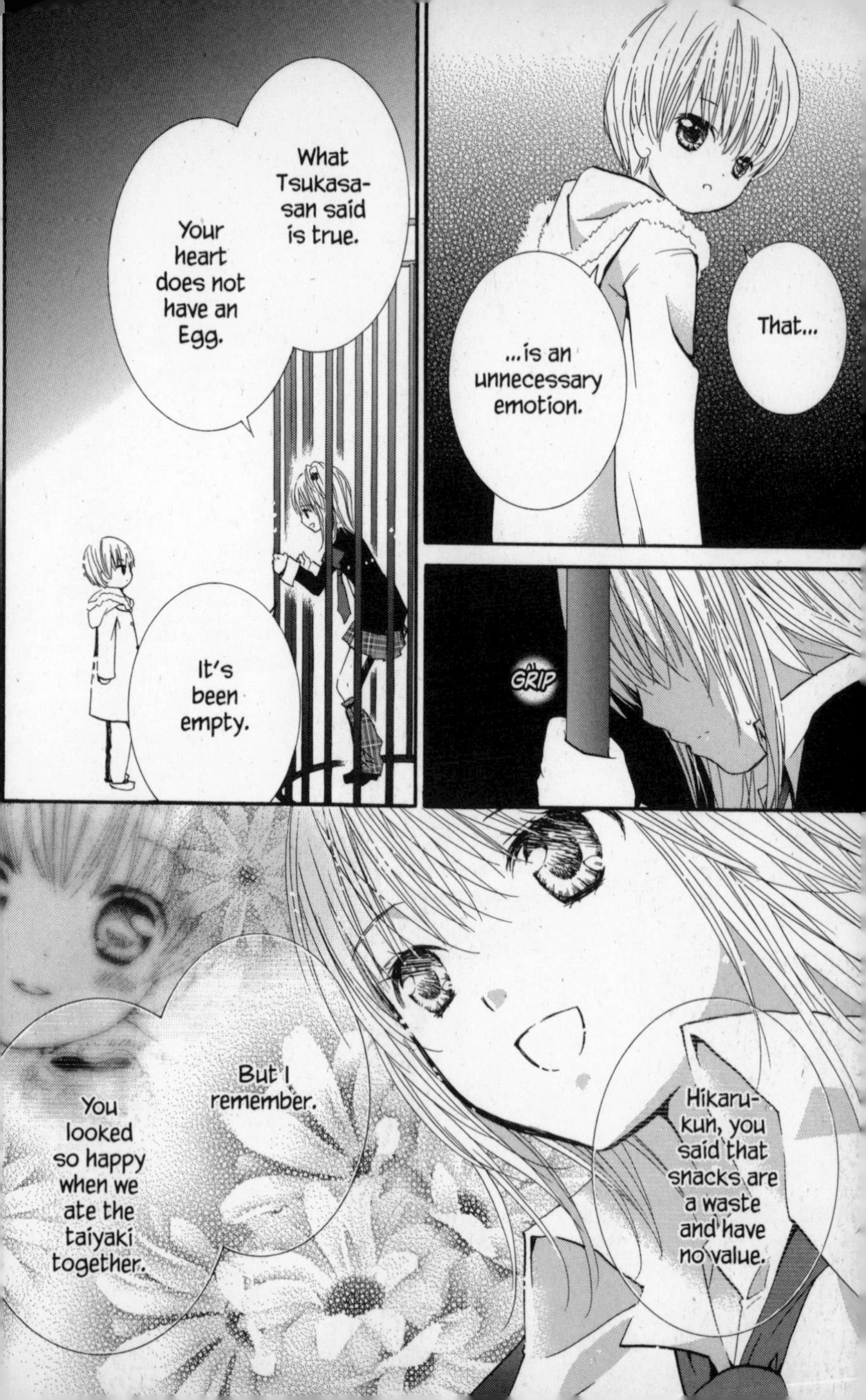
That...
...is an unnecessary emotion.
GRIP
What Tsukasa-san said is true.
Your heart does not have an Egg.
It's been empty.
Hikaru-kun, you said that snacks are a waste and have no value.
But I remember.
You looked so happy when we ate the taiyaki together.

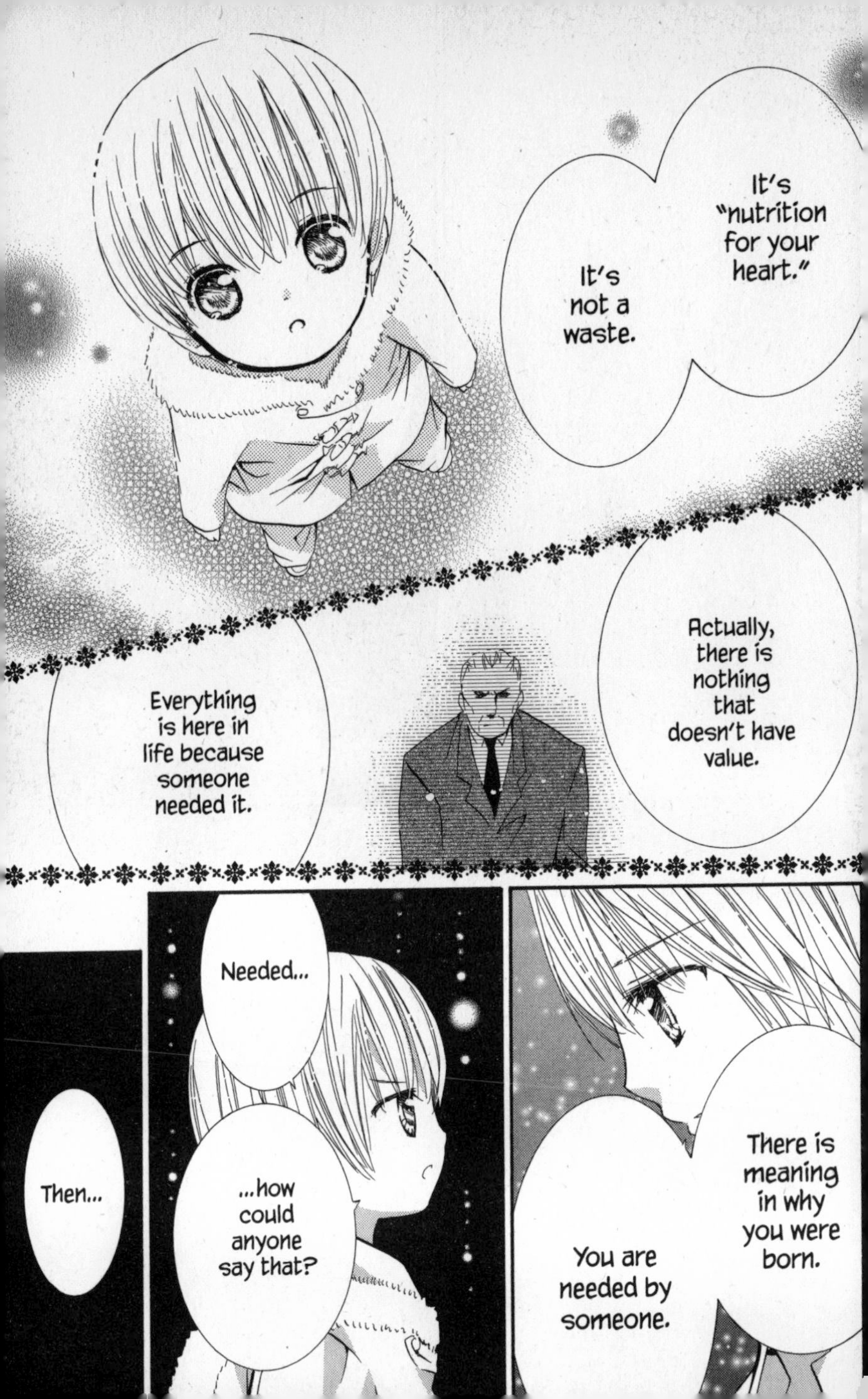

It's "nutrition for your heart."
It's not a waste.
Actually, there is nothing that doesn't have value.
Everything is here in life because someone needed it.
There is meaning in why you were born.
You are needed by someone.
Needed...
Then...
...how could anyone say that?

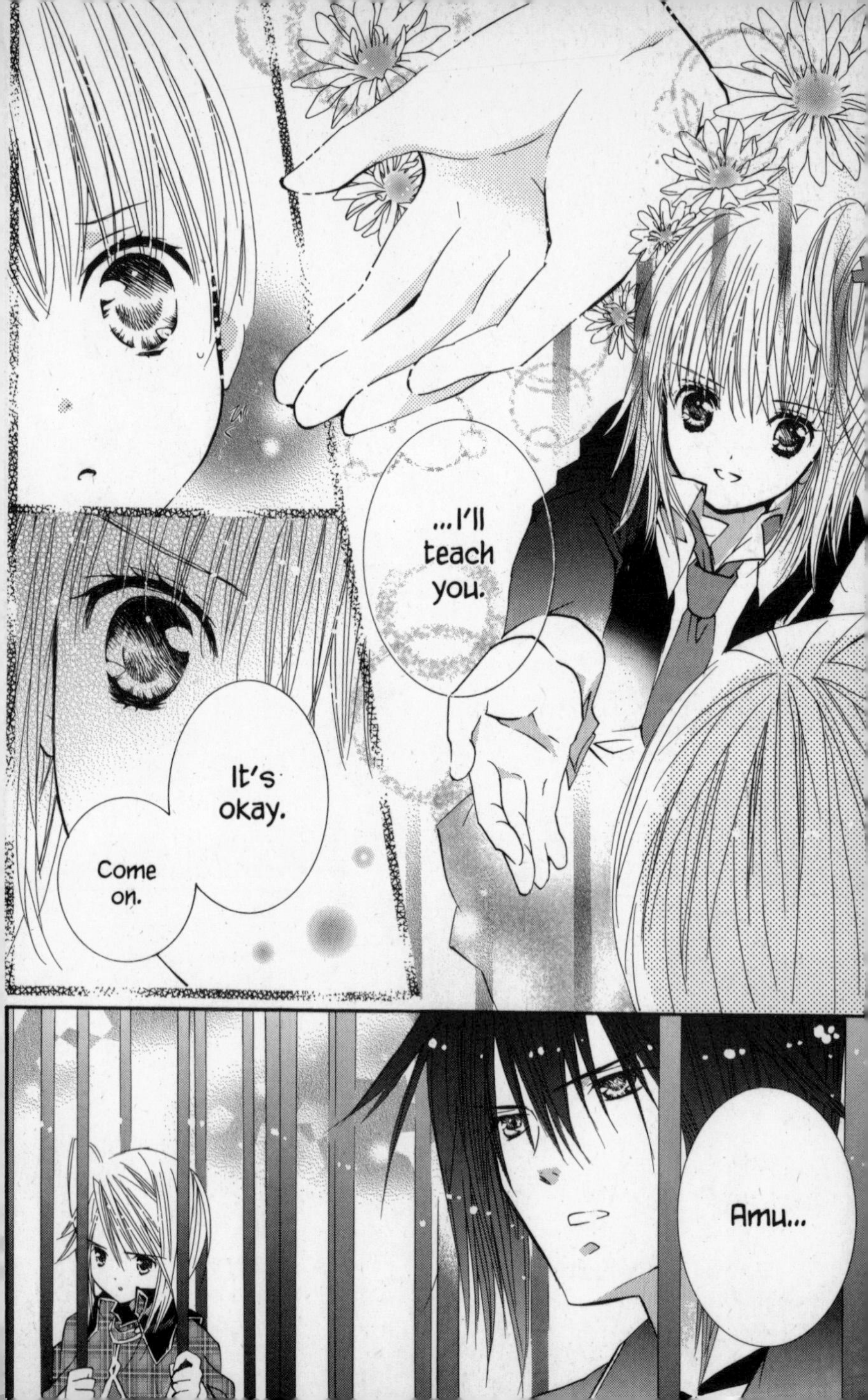
...I'll teach you.
It's okay.
Come on.
Amu...

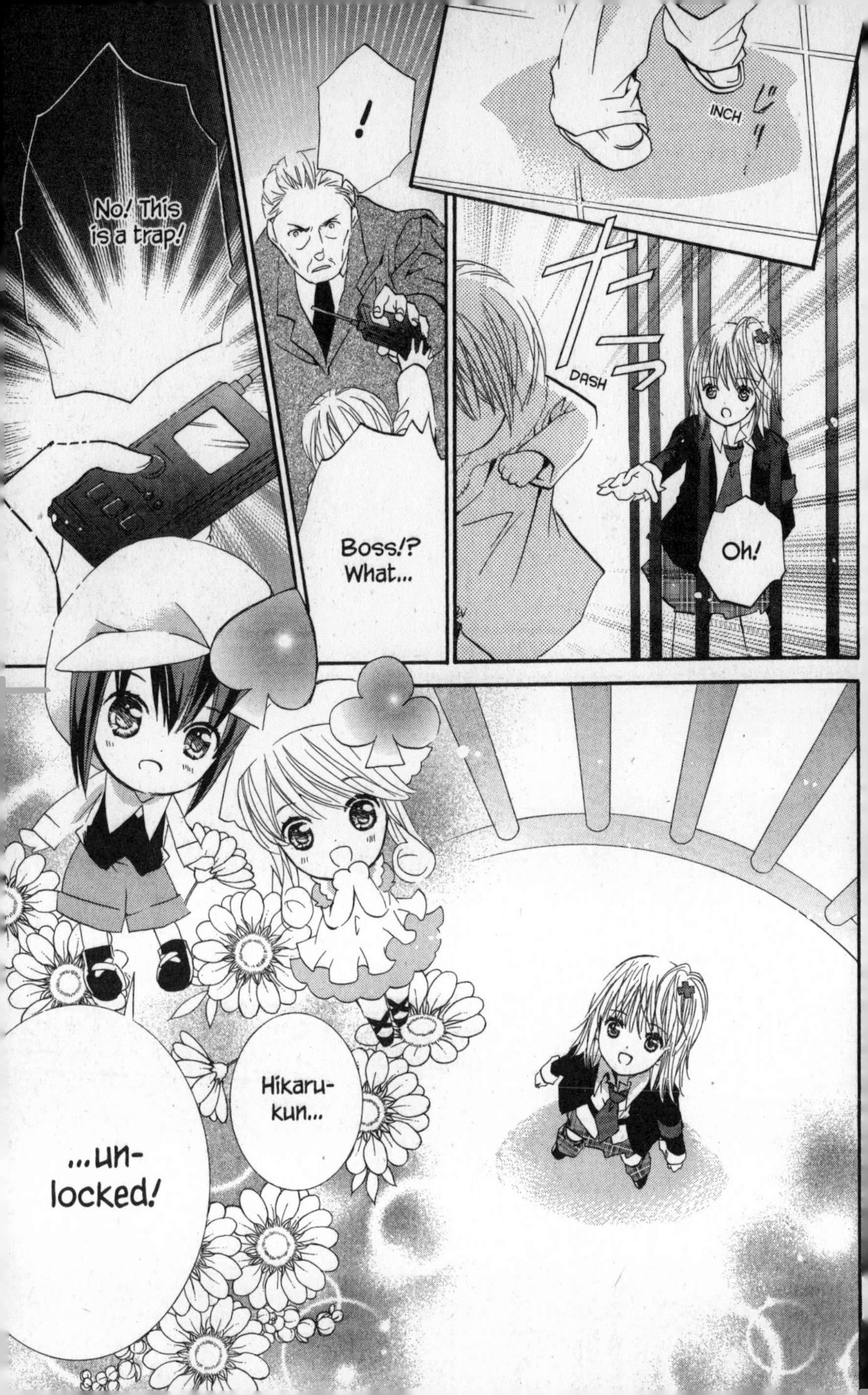
INCH
DASH
Oh!
!
Boss!? What...
No! This is a trap!
Hikaru-kun...
...un-locked!

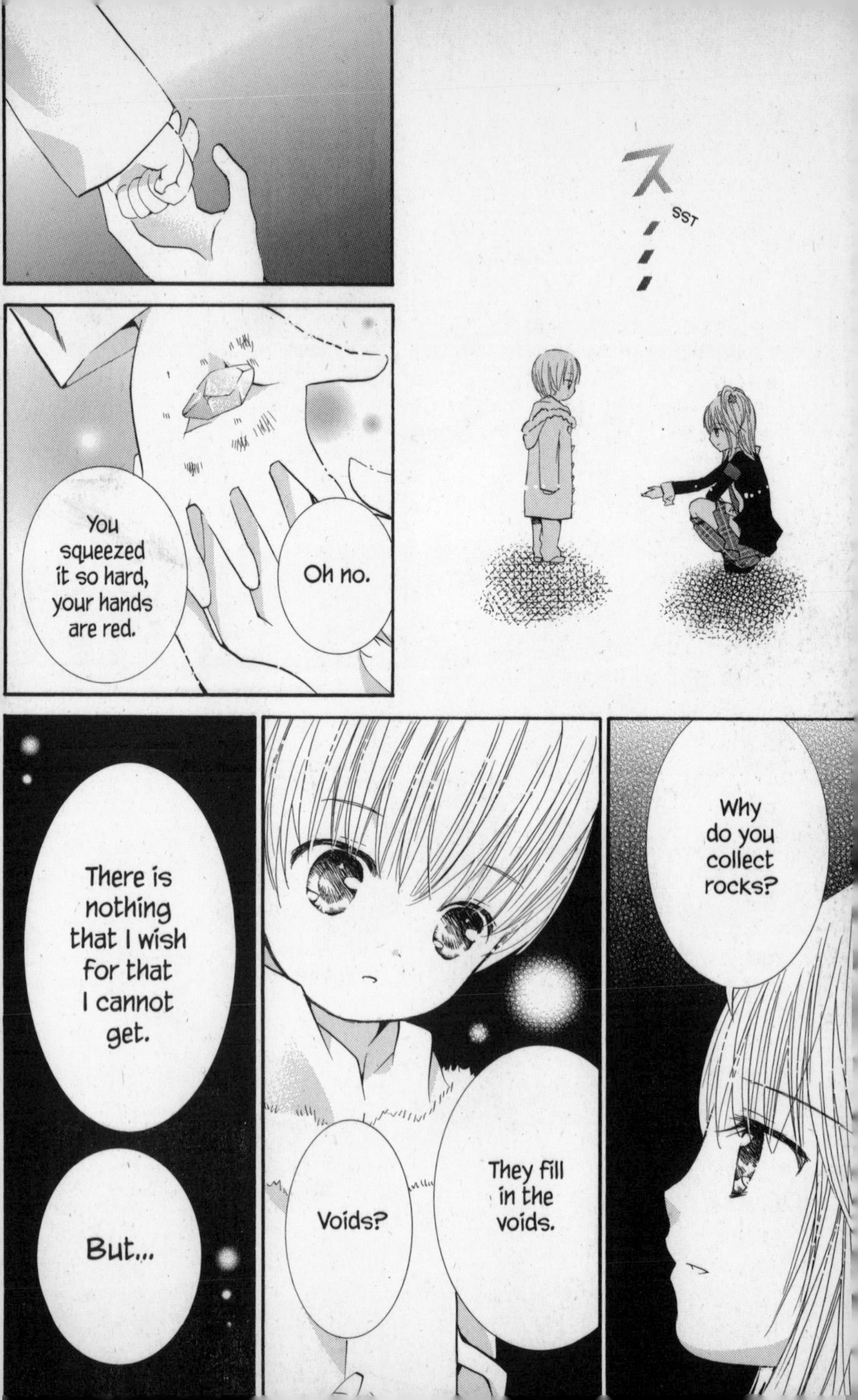
ス
SST
Oh no.
You squeezed it so hard, your hands are red.
Why do you collect rocks?
They fill in the voids.
Voids?
There is nothing that I wish for that I cannot get.
But...

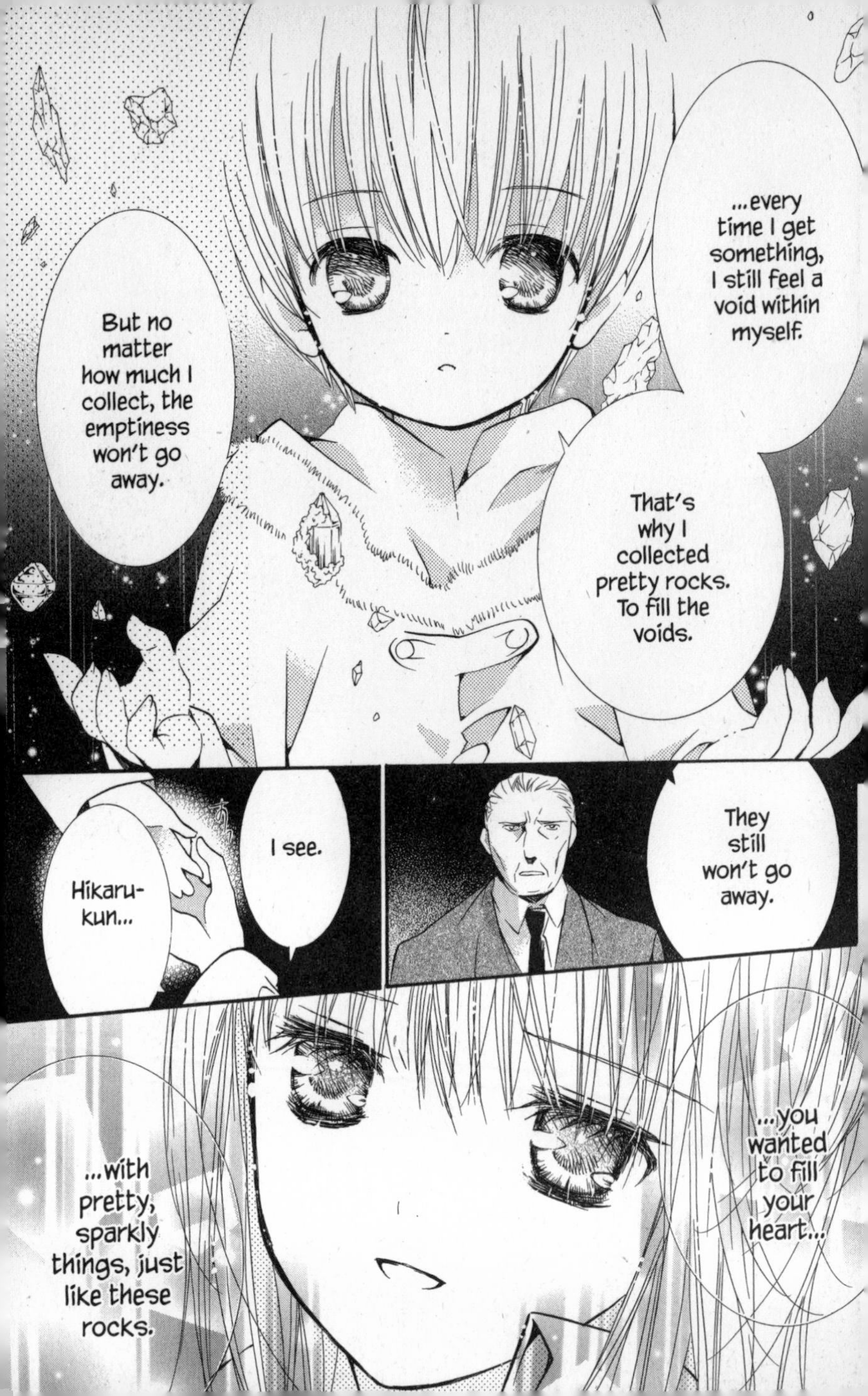
...every time I get something, I still feel a void within myself.
That's why I collected pretty rocks. To fill the voids.
But no matter how much I collect, the emptiness won't go away.
They still won't go away.
I see.
Hikaru-kun...
...you wanted to fill your heart...
...with pretty, sparkly things, just like these rocks.

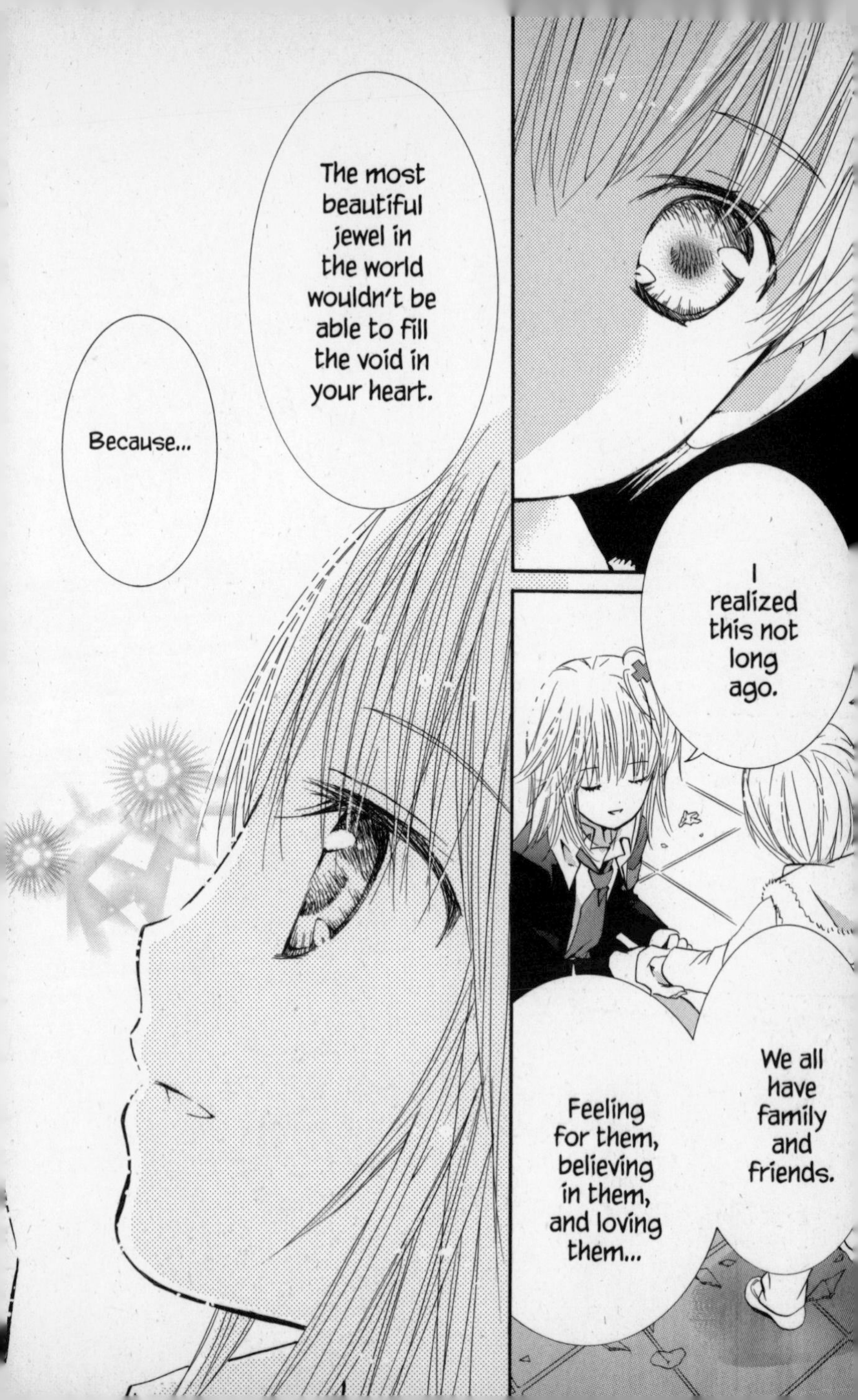
I realized this not long ago.
We all have family and friends.
Feeling for them, believing in them, and loving them...
The most beautiful jewel in the world wouldn't be able to fill the void in your heart.
Because...

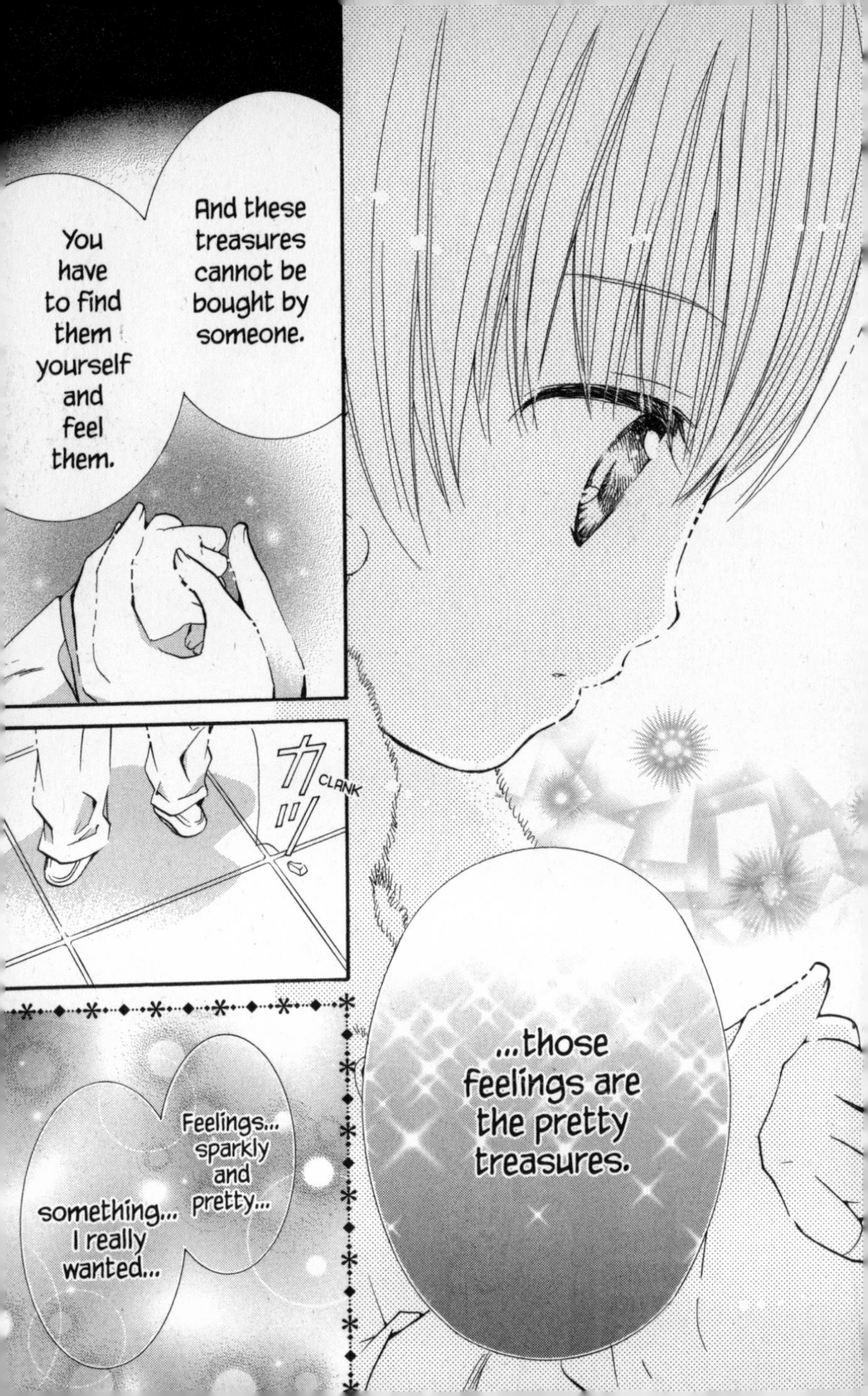
And these treasures cannot be bought by someone.
You have to find them yourself and feel them.
CLANK
Feelings... sparkly and pretty...
something... I really wanted...
...those feelings are the pretty treasures.

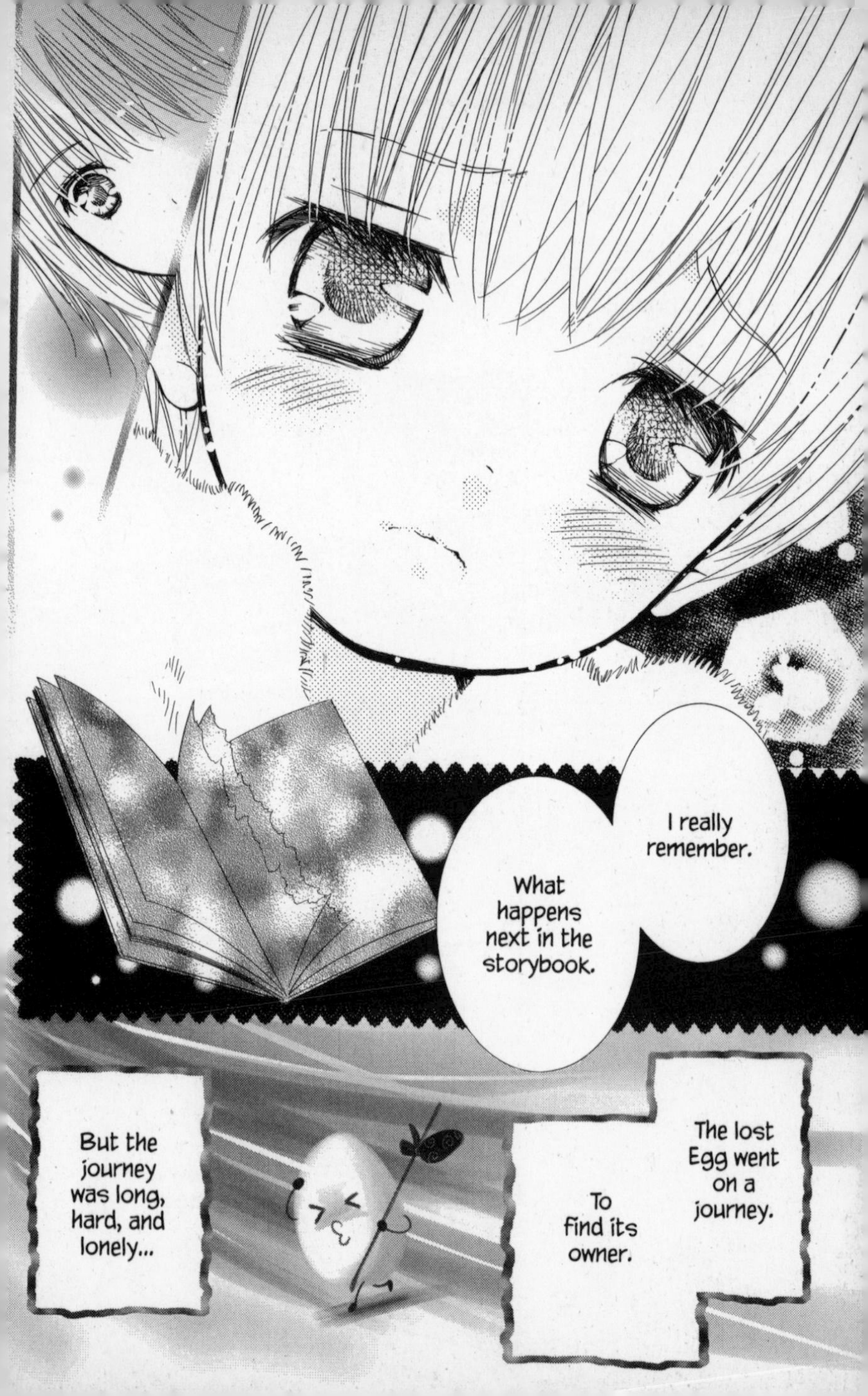
I really remember.
What happens next in the storybook.
The lost Egg went on a journey.
To find its owner.
But the journey was long, hard, and lonely...

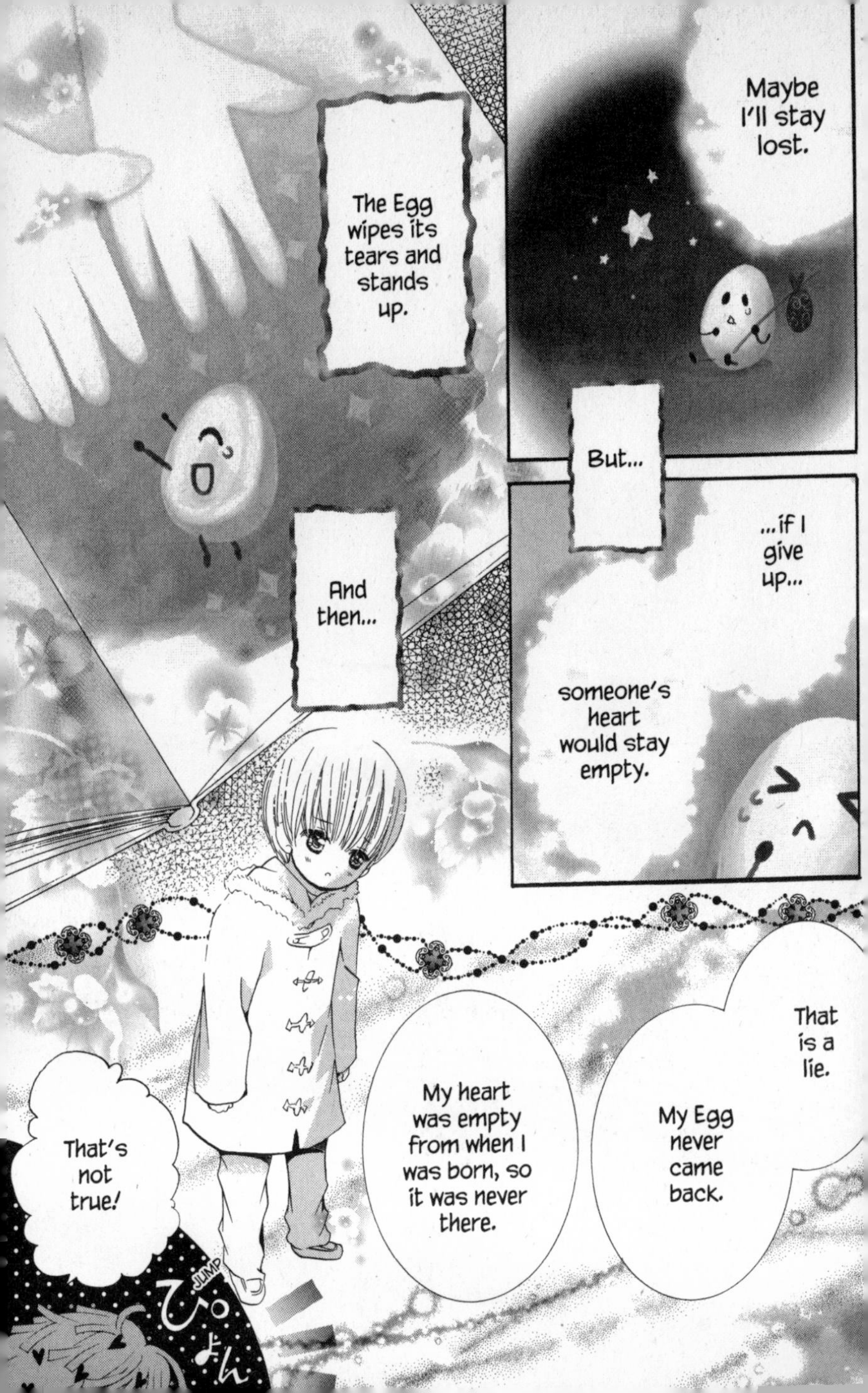
Maybe I'll stay lost.
But...
...if I give up...
someone's heart would stay empty.
The Egg wipes its tears and stands up.
And then...
That is a lie.
My Egg never came back.
My heart was empty from when I was born, so it was never there.
That's not true!
JUMP
ぴょん

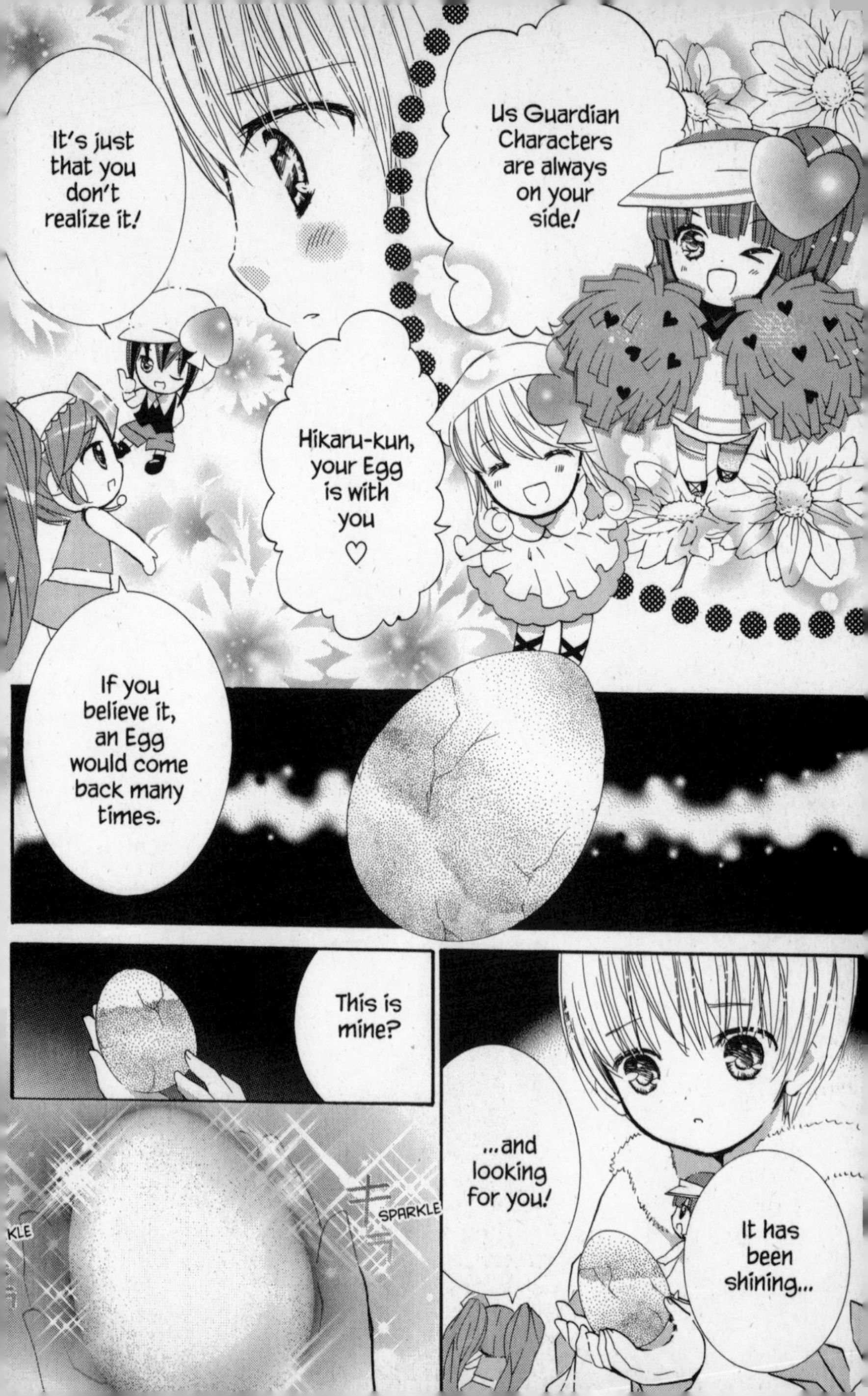
Us Guardian Characters are always on your side!
Hikaru-kun, your Egg is with you ♡
It's just that you don't realize it!
If you believe it, an Egg would come back many times.
It has been shining...
...and looking for you!
This is mine?
SPARKLE
KLE

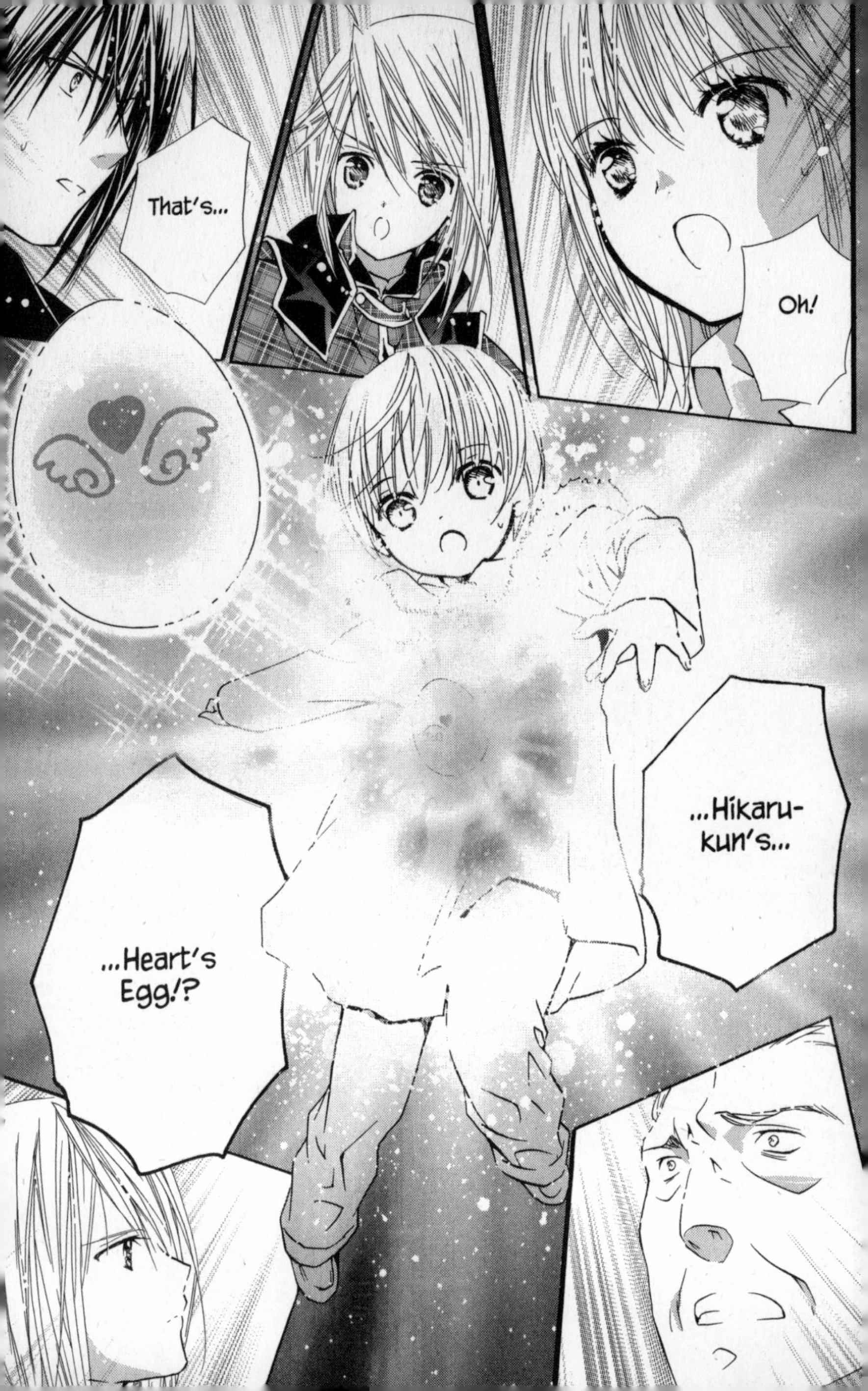
Oh!
That's...
...Hikaru-kun's...
...Heart's Egg!?

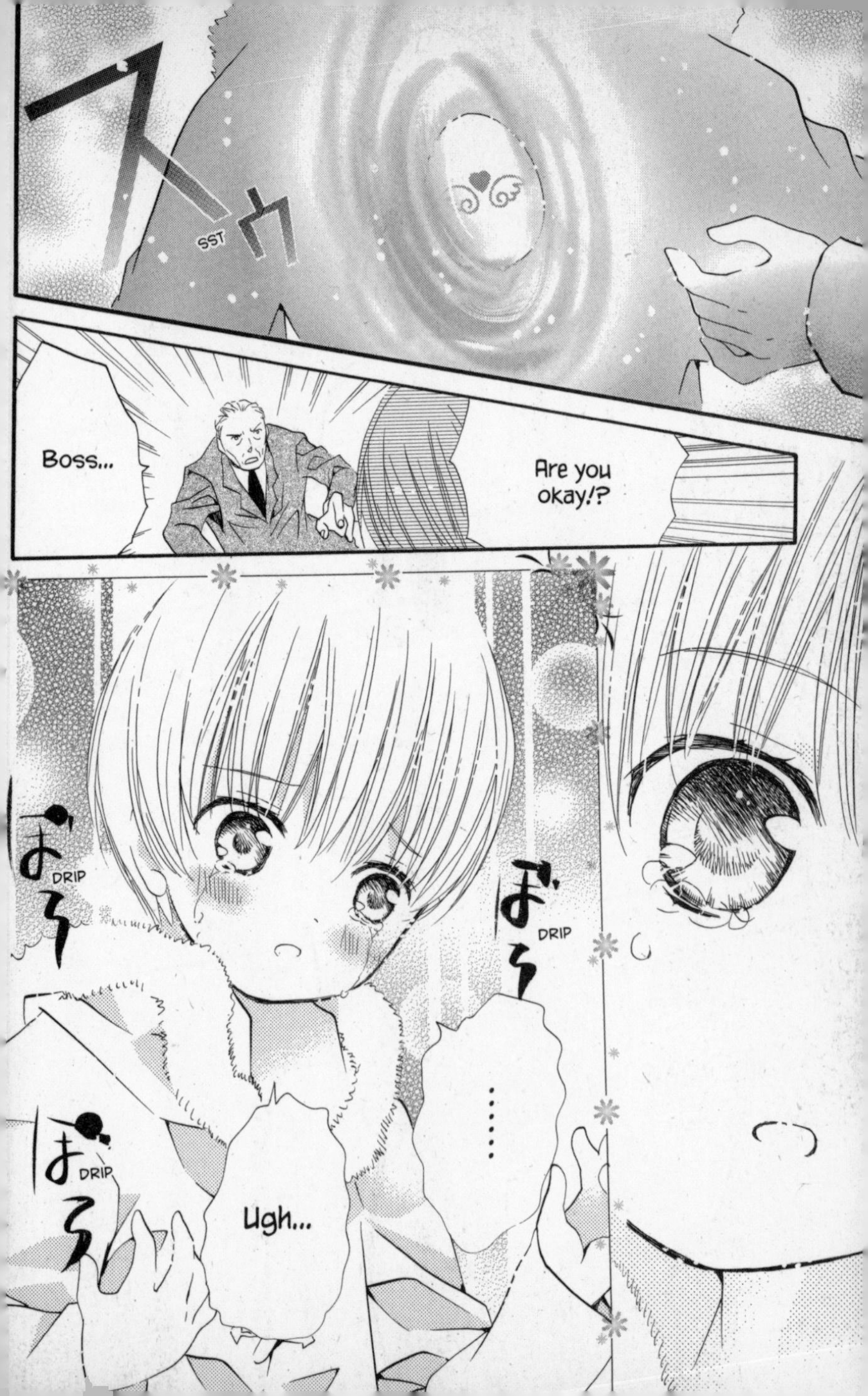
スゥ
SST
Are you okay!?
Boss...
ぽろ
DRIP
......
ぽろ
DRIP
Ugh...
ぽろ
DRIP

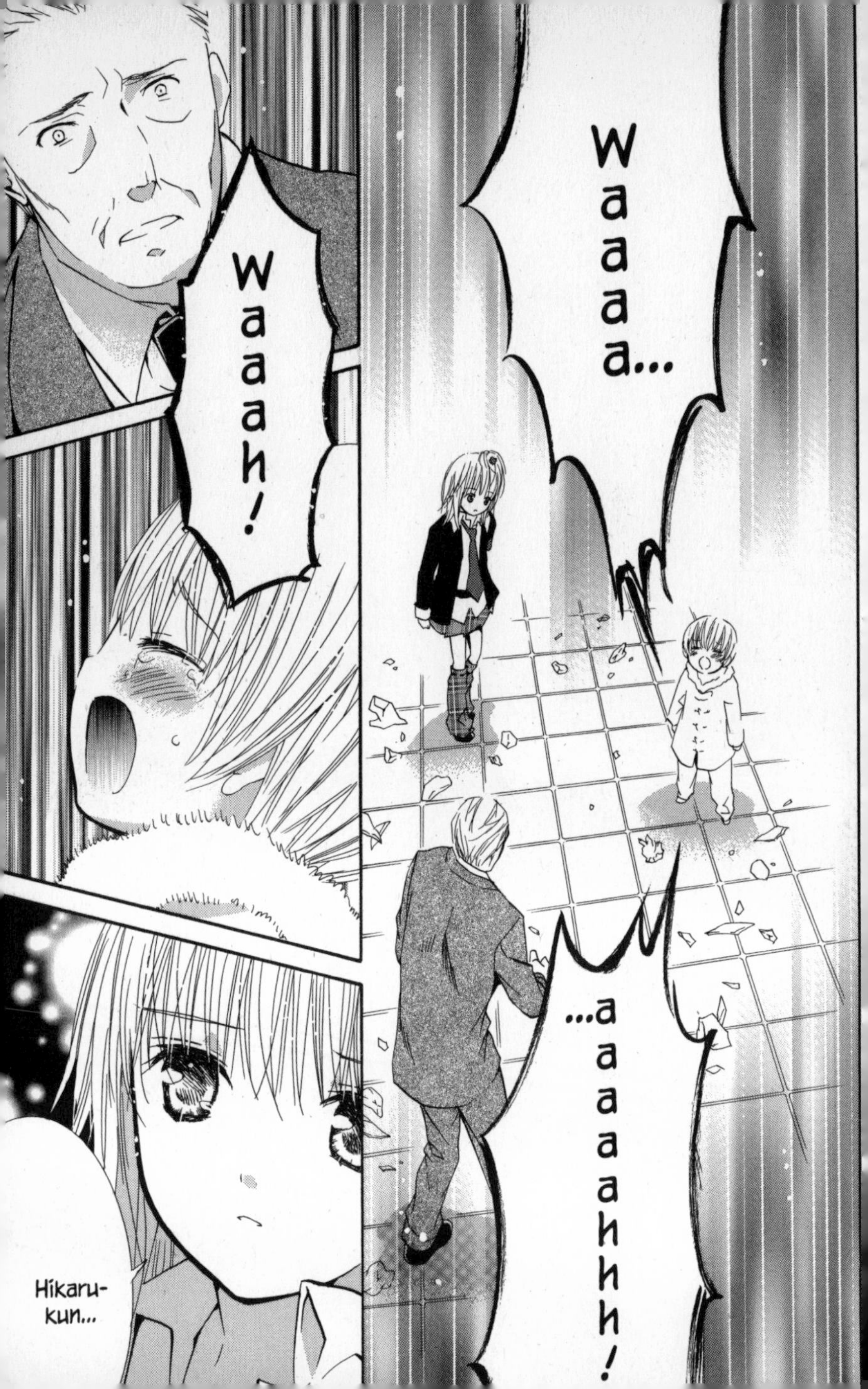

Waaaa...
...aaaaahhh!
Waaah!
Hikaru-kun...

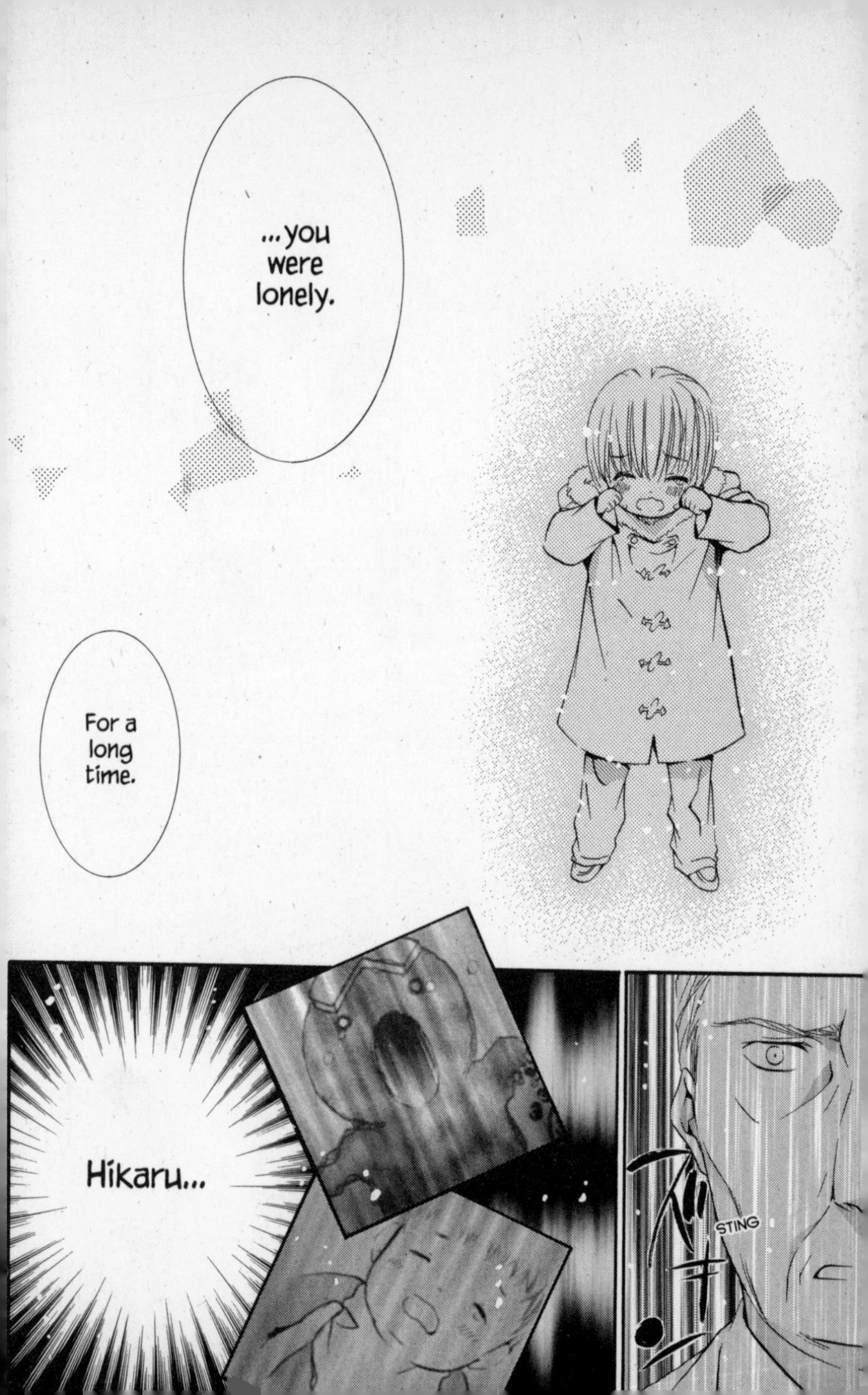
...you were lonely.
For a long time.
STING
Hikaru...

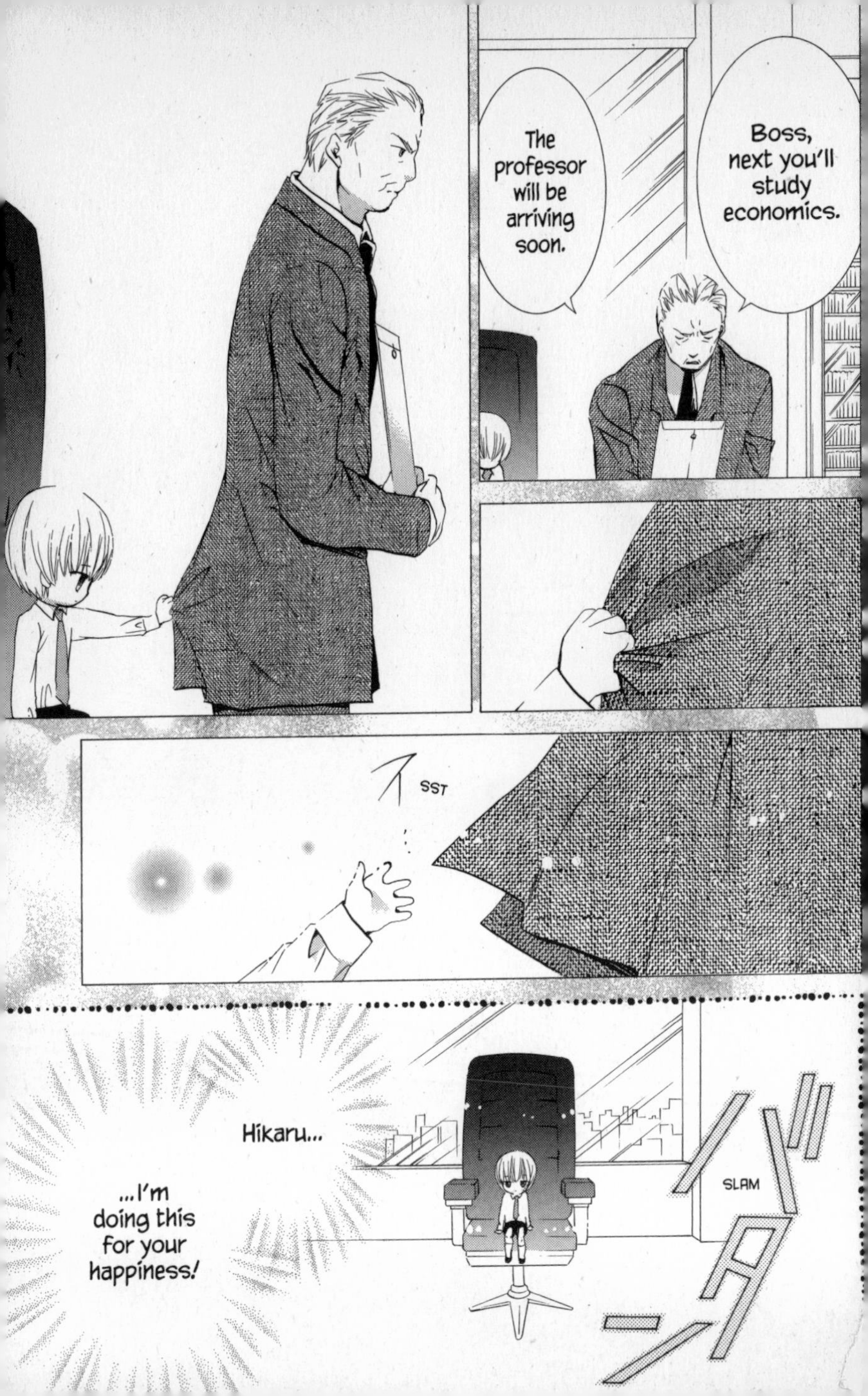
Boss, next you'll study economics.
The professor will be arriving soon.
SST
SLAM
Hikaru...
...I'm doing this for your happiness!

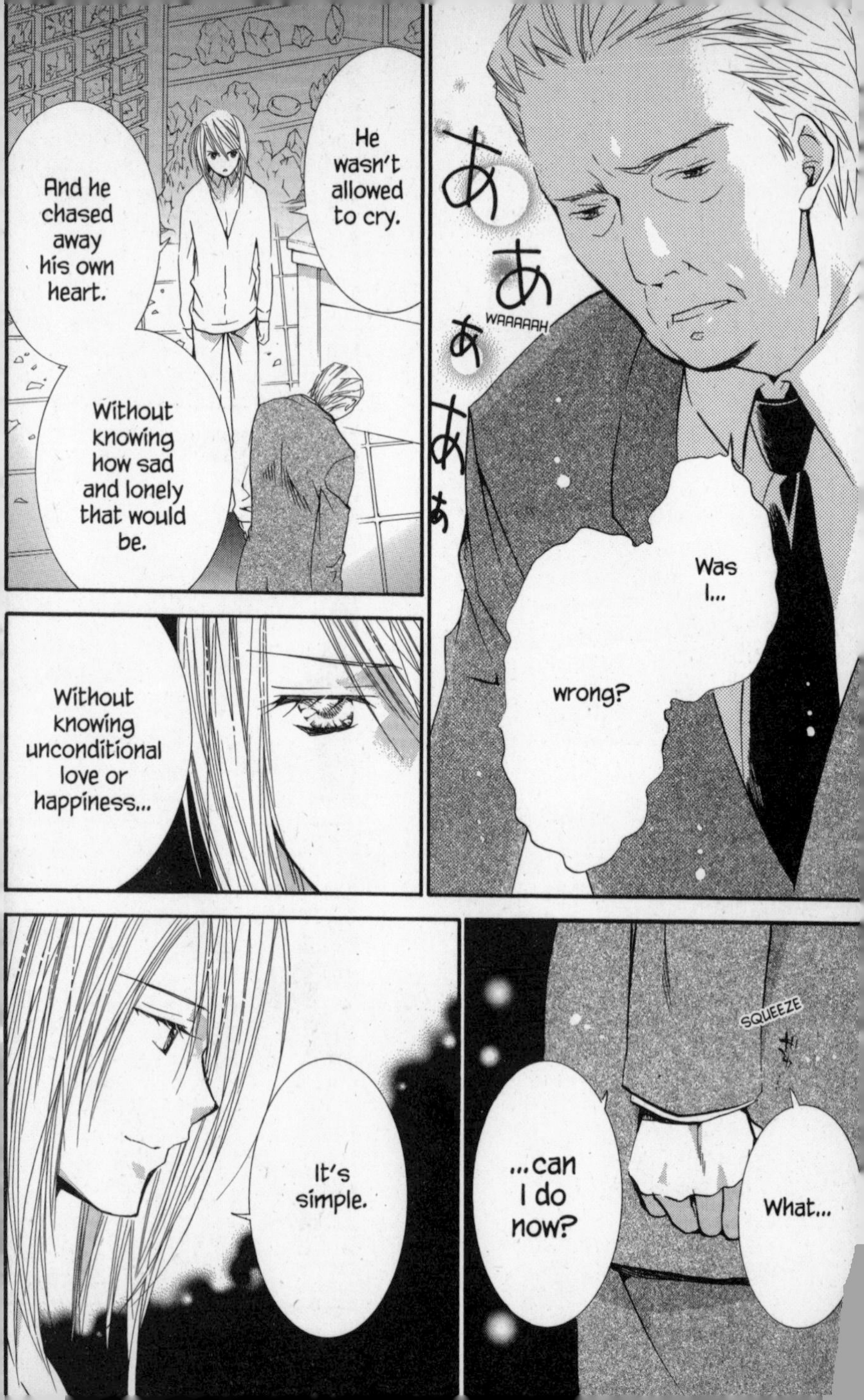
あああああ
WAAAAAH
Was I...
wrong?
He wasn't allowed to cry.
And he chased away his own heart.
Without knowing how sad and lonely that would be.
Without knowing unconditional love or happiness...
SQUEEZE
What...
...can I do now?
It's simple.

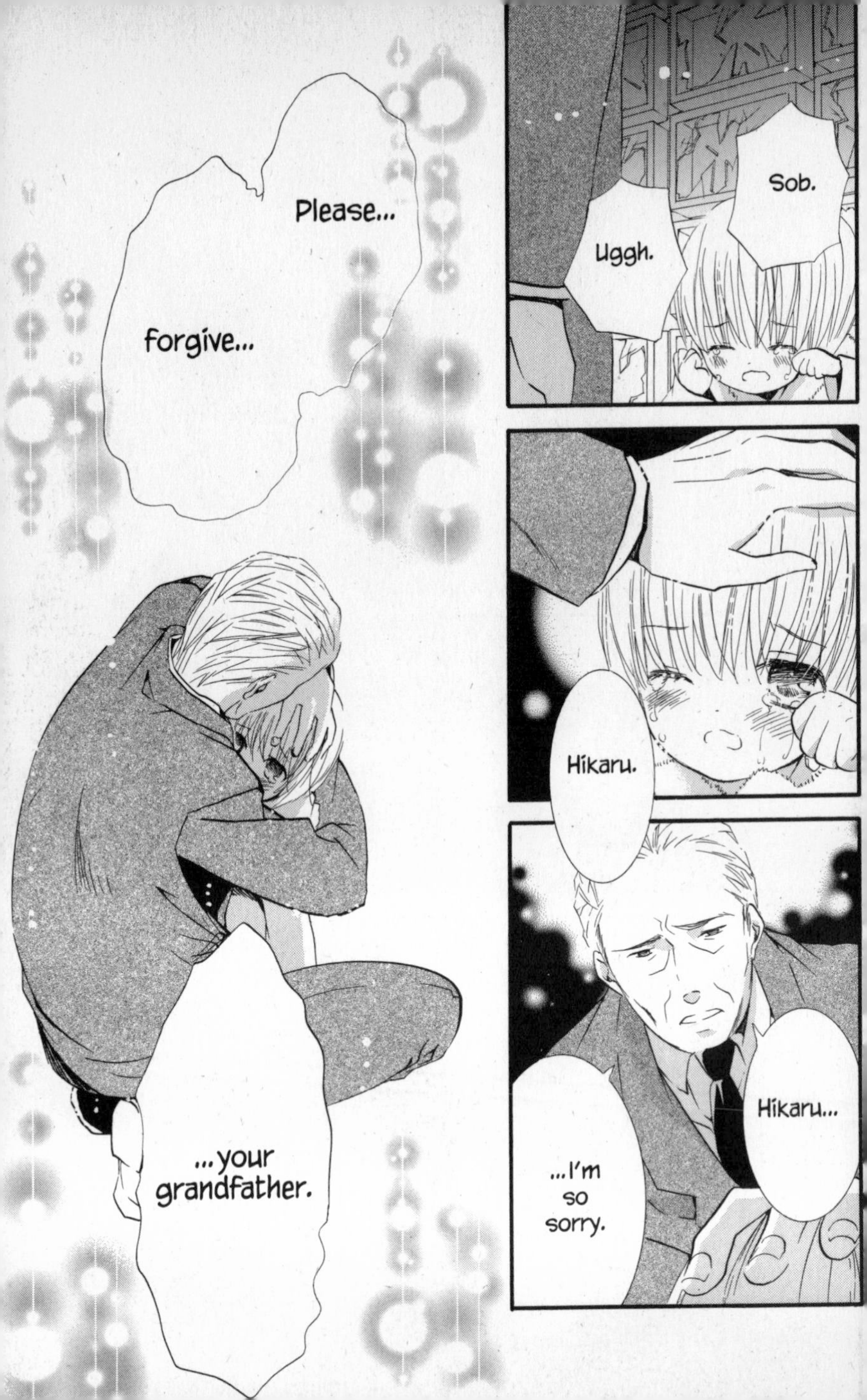
Sob.
Uggh.
Hikaru.
Hikaru...
...I'm so sorry.
Please...
forgive...
...your grandfather.

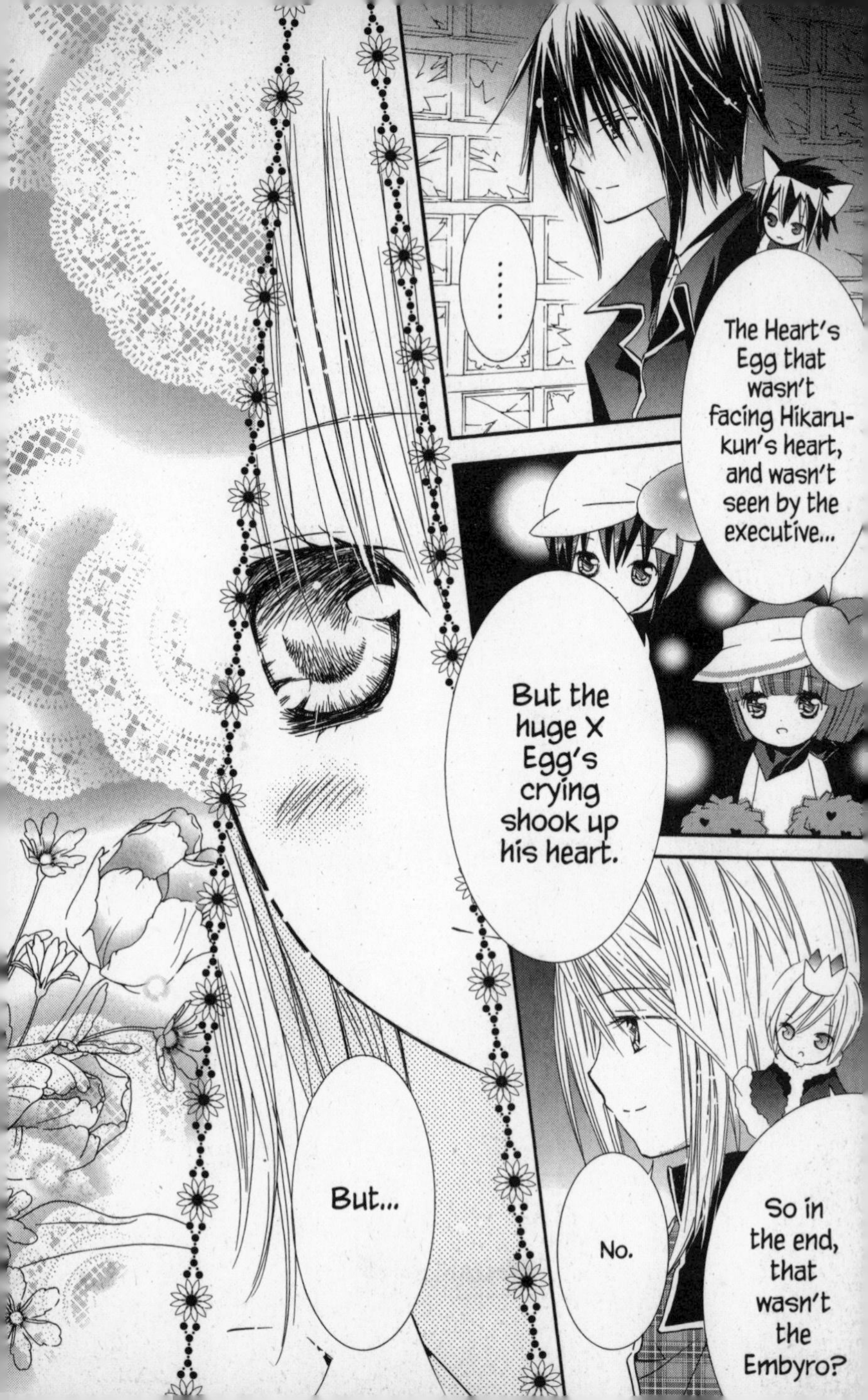
The Heart's Egg that wasn't facing Hikaru-kun's heart, and wasn't seen by the executive...
......
But the huge X Egg's crying shook up his heart.
So in the end, that wasn't the Embyro?
No.
But...

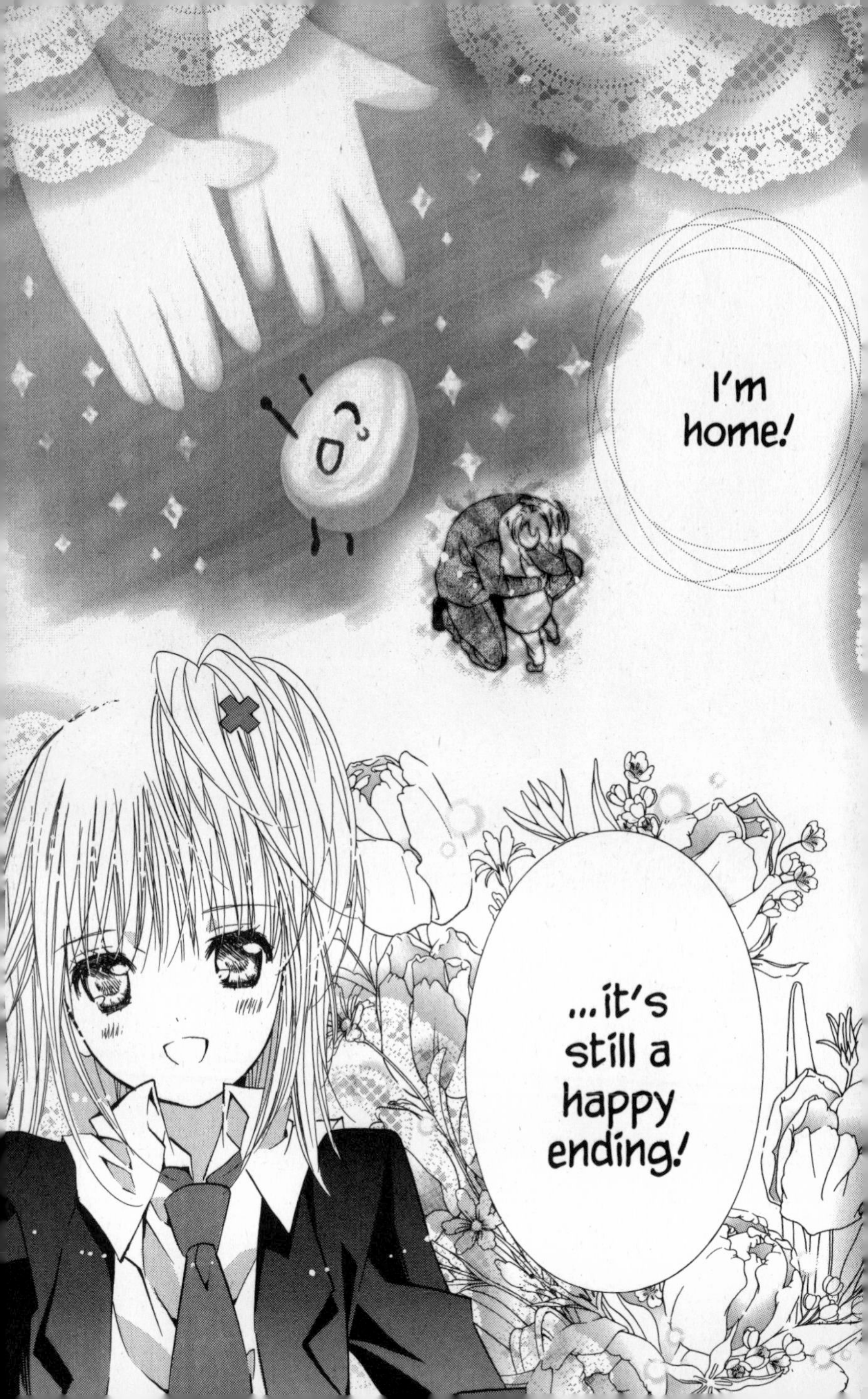
I'm home!
...it's still a happy ending!

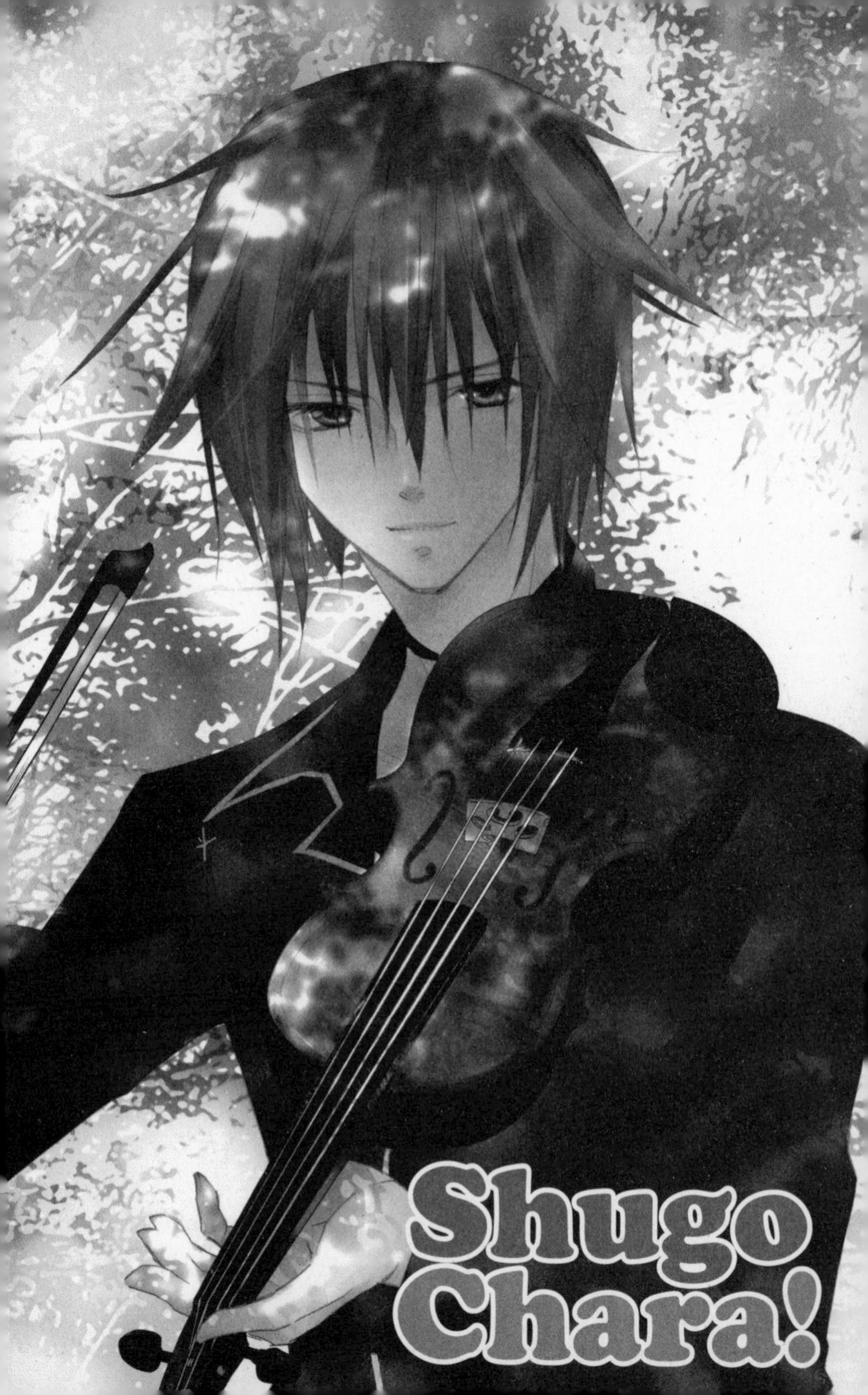
Shugo
Chara!

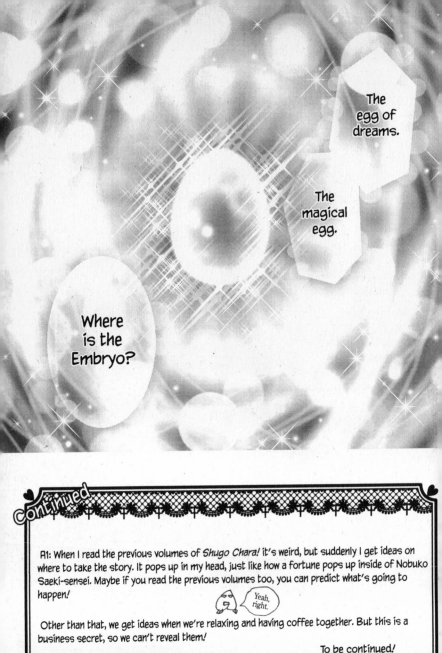

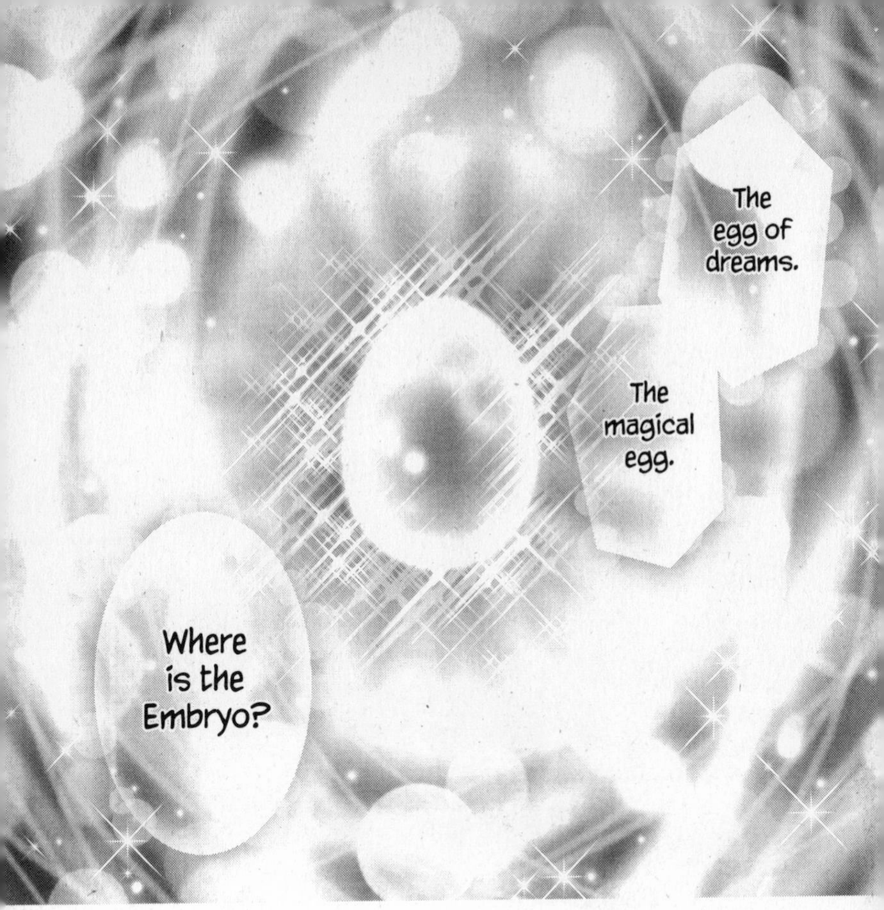
The egg of dreams.
The magical egg.
Where is the Embryo?

Continued

A1: When I read the previous volumes of *Shugo Chara!* it's weird, but suddenly I get ideas on where to take the story. It pops up in my head, just like how a fortune pops up inside of Nobuko Saeki-sensei. Maybe if you read the previous volumes too, you can predict what's going to happen!

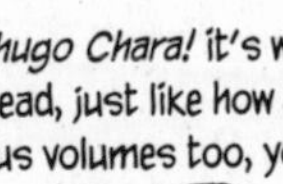
Yeah, right.

Other than that, we get ideas when we're relaxing and having coffee together. But this is a business secret, so we can't reveal them!

To be continued!

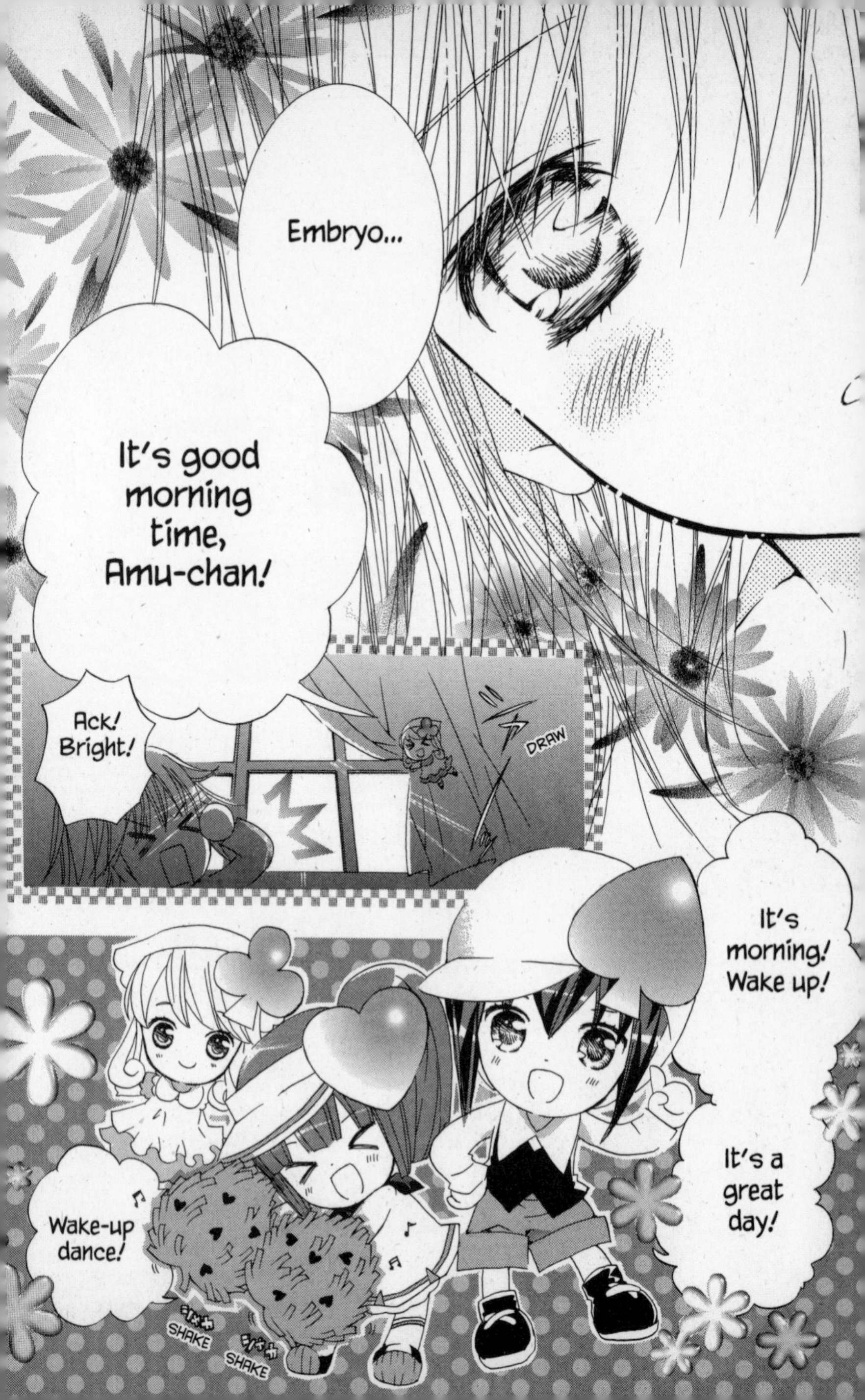
Embryo...
It's good morning time, Amu-chan!
DRAW
Ack! Bright!
It's morning! Wake up!
It's a great day!
Wake-up dance!
SHAKE
SHAKE

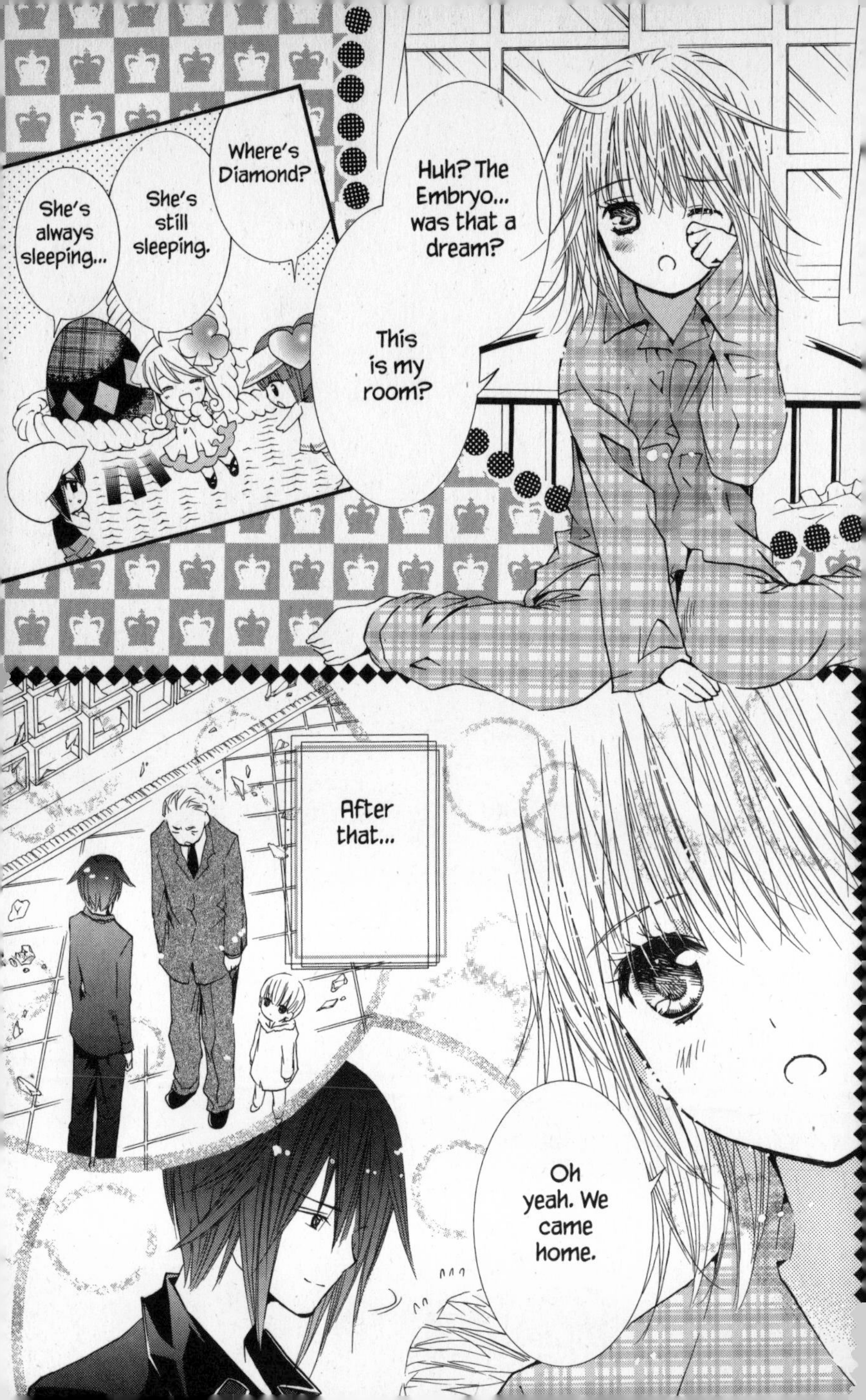
Huh? The Embryo... was that a dream?
This is my room?
Where's Diamond?
She's still sleeping.
She's always sleeping...
Oh yeah. We came home.
After that...

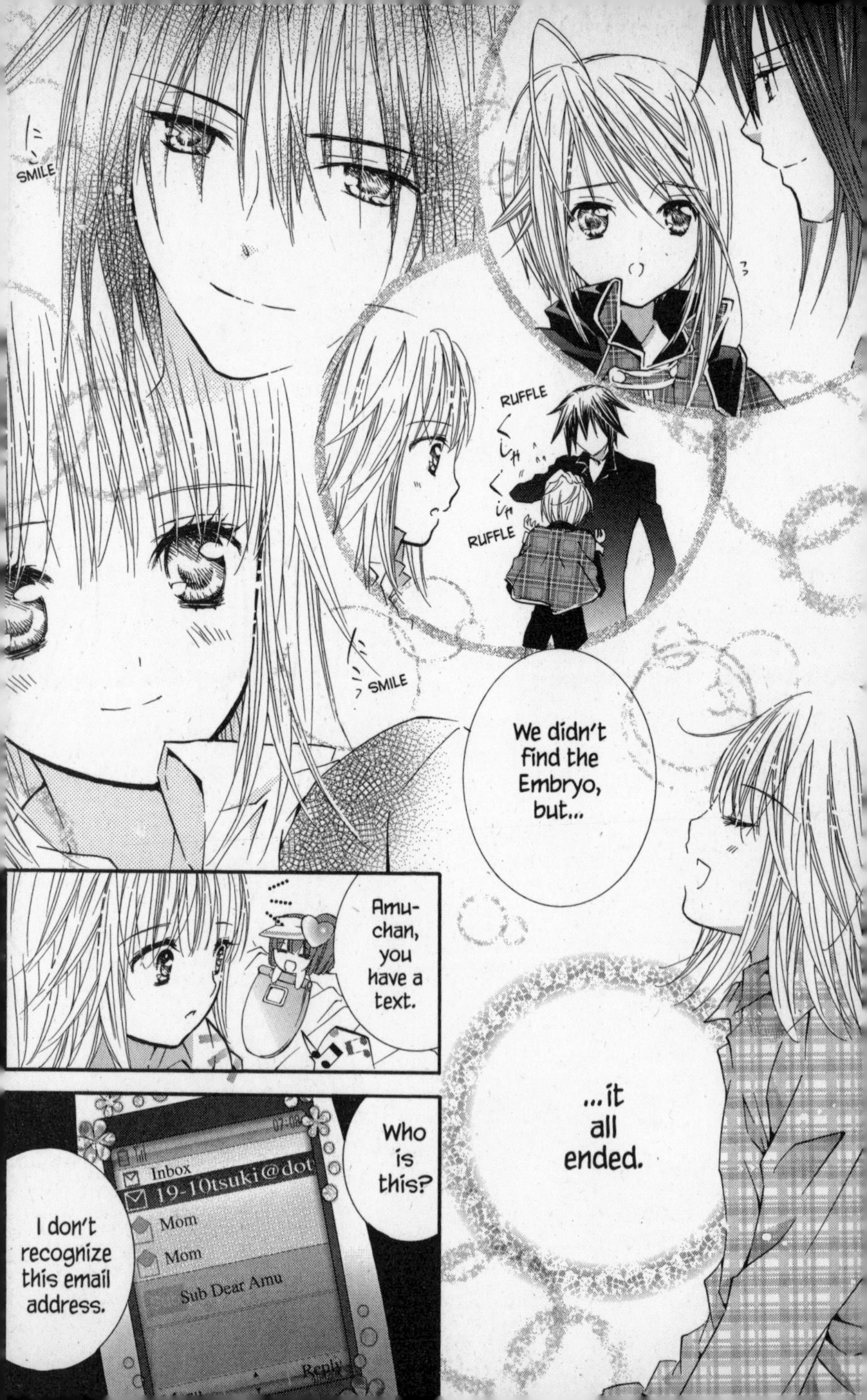
RUFFLE
RUFFLE
We didn't find the Embryo, but...
...it all ended.
SMILE
SMILE
Amu-chan, you have a text.
Who is this?
Inbox
19-10tsuki@dot
Mom
Mom
Sub Dear Amu
Reply
I don't recognize this email address.

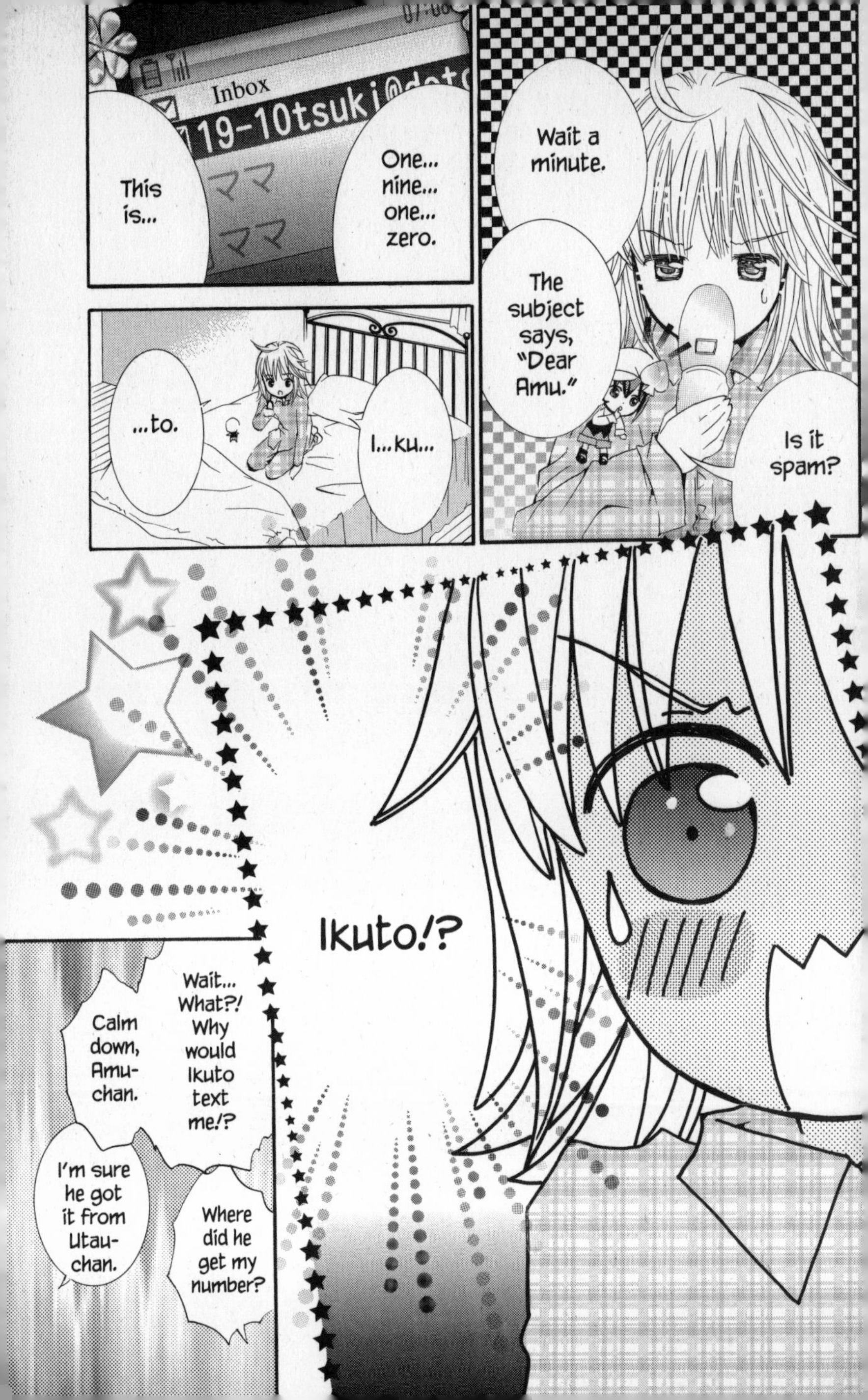
Wait a minute.
The subject says, "Dear Amu."
Is it spam?
Inbox
19-10tsuki@
ママ
ママ
One... nine... one... zero.
This is...
I...ku...
...to.
Ikuto!?
Wait... What?! Why would Ikuto text me!?
Calm down, Amu-chan.
Where did he get my number?
I'm sure he got it from Utau-chan.

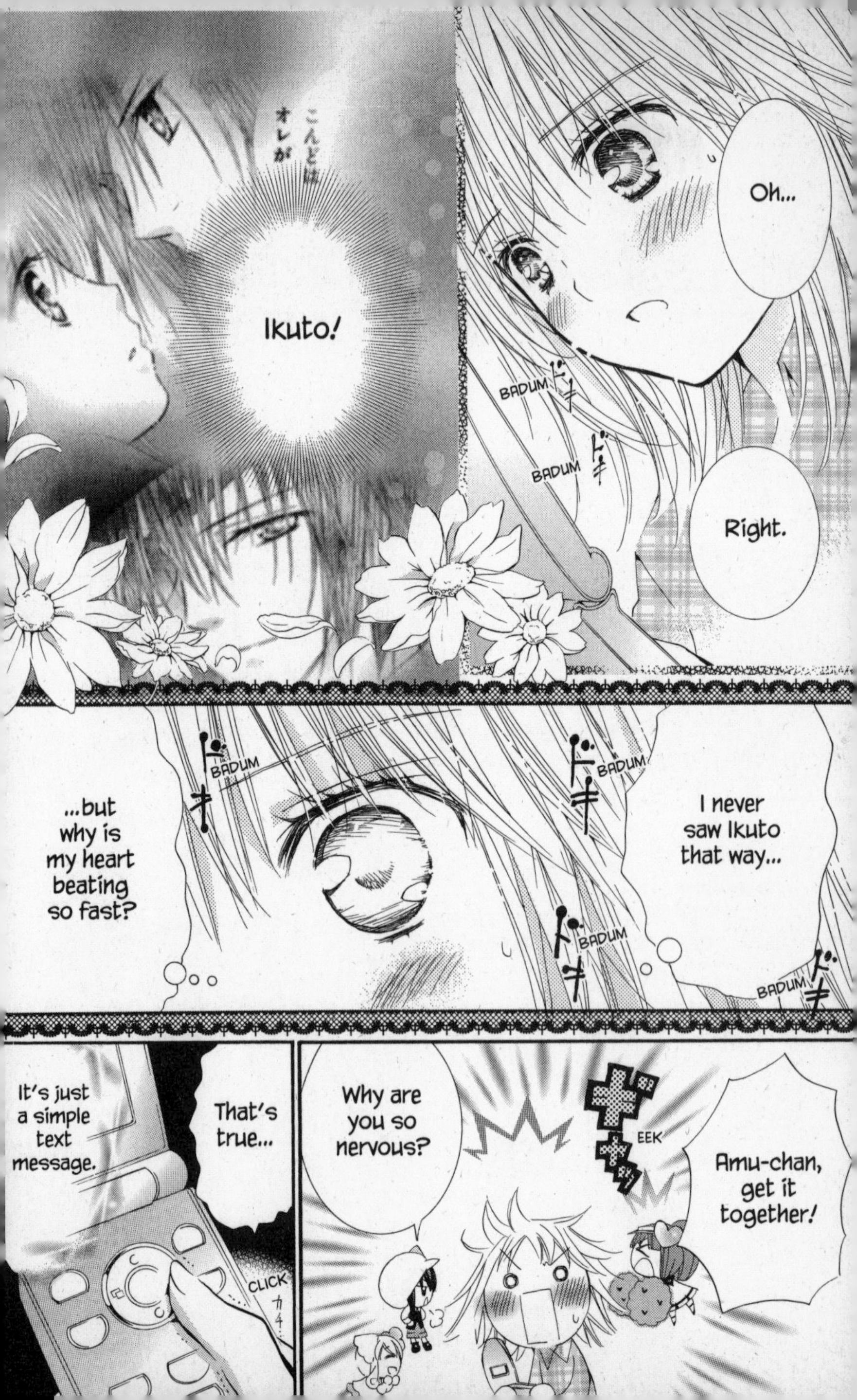
Oh...
Right.
BADUM ドキ
BADUM ドキ
こんどはオレが
Ikuto!
I never saw Ikuto that way...
BADUM ドキ
BADUM ドキ
BADUM ドキ
BADUM ドキ
...but why is my heart beating so fast?
Amu-chan, get it together!
EEK
Why are you so nervous?
That's true...
It's just a simple text message.
CLICK カチ…

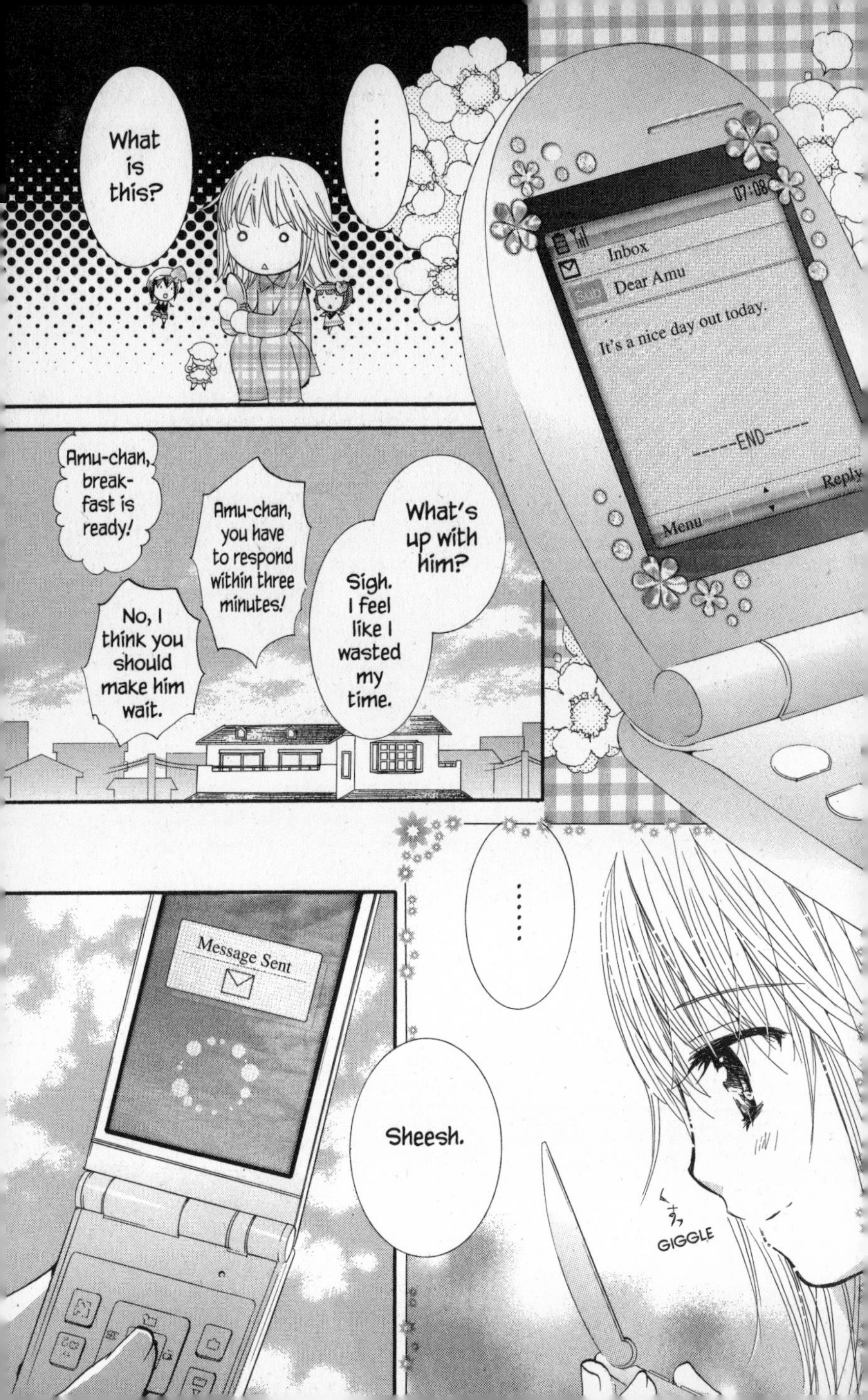
07:08
Inbox
Dear Amu
It's a nice day out today.
------END------
Reply
Menu
......
What is this?
What's up with him?
Sigh. I feel like I wasted my time.
Amu-chan, you have to respond within three minutes!
Amu-chan, breakfast is ready!
No, I think you should make him wait.
......
Sheesh.
くすっ
GIGGLE
Message Sent

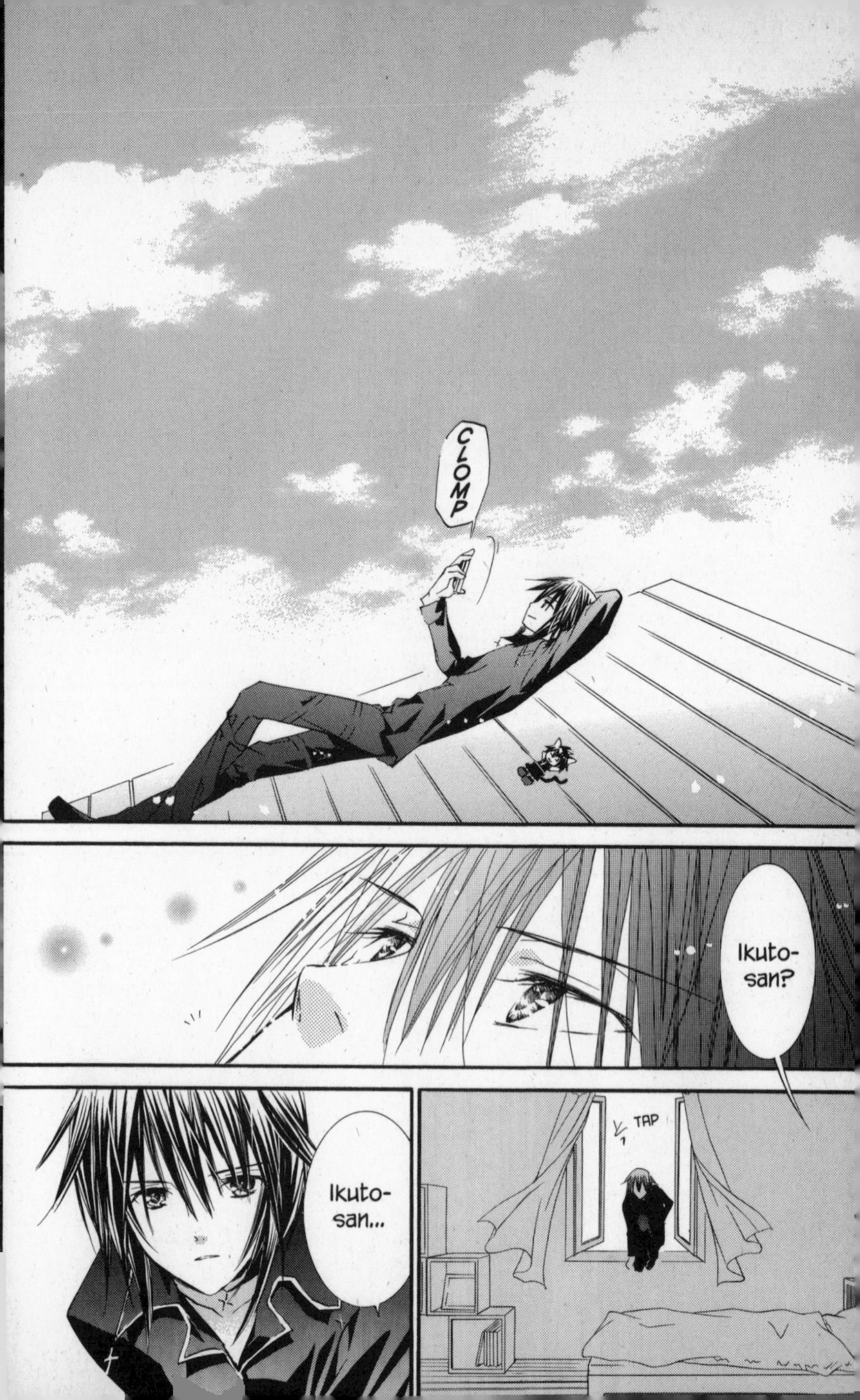
CLOMP
Ikuto-san?
TAP
Ikuto-san...

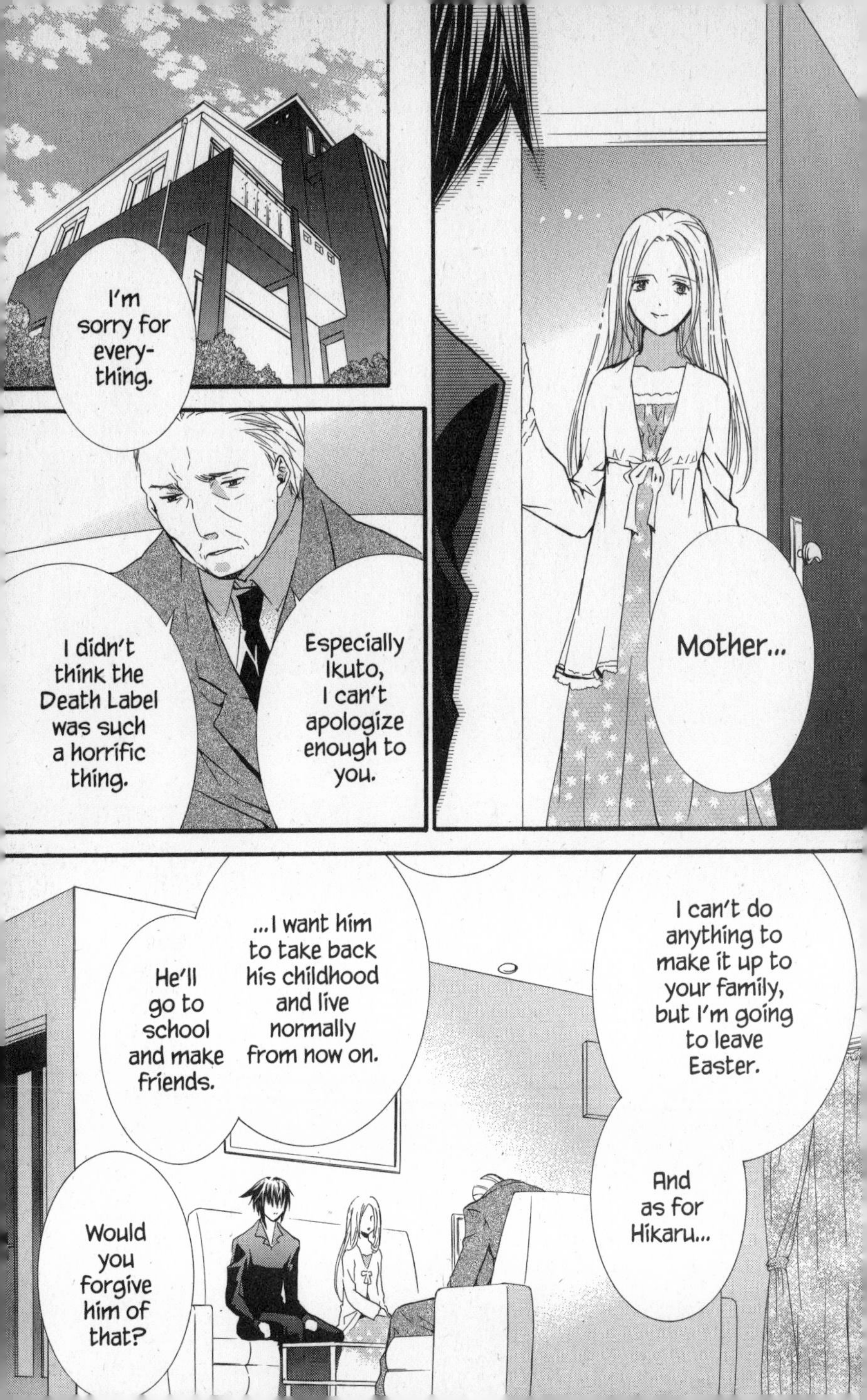
Mother...
I'm sorry for every-thing.
Especially Ikuto, I can't apologize enough to you.
I didn't think the Death Label was such a horrific thing.
I can't do anything to make it up to your family, but I'm going to leave Easter.
And as for Hikaru...
...I want him to take back his childhood and live normally from now on.
He'll go to school and make friends.
Would you forgive him of that?

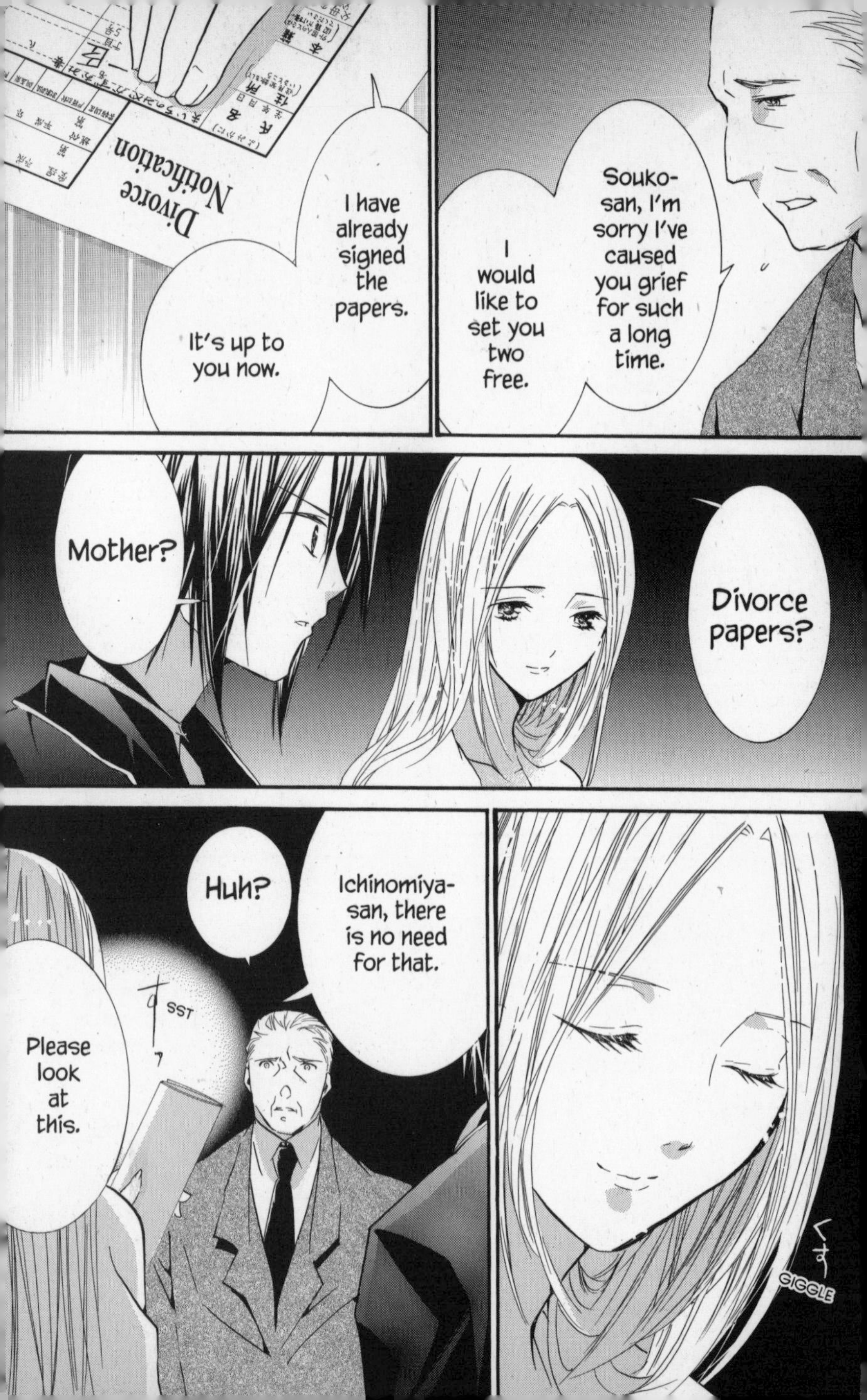
Souko-san, I'm sorry I've caused you grief for such a long time.
I would like to set you two free.
I have already signed the papers.
It's up to you now.
Divorce Notification
Divorce papers?
Mother?
くす
GIGGLE
Ichinomiya-san, there is no need for that.
Huh?
....
SST
Please look at this.

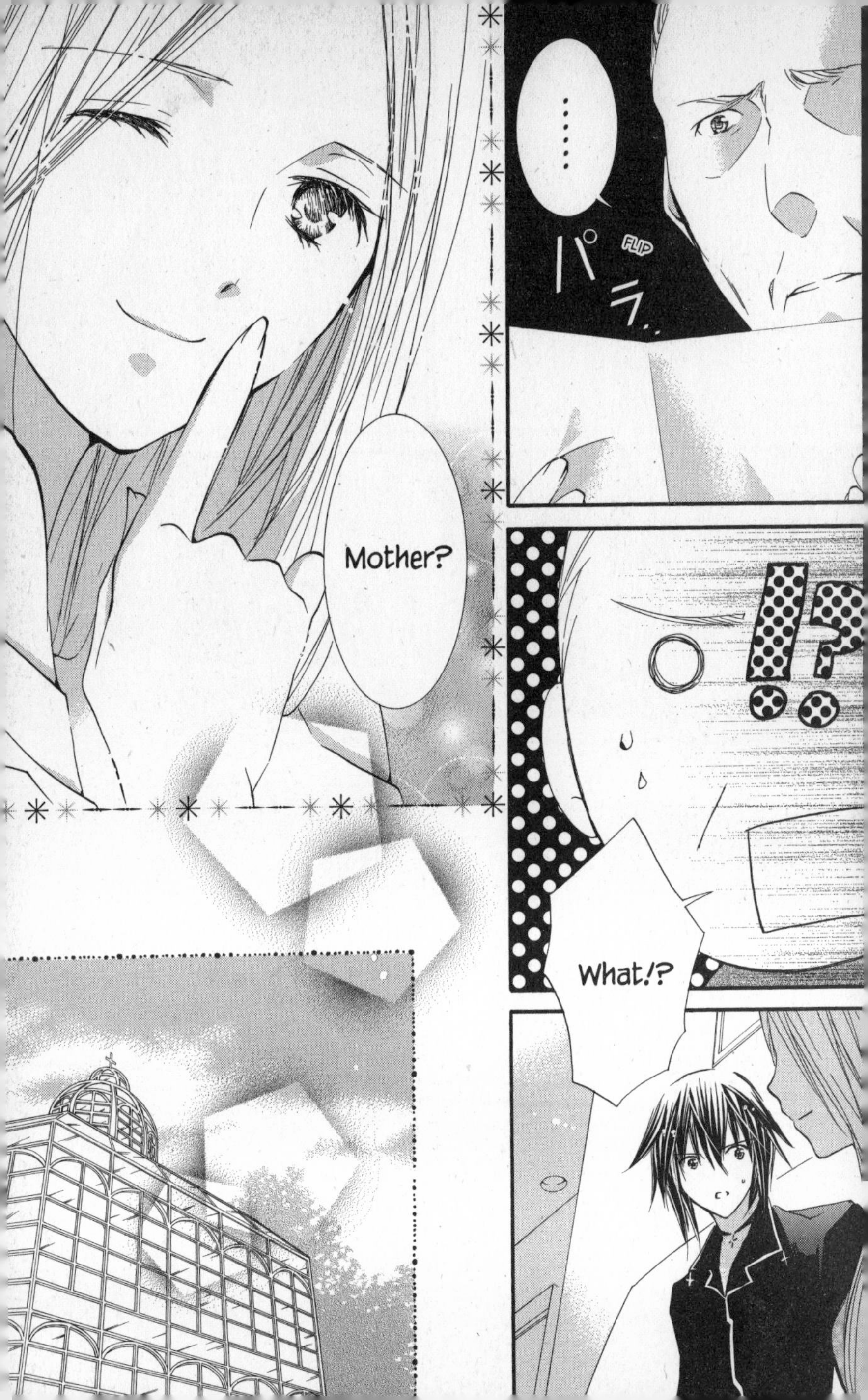
……
パラ..
FLIP
!?
What!?
Mother?

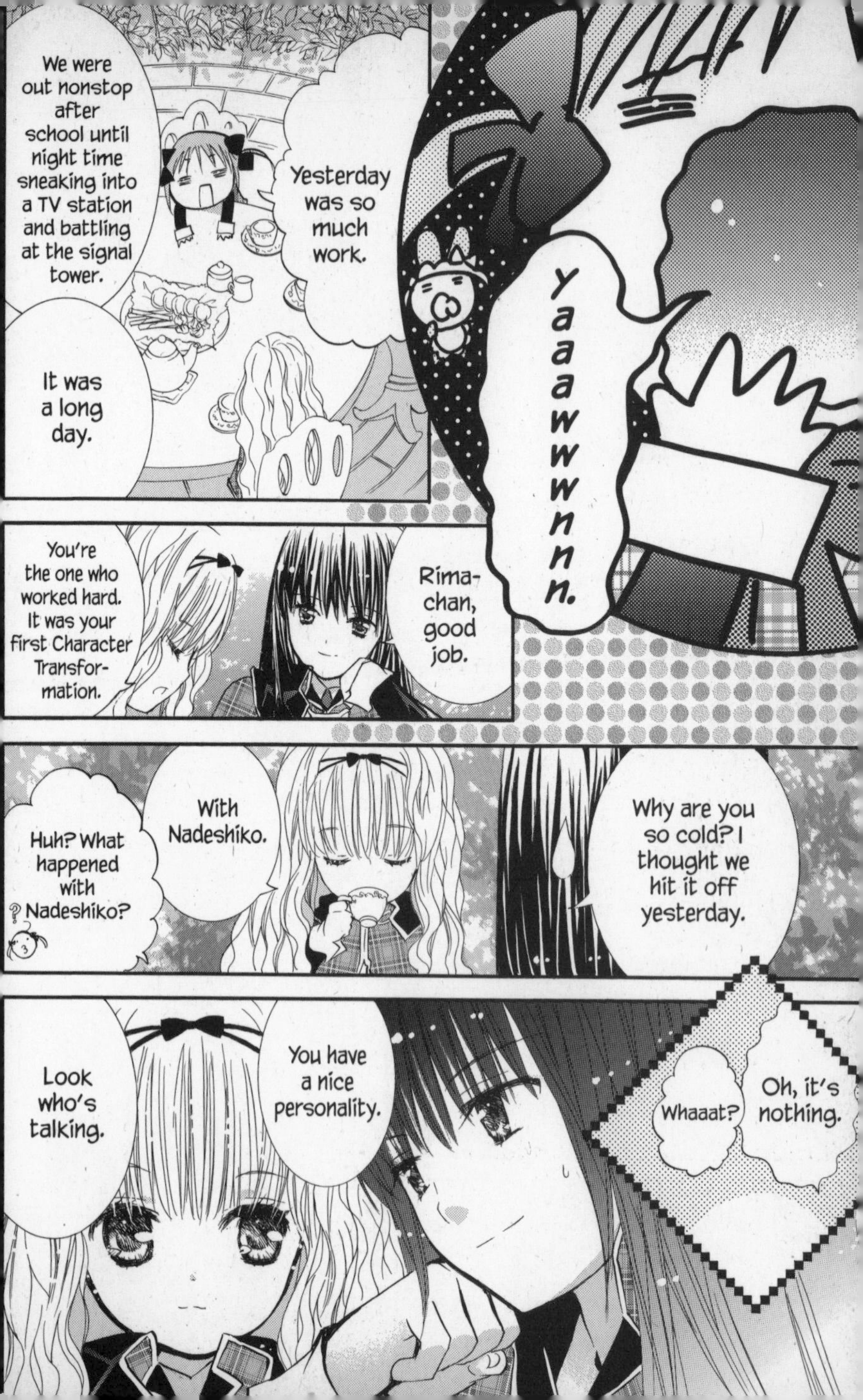
Yaaaawwwwnnn.
Yesterday was so much work.
We were out nonstop after school until night time sneaking into a TV station and battling at the signal tower.
It was a long day.
Rima-chan, good job.
You're the one who worked hard. It was your first Character Transformation.
Why are you so cold? I thought we hit it off yesterday.
With Nadeshiko.
Huh? What happened with Nadeshiko?
Oh, it's nothing.
Whaaat?
You have a nice personality.
Look who's talking.

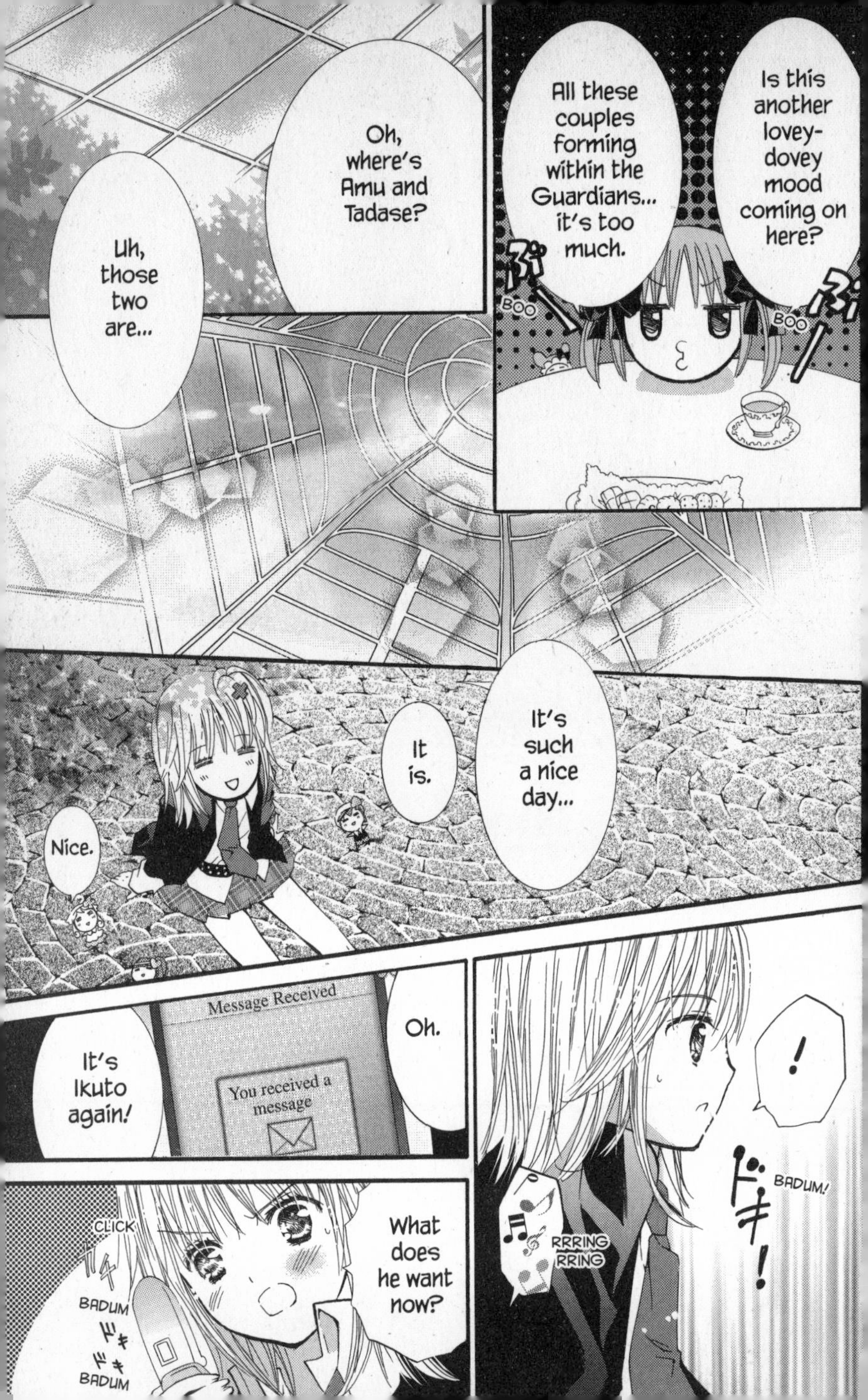

Is this another lovey-dovey mood coming on here?
BOO
All these couples forming within the Guardians... it's too much.
BOO
Oh, where's Amu and Tadase?
Uh, those two are...
It's such a nice day...
It is.
Nice.
!
BADUM!
RRRING RRING
Oh.
Message Received
You received a message
It's Ikuto again!
What does he want now?
CLICK
BADUM
BADUM

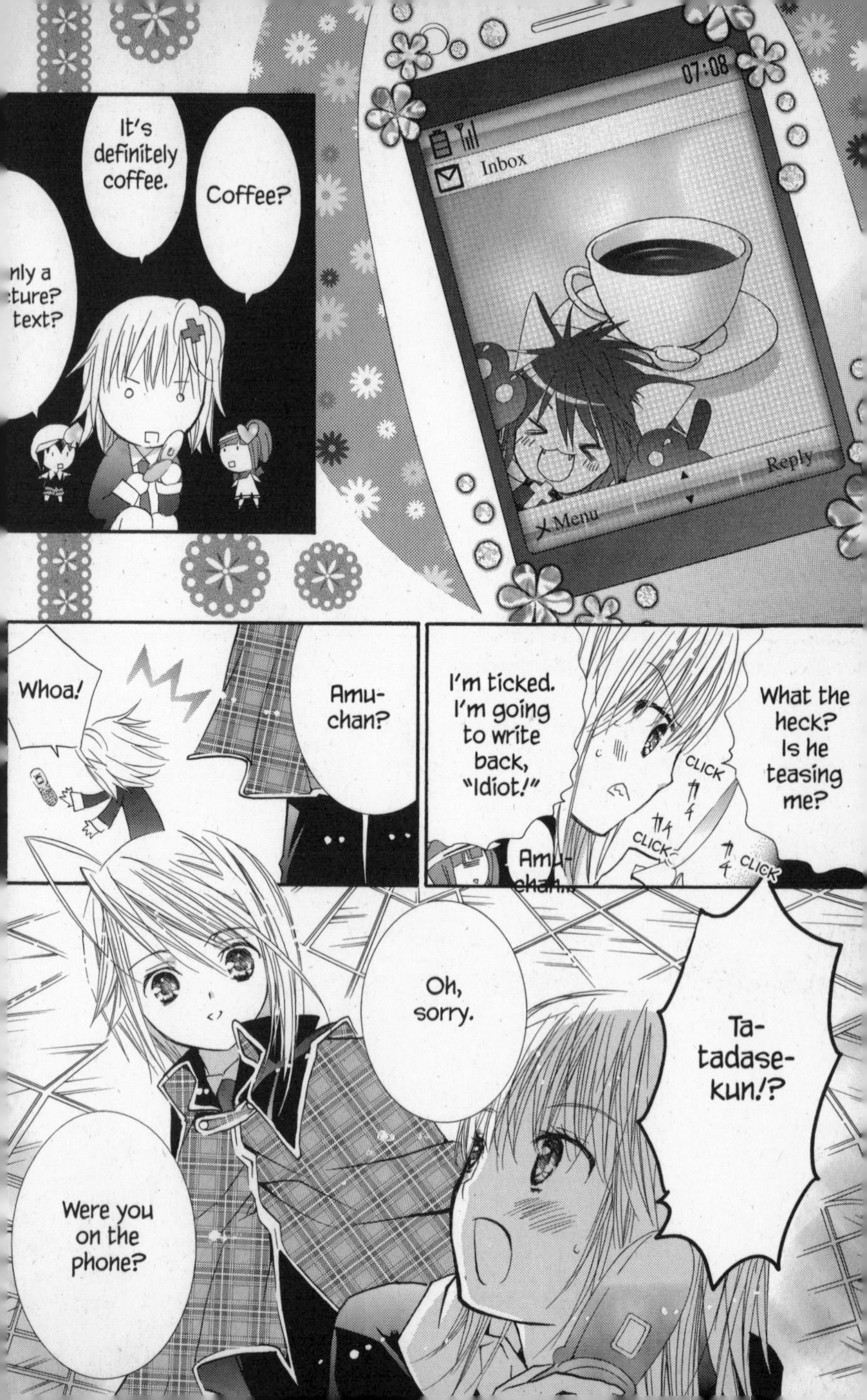

07:08
Inbox
Reply
Menu
Coffee?
It's definitely coffee.
nly a ture? text?
What the heck? Is he teasing me?
CLICK
CLICK
CLICK
I'm ticked. I'm going to write back, "Idiot!"
Amu-chan...
Amu-chan?
Whoa!
Ta-tadase-kun!?
Oh, sorry.
Were you on the phone?

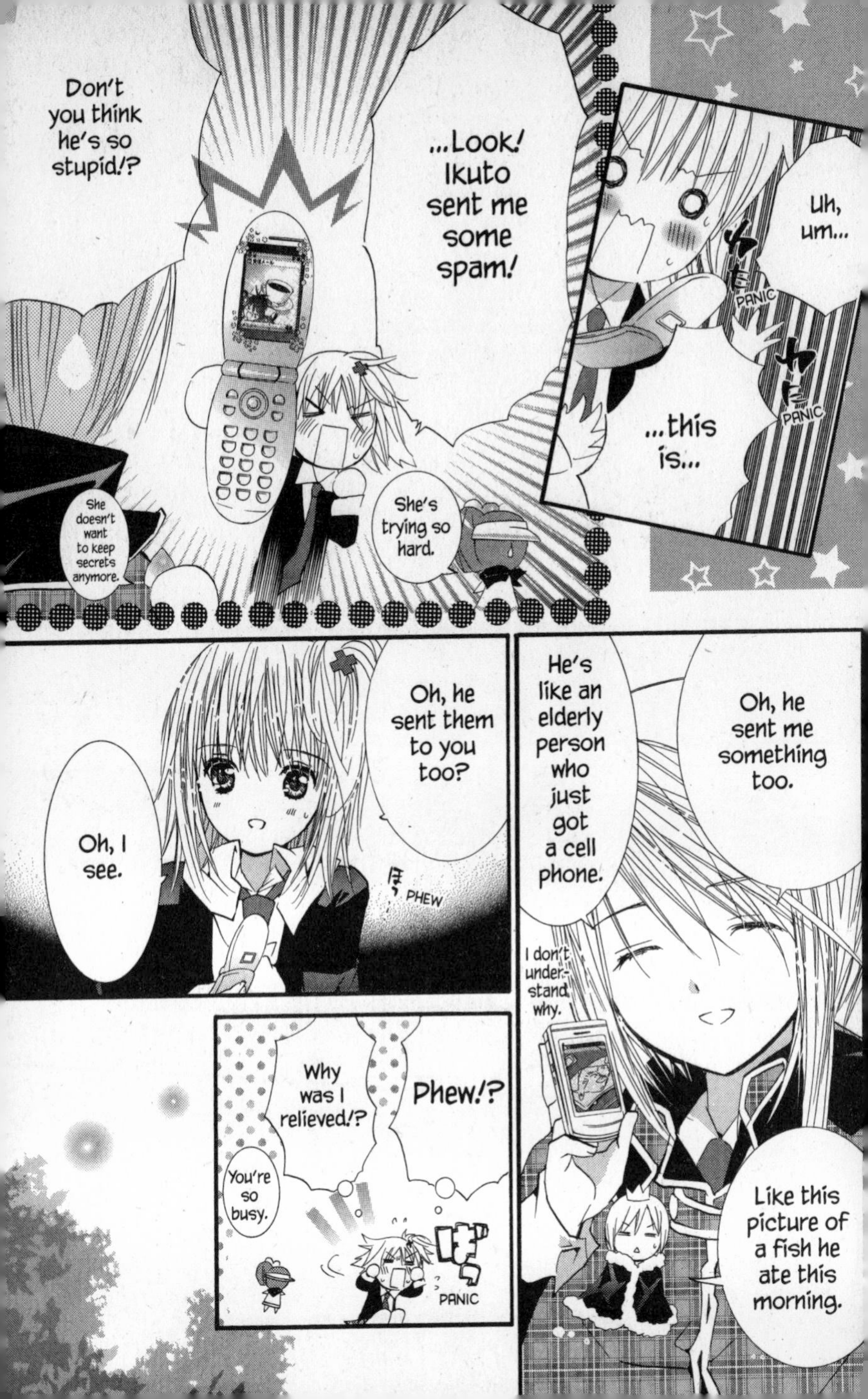
Uh, um...
PANIC
PANIC
...this is...
...Look! Ikuto sent me some spam!
Don't you think he's so stupid!?
She's trying so hard.
She doesn't want to keep secrets anymore.
Oh, he sent me something too.
He's like an elderly person who just got a cell phone.
I don't under-stand why.
Like this picture of a fish he ate this morning.
Oh, he sent them to you too?
PHEW
Oh, I see.
Phew!?
Why was I relieved!?
PANIC
You're so busy.

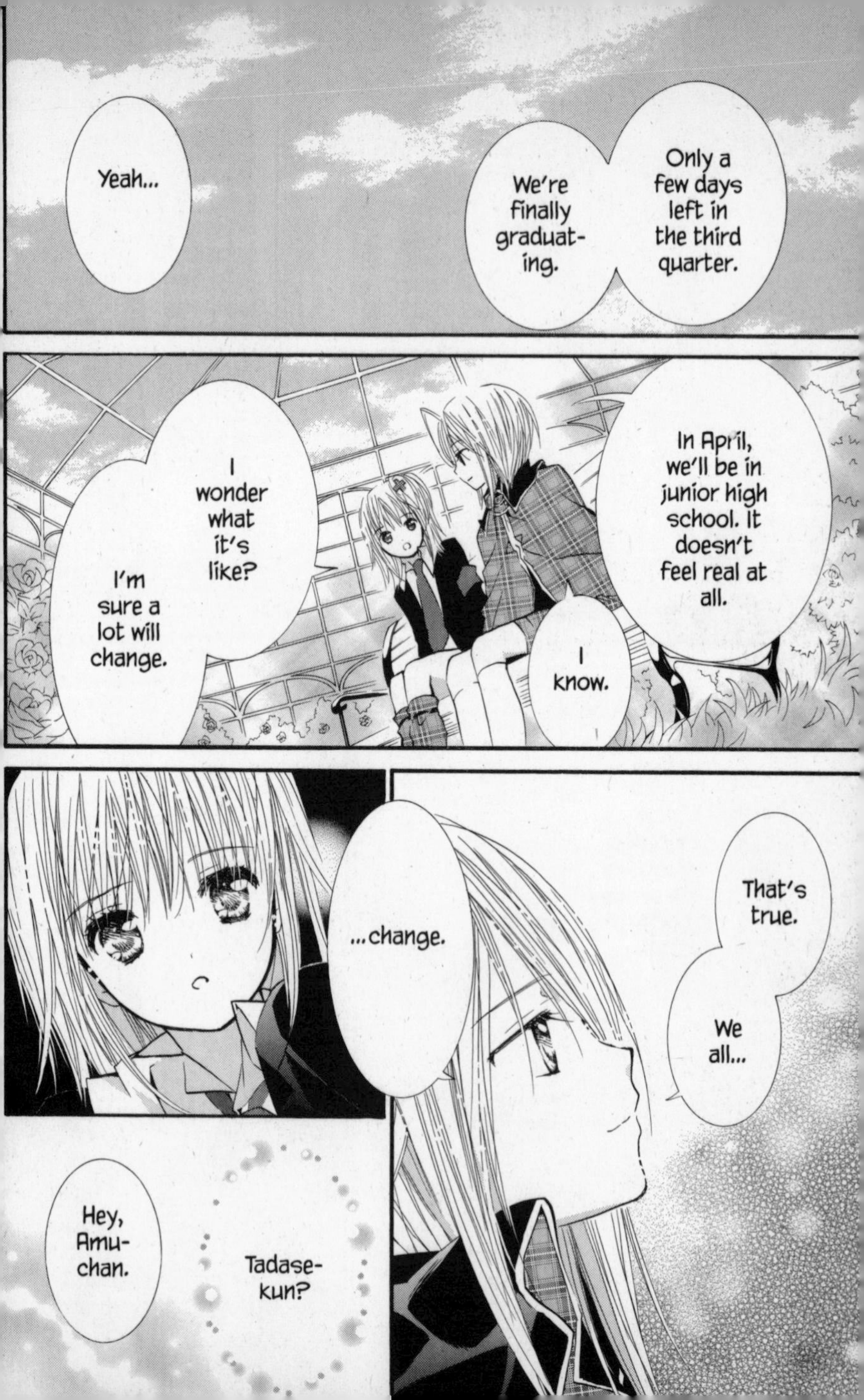
Only a few days left in the third quarter.
We're finally graduat-ing.
Yeah...
In April, we'll be in junior high school. It doesn't feel real at all.
I know.
I wonder what it's like?
I'm sure a lot will change.
That's true.
We all...
...change.
Hey, Amu-chan.
Tadase-kun?

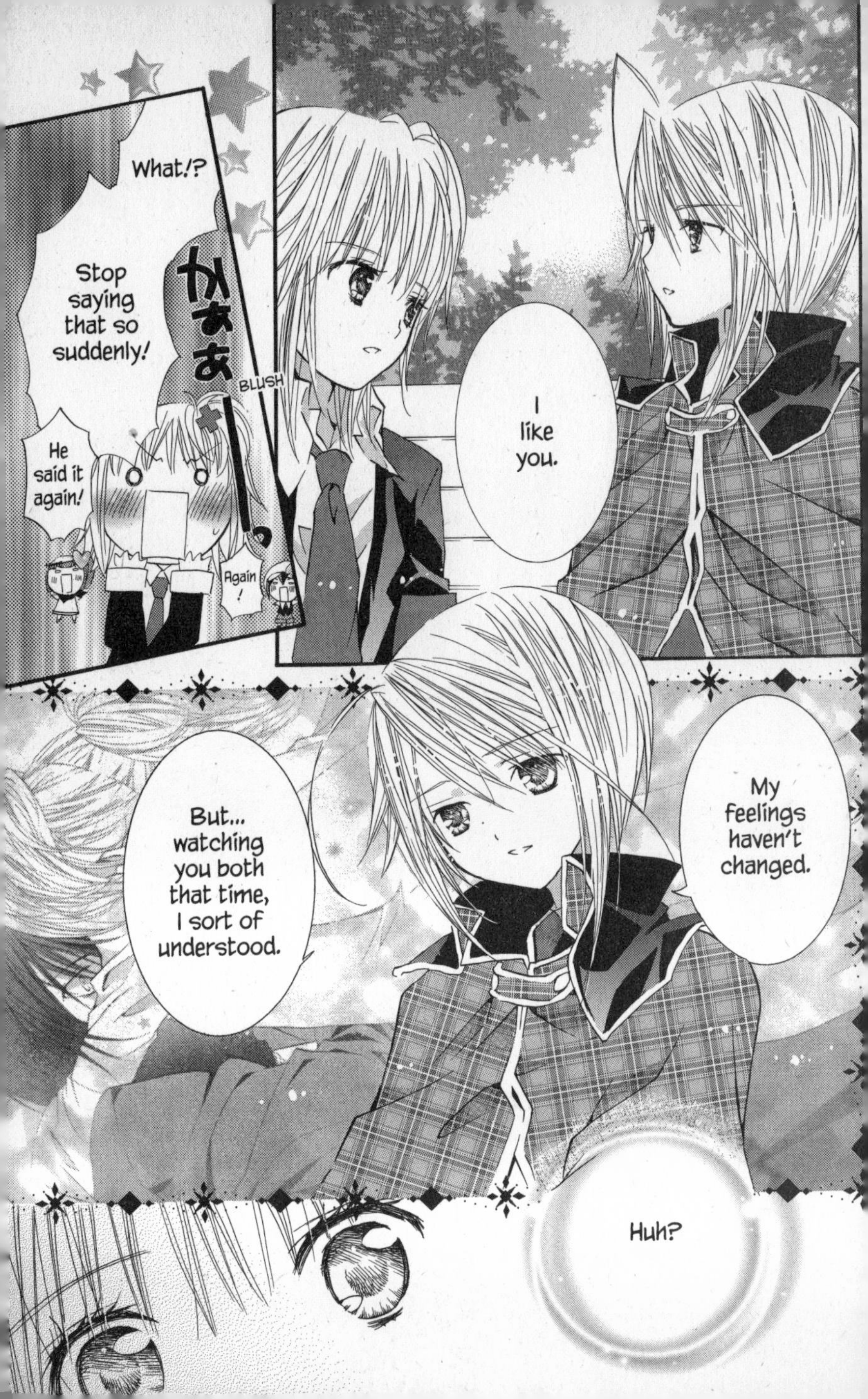
I like you.
What!?
かぁぁ
BLUSH
Stop saying that so suddenly!
Again!
He said it again!
My feelings haven't changed.
But... watching you both that time, I sort of understood.
Huh?

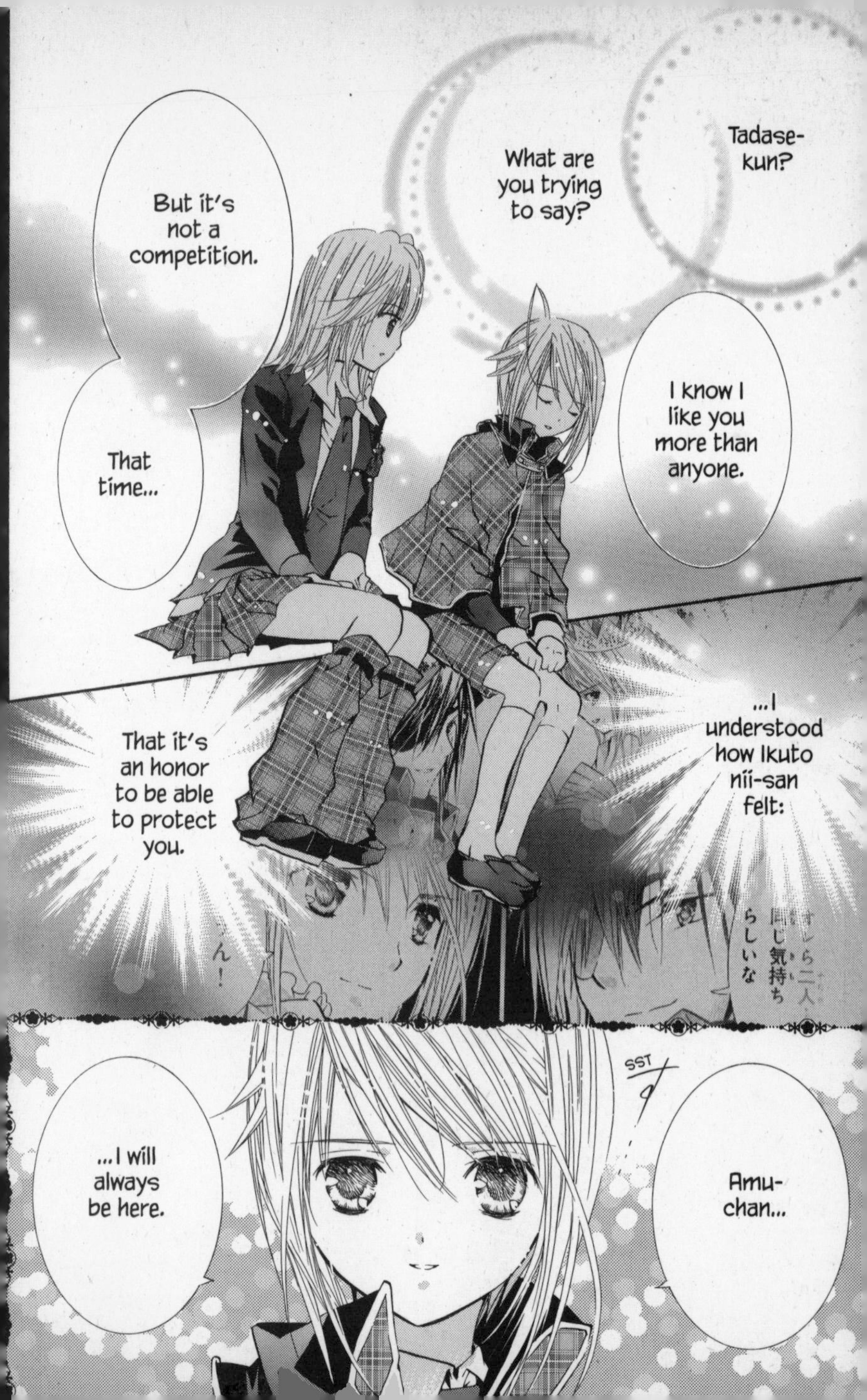

Tadase-kun?
What are you trying to say?
I know I like you more than anyone.
But it's not a competition.
That time...
...I understood how Ikuto nii-san felt:
That it's an honor to be able to protect you.
SST
Amu-chan...
...I will always be here.

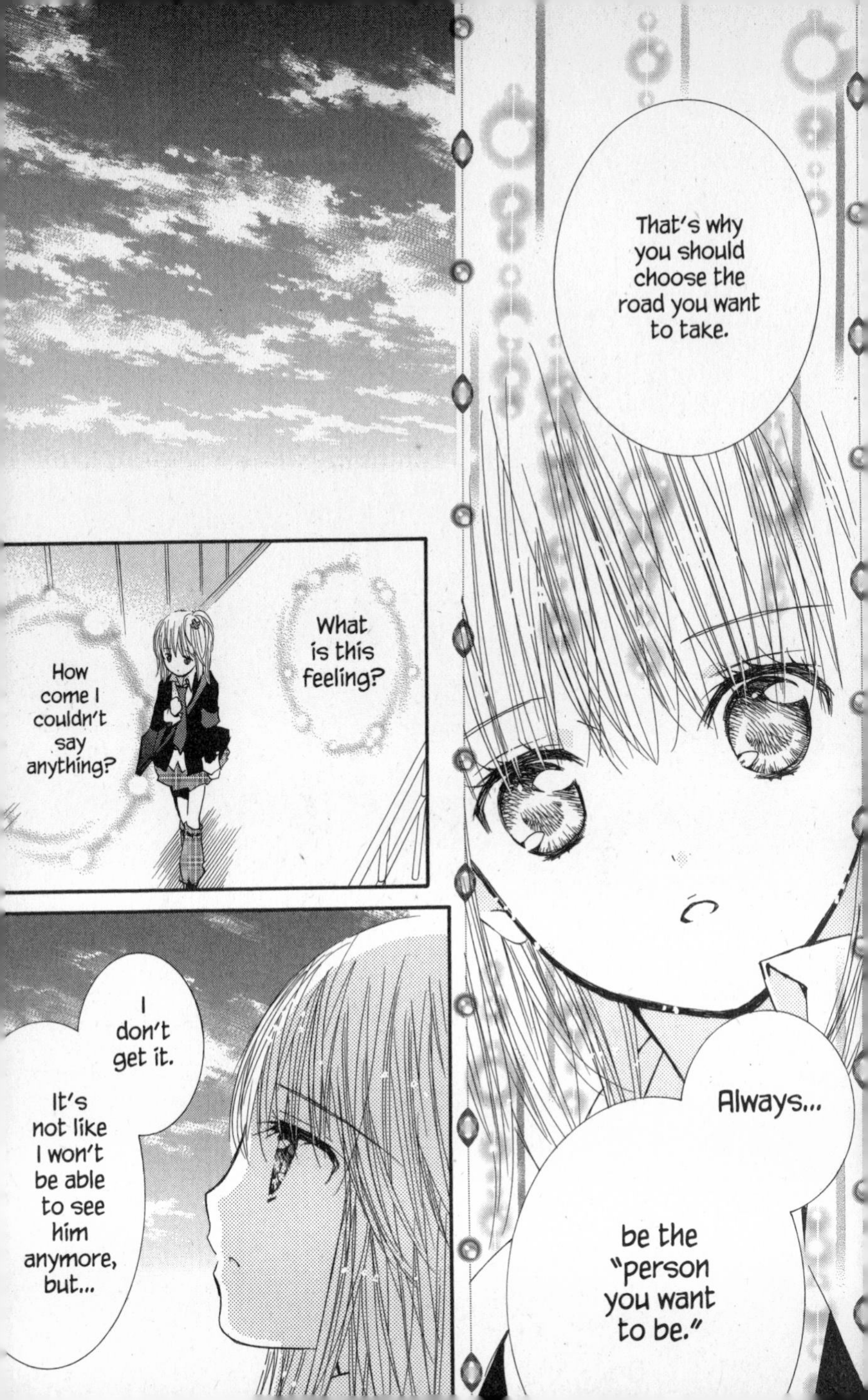
That's why you should choose the road you want to take.
Always...
be the "person you want to be."
What is this feeling?
How come I couldn't say anything?
I don't get it.
It's not like I won't be able to see him anymore, but...

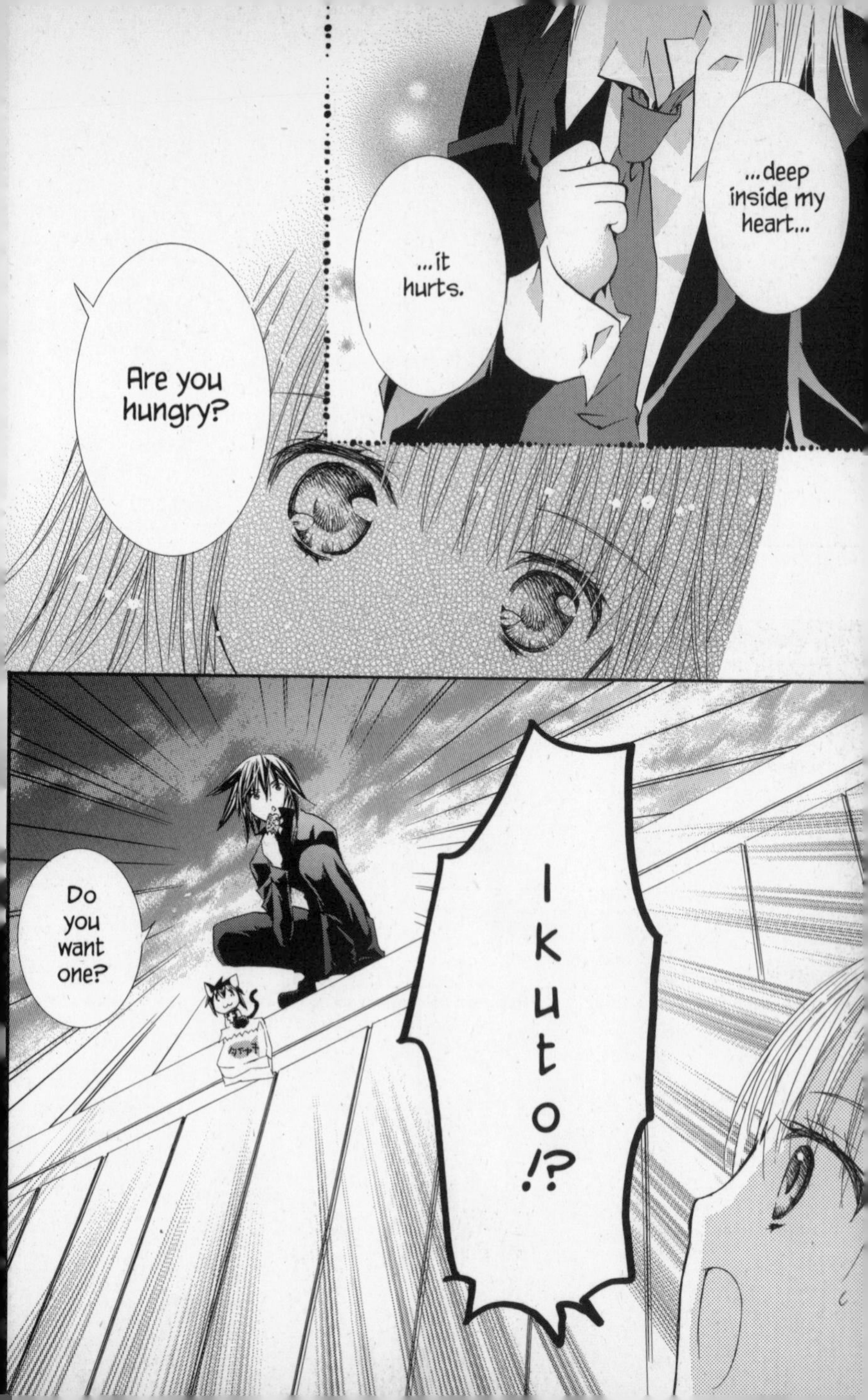
...deep inside my heart...
...it hurts.
Are you hungry?
Ikuto!?
Do you want one?

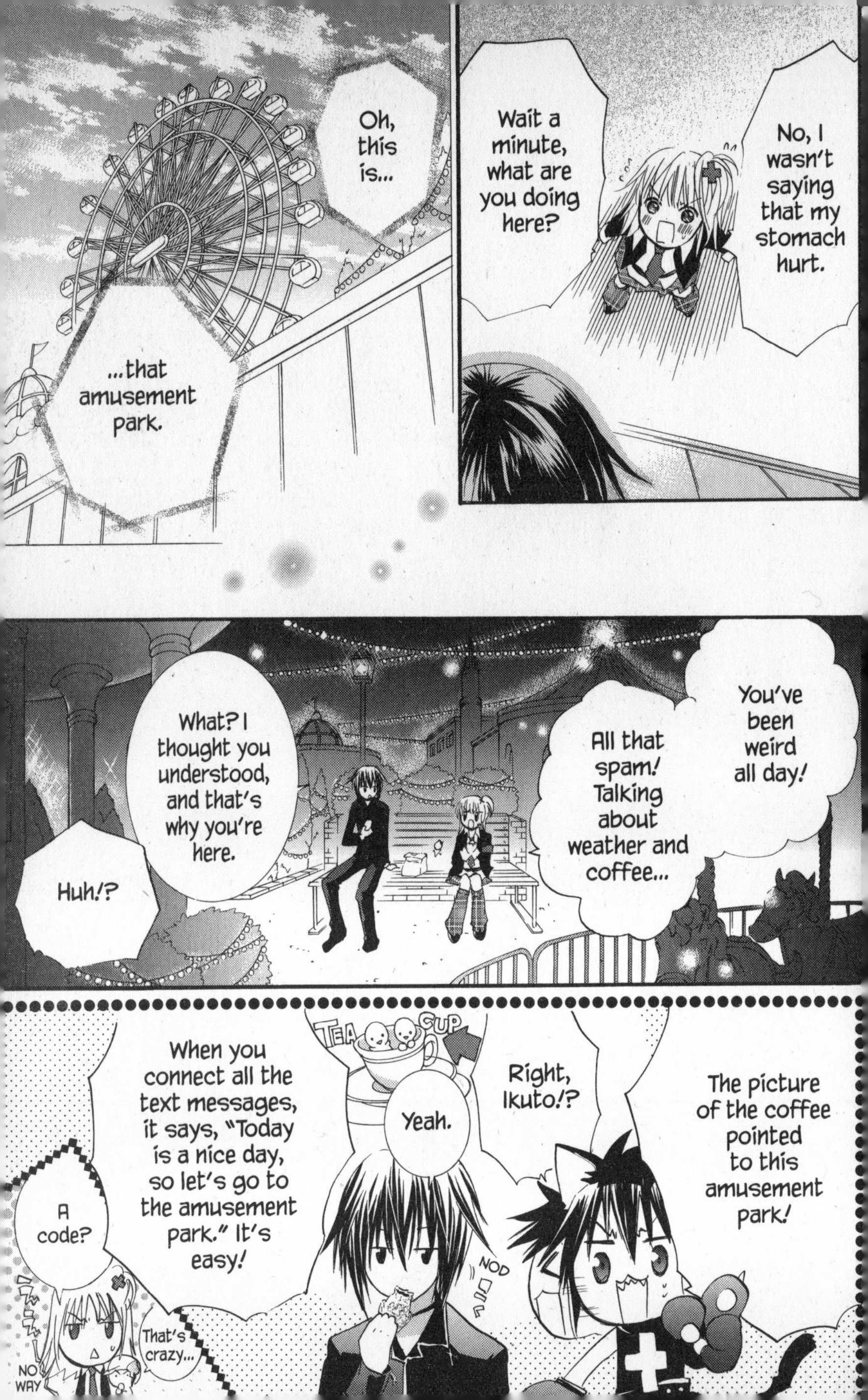
No, I wasn't saying that my stomach hurt.
Wait a minute, what are you doing here?
Oh, this is...
...that amusement park.
You've been weird all day!
All that spam! Talking about weather and coffee...
What? I thought you understood, and that's why you're here.
Huh!?
The picture of the coffee pointed to this amusement park!
Right, Ikuto!?
NOD
Yeah.
TEA CUP
When you connect all the text messages, it says, "Today is a nice day, so let's go to the amusement park." It's easy!
A code?
That's crazy...
NO WAY

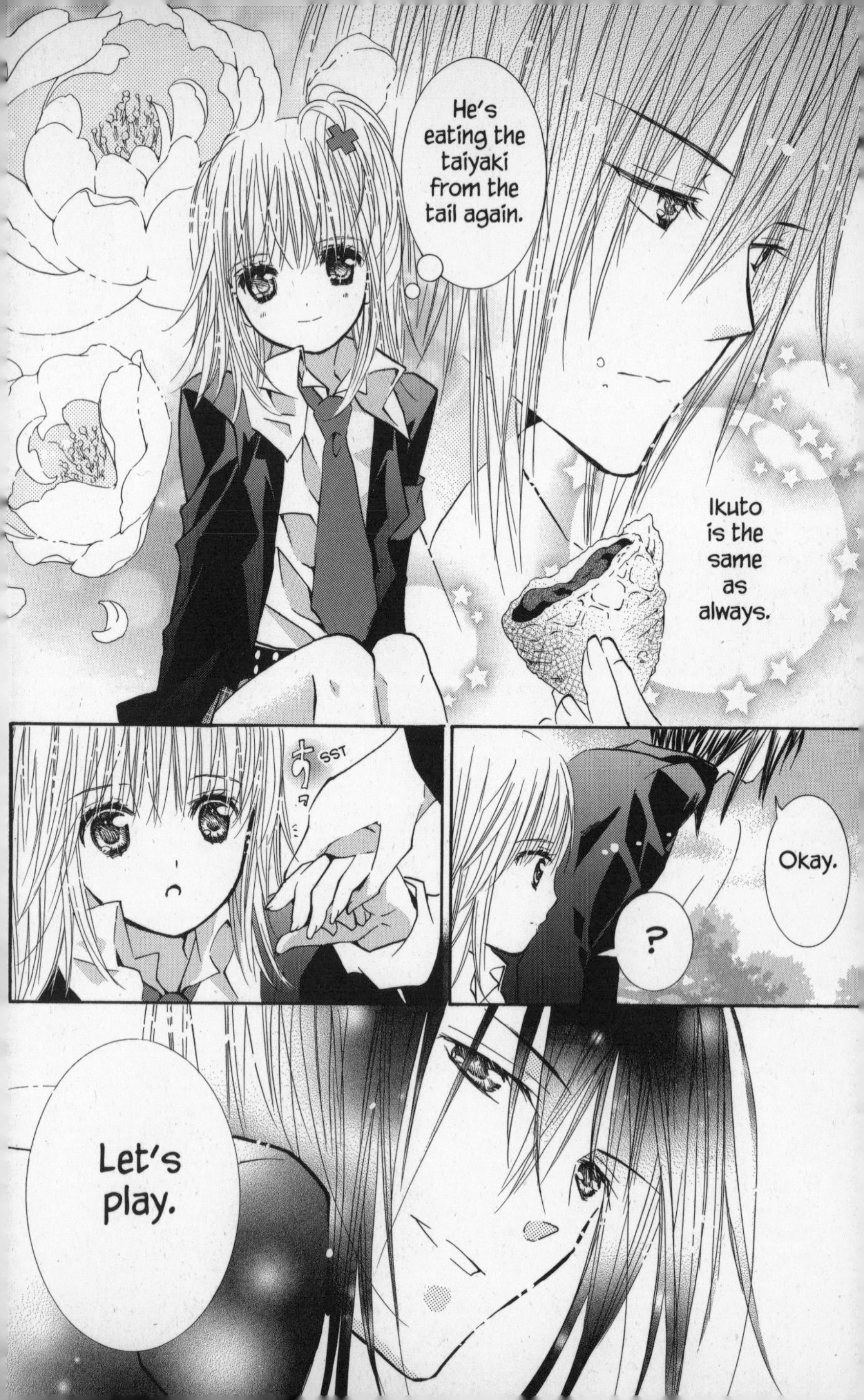
He's eating the taiyaki from the tail again.
Ikuto is the same as always.
Okay.
?
SST
Let's play.

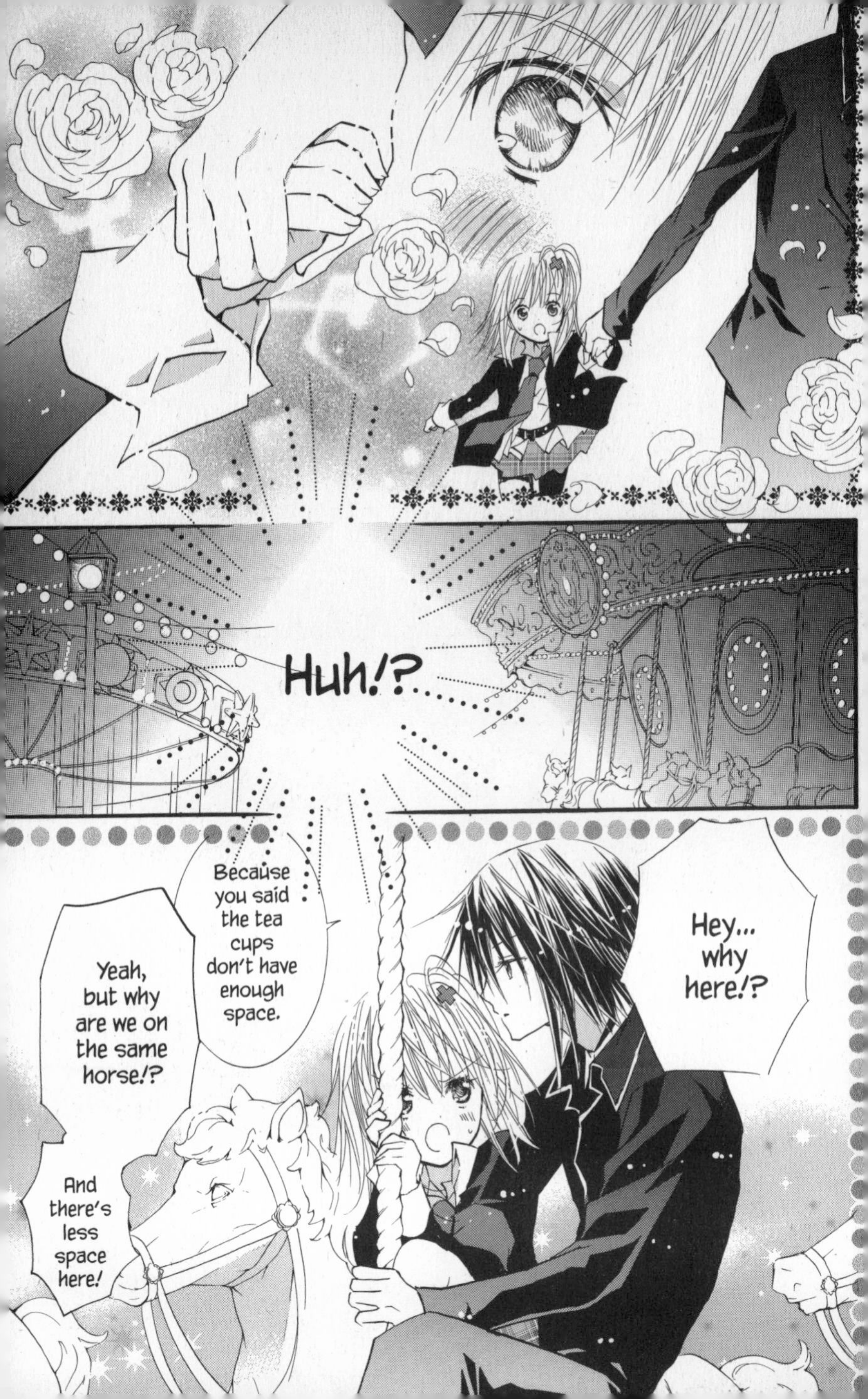
Huh!?
Hey... why here!?
Because you said the tea cups don't have enough space.
Yeah, but why are we on the same horse!?
And there's less space here!

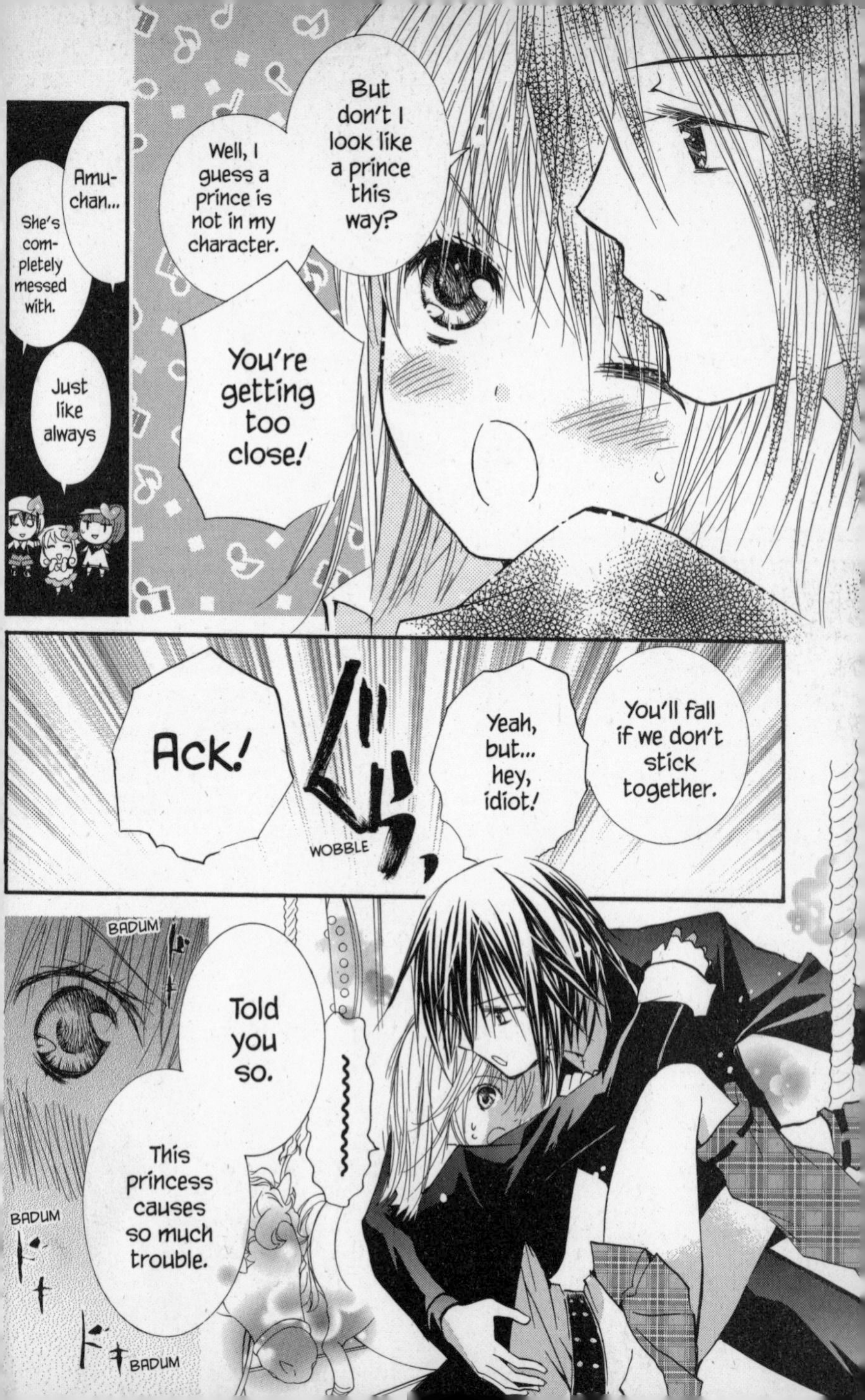
But don't I look like a prince this way?
Well, I guess a prince is not in my character.
You're getting too close!
Amu-chan...
She's completely messed with.
Just like always
You'll fall if we don't stick together.
Yeah, but... hey, idiot!
WOBBLE
Ack!
Told you so.
This princess causes so much trouble.
BADUM
BADUM
BADUM

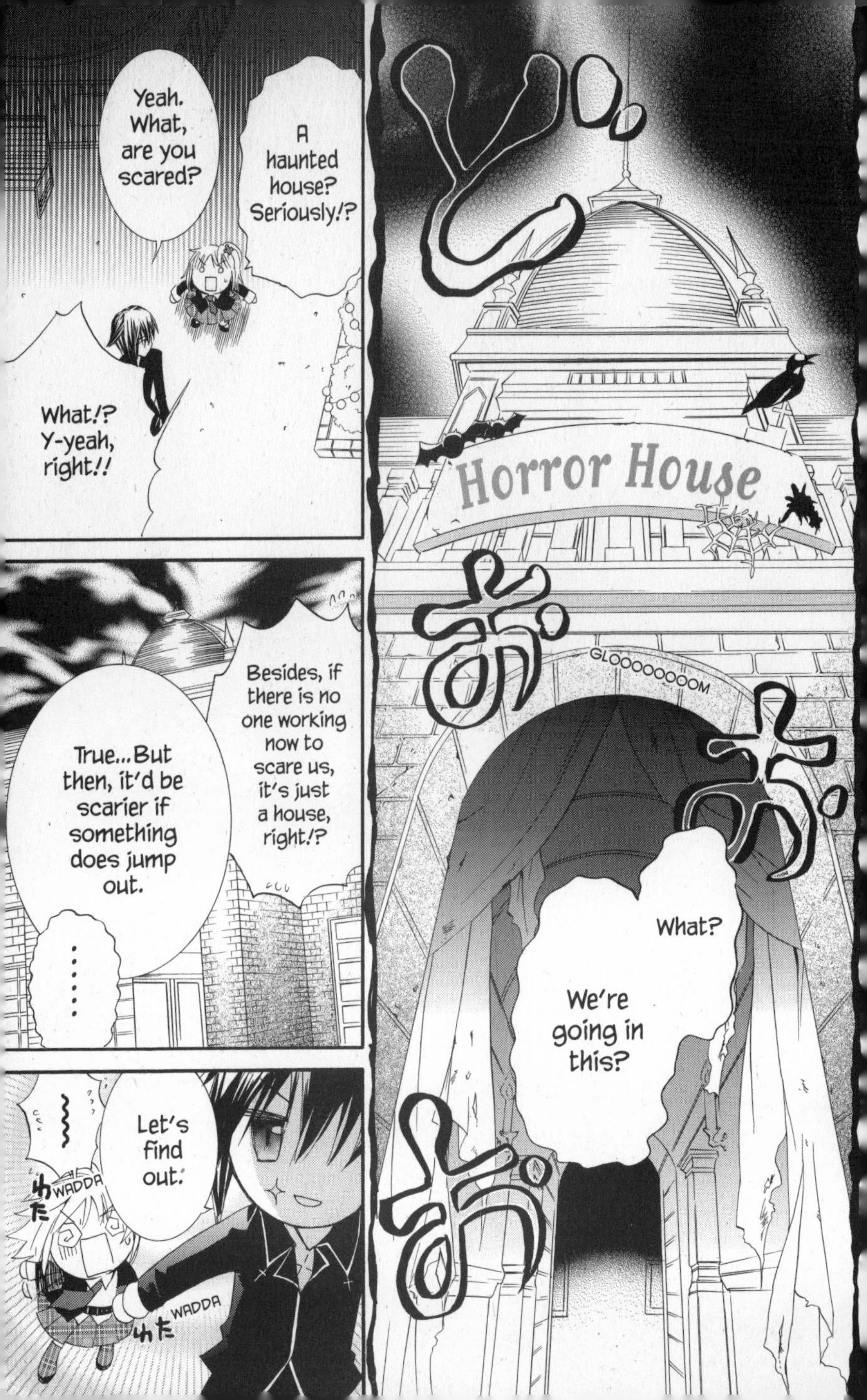
Horror House
GLOOOOOOOOM
What?
We're going in this?
A haunted house? Seriously!?
Yeah. What, are you scared?
What!? Y-yeah, right!!
Besides, if there is no one working now to scare us, it's just a house, right!?
True...But then, it'd be scarier if something does jump out.
......
Let's find out.
WADDA
WADDA

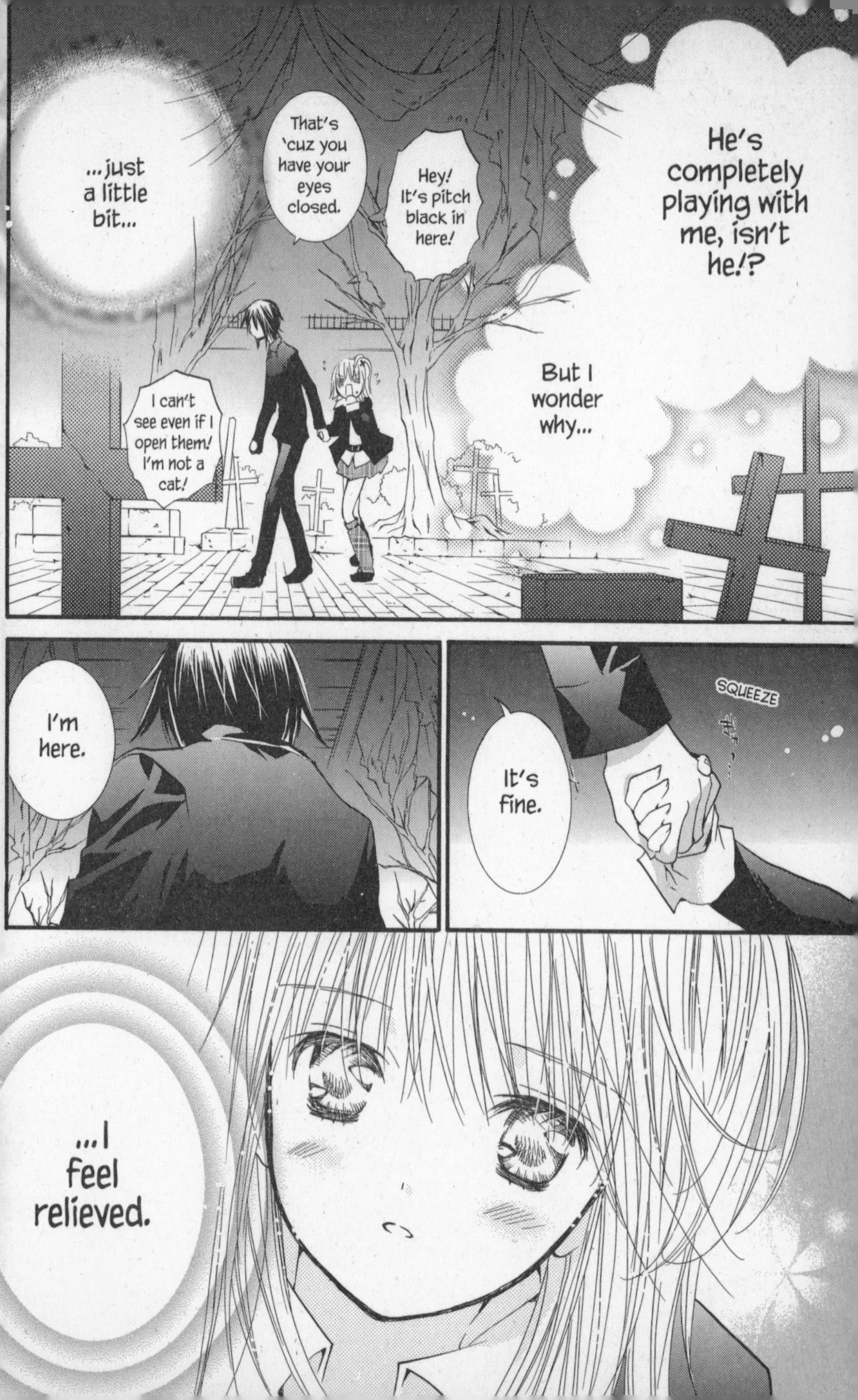
He's completely playing with me, isn't he!?
Hey! It's pitch black in here!
That's 'cuz you have your eyes closed.
...just a little bit...
But I wonder why...
I can't see even if I open them! I'm not a cat!
SQUEEZE
It's fine.
I'm here.
...I feel relieved.

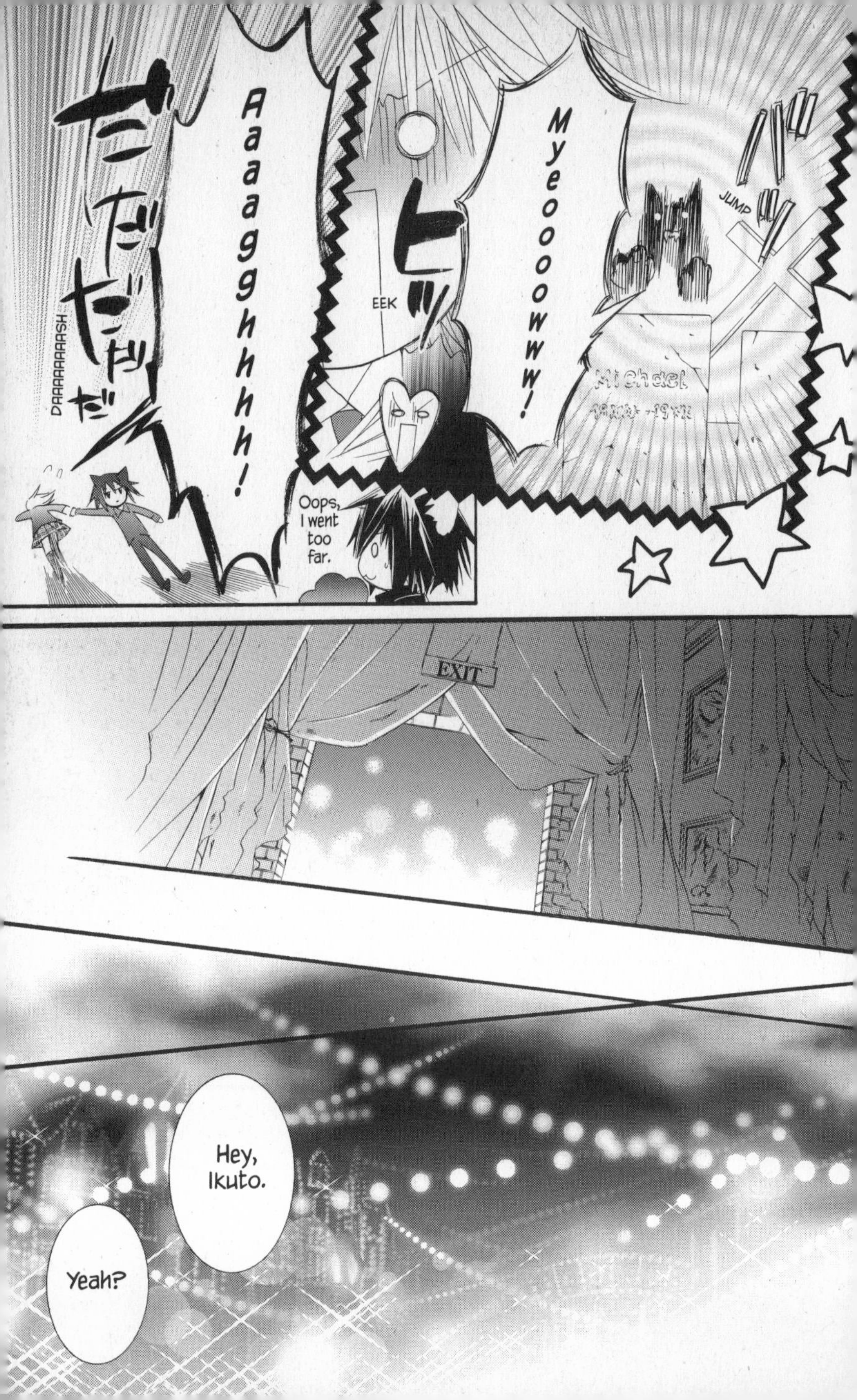
JUMP
Myeoooowww!
EEK
Aaaagghhhhh!
Oops, I went too far.
DAAAAAAAASH
EXIT
Hey, Ikuto.
Yeah?

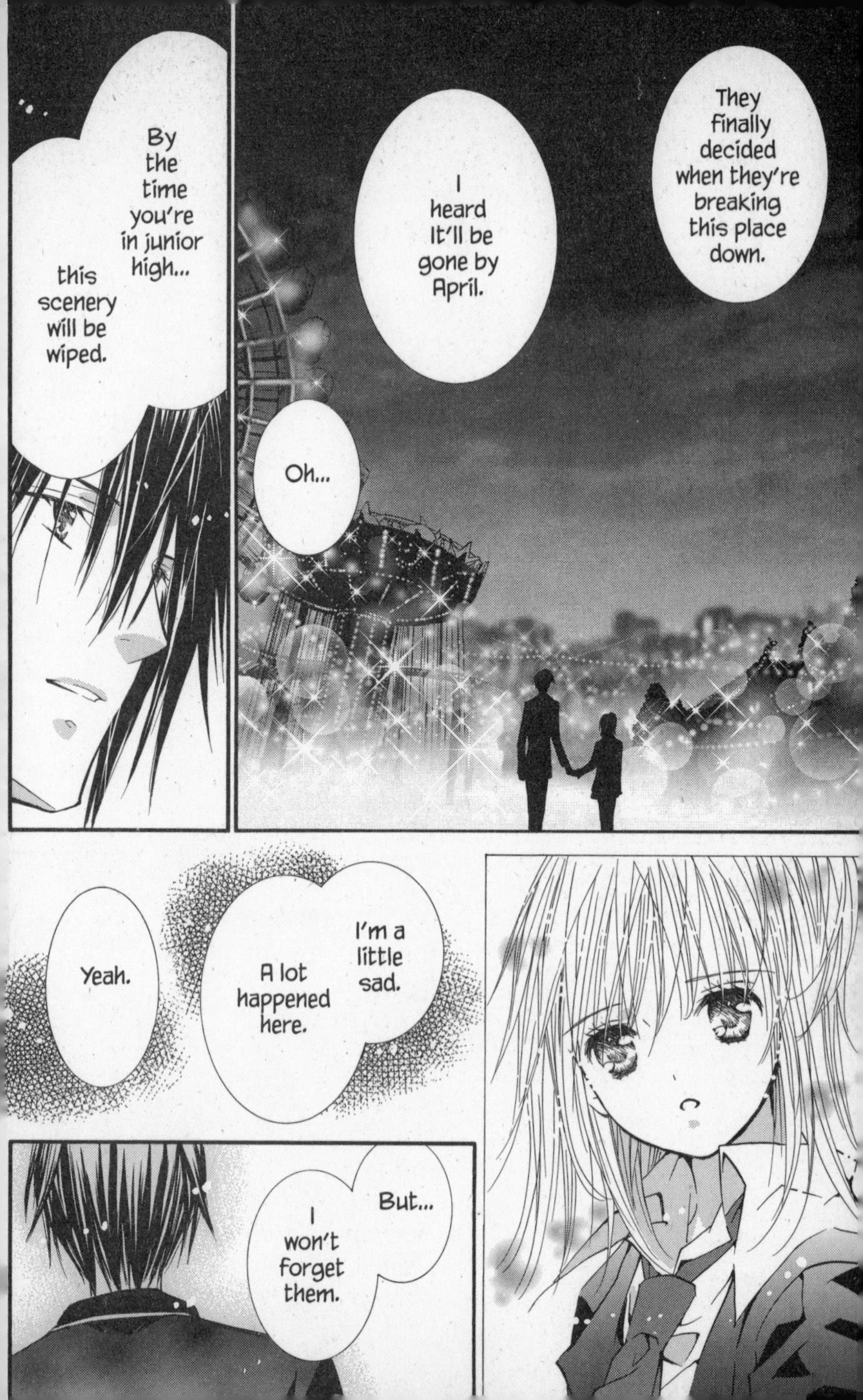
They finally decided when they're breaking this place down.
I heard It'll be gone by April.
Oh...
By the time you're in junior high...
this scenery will be wiped.
I'm a little sad.
A lot happened here.
Yeah.
But...
I won't forget them.

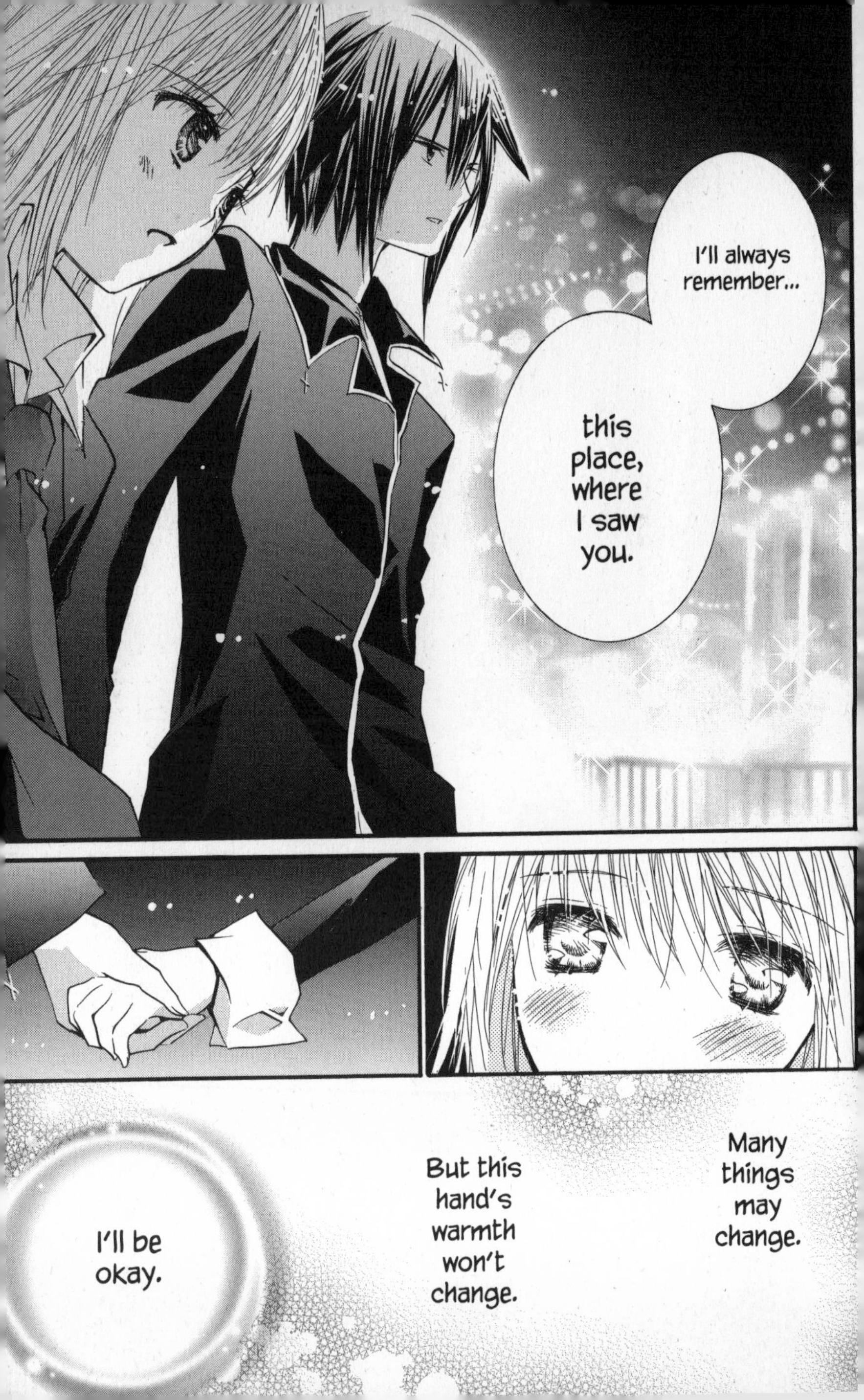
I'll always remember...
this place, where I saw you.
Many things may change.
But this hand's warmth won't change.
I'll be okay.

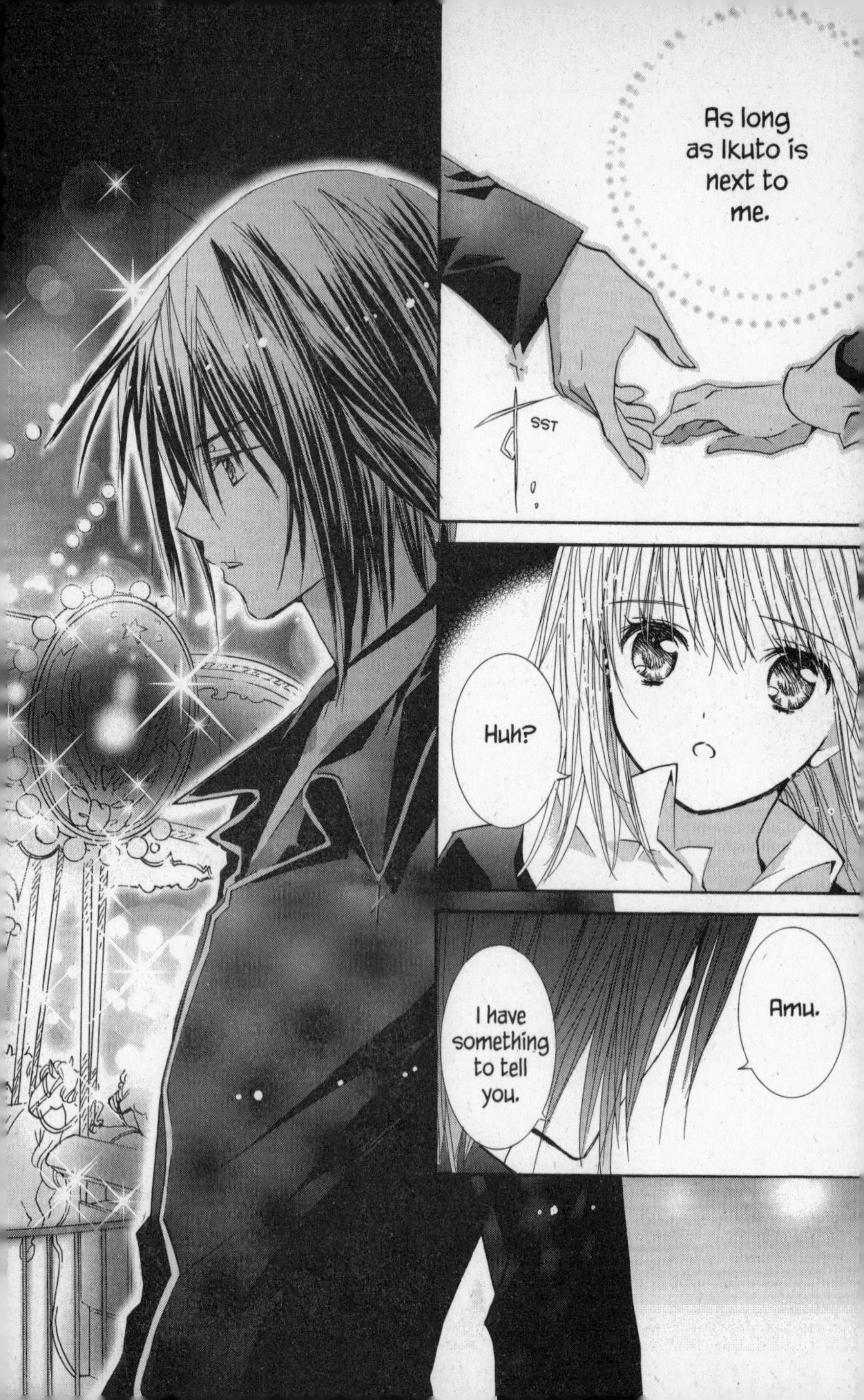
As long as Ikuto is next to me.
SST
Huh?
Amu.
I have something to tell you.

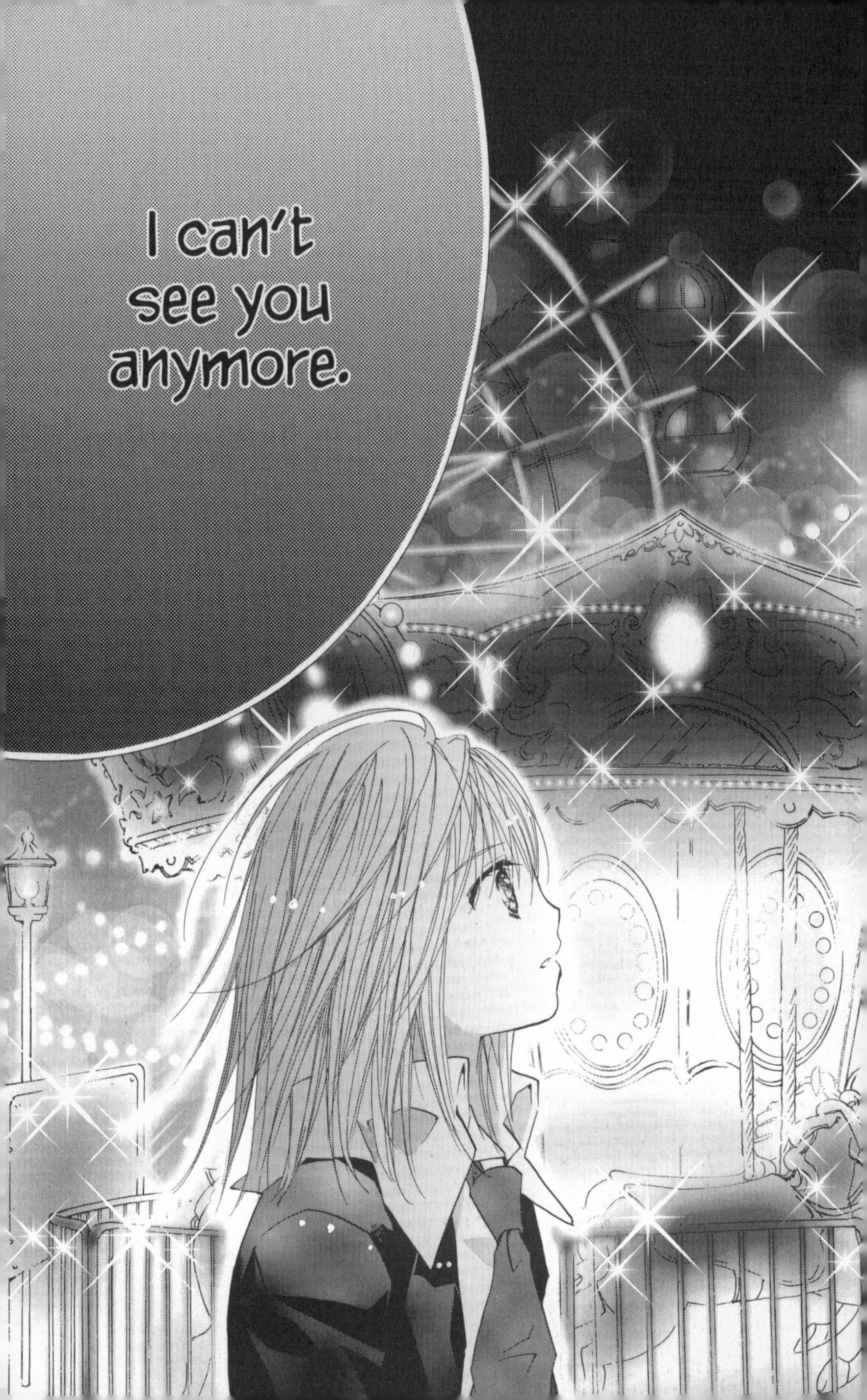
I can't see you anymore.

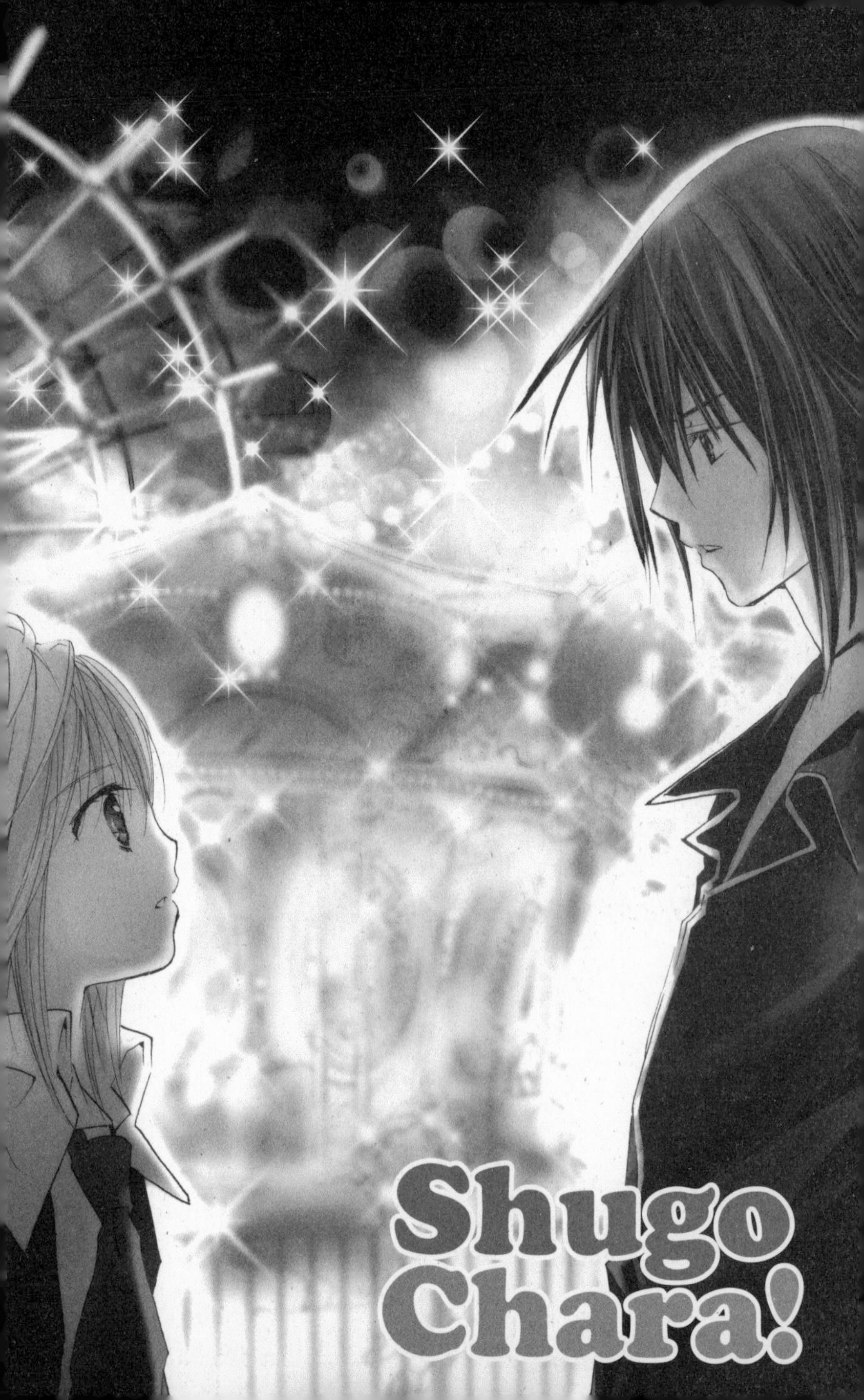
Shugo
Chara!

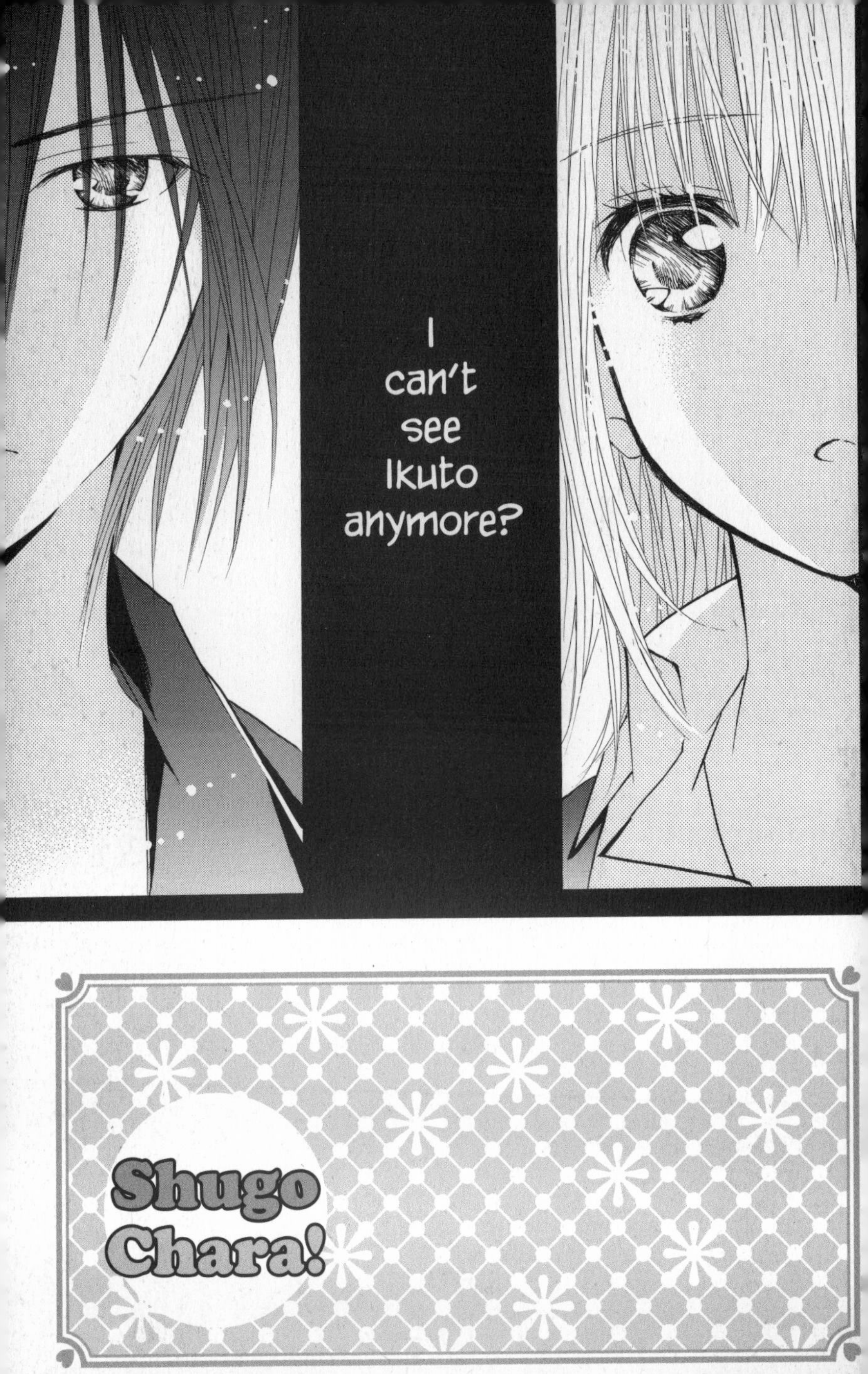
I can't see Ikuto anymore?

Shugo Chara!

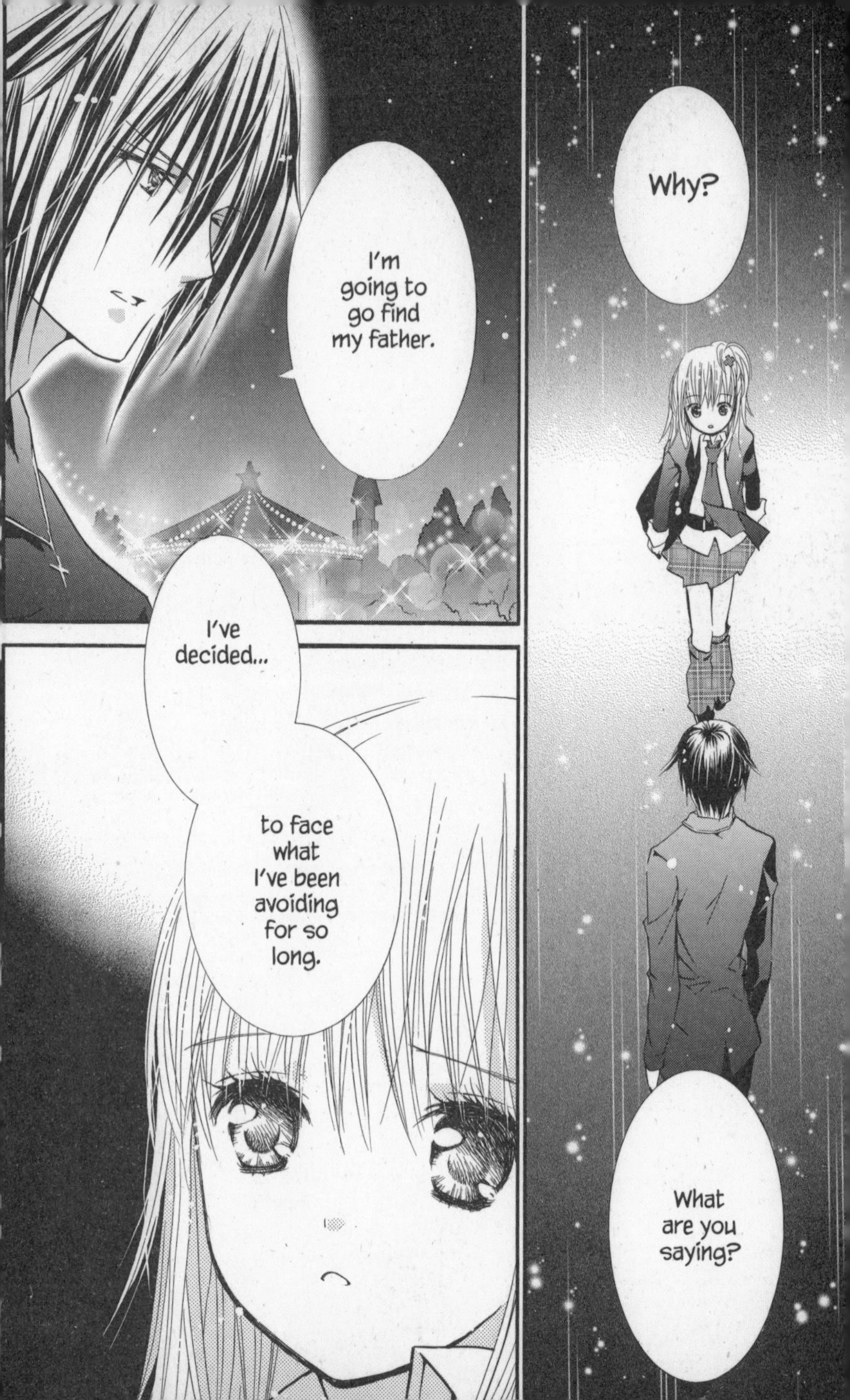
Why?
What are you saying?
I'm going to go find my father.
I've decided...
to face what I've been avoiding for so long.

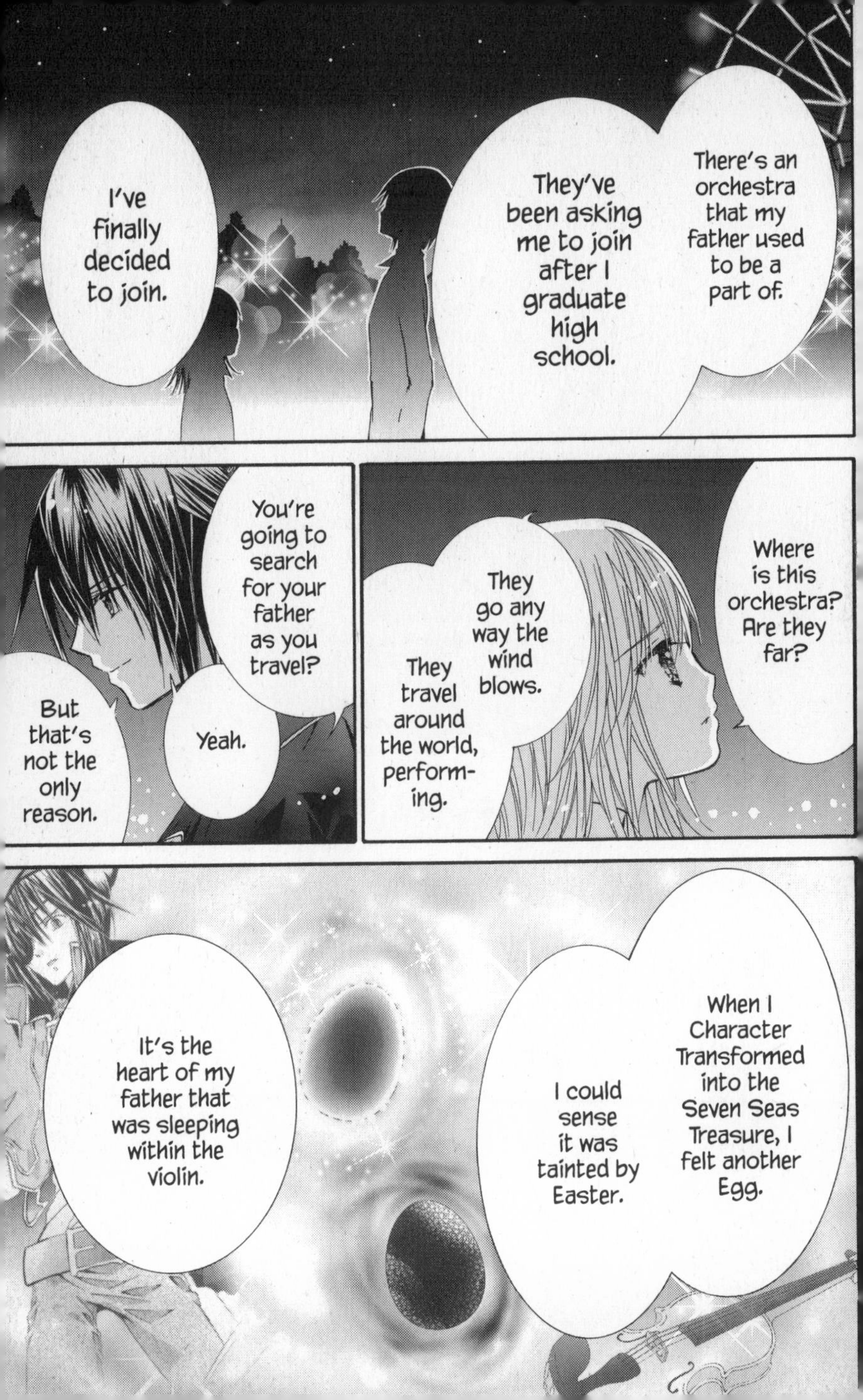
There's an orchestra that my father used to be a part of.
They've been asking me to join after I graduate high school.
I've finally decided to join.
Where is this orchestra? Are they far?
They go any way the wind blows.
They travel around the world, perform-ing.
You're going to search for your father as you travel?
Yeah.
But that's not the only reason.
When I Character Transformed into the Seven Seas Treasure, I felt another Egg.
I could sense it was tainted by Easter.
It's the heart of my father that was sleeping within the violin.

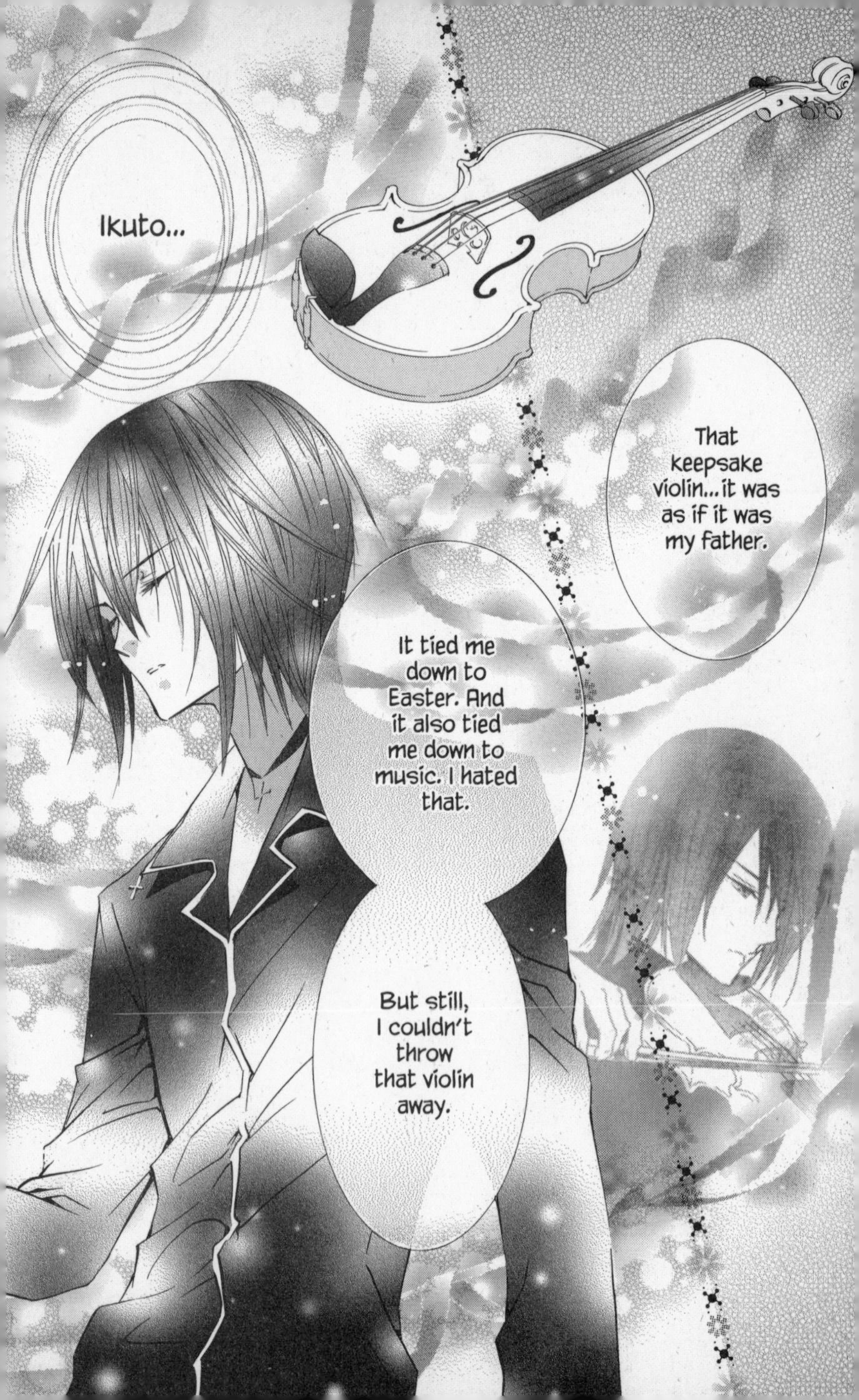
Ikuto...
That keepsake violin...it was as if it was my father.
It tied me down to Easter. And it also tied me down to music. I hated that.
But still, I couldn't throw that violin away.

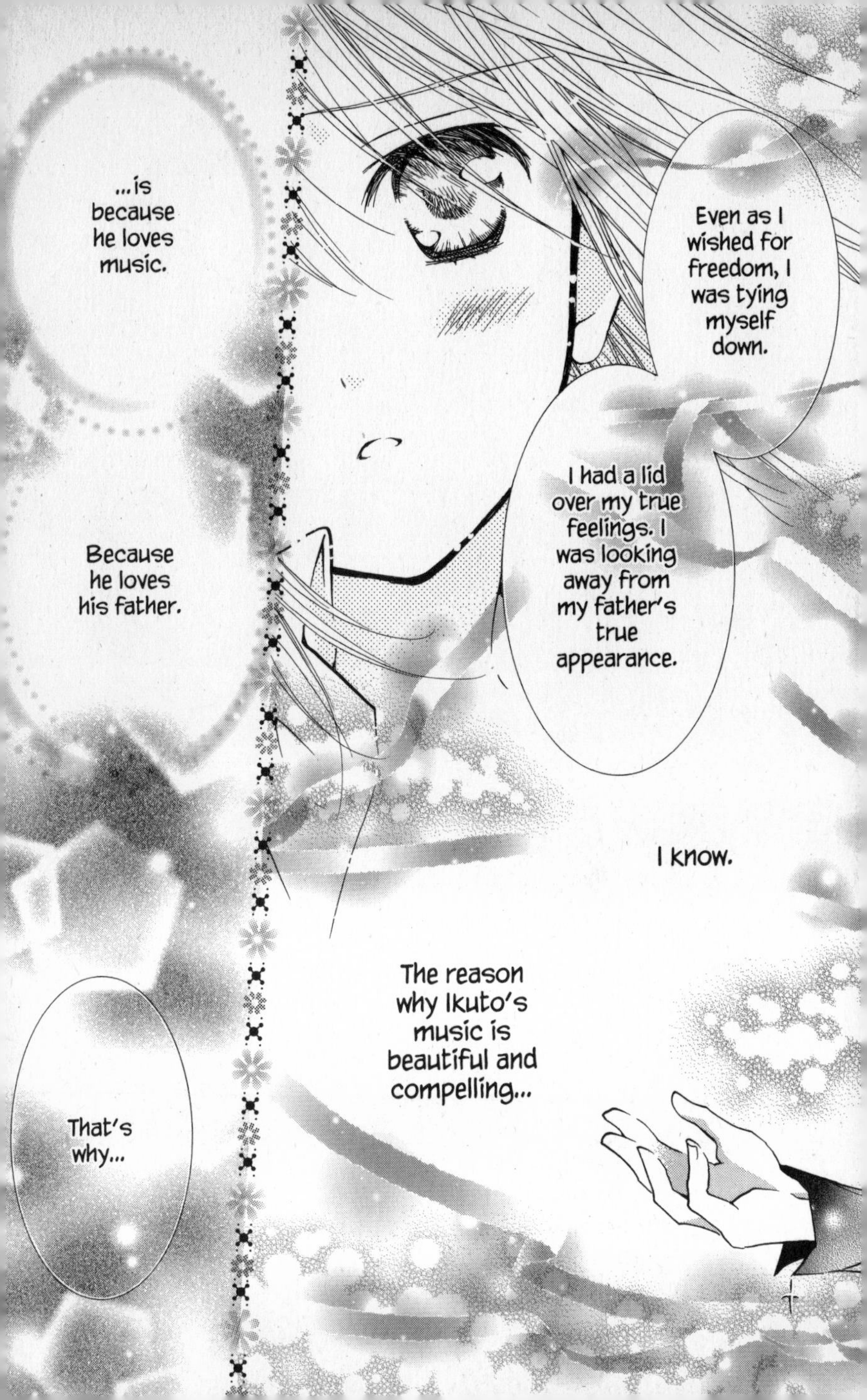
Even as I wished for freedom, I was tying myself down.
I had a lid over my true feelings. I was looking away from my father's true appearance.
I know.
The reason why Ikuto's music is beautiful and compelling...
...is because he loves music.
Because he loves his father.
That's why...

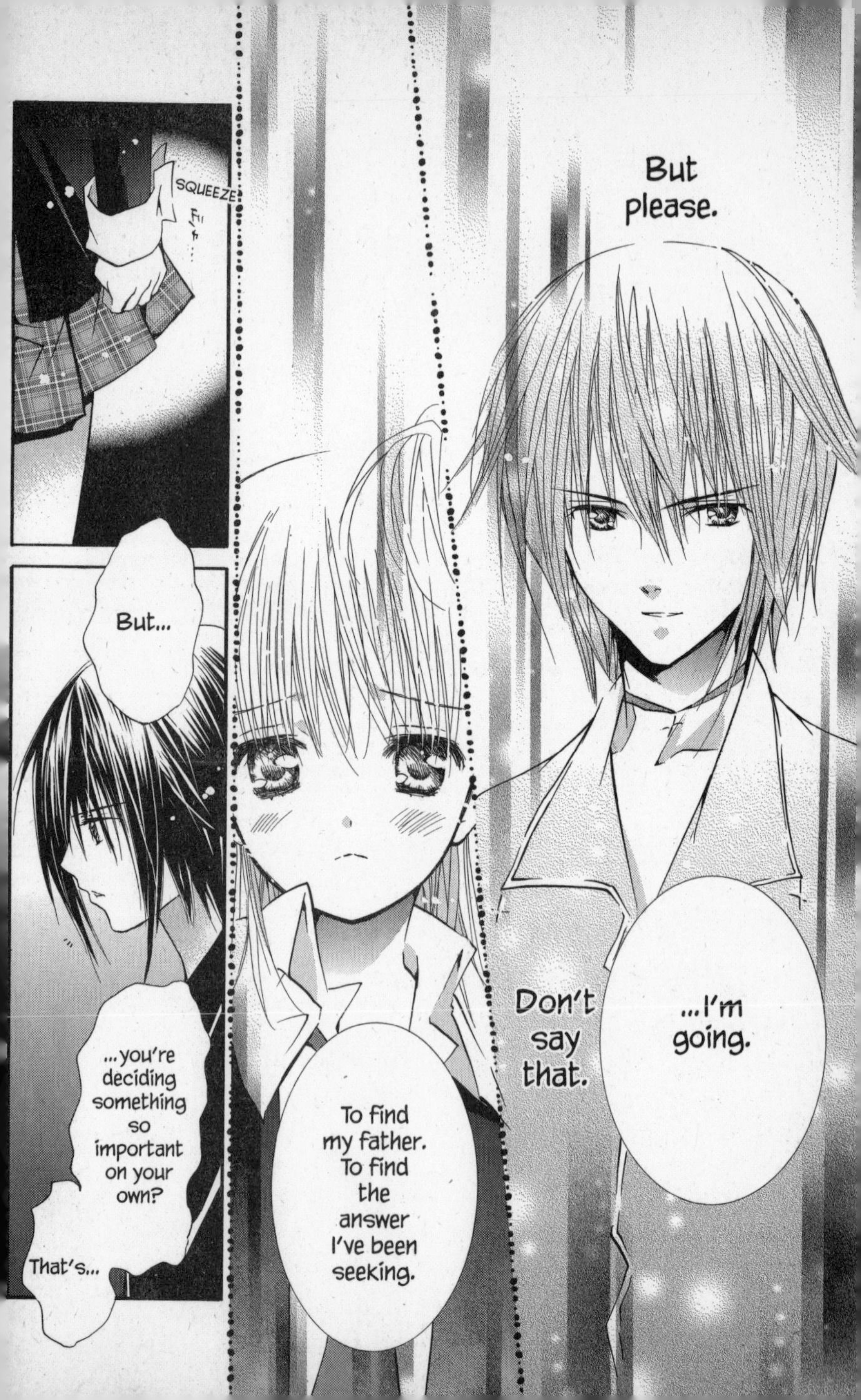
But please.
...I'm going.
Don't say that.
To find my father. To find the answer I've been seeking.
SQUEEZE
But...
...you're deciding something so important on your own?
That's...

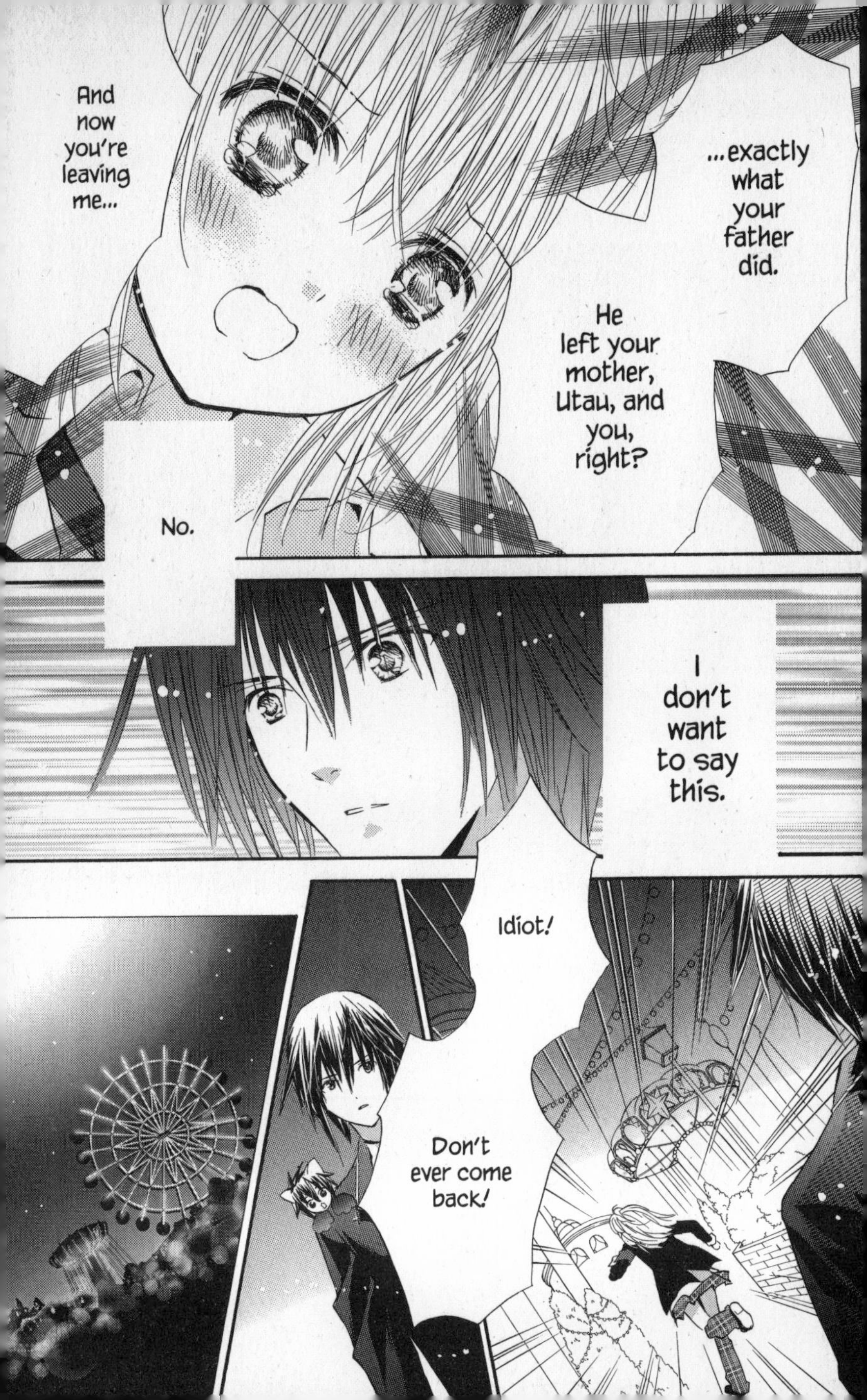
And now you're leaving me...
...exactly what your father did.
He left your mother, Utau, and you, right?
No.
I don't want to say this.
Idiot!
Don't ever come back!

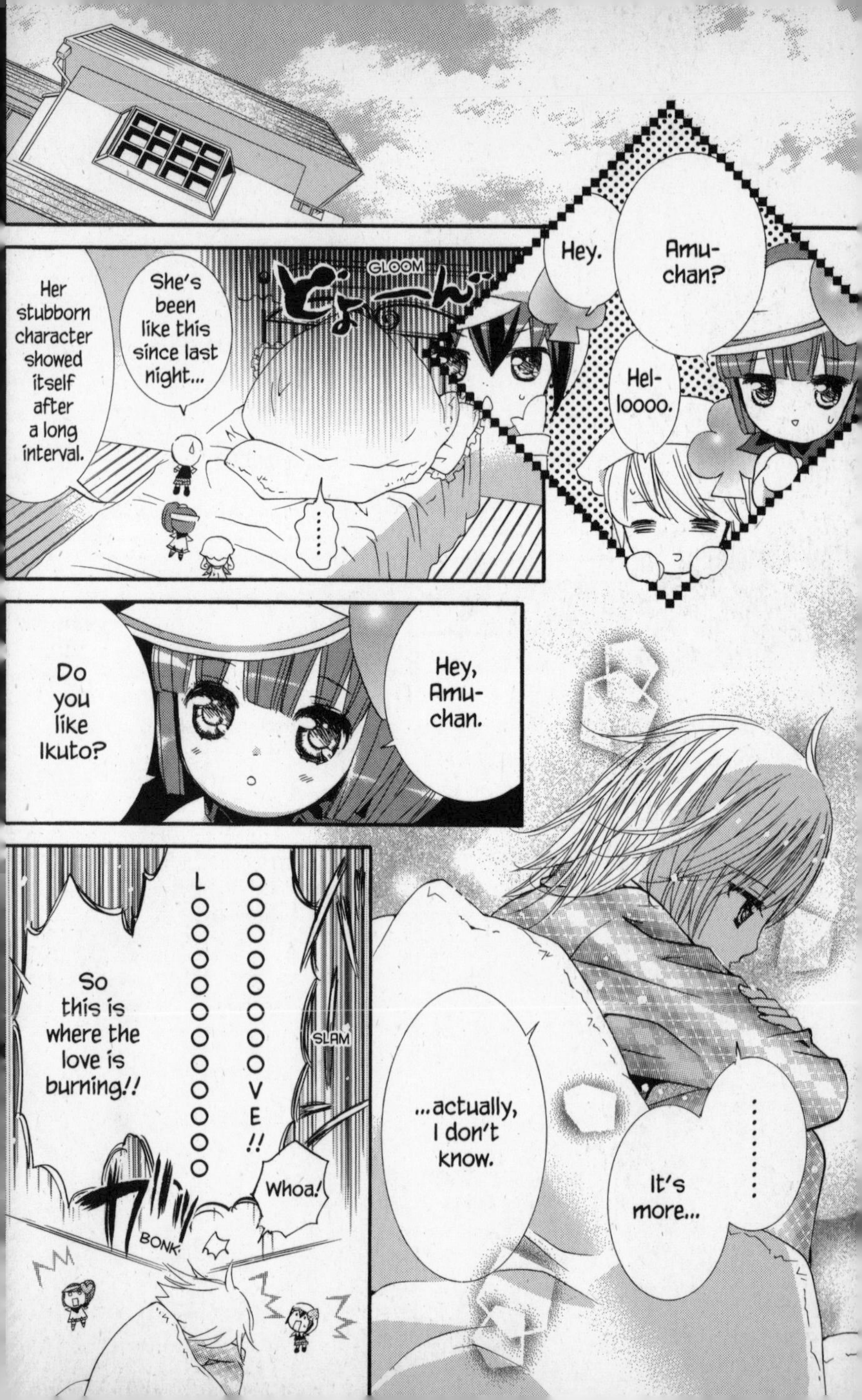
Amu-chan?
Hey.
Hel-loooo.
GLOOM
She's been like this since last night...
Her stubborn character showed itself after a long interval.
......
Hey, Amu-chan.
Do you like Ikuto?
......
It's more...
...actually, I don't know.
OOOOOOOOOVE!!
LOOOOOOOOOOOOO
So this is where the love is burning!!
SLAM
Whoa!
BONK

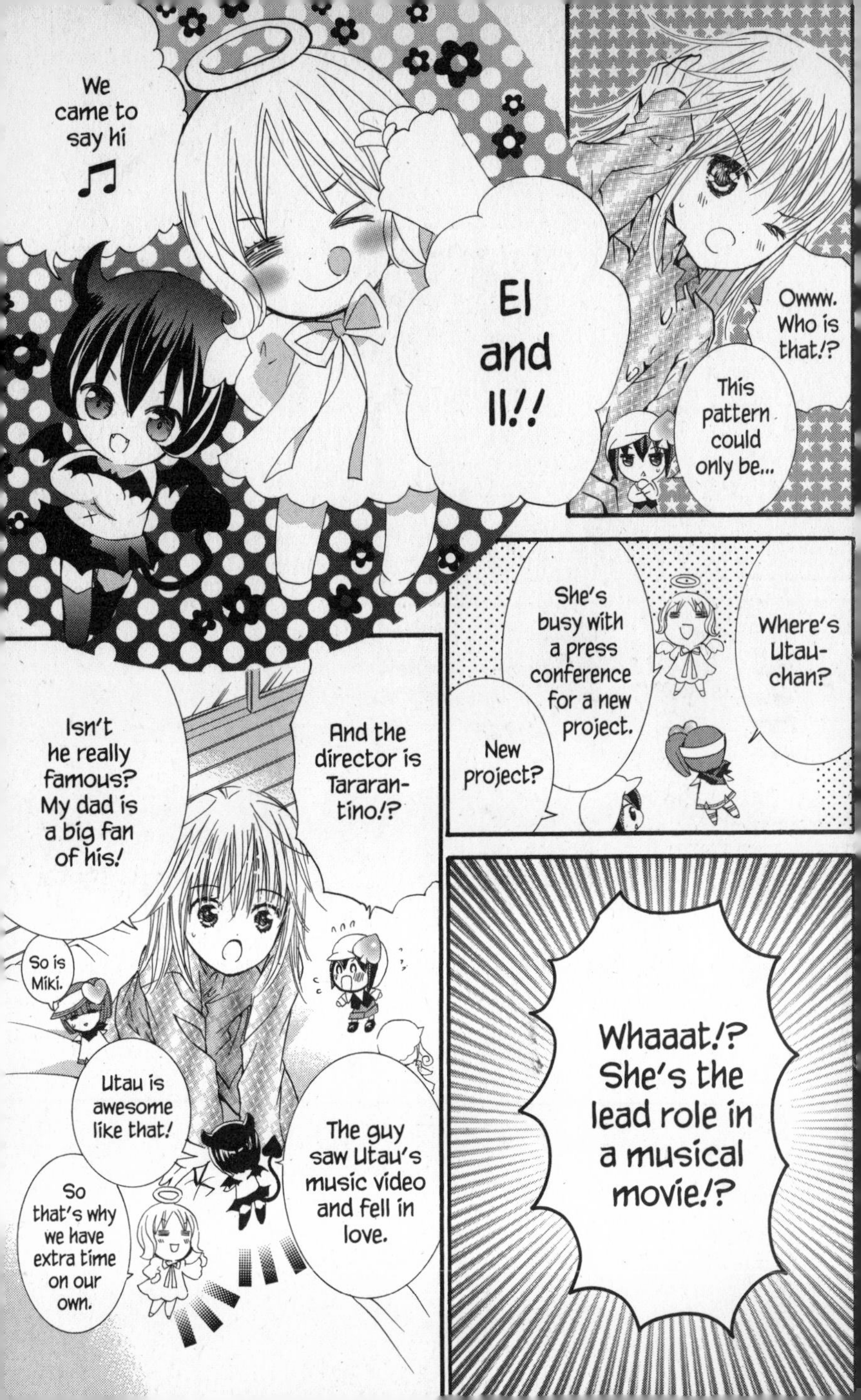

Owww. Who is that!?
This pattern could only be...
El and Il!!
We came to say hi ♫
Where's Utau-chan?
She's busy with a press conference for a new project.
New project?
Whaaat!? She's the lead role in a musical movie!?
And the director is Tararantino!?
Isn't he really famous? My dad is a big fan of his!
So is Miki.
The guy saw Utau's music video and fell in love.
Utau is awesome like that!
So that's why we have extra time on our own.

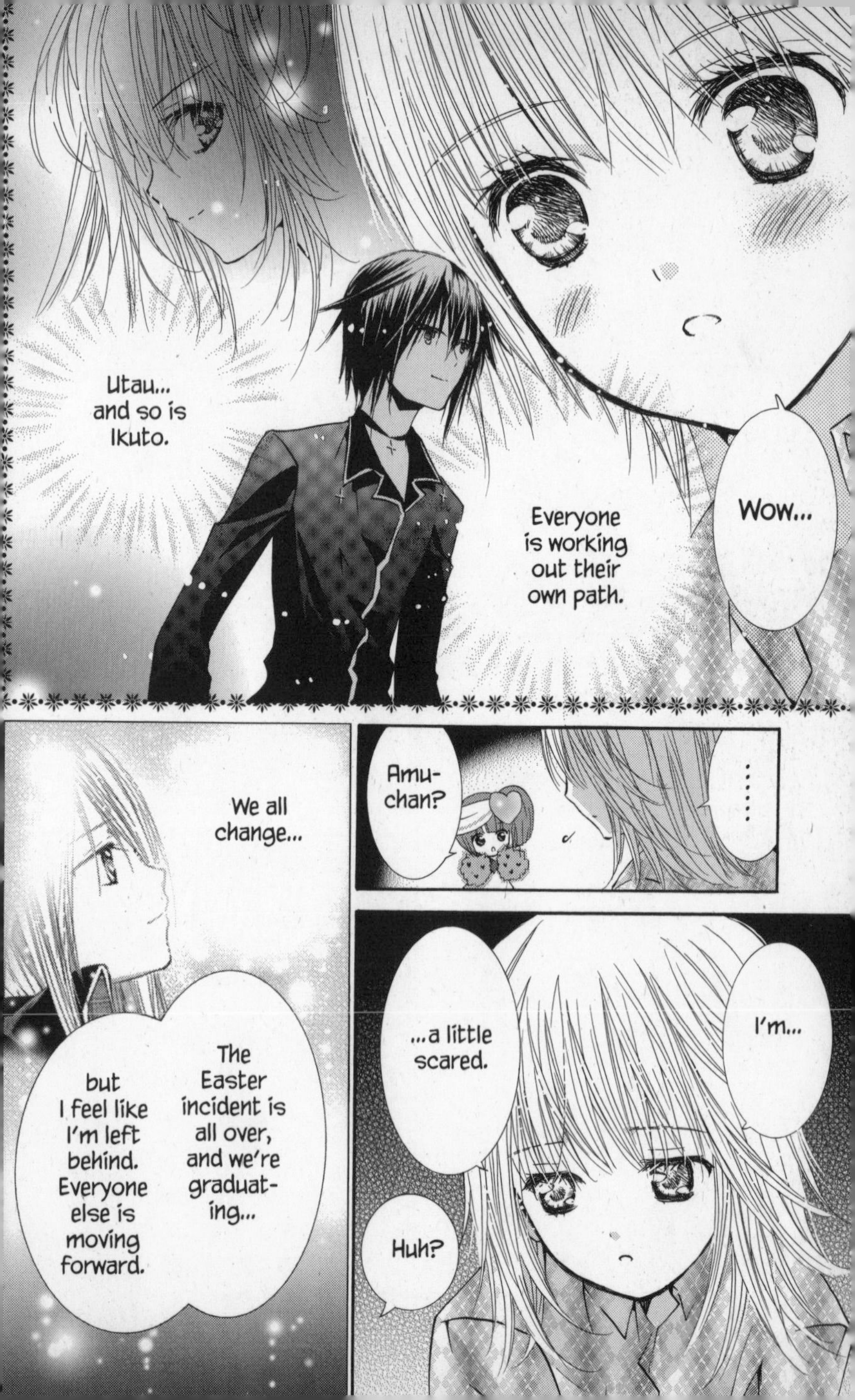
Wow...
Everyone is working out their own path.
Utau... and so is Ikuto.
......
Amu-chan?
I'm...
...a little scared.
Huh?
We all change...
The Easter incident is all over, and we're graduat-ing...
but I feel like I'm left behind. Everyone else is moving forward.

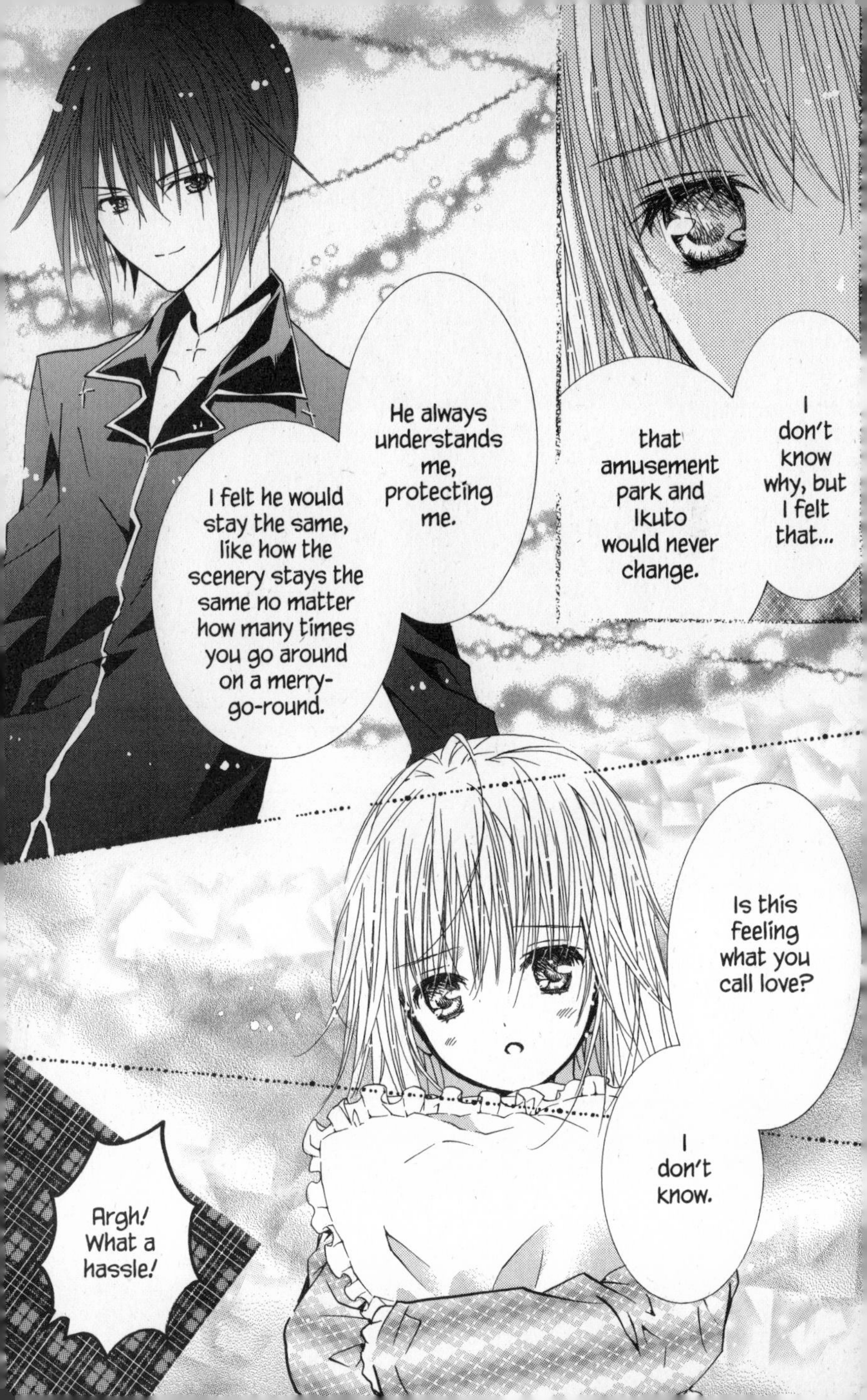
I don't know why, but I felt that...
that amusement park and Ikuto would never change.
He always understands me, protecting me.
I felt he would stay the same, like how the scenery stays the same no matter how many times you go around on a merry-go-round.
Is this feeling what you call love?
I don't know.
Argh! What a hassle!

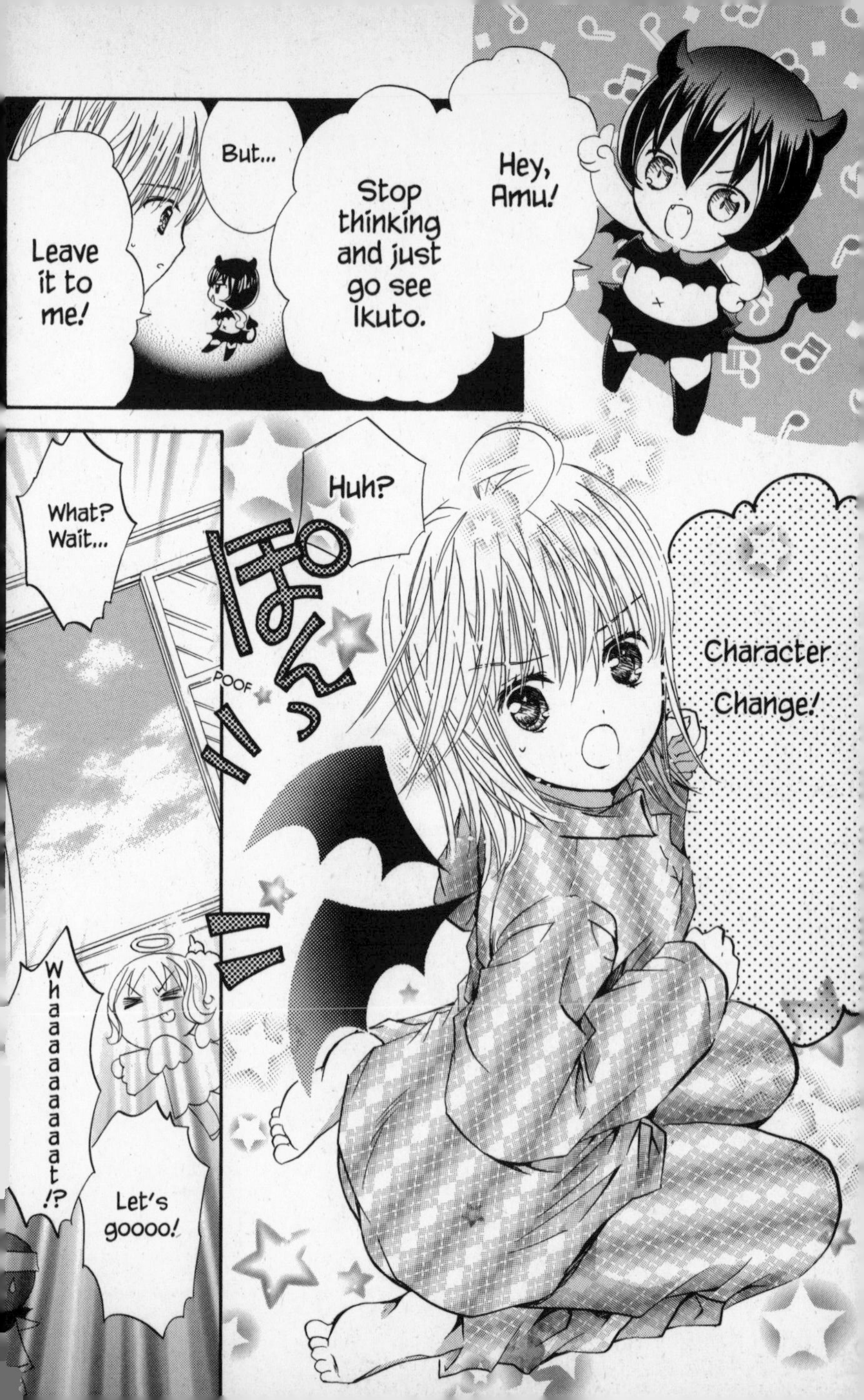
Hey, Amu!
Stop thinking and just go see Ikuto.
But...
Leave it to me!
Character Change!
Huh?
ぽんっ!!
POOF
What? Wait...
Whaaaaaaaaaat!?
Let's goooo!

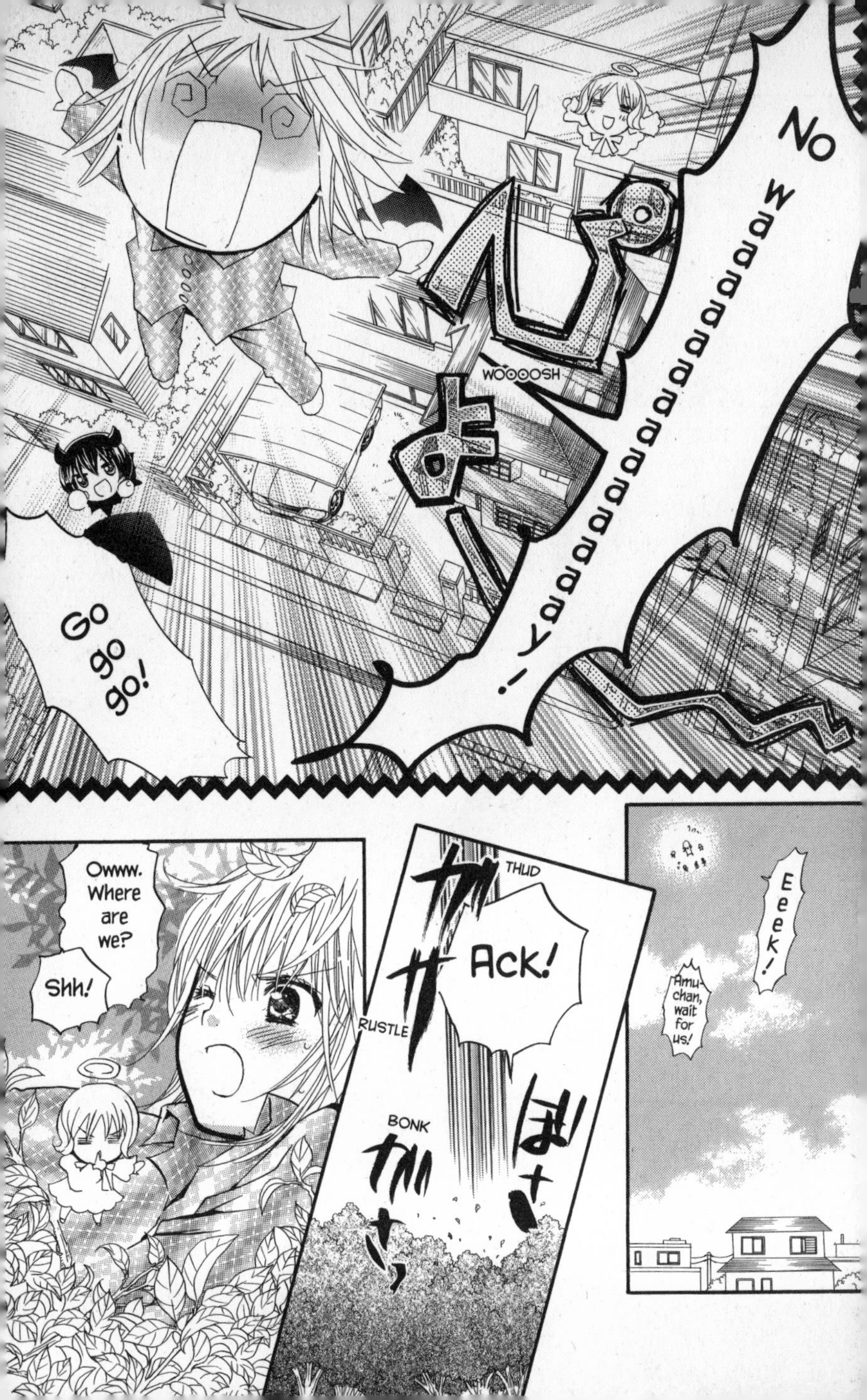
No waaaaaaaaaaaaaaaaaaay!
WOOOOSH
Go go go!
Eeeek!
Amu-chan, wait for us!
THUD
Ack!
RUSTLE
BONK
Owww. Where are we?
Shh!

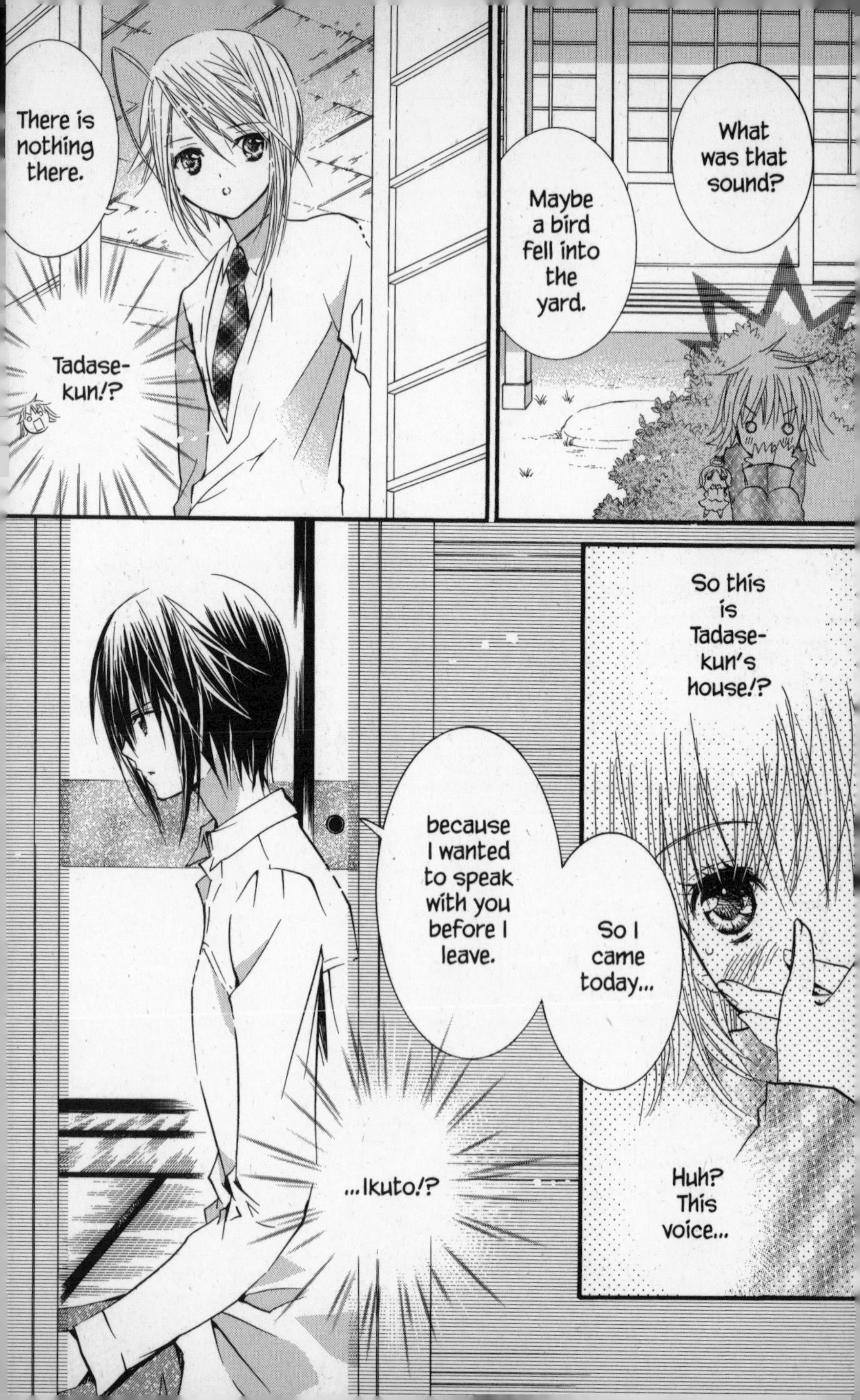
What was that sound?
Maybe a bird fell into the yard.
There is nothing there.
Tadase-kun!?
So this is Tadase-kun's house!?
Huh? This voice...
So I came today...
because I wanted to speak with you before I leave.
...Ikuto!?

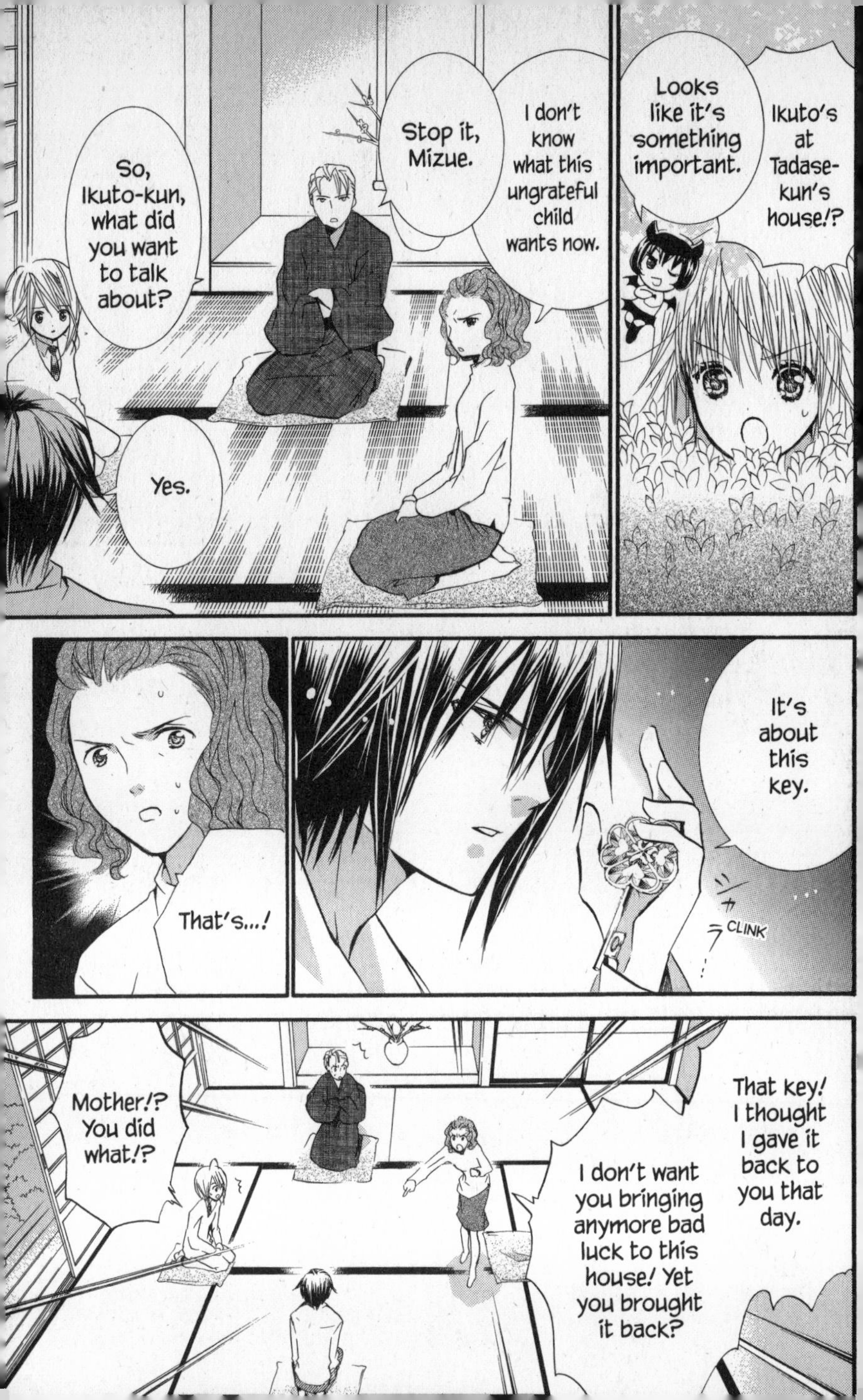
Ikuto's at Tadase-kun's house!?
Looks like it's something important.
I don't know what this ungrateful child wants now.
Stop it, Mizue.
So, Ikuto-kun, what did you want to talk about?
Yes.
It's about this key.
CLINK
That's...!
That key! I thought I gave it back to you that day.
I don't want you bringing anymore bad luck to this house! Yet you brought it back?
Mother!? You did what!?

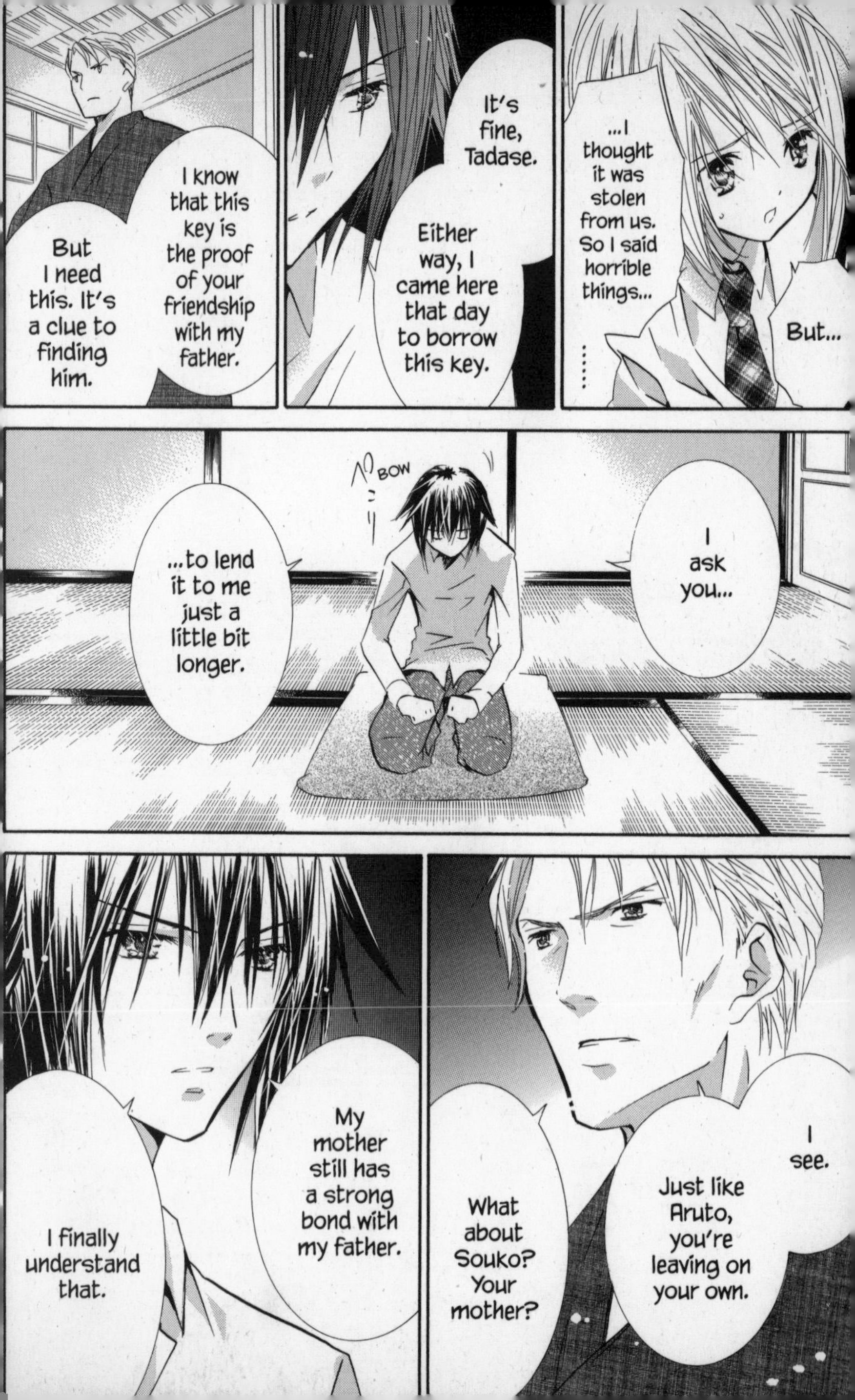
But...
...I thought it was stolen from us. So I said horrible things...
......
It's fine, Tadase.
Either way, I came here that day to borrow this key.
I know that this key is the proof of your friendship with my father.
But I need this. It's a clue to finding him.
I ask you...
BOW
...to lend it to me just a little bit longer.
I see.
Just like Aruto, you're leaving on your own.
What about Souko? Your mother?
My mother still has a strong bond with my father.
I finally understand that.

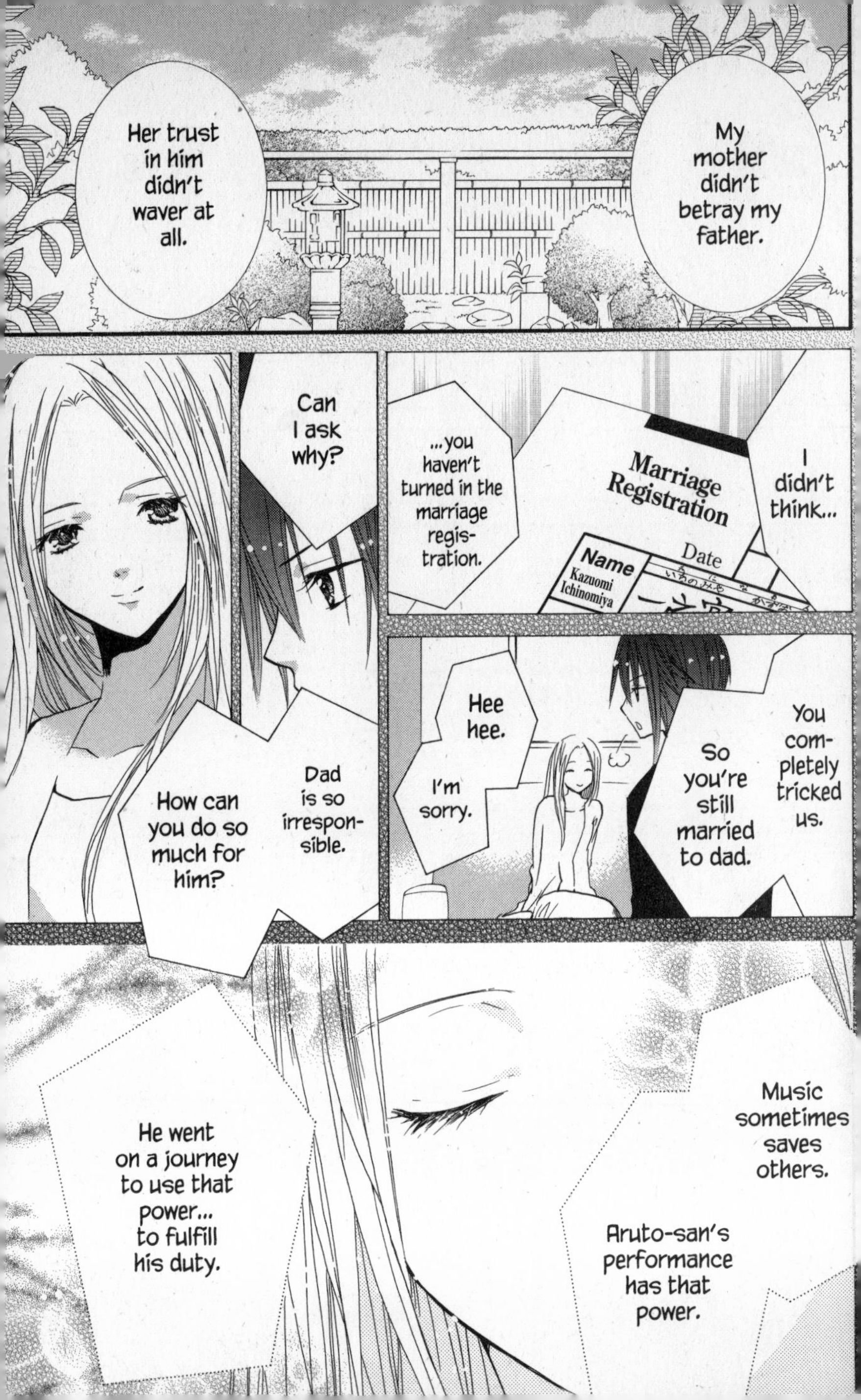
My mother didn't betray my father.
Her trust in him didn't waver at all.
I didn't think...
...you haven't turned in the marriage registration.
Marriage Registration
Date
Name
Kazuomi Ichinomiya
You completely tricked us.
So you're still married to dad.
Hee hee.
I'm sorry.
Can I ask why?
Dad is so irresponsible.
How can you do so much for him?
Music sometimes saves others.
Aruto-san's performance has that power.
He went on a journey to use that power... to fulfill his duty.

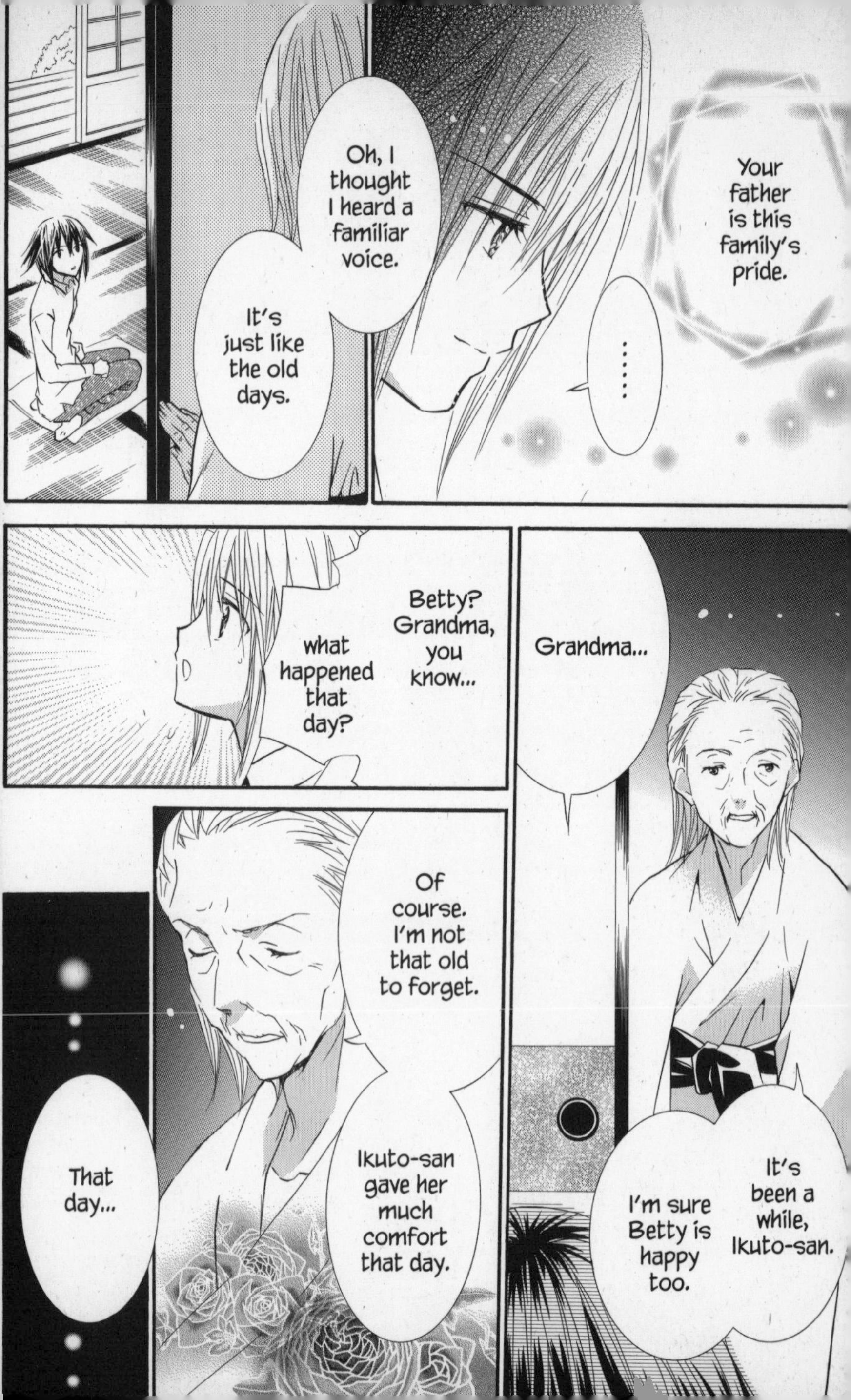
Your father is this family's pride.
......
Oh, I thought I heard a familiar voice.
It's just like the old days.
Grandma...
It's been a while, Ikuto-san.
I'm sure Betty is happy too.
Betty? Grandma, you know...
what happened that day?
Of course. I'm not that old to forget.
Ikuto-san gave her much comfort that day.
That day...

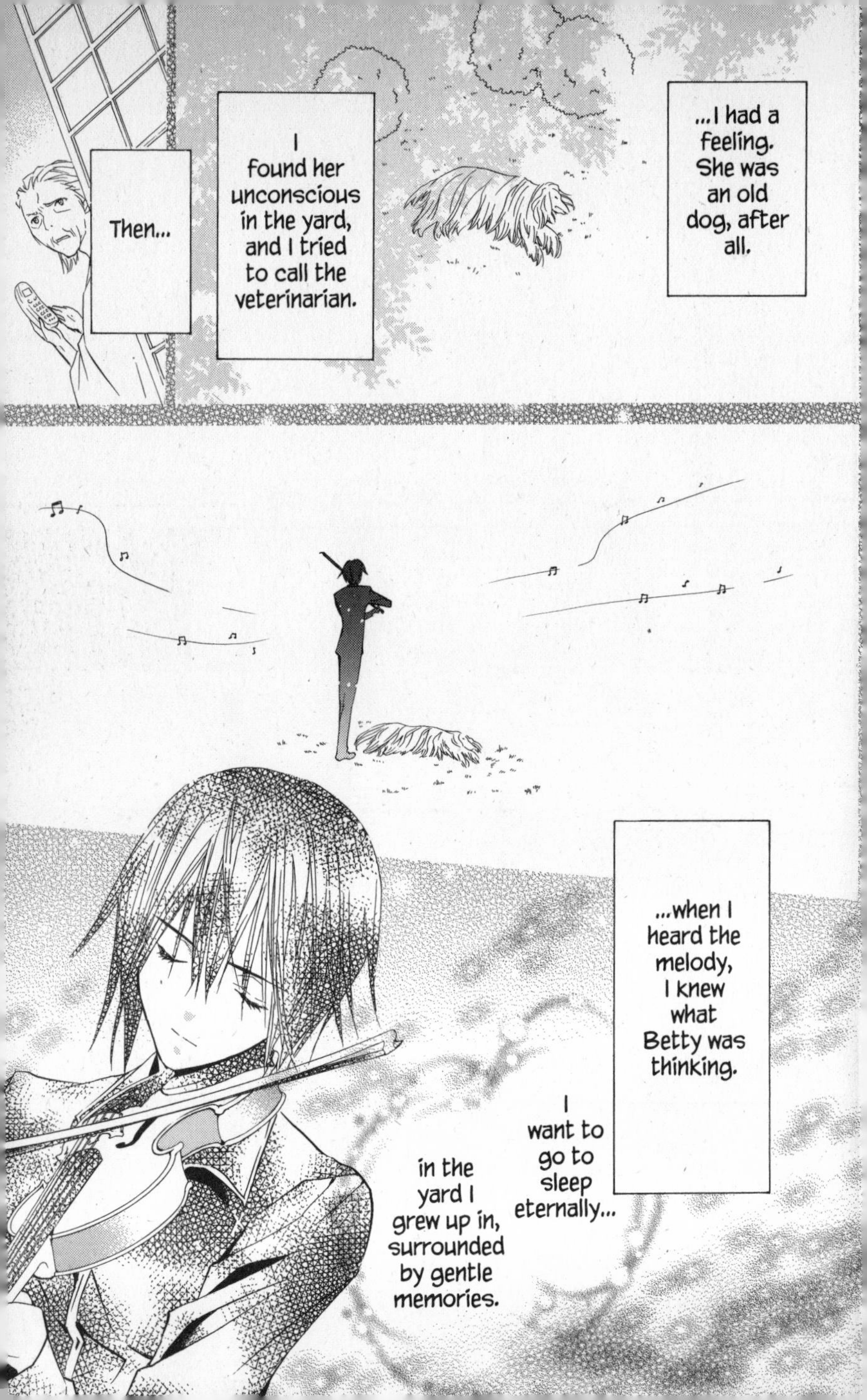
...I had a feeling. She was an old dog, after all.
I found her unconscious in the yard, and I tried to call the veterinarian.
Then...
...when I heard the melody, I knew what Betty was thinking.
I want to go to sleep eternally...
in the yard I grew up in, surrounded by gentle memories.

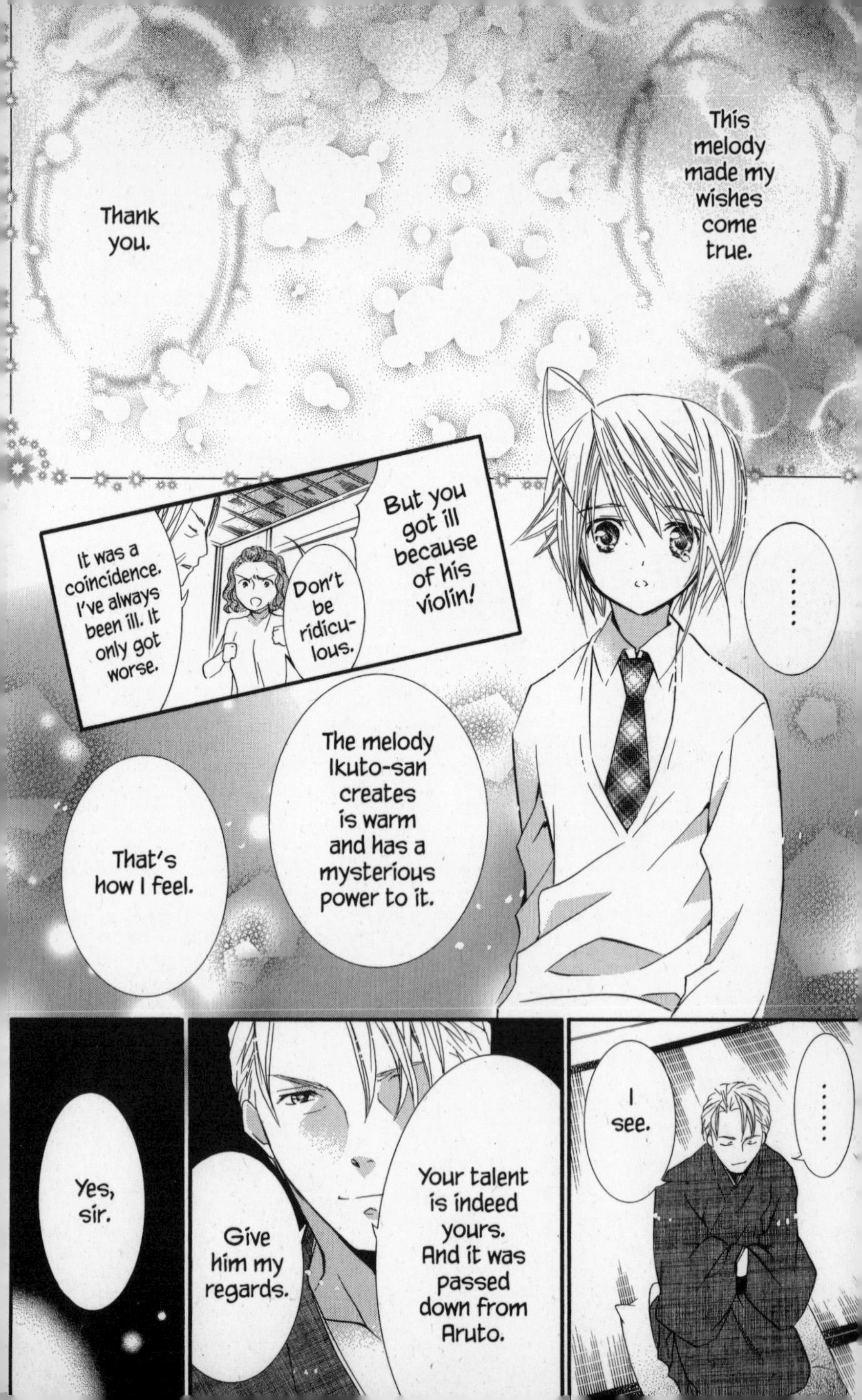
This melody made my wishes come true.
Thank you.
......
But you got ill because of his violin!
Don't be ridiculous.
It was a coincidence. I've always been ill. It only got worse.
The melody Ikuto-san creates is warm and has a mysterious power to it.
That's how I feel.
......
I see.
Your talent is indeed yours. And it was passed down from Aruto.
Give him my regards.
Yes, sir.

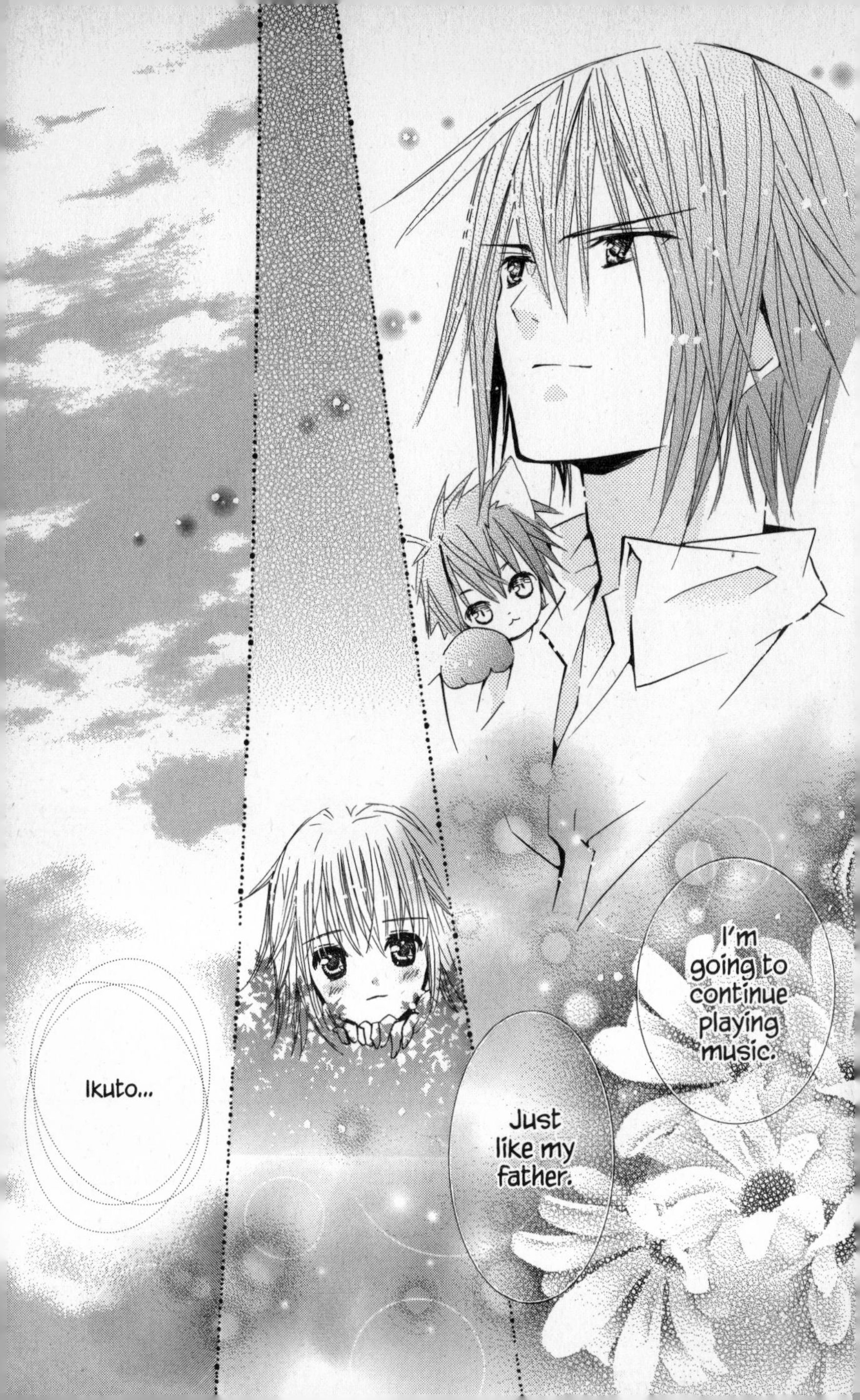
I'm going to continue playing music.
Just like my father.
Ikuto...

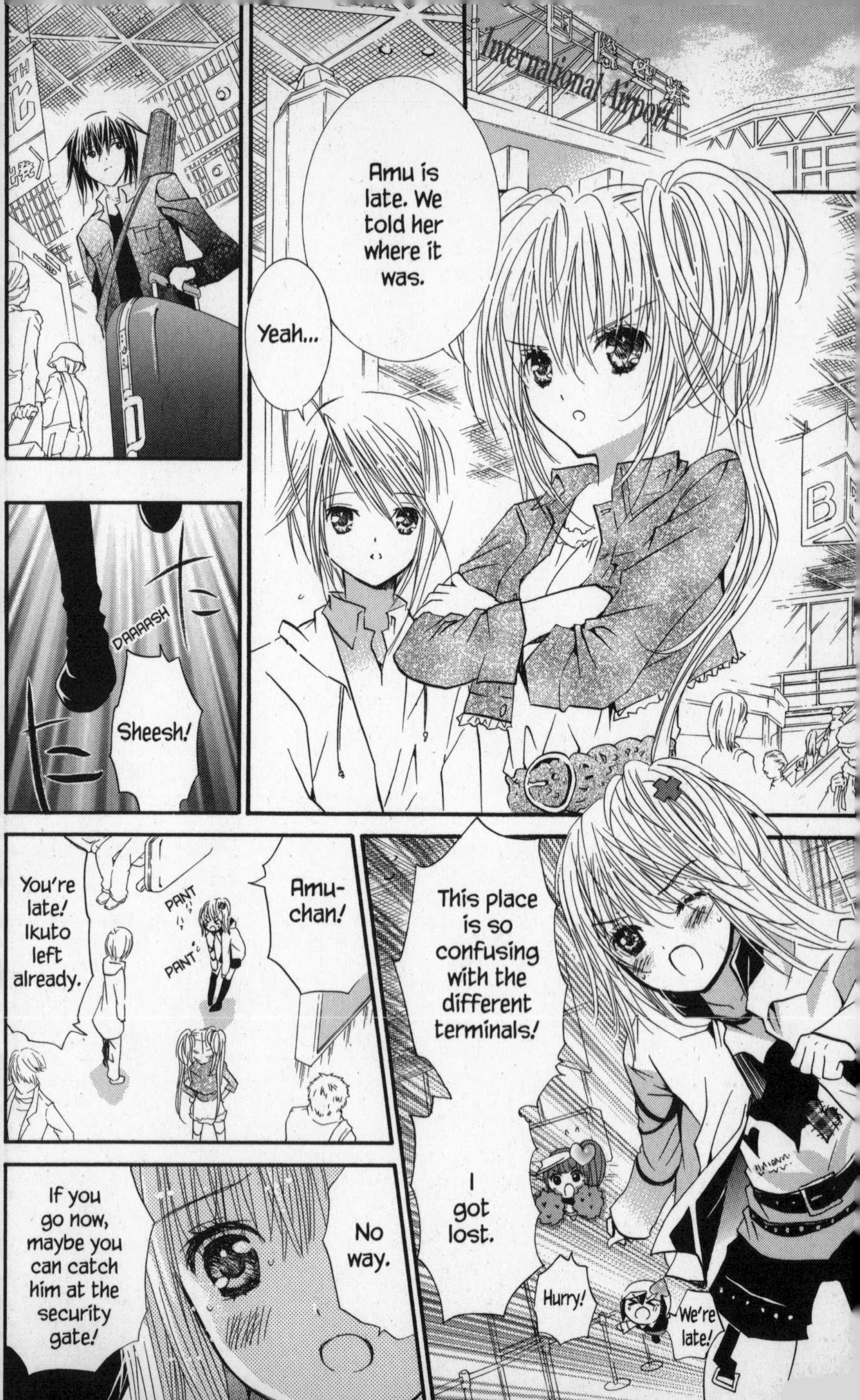
International Airport
Amu is late. We told her where it was.
Yeah...
DAAAASH
Sheesh!
This place is so confusing with the different terminals!
I got lost.
Hurry!
We're late!
Amu-chan!
You're late! Ikuto left already.
PANT
PANT
No way.
If you go now, maybe you can catch him at the security gate!

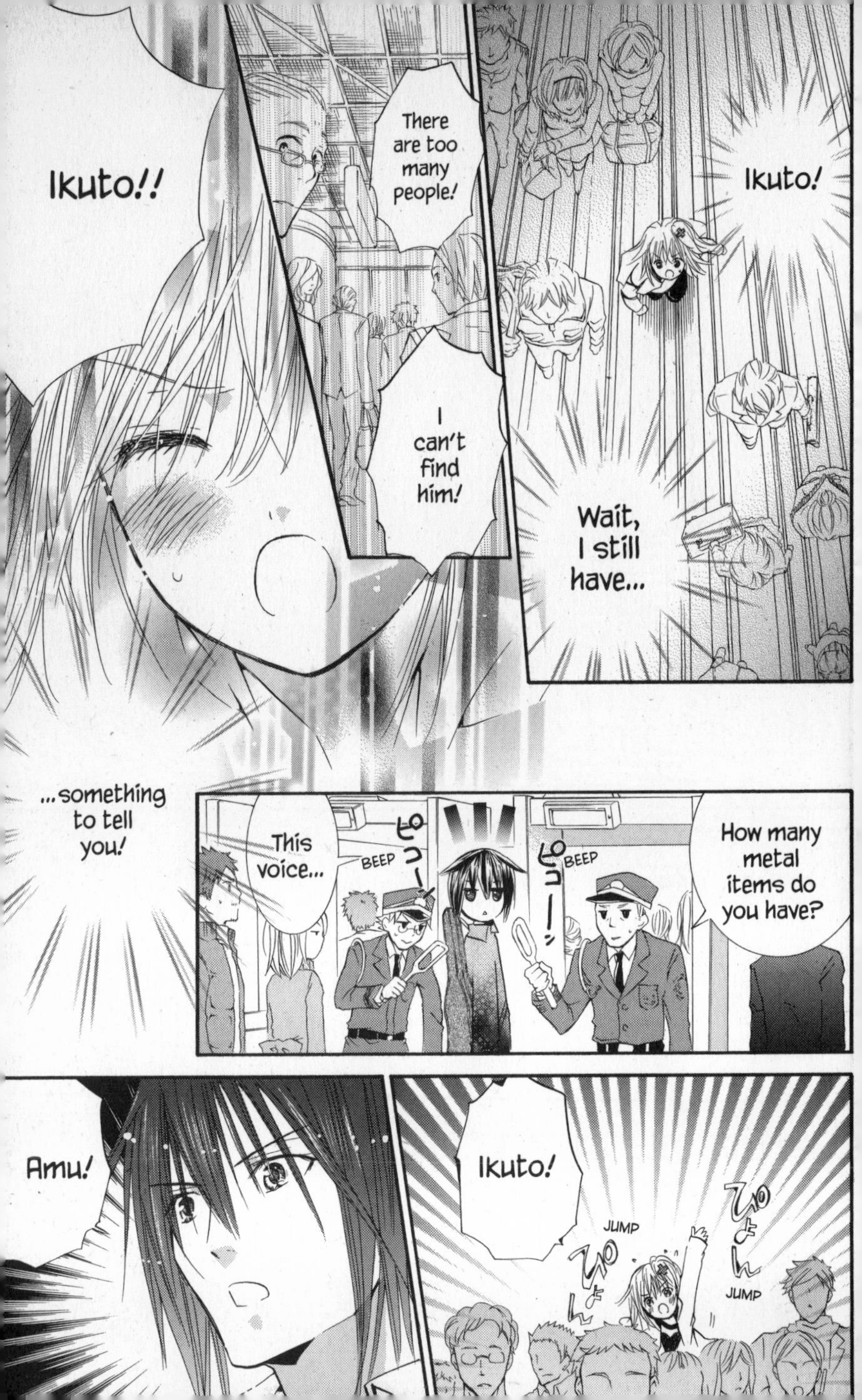
Ikuto!
Wait, I still have...
There are too many people!
I can't find him!
Ikuto!!
...something to tell you!
How many metal items do you have?
BEEP
BEEP
This voice...
Ikuto!
JUMP
JUMP
Amu!

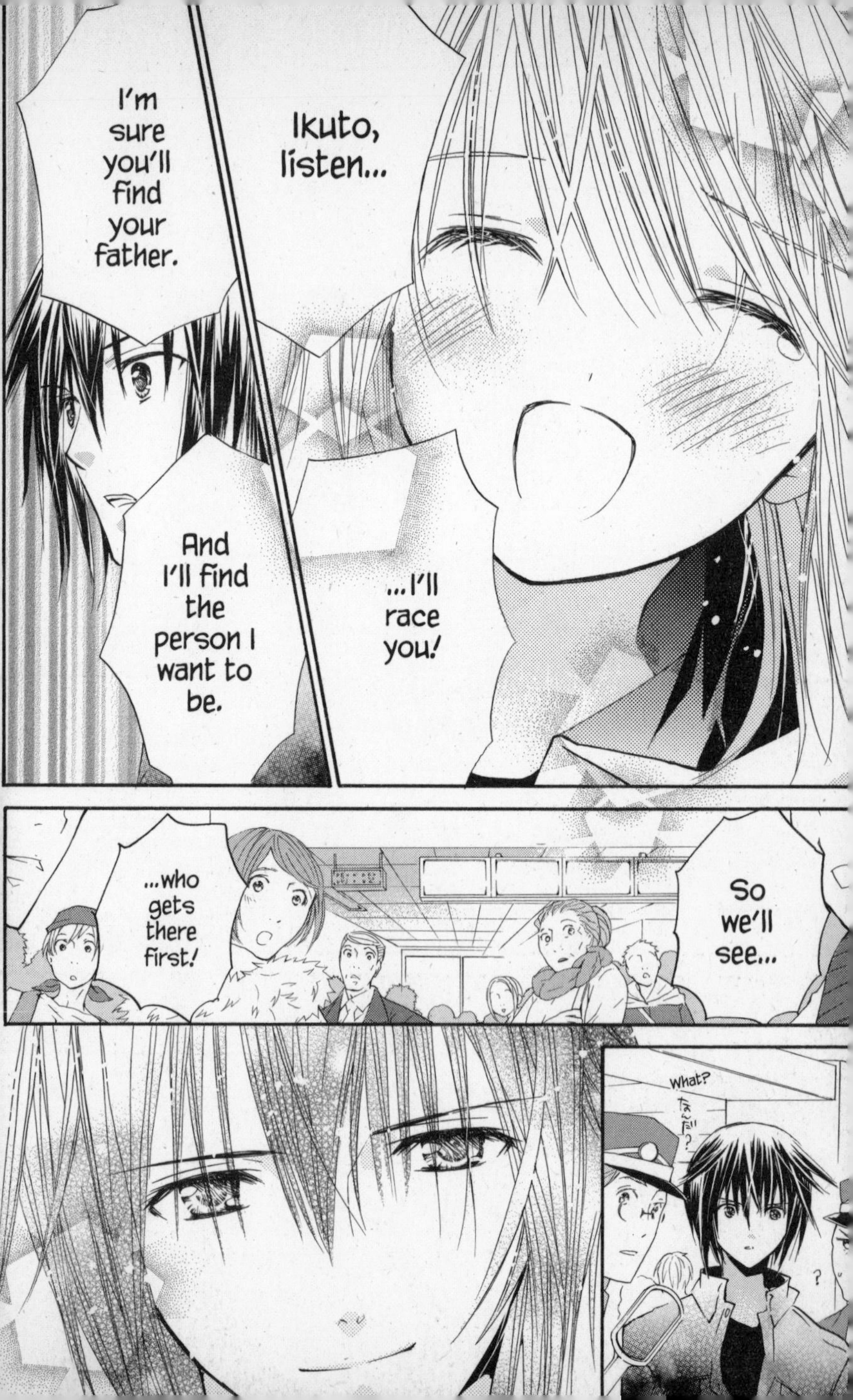
Ikuto, listen...
...I'll race you!
I'm sure you'll find your father.
And I'll find the person I want to be.
So we'll see...
...who gets there first!
What?
なんだ？
?

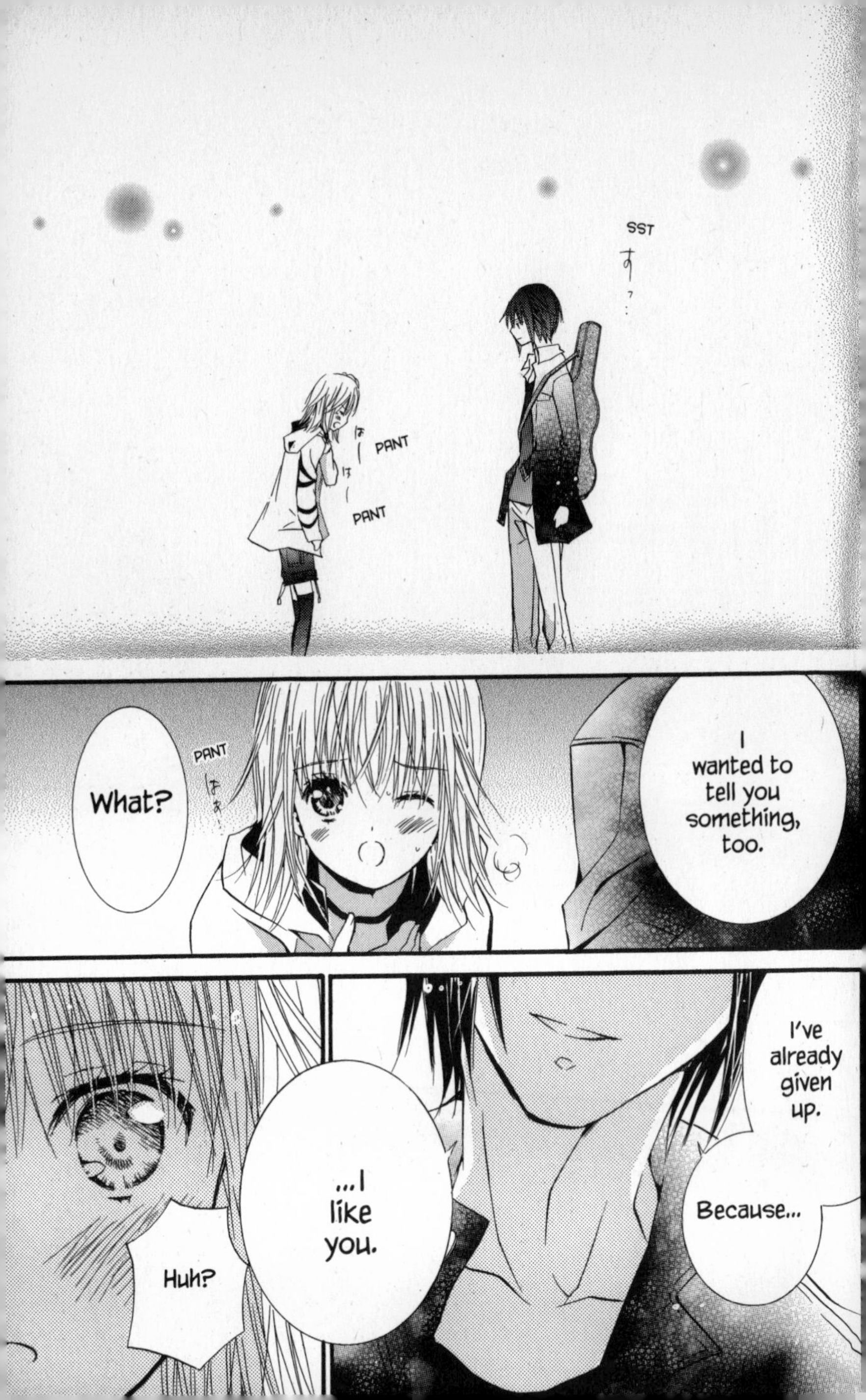
SST
PANT
PANT
I wanted to tell you something, too.
PANT
What?
I've already given up.
Because...
...I like you.
Huh?

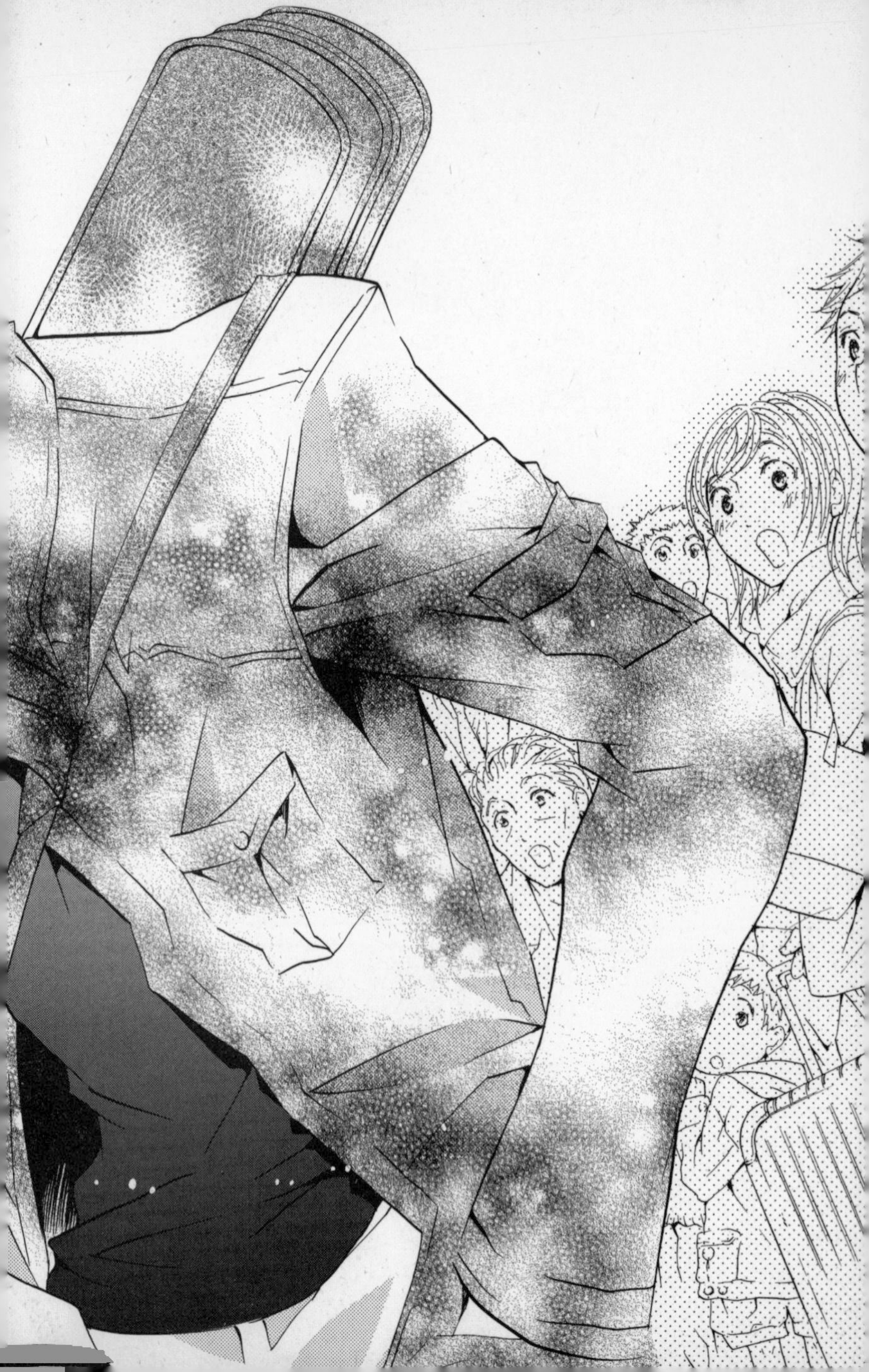

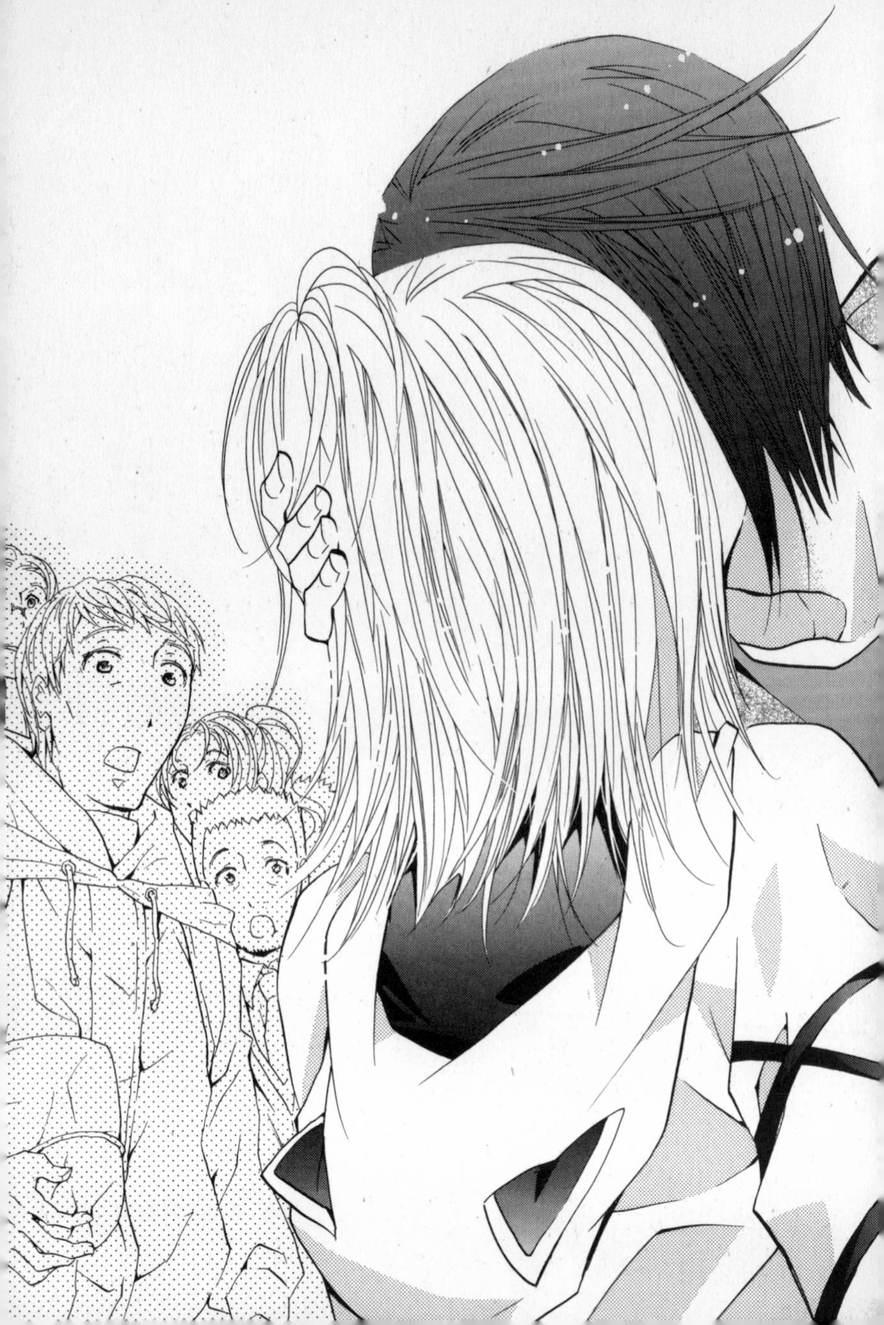

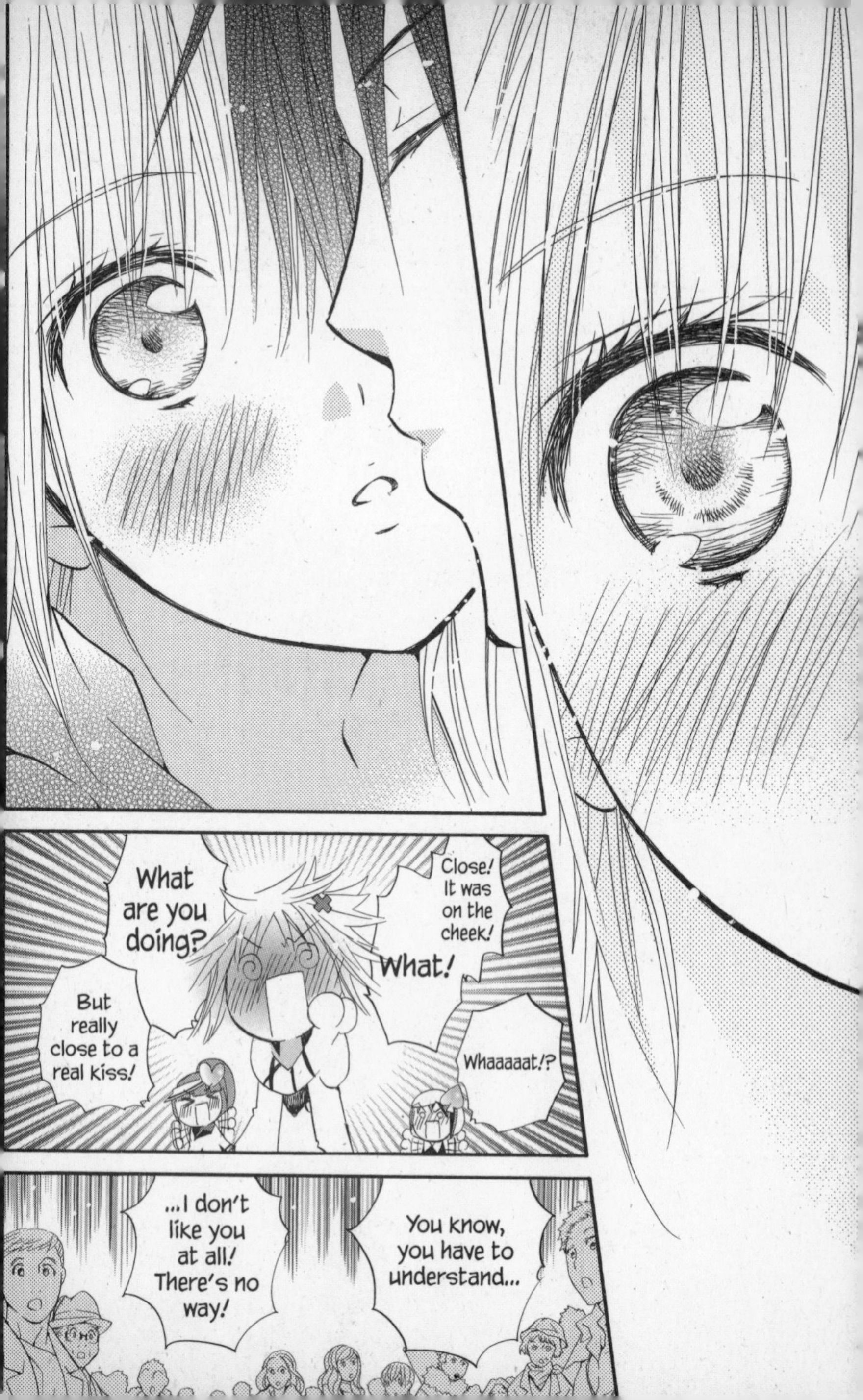

Close! It was on the cheek!
What are you doing?
What!
Whaaaaat!?
But really close to a real kiss!
You know, you have to understand...
...I don't like you at all! There's no way!

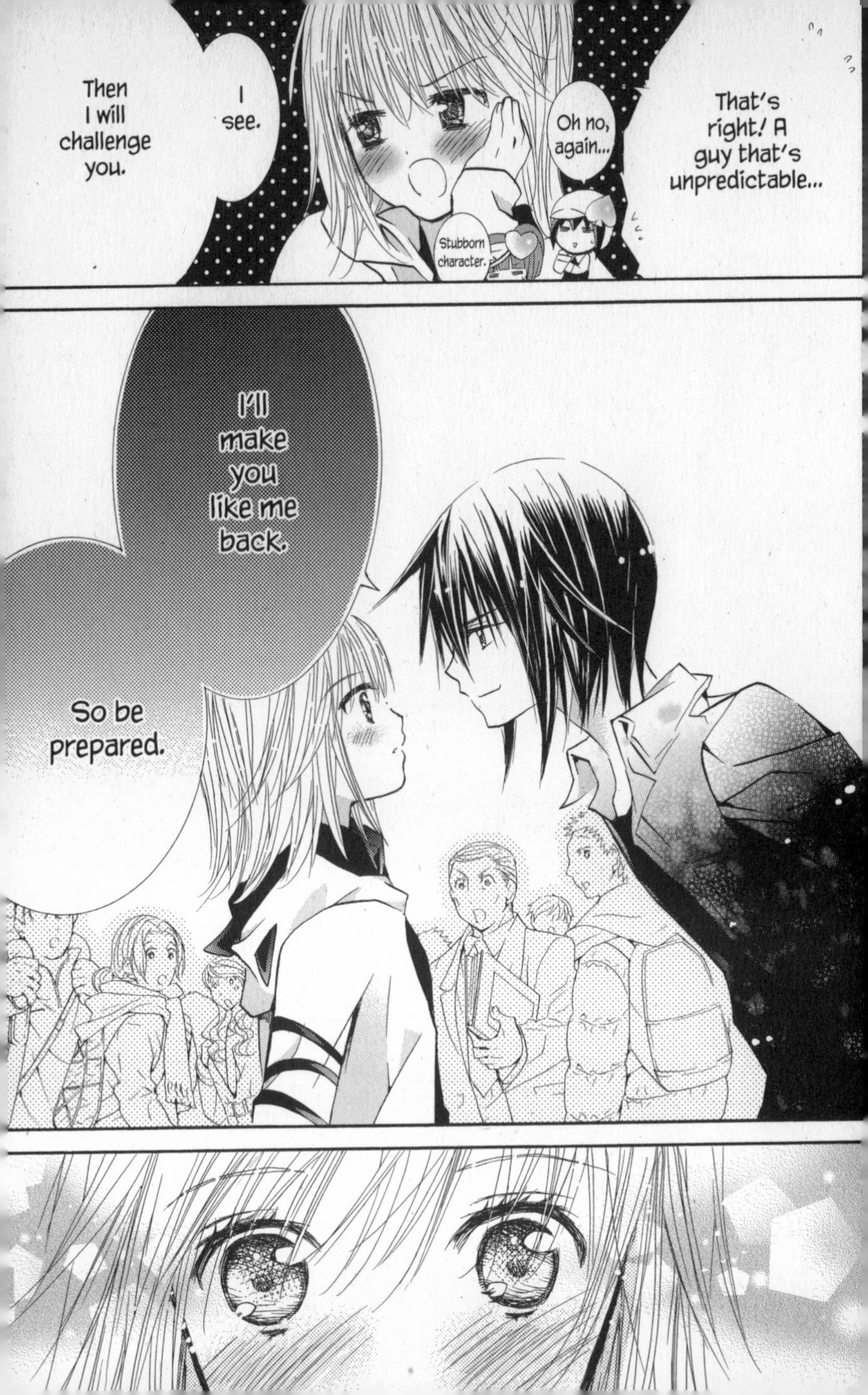
That's right! A guy that's unpredictable...
Oh no, again...
Stubborn character.
I see.
Then I will challenge you.
I'll make you like me back.
So be prepared.

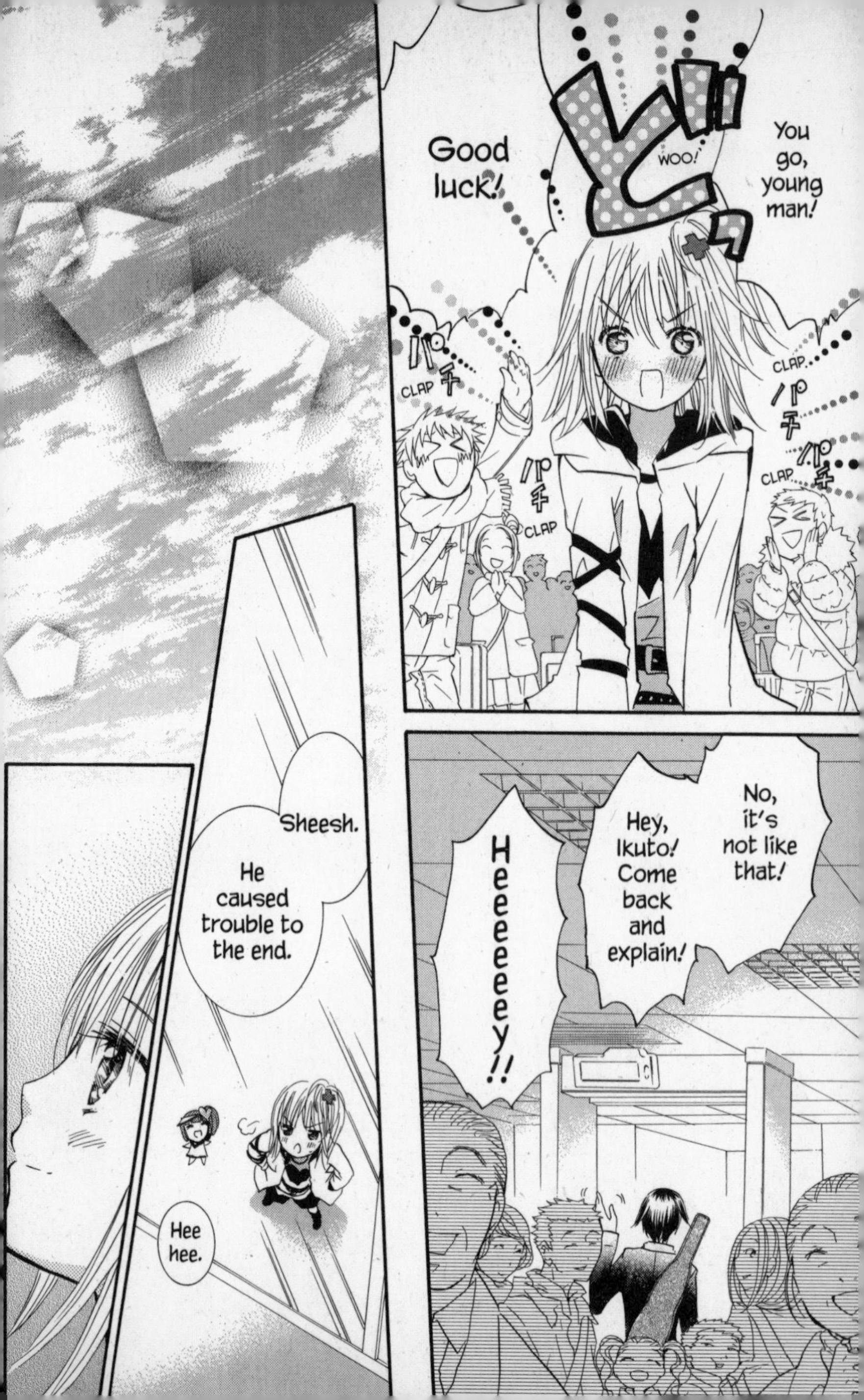
You go, young man!
WOO!
Good luck!
CLAP
CLAP
CLAP
CLAP
CLAP
No, it's not like that!
Hey, Ikuto! Come back and explain!
Heeeeeeey!!
Sheesh.
He caused trouble to the end.
Hee hee.

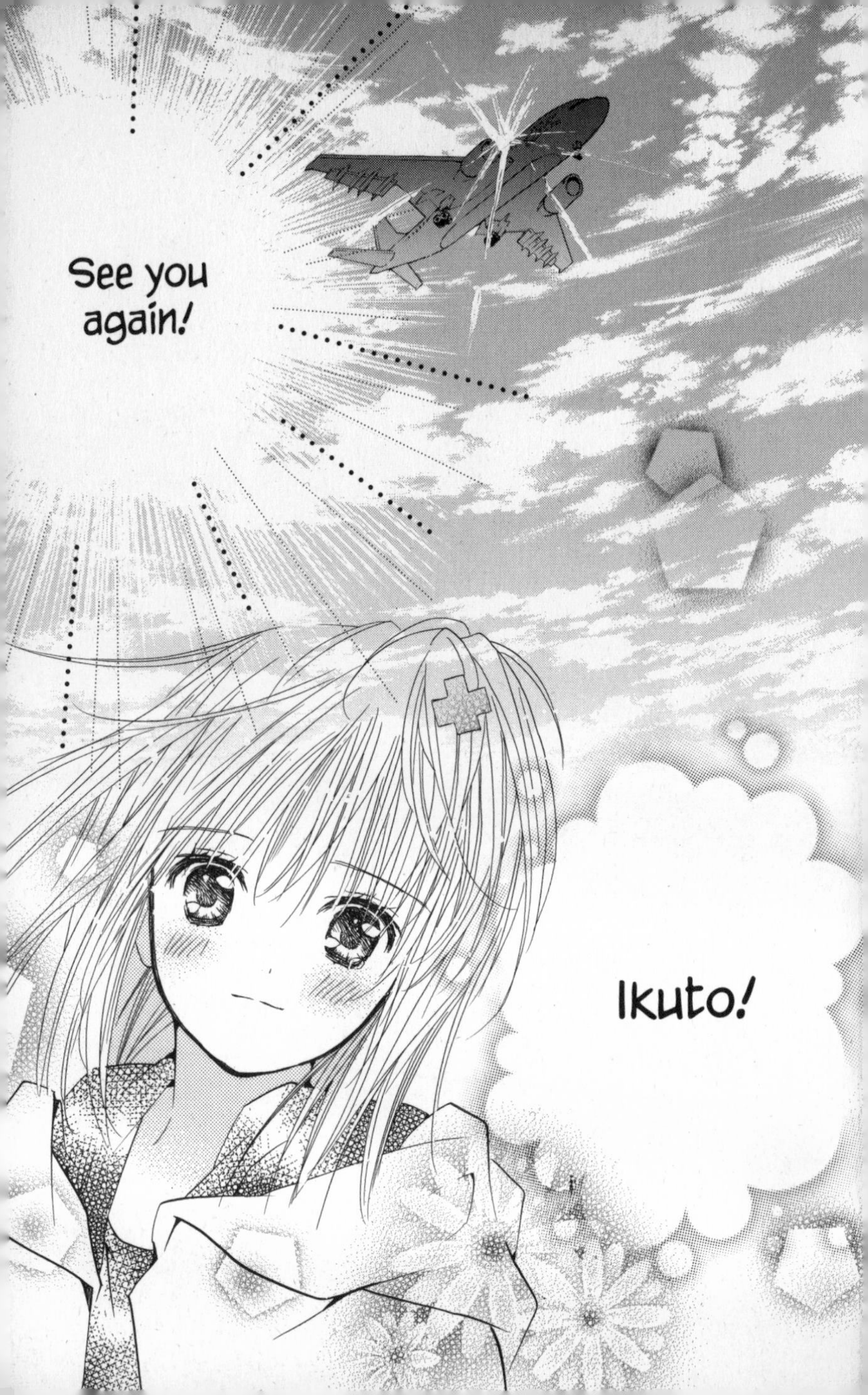
See you again!
Ikuto!

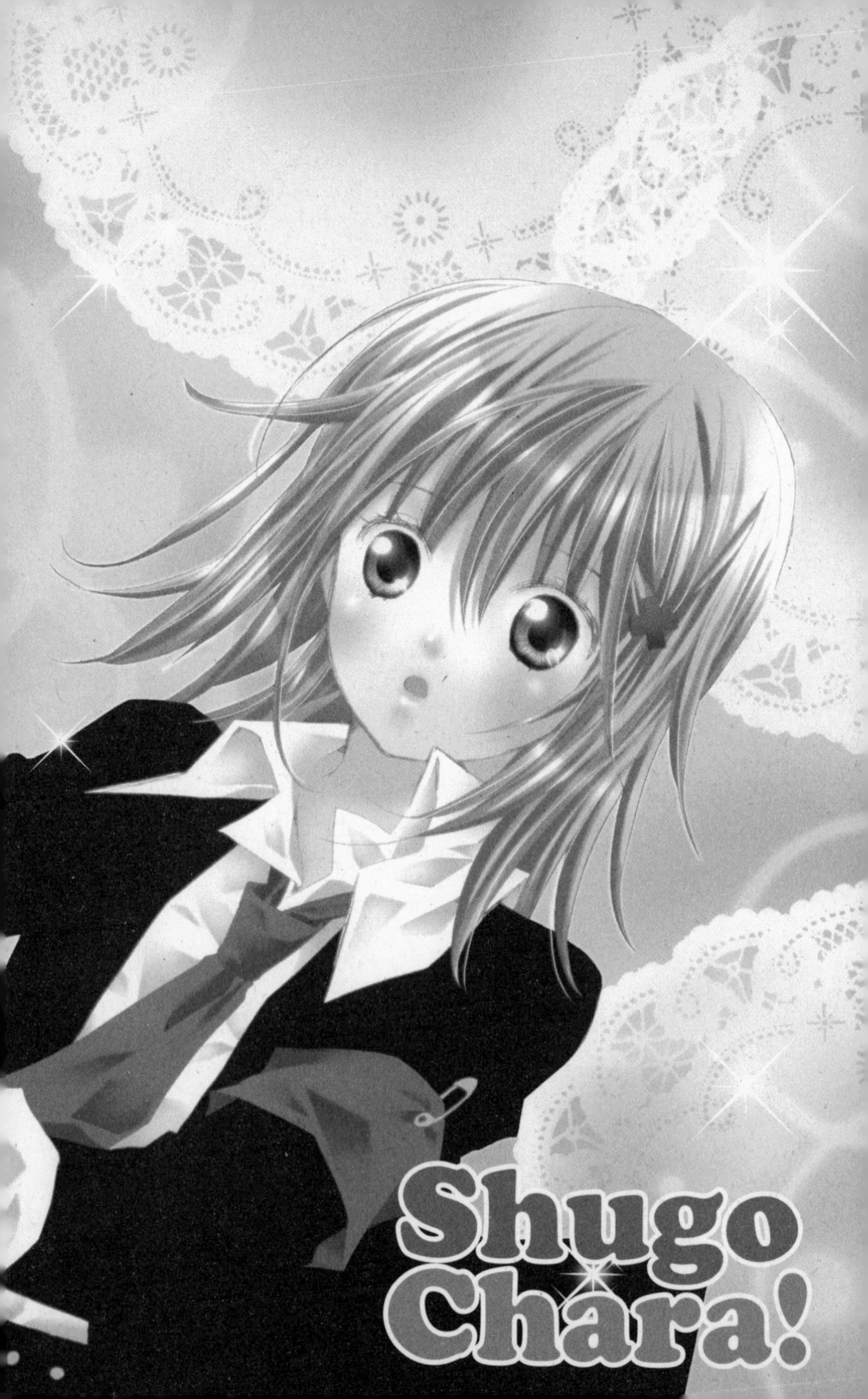
Shugo
Chara!

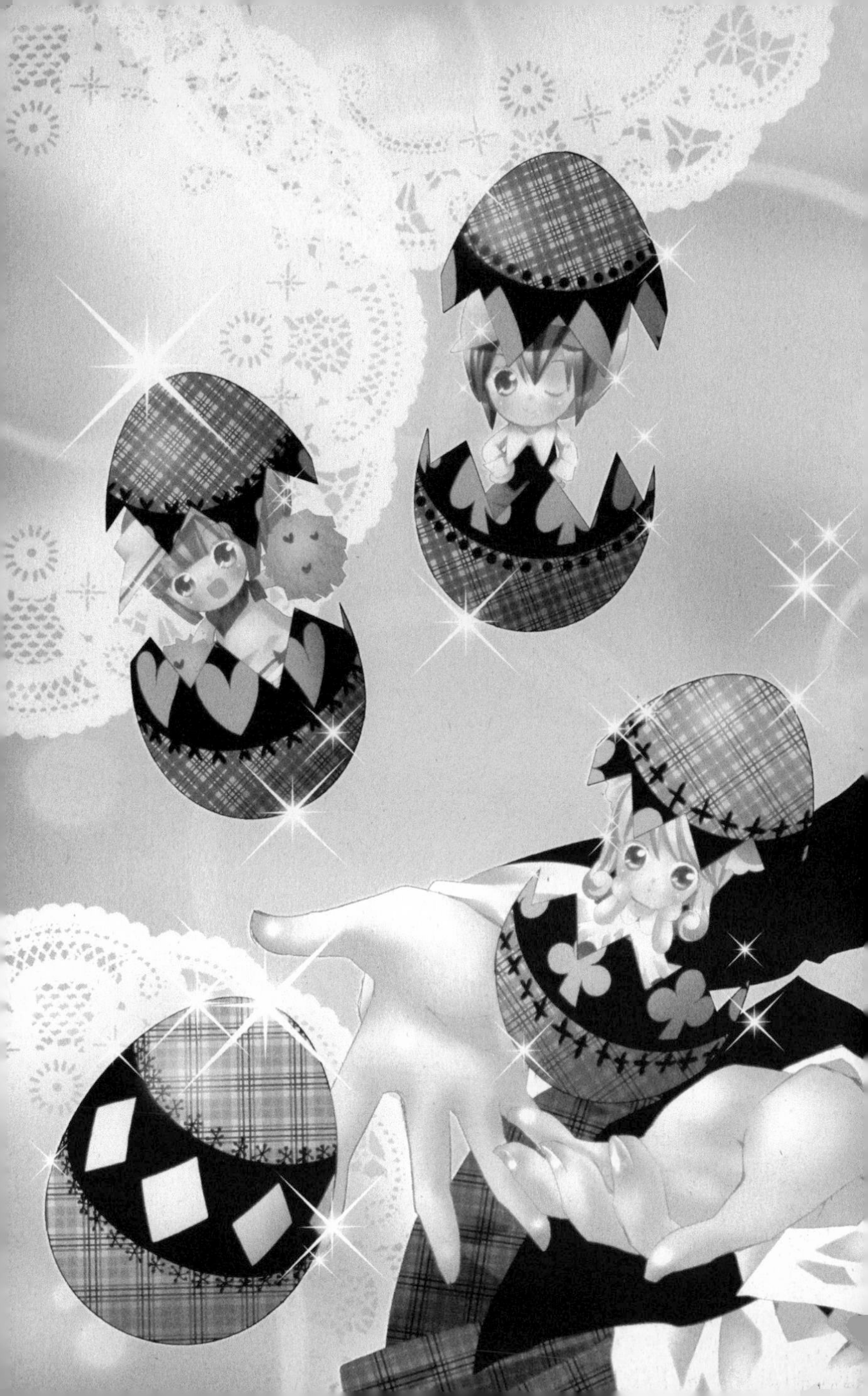

Shugo Chara!

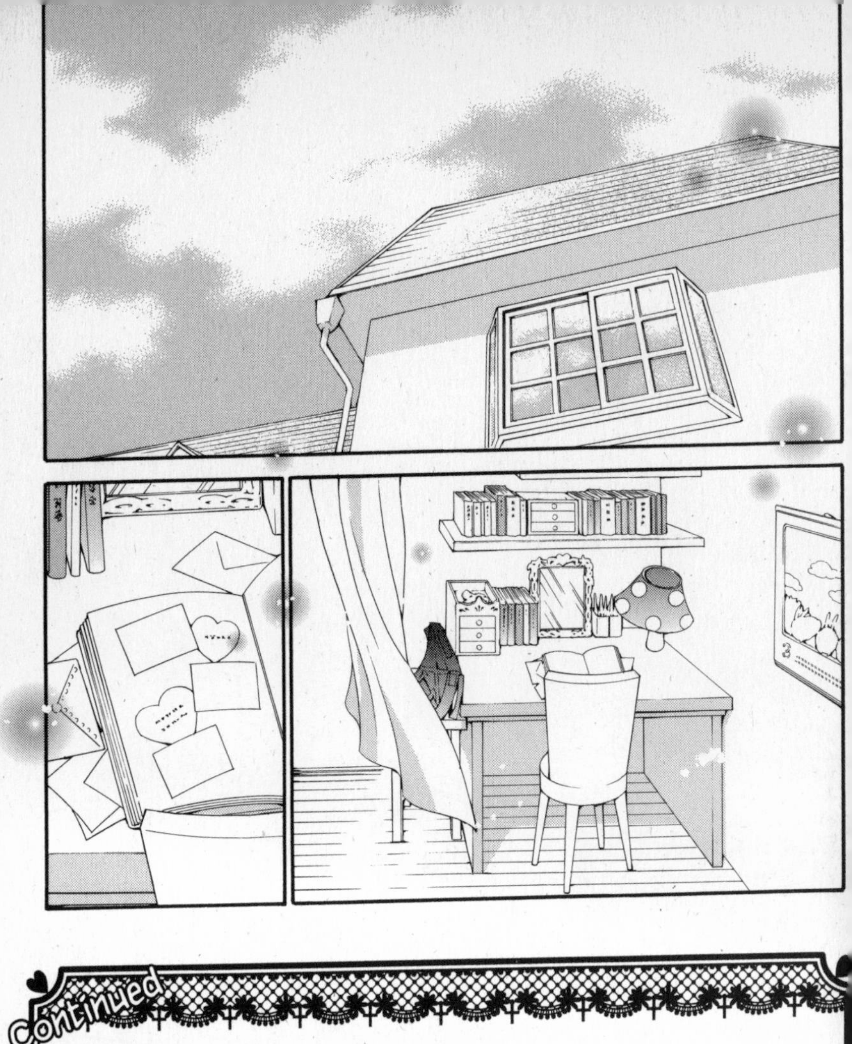

Continued

Q2: Do you read a lot of books and/or manga?

A2: I do! I read a lot. And I mean, a LOT. I've loved to read since I was a kid, and when I was in elementary school I was awarded the champion of readers once. I believe if you continue to read, even as an adult, it gives you a different kind of nourishment for your mind.

Q3: Have you been watching the Shugo Chara! anime?

A3: Of course! 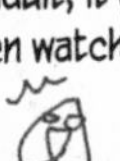 And I am currently watching the new *"Shugo Chara Party!"* as well!

Please watch it!

So that's it for this volume. I'll see you in volume 11!

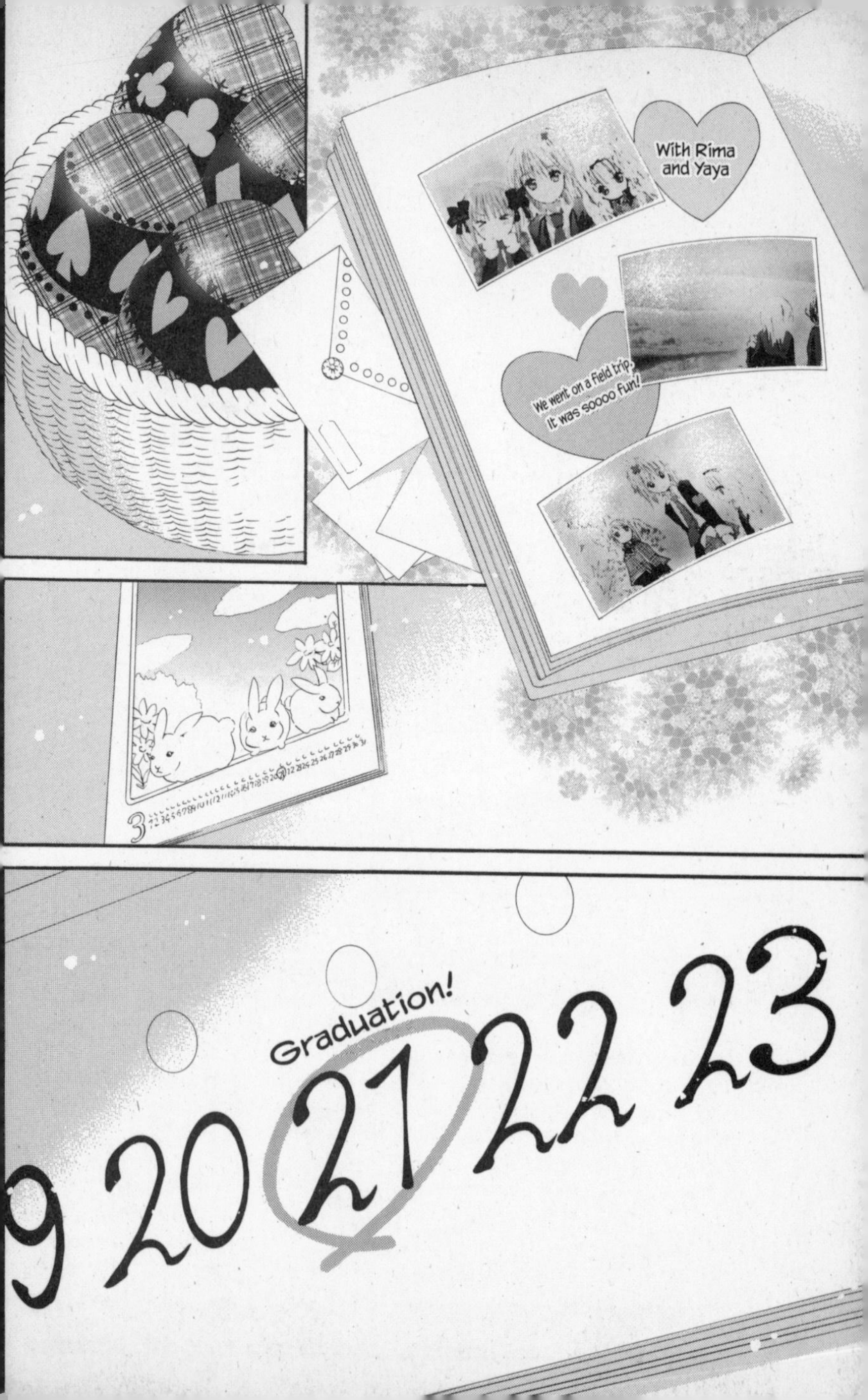
With Rima and Yaya
We went on a field trip. It was soooo fun!
Graduation!
9 20 21 22 23

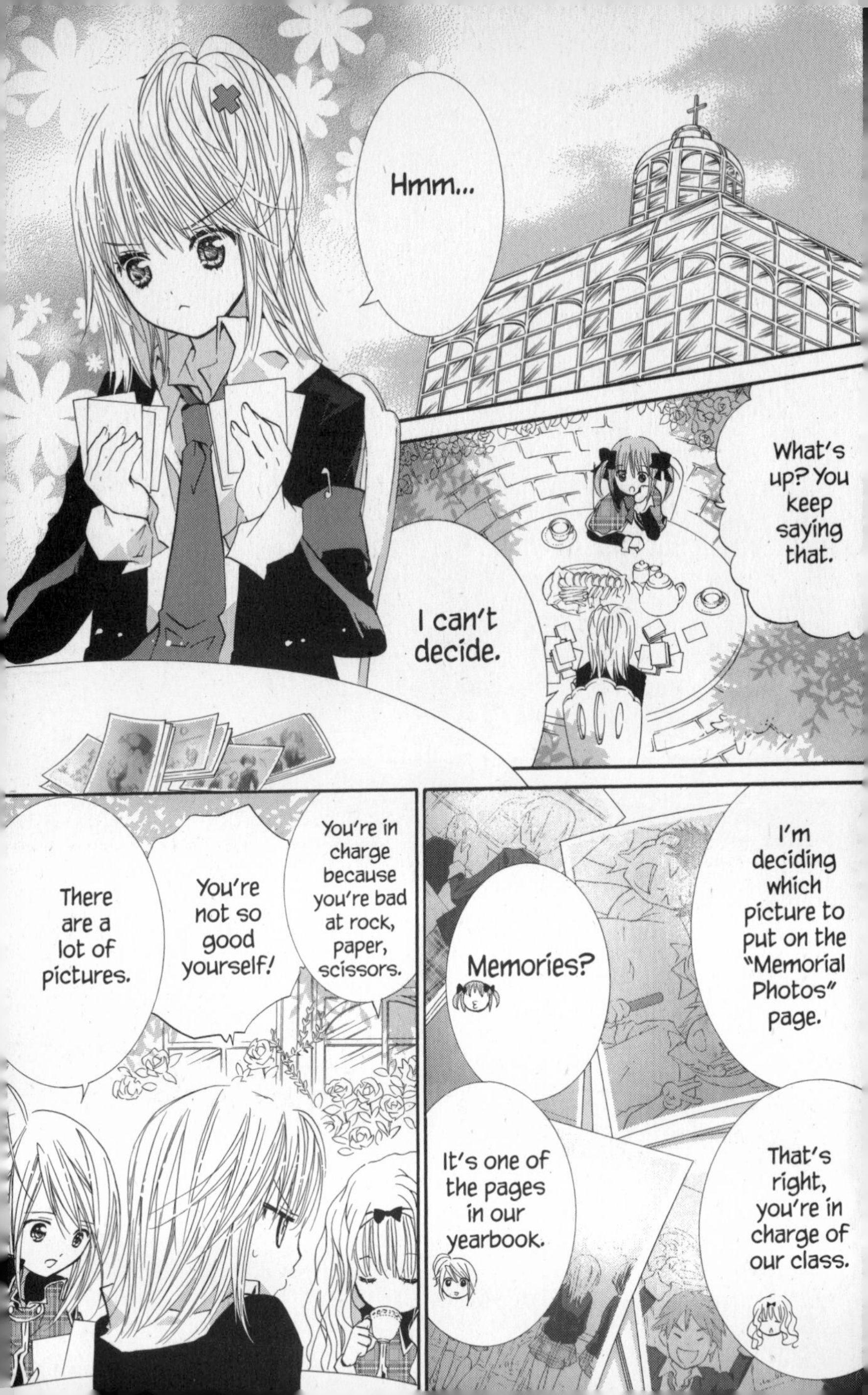
Hmm...
What's up? You keep saying that.
I can't decide.
I'm deciding which picture to put on the "Memorial Photos" page.
Memories?
That's right, you're in charge of our class.
It's one of the pages in our yearbook.
You're in charge because you're bad at rock, paper, scissors.
You're not so good yourself!
There are a lot of pictures.

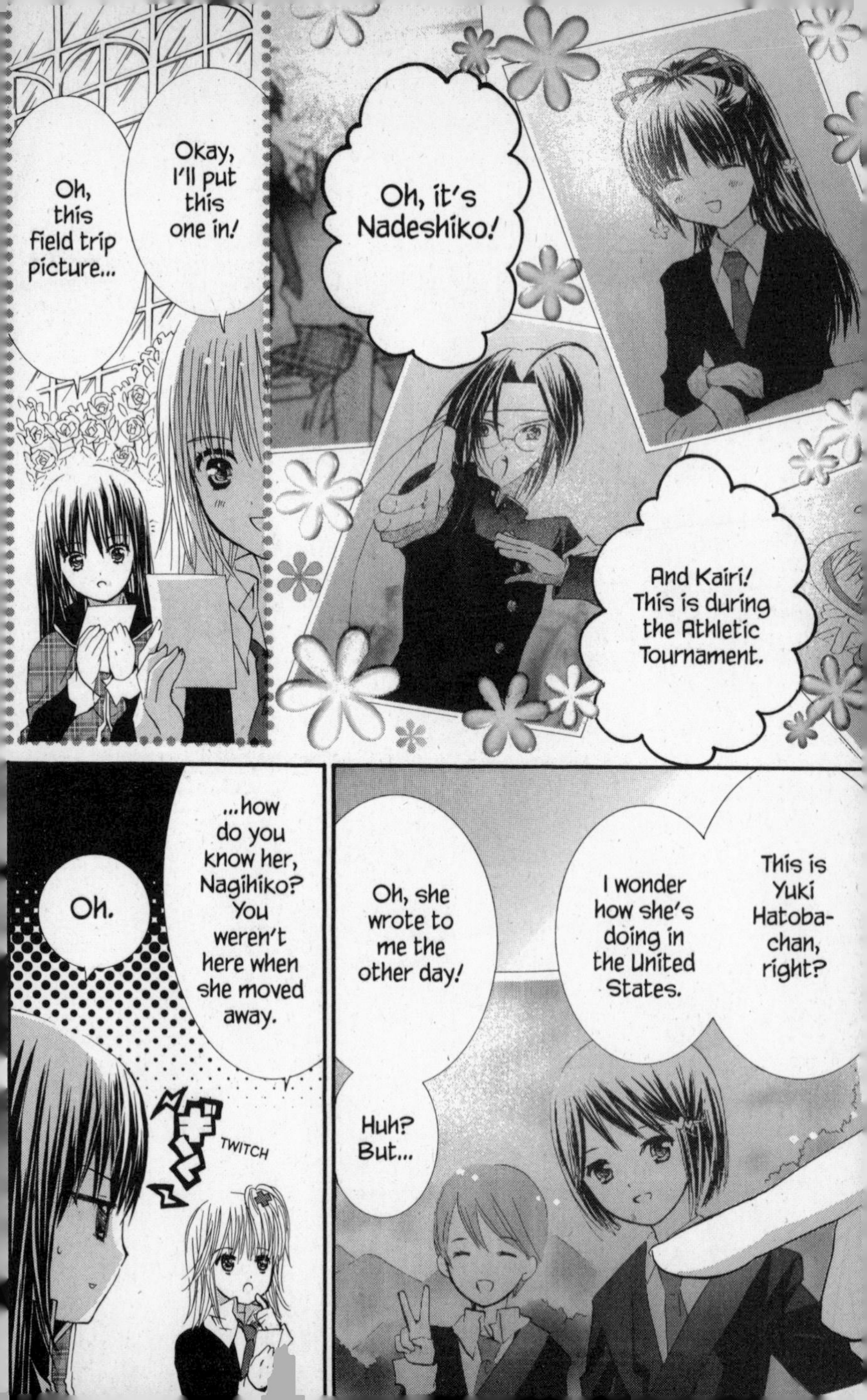

Oh, it's Nadeshiko!
And Kairi! This is during the Athletic Tournament.
Okay, I'll put this one in!
Oh, this field trip picture...
This is Yuki Hatoba-chan, right?
I wonder how she's doing in the United States.
Oh, she wrote to me the other day!
Huh? But...
...how do you know her, Nagihiko? You weren't here when she moved away.
Oh.
TWITCH

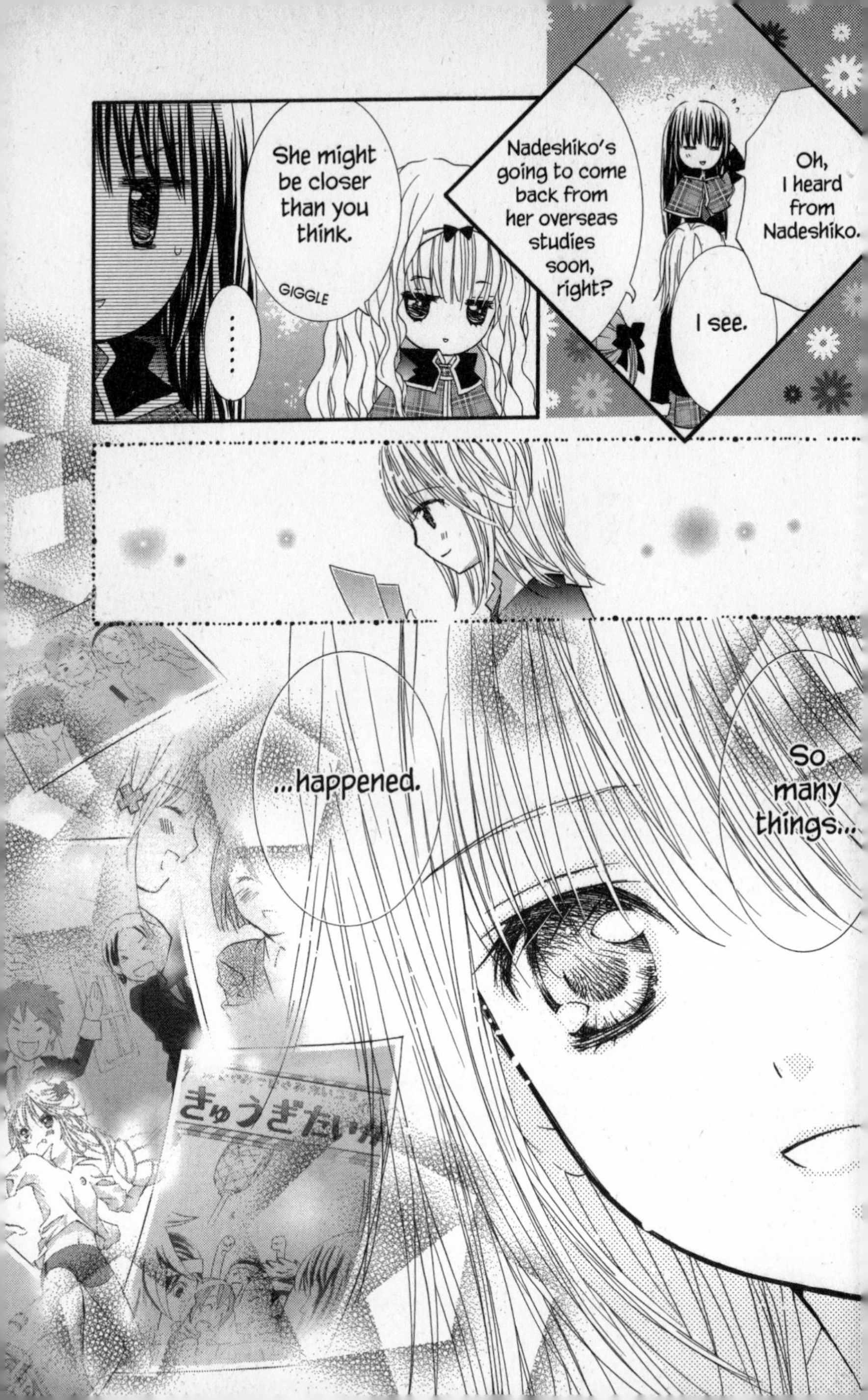

Nadeshiko's going to come back from her overseas studies soon, right?
Oh, I heard from Nadeshiko.
I see.
She might be closer than you think.
GIGGLE
......
So many things...
...happened.
きゅうぎたいか

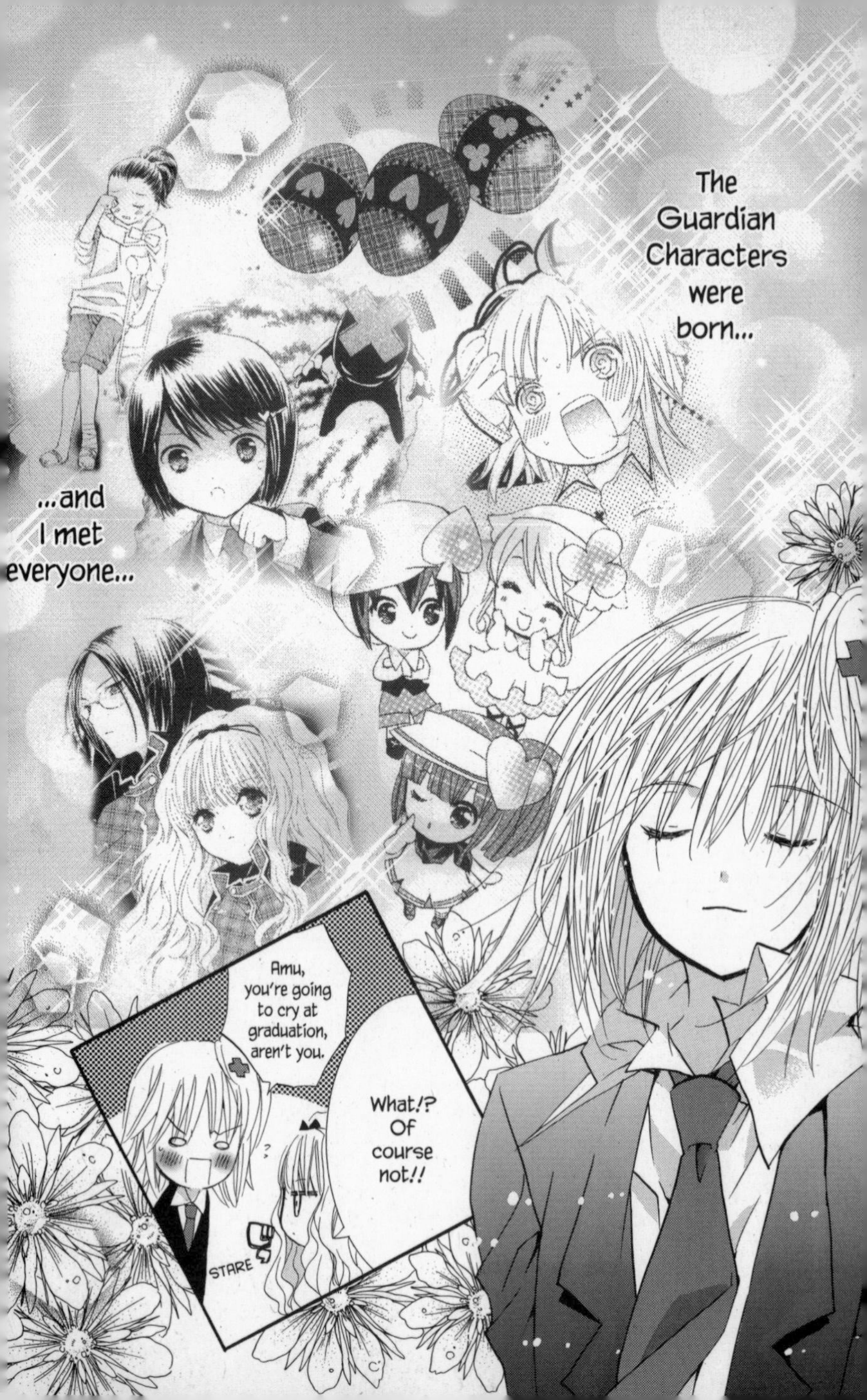
The Guardian Characters were born...
...and I met everyone...
Amu, you're going to cry at graduation, aren't you.
What!? Of course not!!
STARE

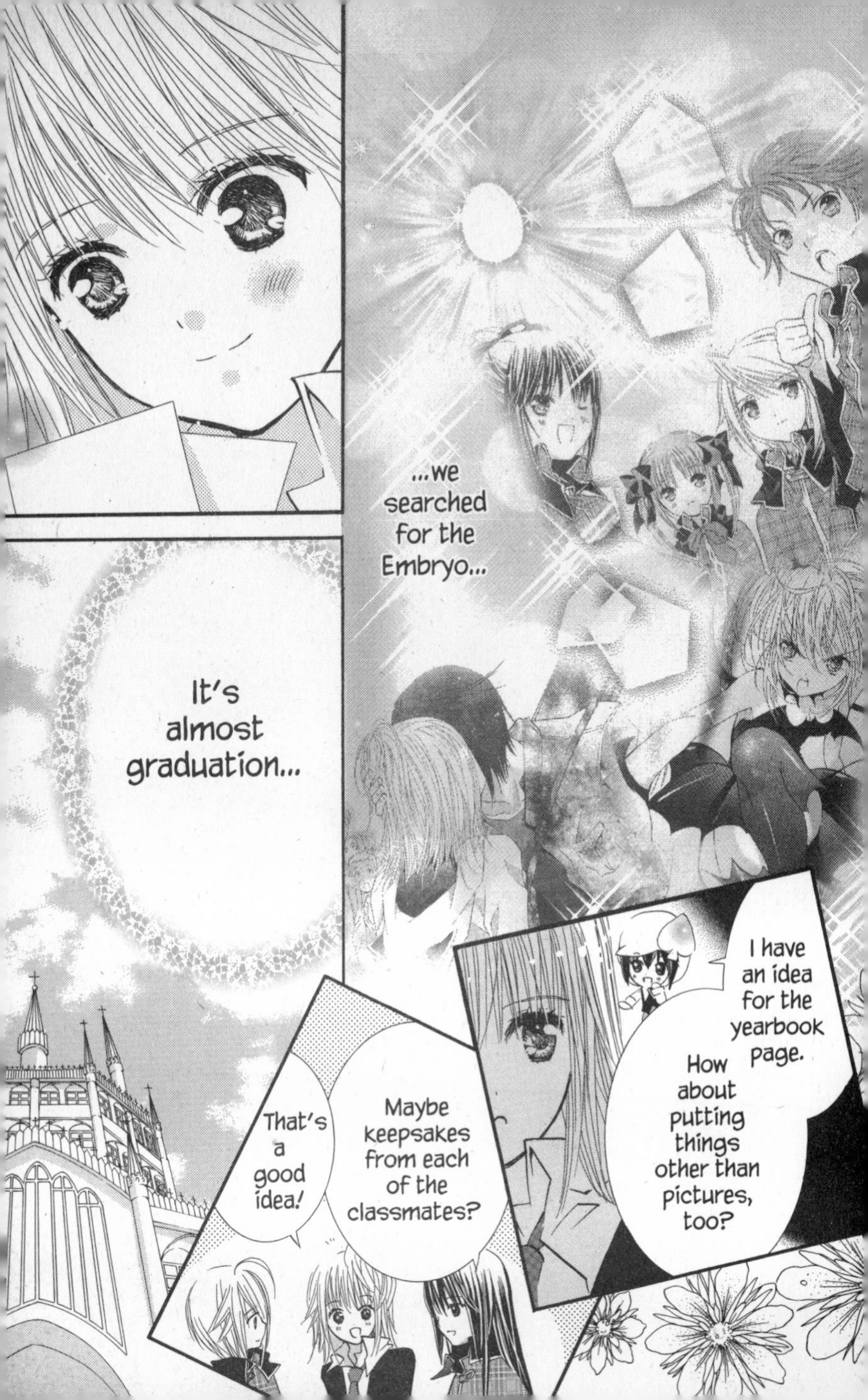
...we searched for the Embryo...
It's almost graduation...
I have an idea for the yearbook page.
How about putting things other than pictures, too?
Maybe keepsakes from each of the classmates?
That's a good idea!

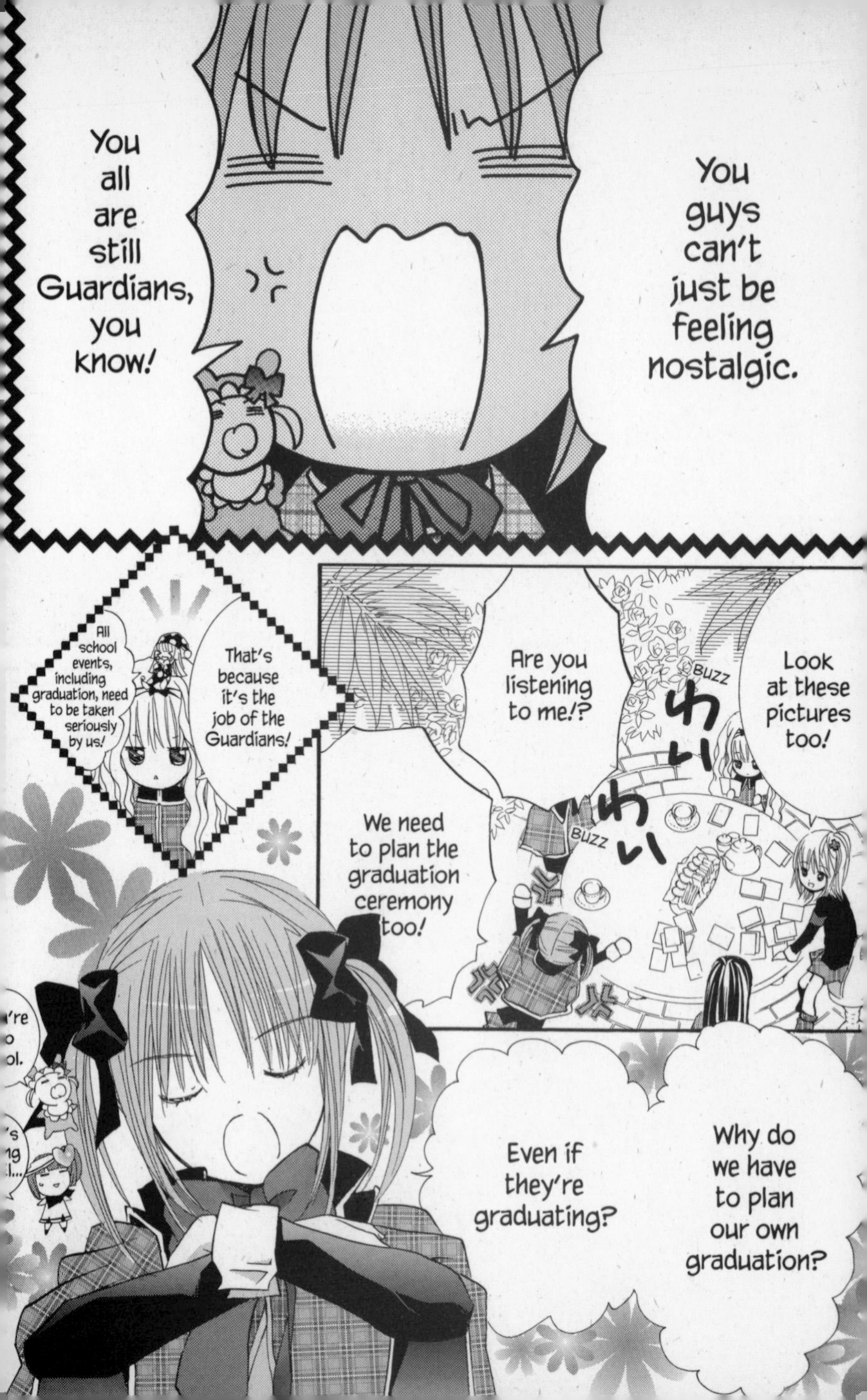
You guys can't just be feeling nostalgic.
You all are still Guardians, you know!
Look at these pictures too!
BUZZ
わい
わい
BUZZ
Are you listening to me!?
We need to plan the graduation ceremony too!
That's because it's the job of the Guardians!
All school events, including graduation, need to be taken seriously by us!
Why do we have to plan our own graduation?
Even if they're graduating?

Shugo Chara!

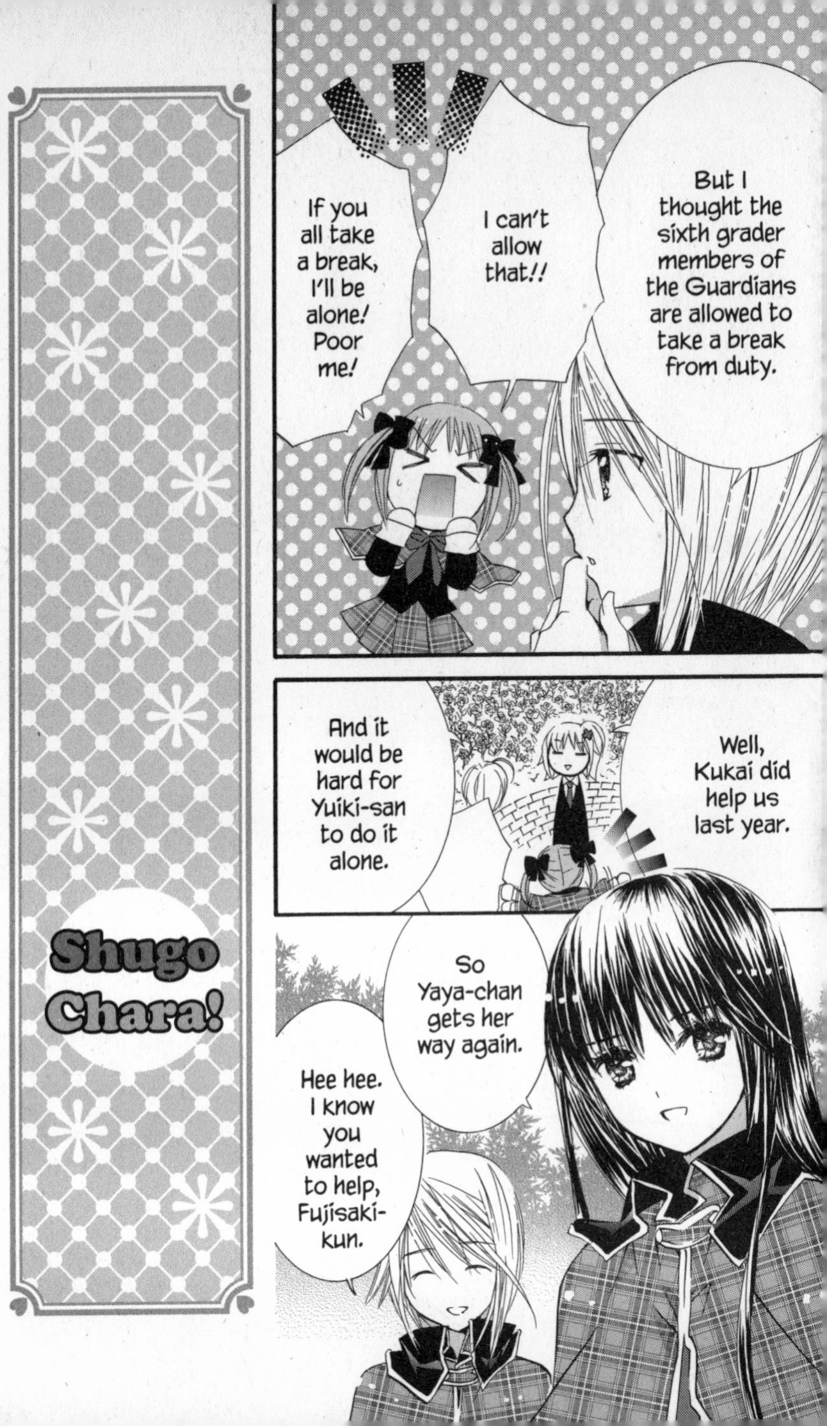
But I thought the sixth grader members of the Guardians are allowed to take a break from duty.
I can't allow that!!
If you all take a break, I'll be alone! Poor me!
Well, Kukai did help us last year.
And it would be hard for Yuiki-san to do it alone.
So Yaya-chan gets her way again.
Hee hee. I know you wanted to help, Fujisaki-kun.

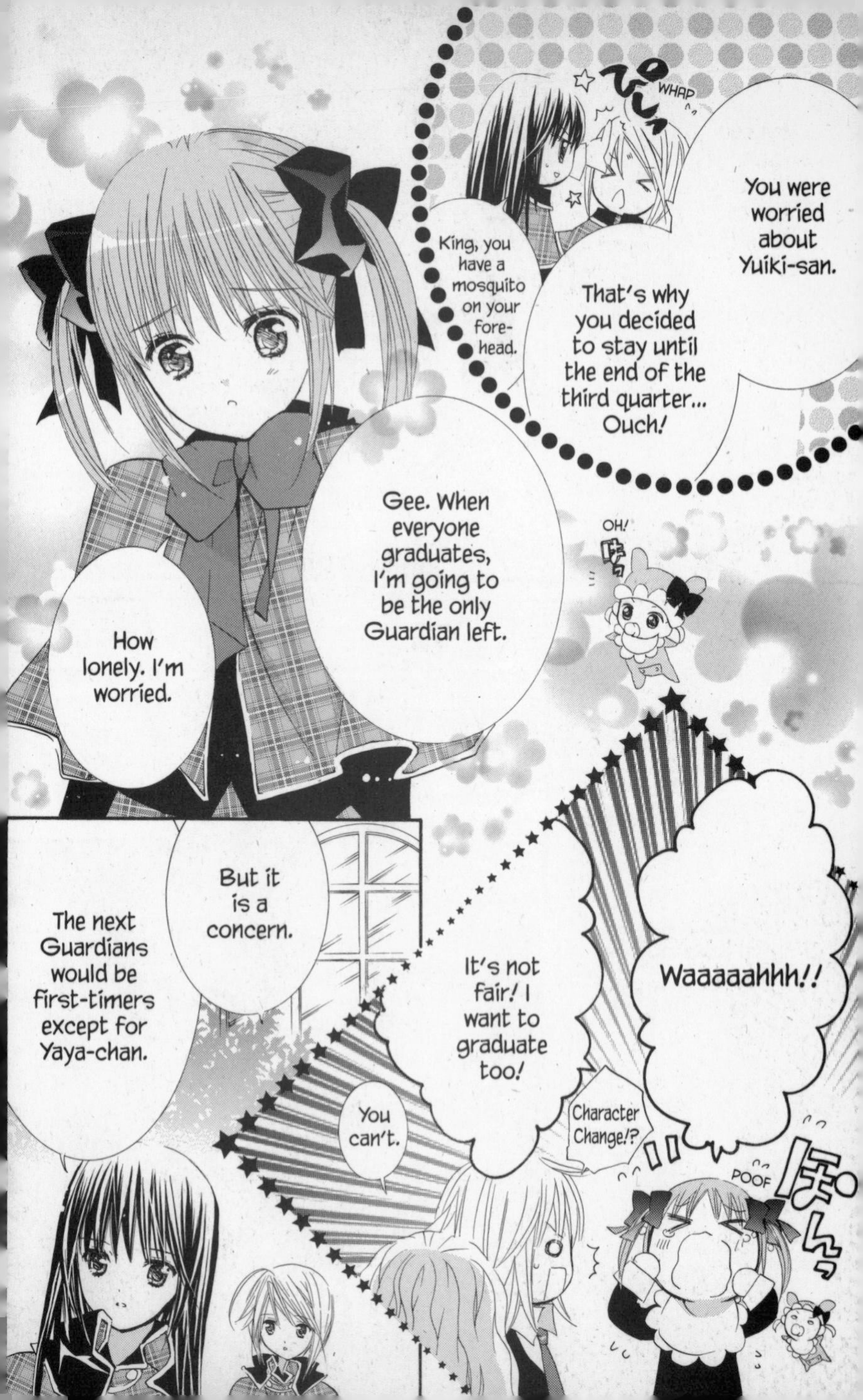

WHAP
You were worried about Yuiki-san.
That's why you decided to stay until the end of the third quarter... Ouch!
King, you have a mosquito on your forehead.
OH!
Gee. When everyone graduates, I'm going to be the only Guardian left.
How lonely. I'm worried.
...
Waaaaahhh!!
It's not fair! I want to graduate too!
POOF
Character Change!?
You can't.
But it is a concern.
The next Guardians would be first-timers except for Yaya-chan.

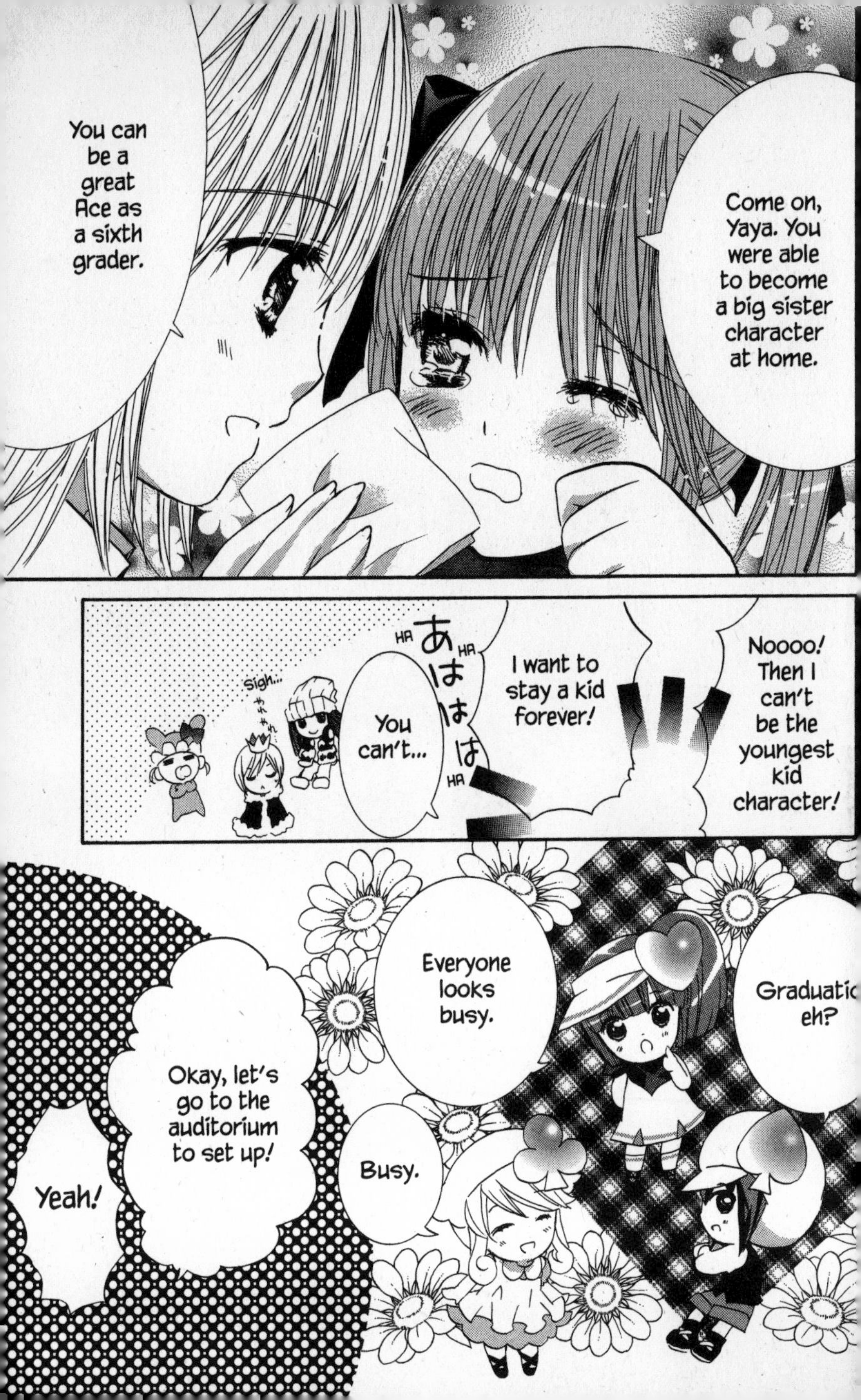
Come on, Yaya. You were able to become a big sister character at home.
You can be a great Ace as a sixth grader.
Noooo! Then I can't be the youngest kid character!
I want to stay a kid forever!
HA HA HA
あははは
You can't...
Sigh...
Graduati eh?
Everyone looks busy.
Busy.
Okay, let's go to the auditorium to set up!
Yeah!

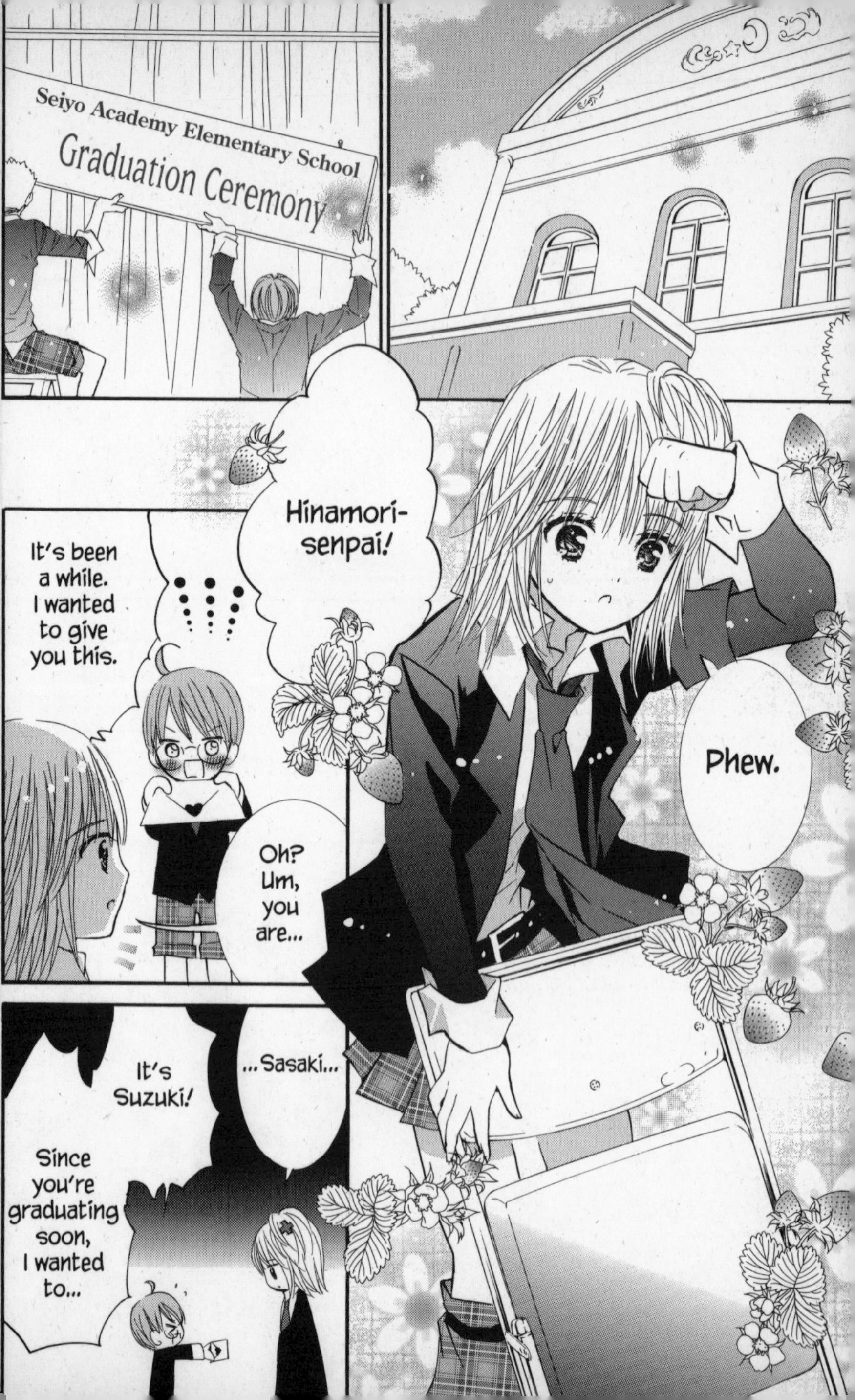
Seiyo Academy Elementary School
Graduation Ceremony
Hinamori-senpai!
Phew.
It's been a while. I wanted to give you this.
...
Oh? Um, you are...
...Sasaki...
It's Suzuki!
Since you're graduating soon, I wanted to...

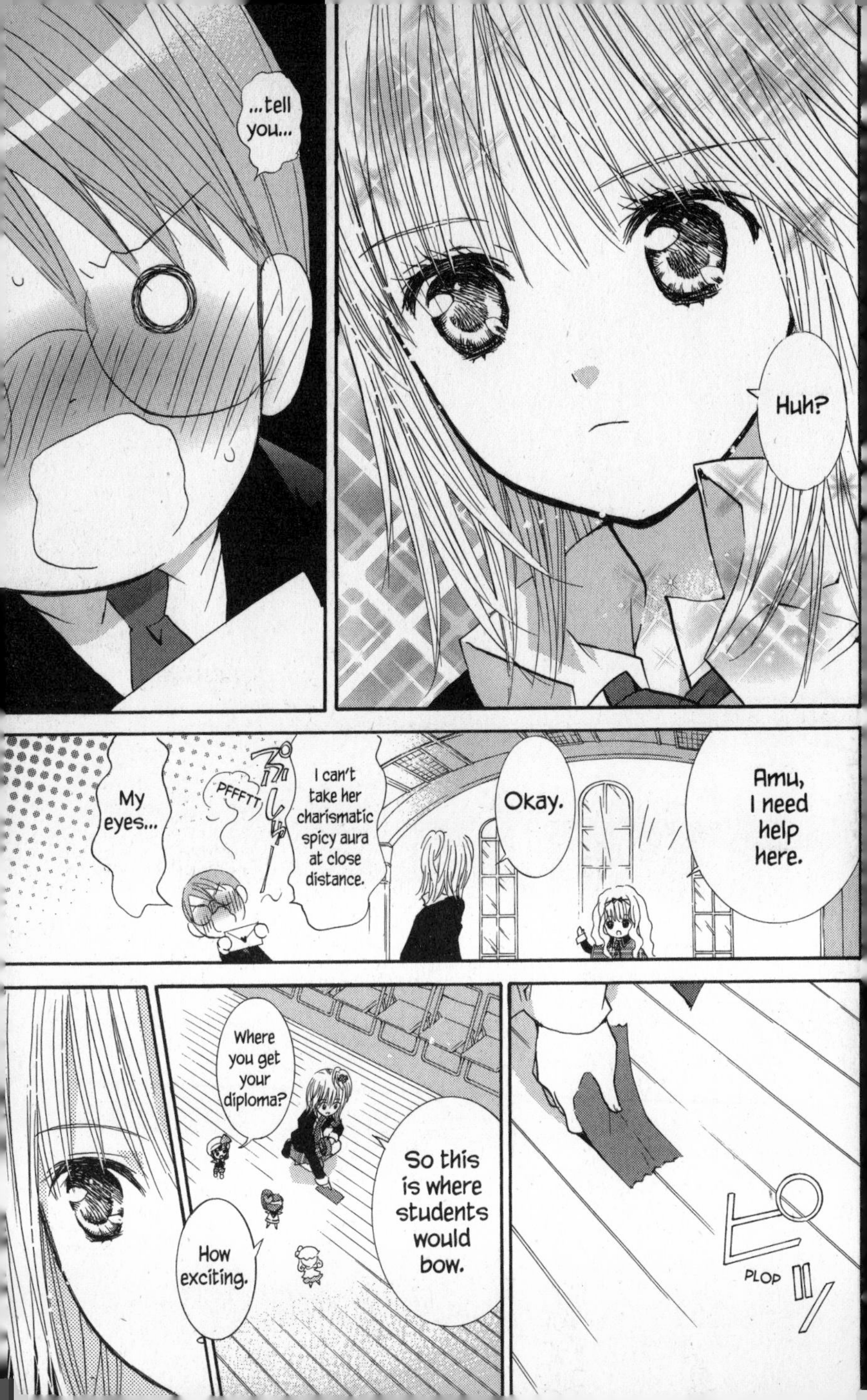
Huh?
...tell you...
Amu, I need help here.
Okay.
I can't take her charismatic spicy aura at close distance.
PFFFTT
My eyes...
PLOP
So this is where students would bow.
Where you get your diploma?
How exciting.

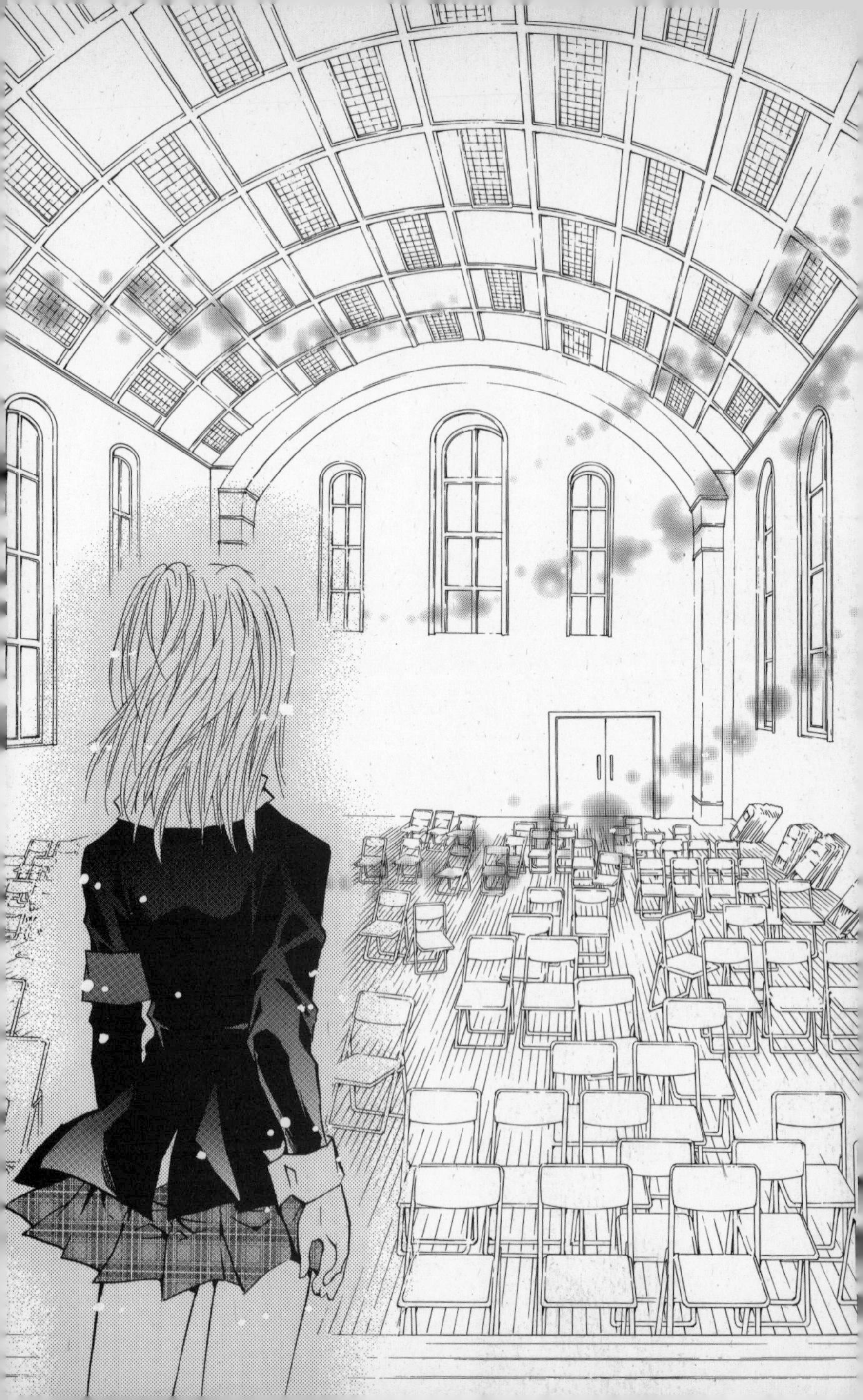

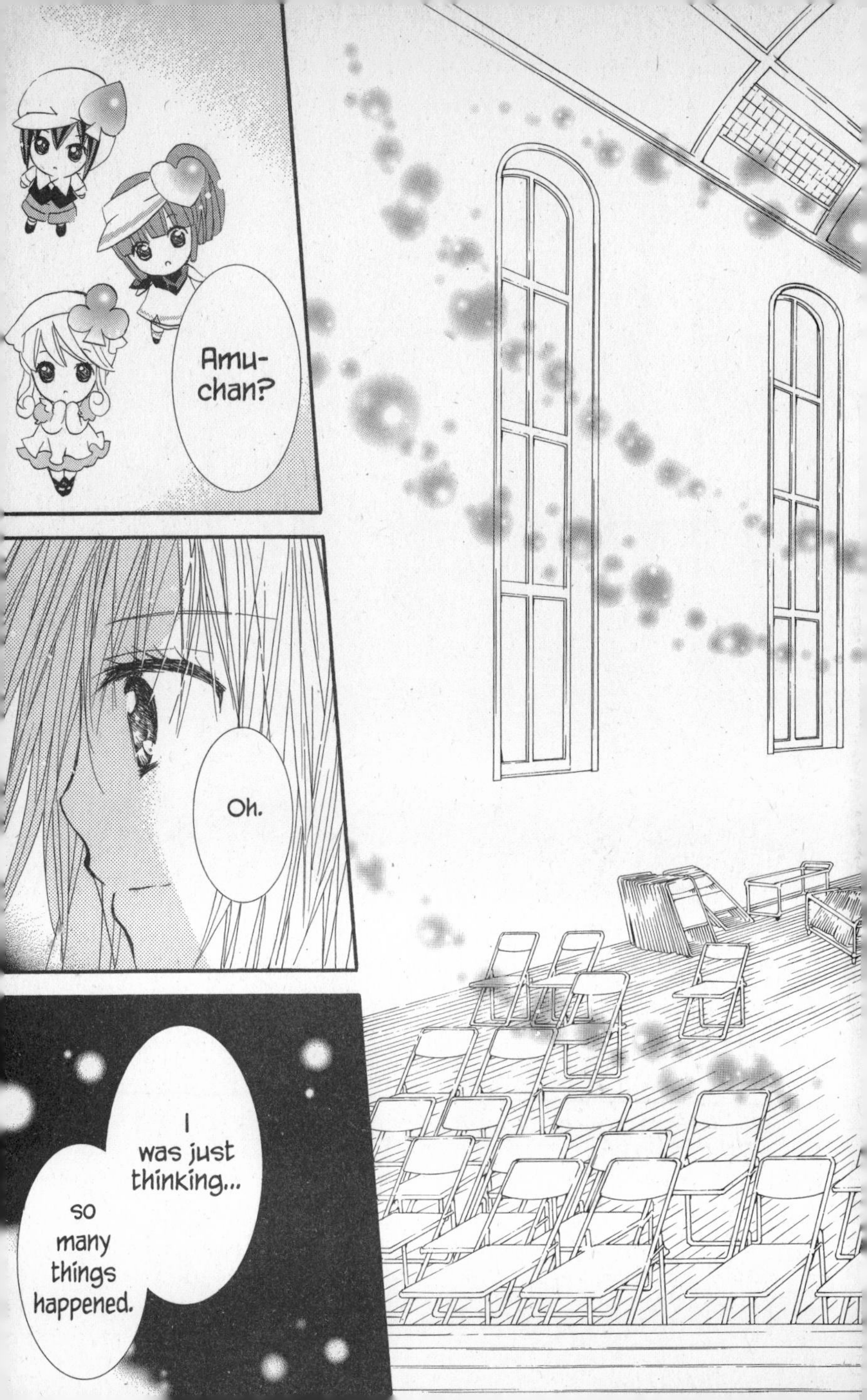
Amu-chan?
Oh.
I was just thinking...
so many things happened.

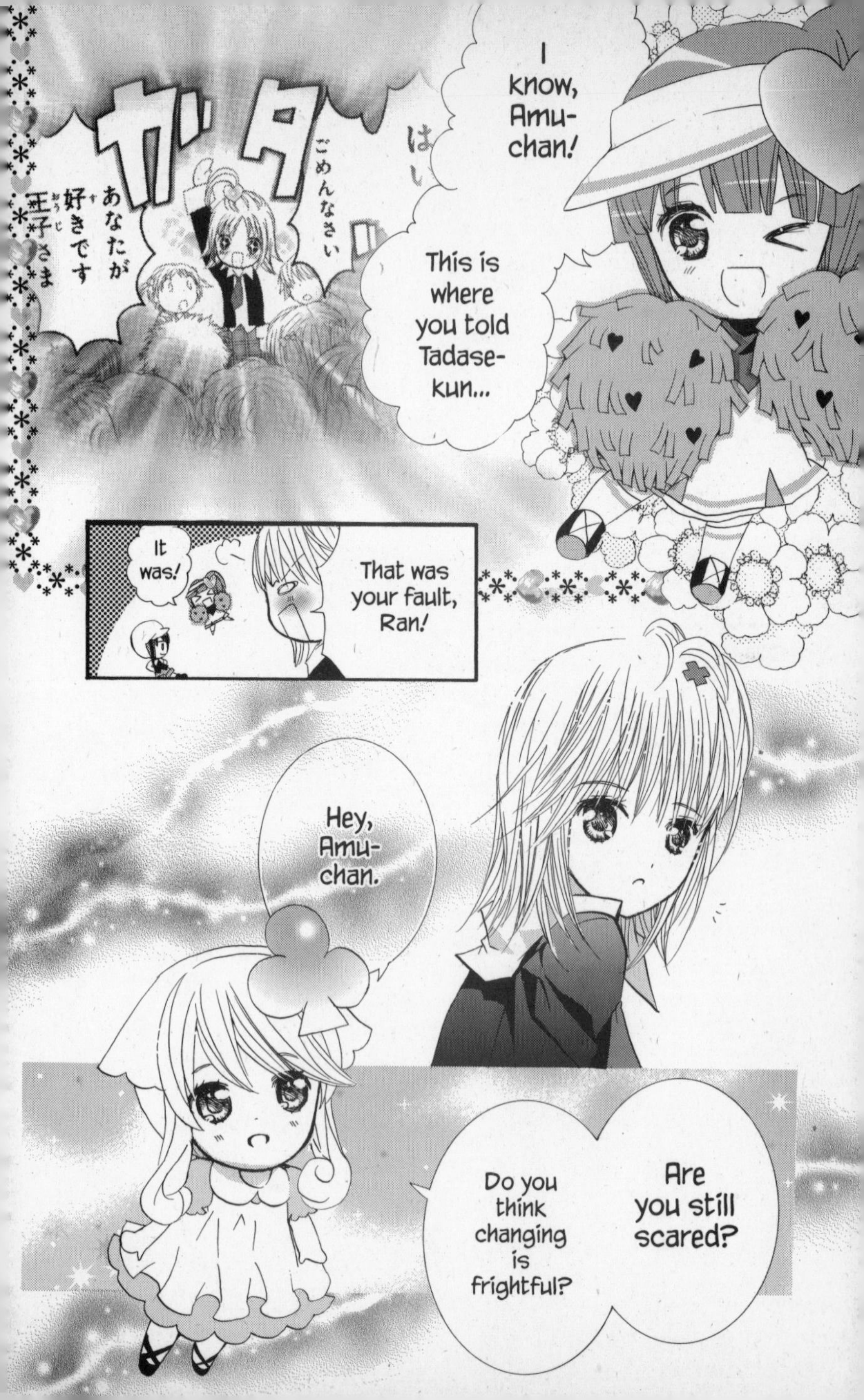
I know, Amu-chan!
This is where you told Tadase-kun...
はい
ごめんなさい
ガタ
あなたが好きです王子さま
That was your fault, Ran!
It was!
Hey, Amu-chan.
Are you still scared?
Do you think changing is frightful?

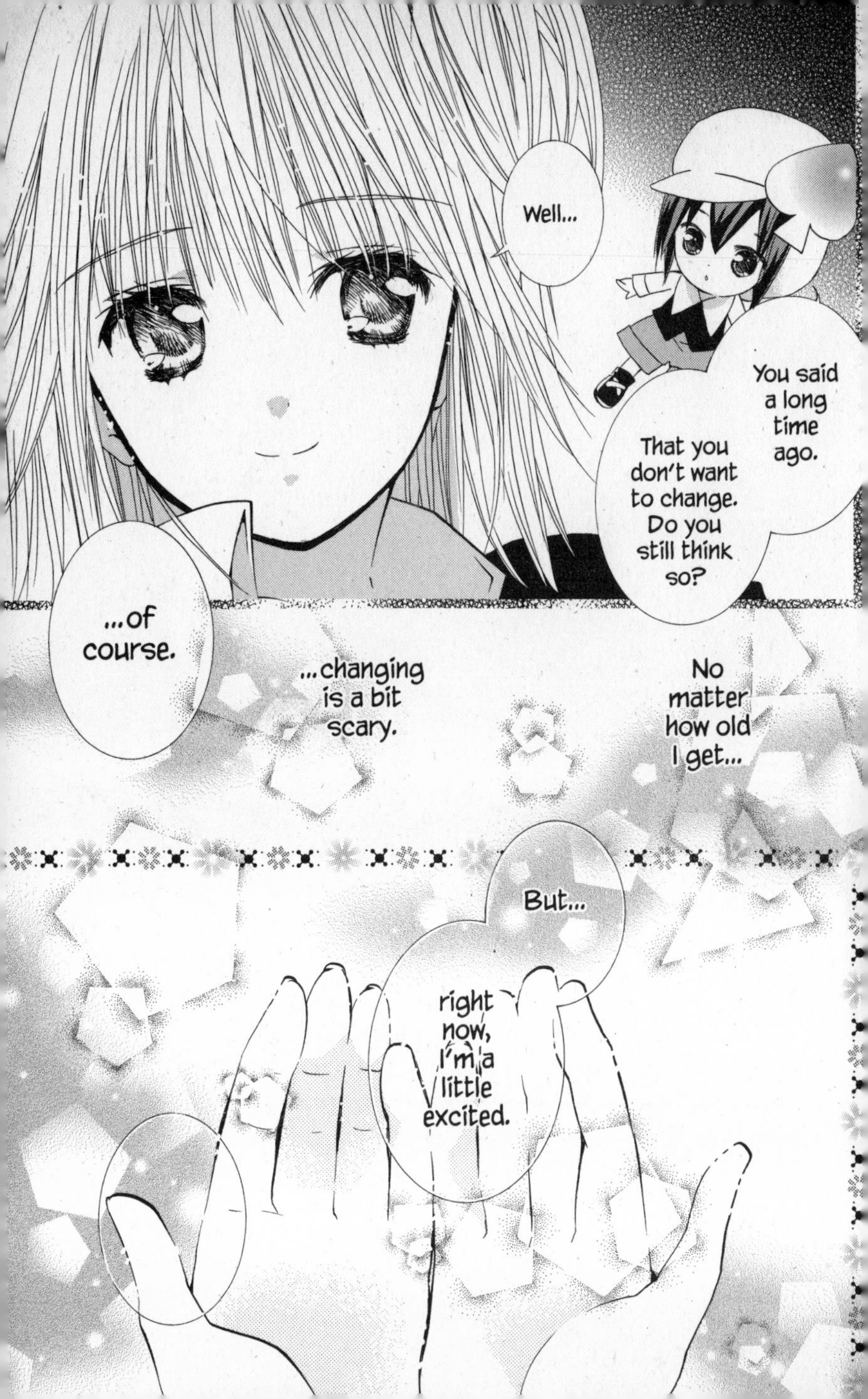
You said a long time ago.
That you don't want to change. Do you still think so?
Well...
...of course.
No matter how old I get...
...changing is a bit scary.
But...
right now, I'm a little excited.

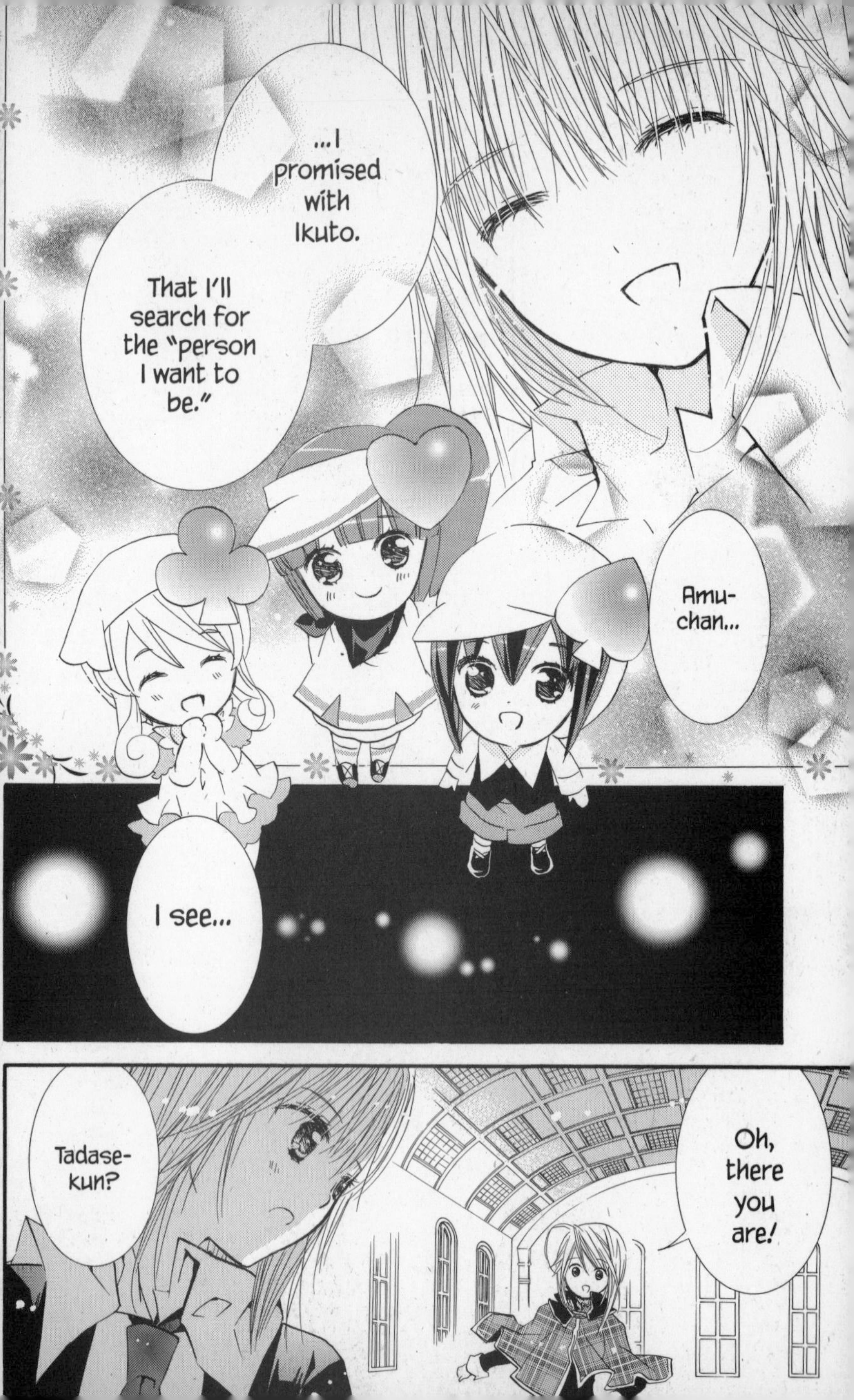
...I promised with Ikuto.
That I'll search for the "person I want to be."
Amu-chan...
I see...
Oh, there you are!
Tadase-kun?

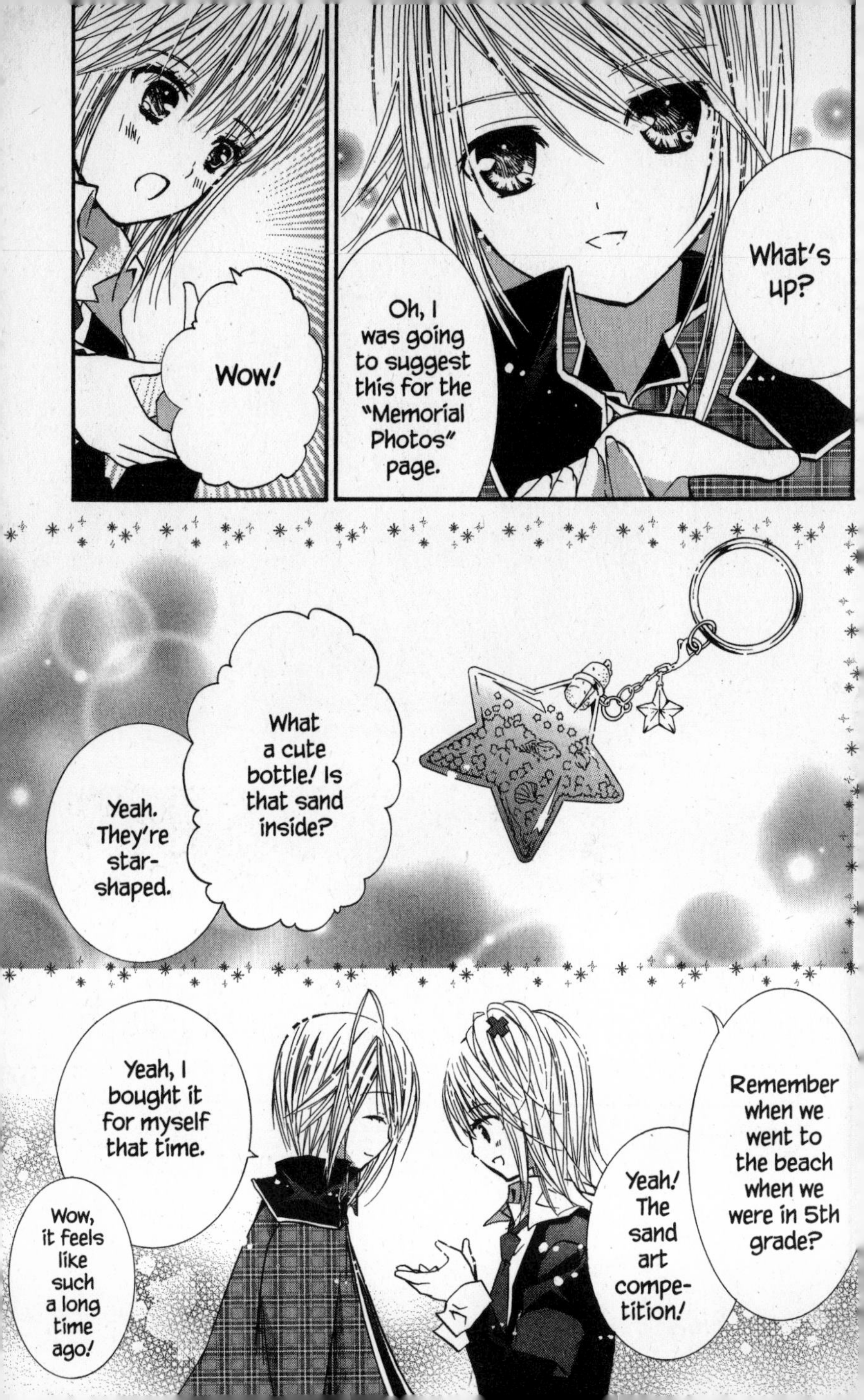
What's up?
Oh, I was going to suggest this for the "Memorial Photos" page.
Wow!
What a cute bottle! Is that sand inside?
Yeah. They're star-shaped.
Remember when we went to the beach when we were in 5th grade?
Yeah! The sand art competition!
Yeah, I bought it for myself that time.
Wow, it feels like such a long time ago!

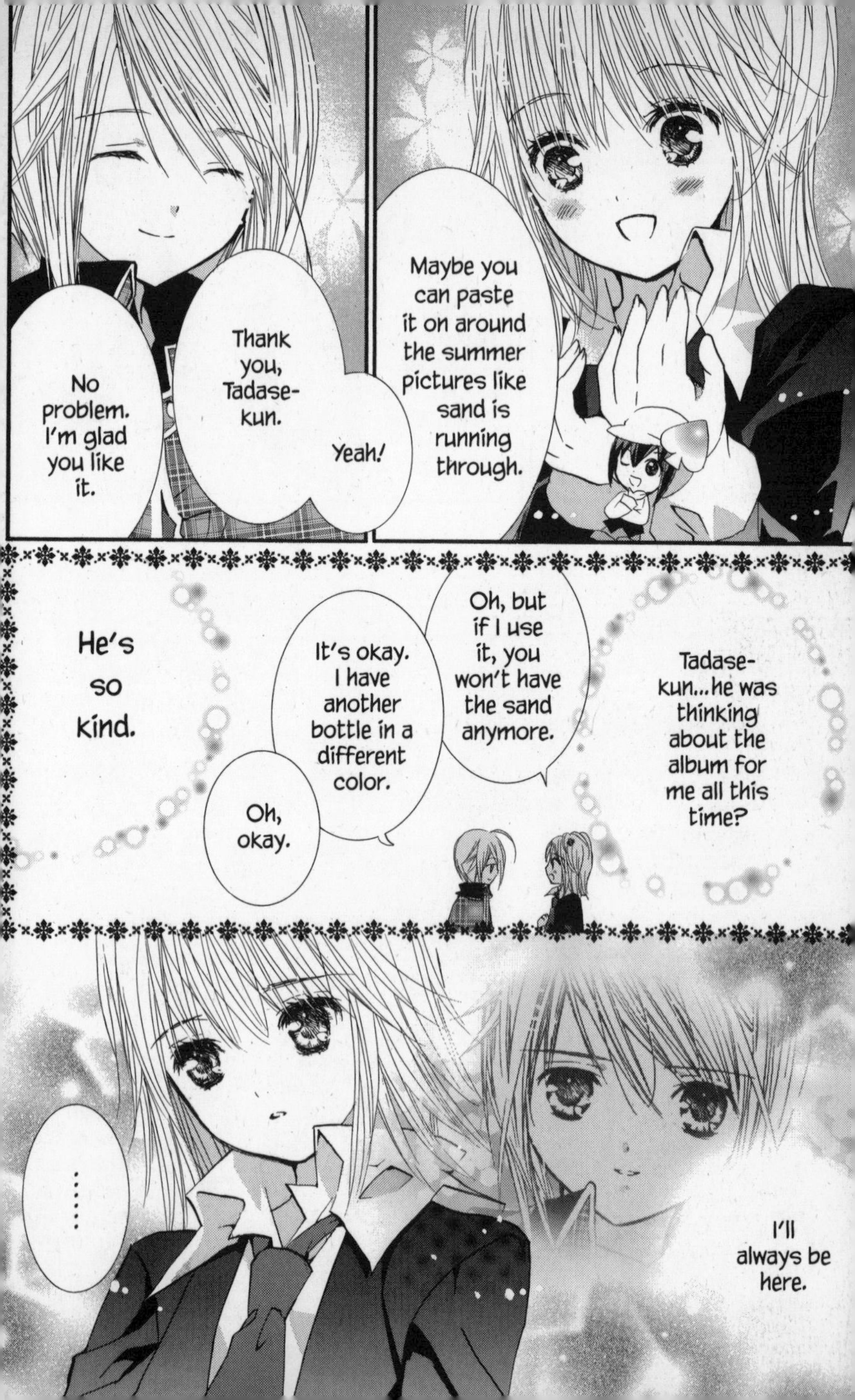
Maybe you can paste it on around the summer pictures like sand is running through.
Yeah!
Thank you, Tadase-kun.
No problem. I'm glad you like it.
Tadase-kun...he was thinking about the album for me all this time?
Oh, but if I use it, you won't have the sand anymore.
It's okay. I have another bottle in a different color.
Oh, okay.
He's so kind.
I'll always be here.
......

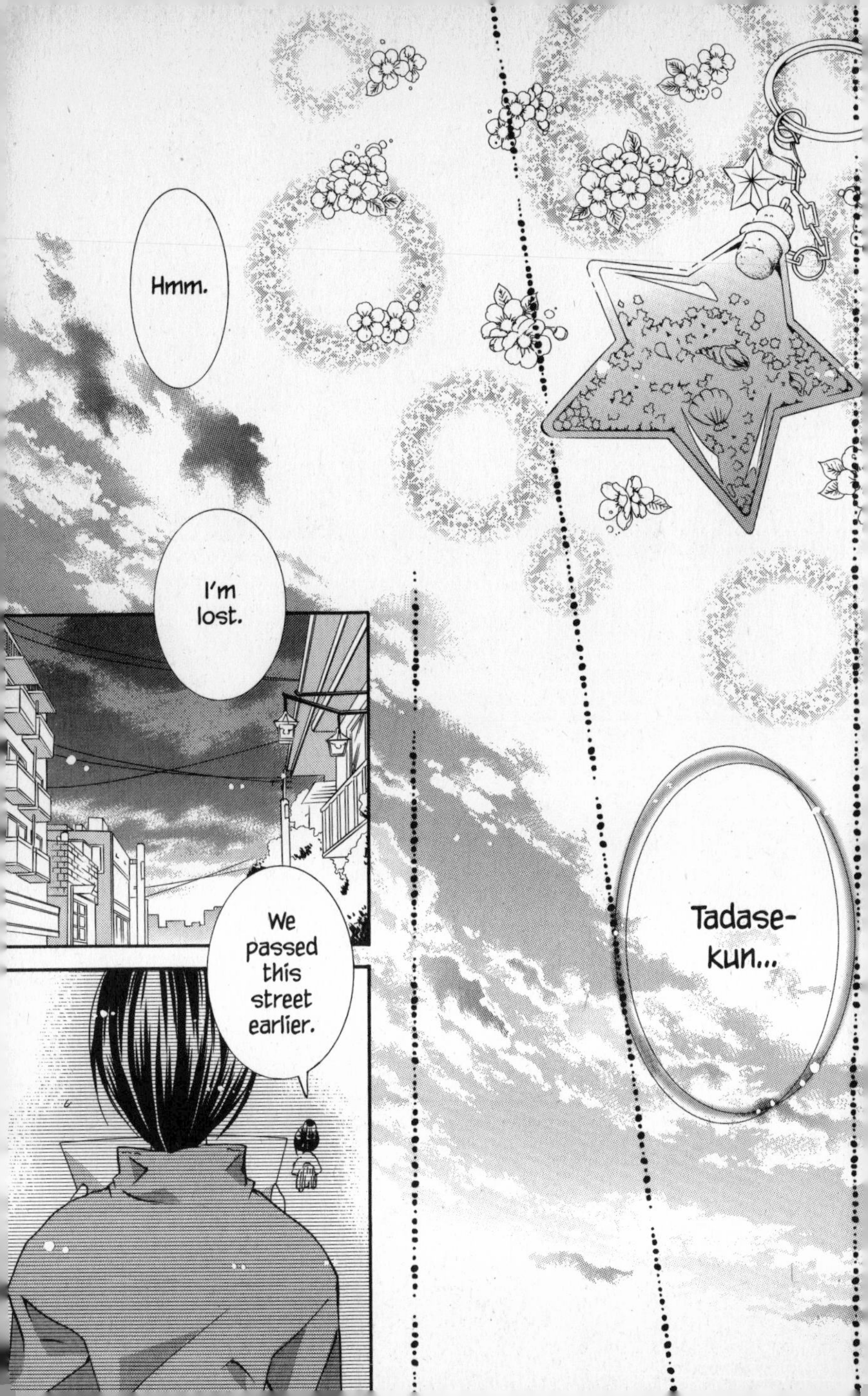
Tadase-kun...
Hmm.
I'm lost.
We passed this street earlier.

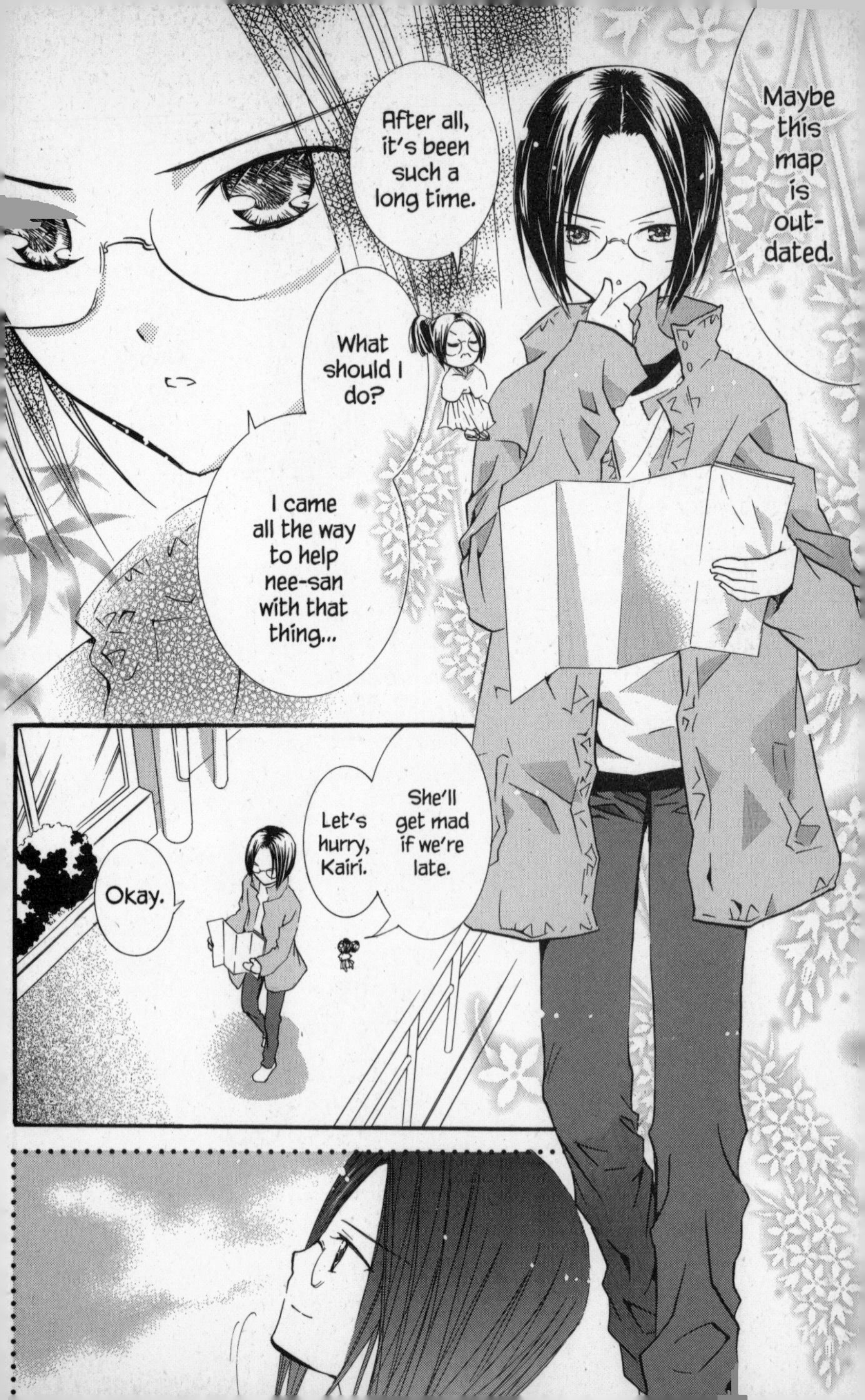
Maybe this map is out-dated.
After all, it's been such a long time.
What should I do?
I came all the way to help nee-san with that thing...
She'll get mad if we're late.
Let's hurry, Kairi.
Okay.

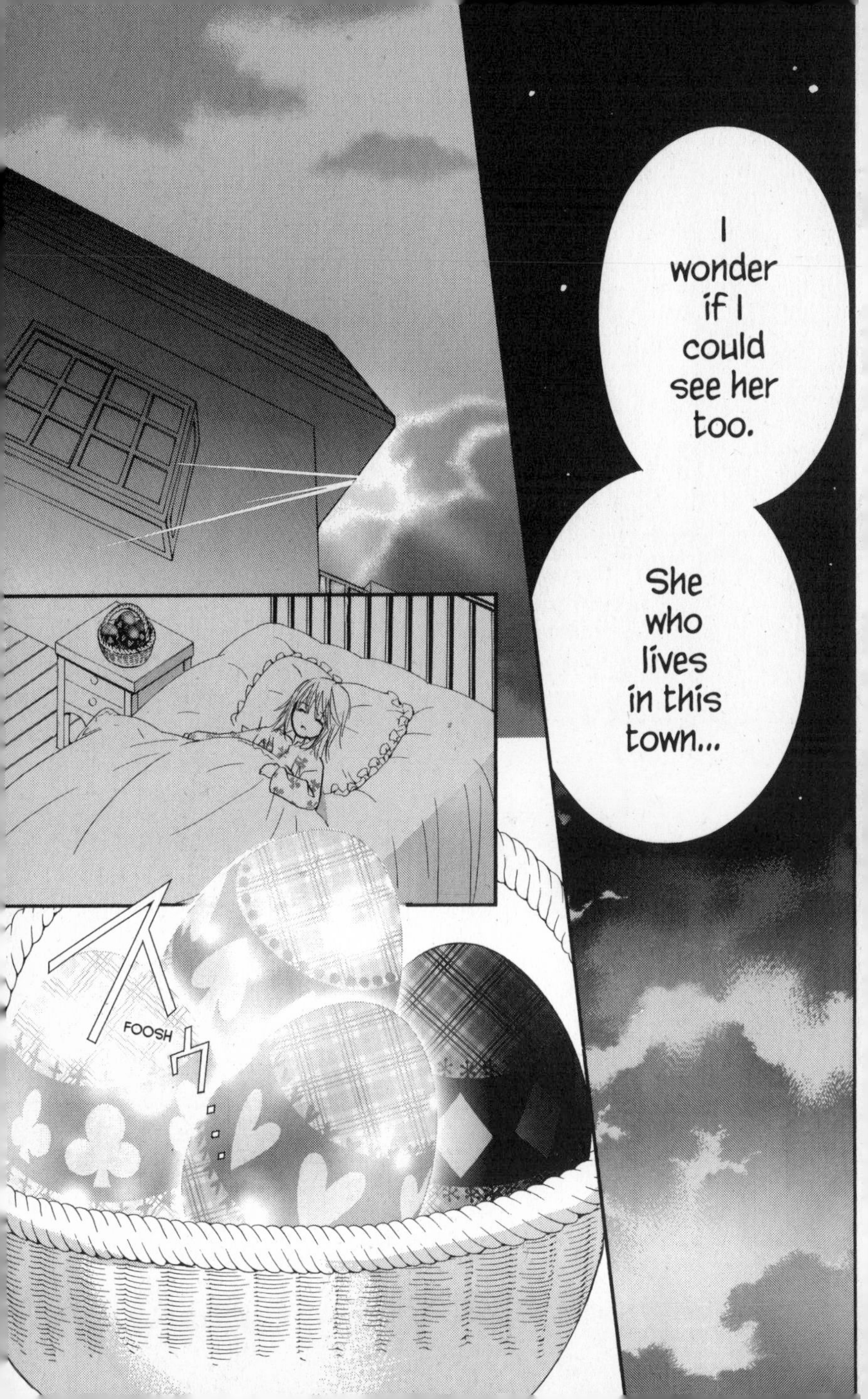
I wonder if I could see her too.
She who lives in this town...
FOOSH

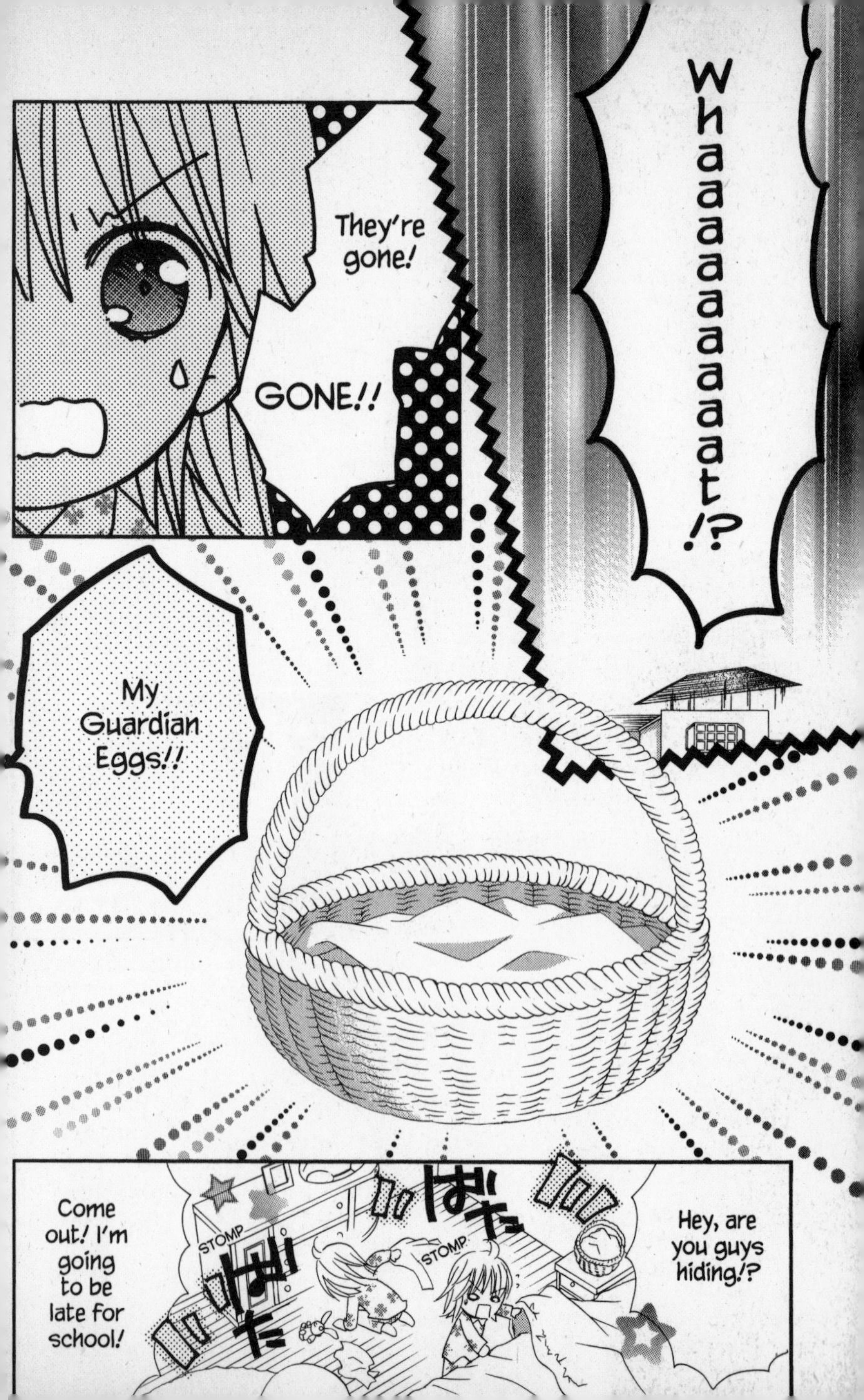
Whaaaaaaaat!?
They're gone!
GONE!!
My Guardian Eggs!!
Hey, are you guys hiding!?
STOMP
STOMP
Come out! I'm going to be late for school!

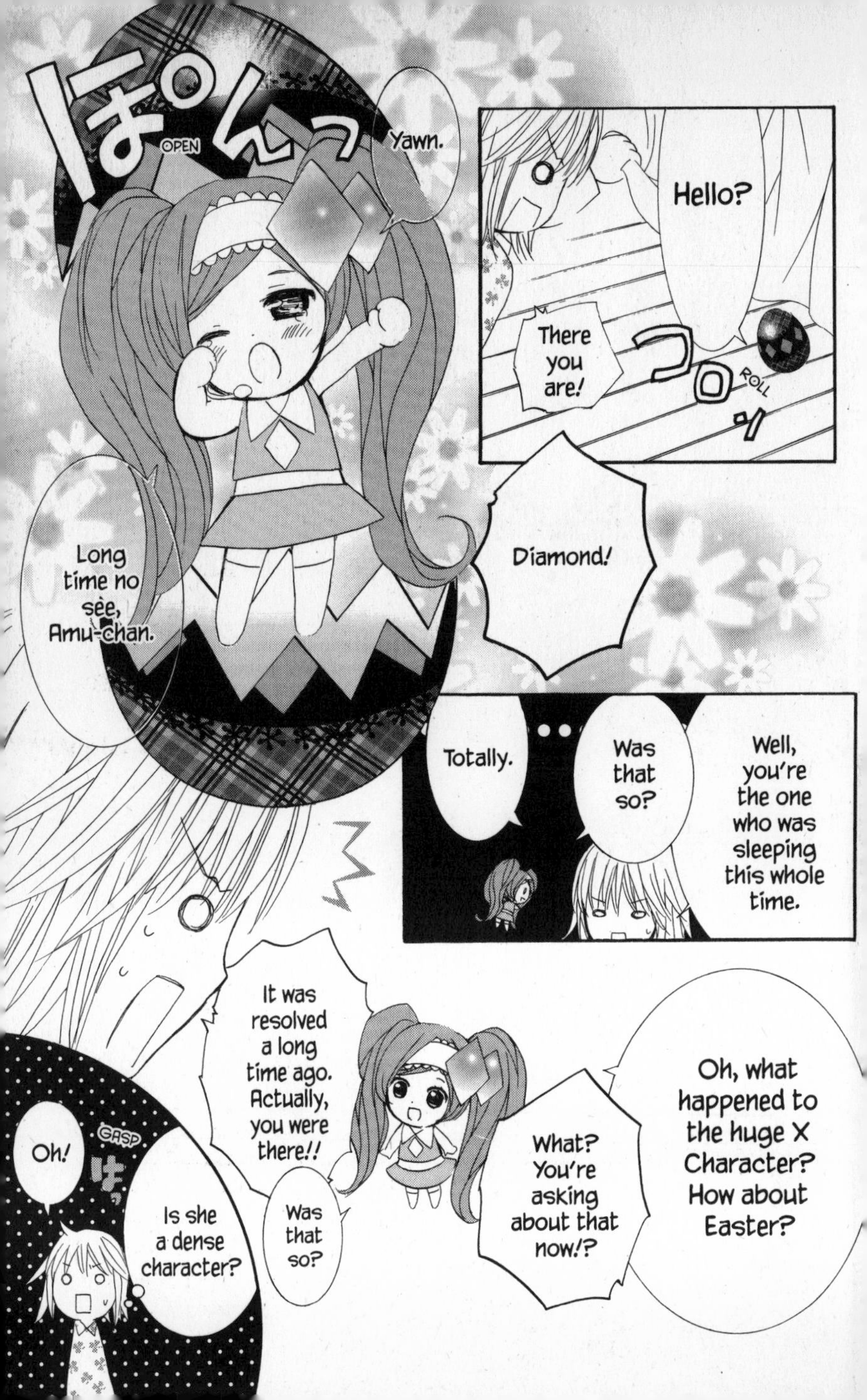

Hello?
There you are!
コロッ
ROLL
ぽんっ
OPEN
Yawn.
Diamond!
Long time no see, Amu-chan.
Well, you're the one who was sleeping this whole time.
Was that so?
Totally.
...
Oh, what happened to the huge X Character? How about Easter?
What? You're asking about that now!?
It was resolved a long time ago. Actually, you were there!!
Was that so?
は,
GASP
Oh!
Is she a dense character?

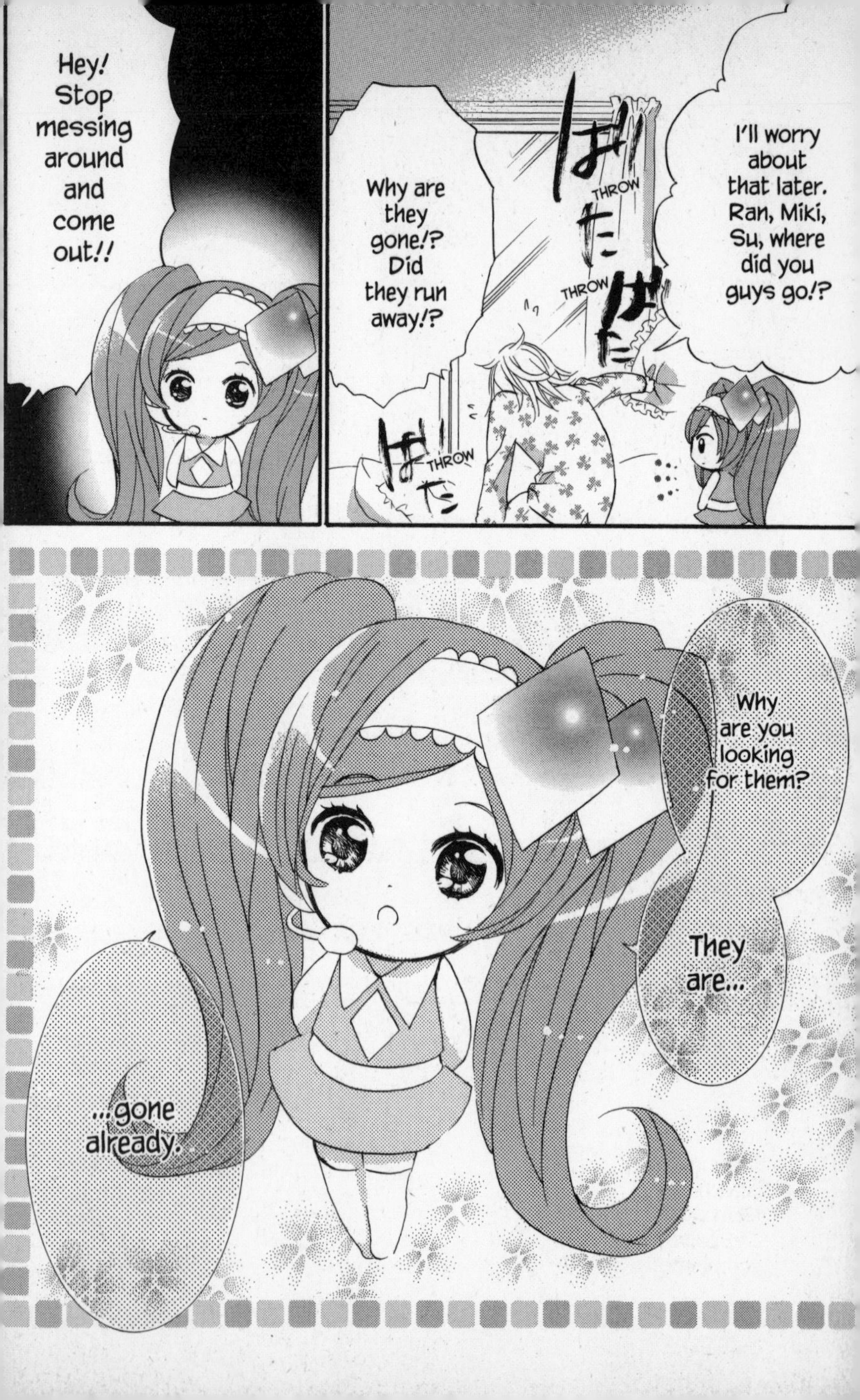
I'll worry about that later. Ran, Miki, Su, where did you guys go!?
THROW
THROW
Why are they gone!? Did they run away!?
THROW
Hey! Stop messing around and come out!!
Why are you looking for them?
They are...
...gone already.

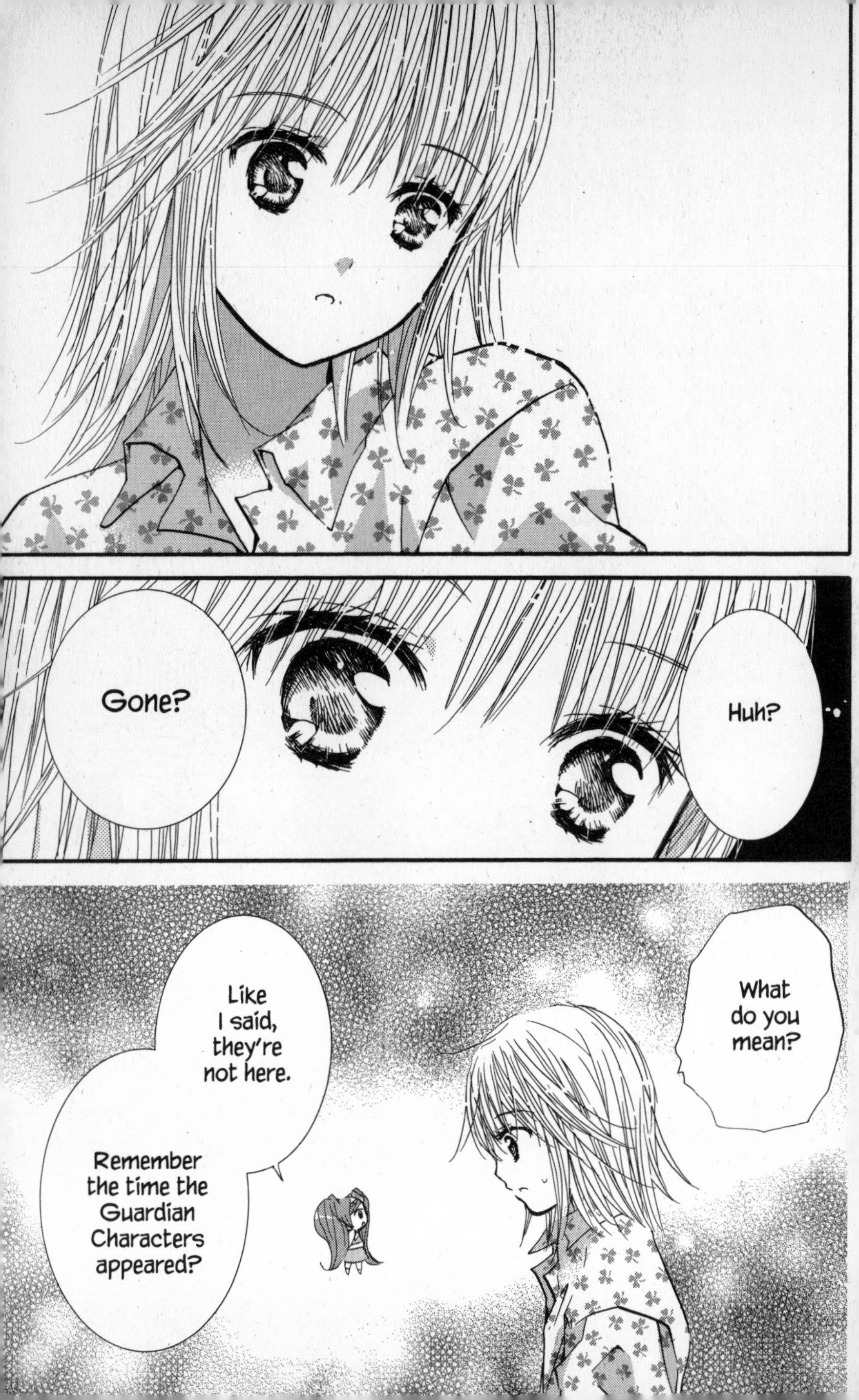
Huh?
Gone?
What do you mean?
Like I said, they're not here.
Remember the time the Guardian Characters appeared?

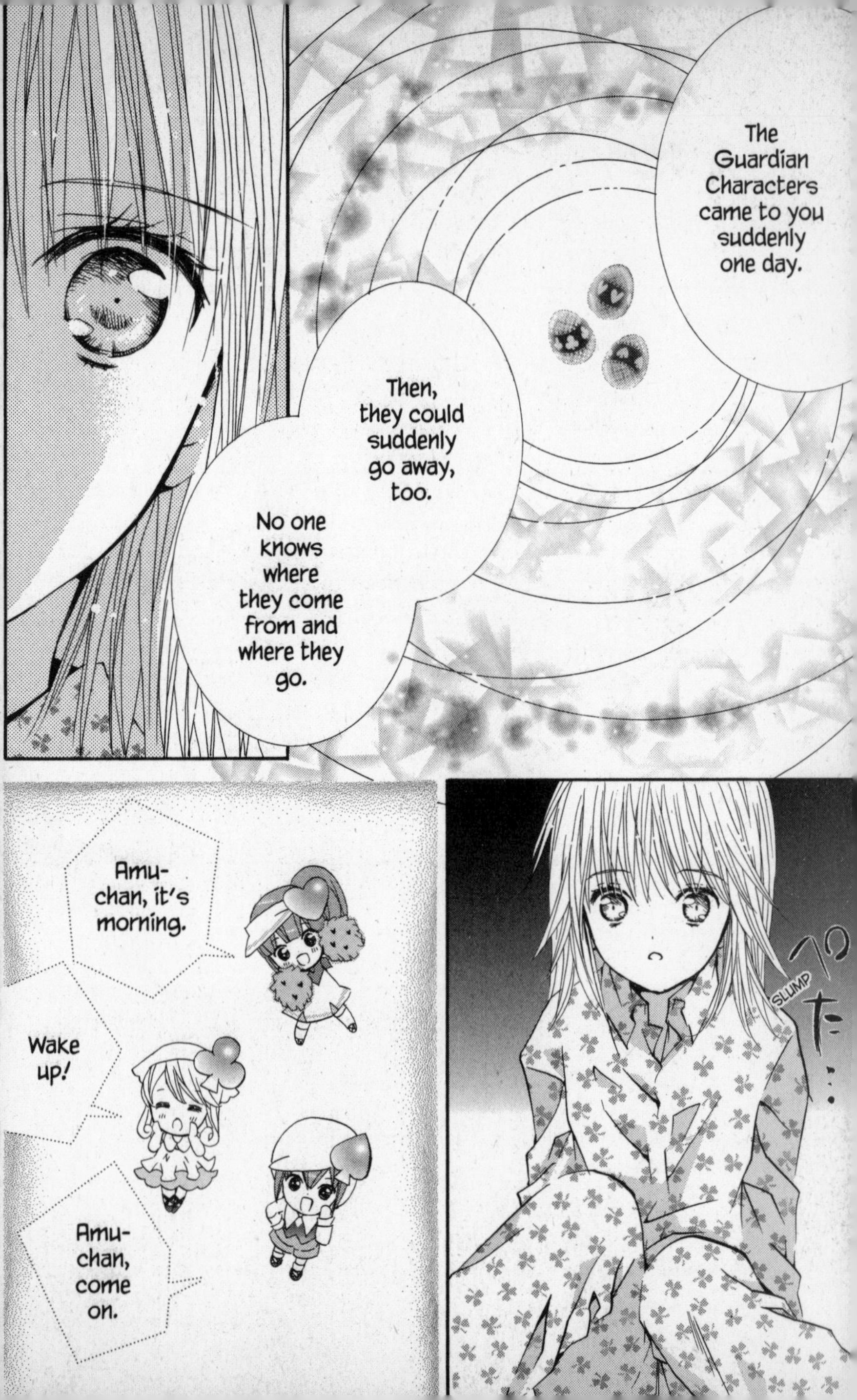
The Guardian Characters came to you suddenly one day.
Then, they could suddenly go away, too.
No one knows where they come from and where they go.
へた…
SLUMP
Amu-chan, it's morning.
Wake up!
Amu-chan, come on.

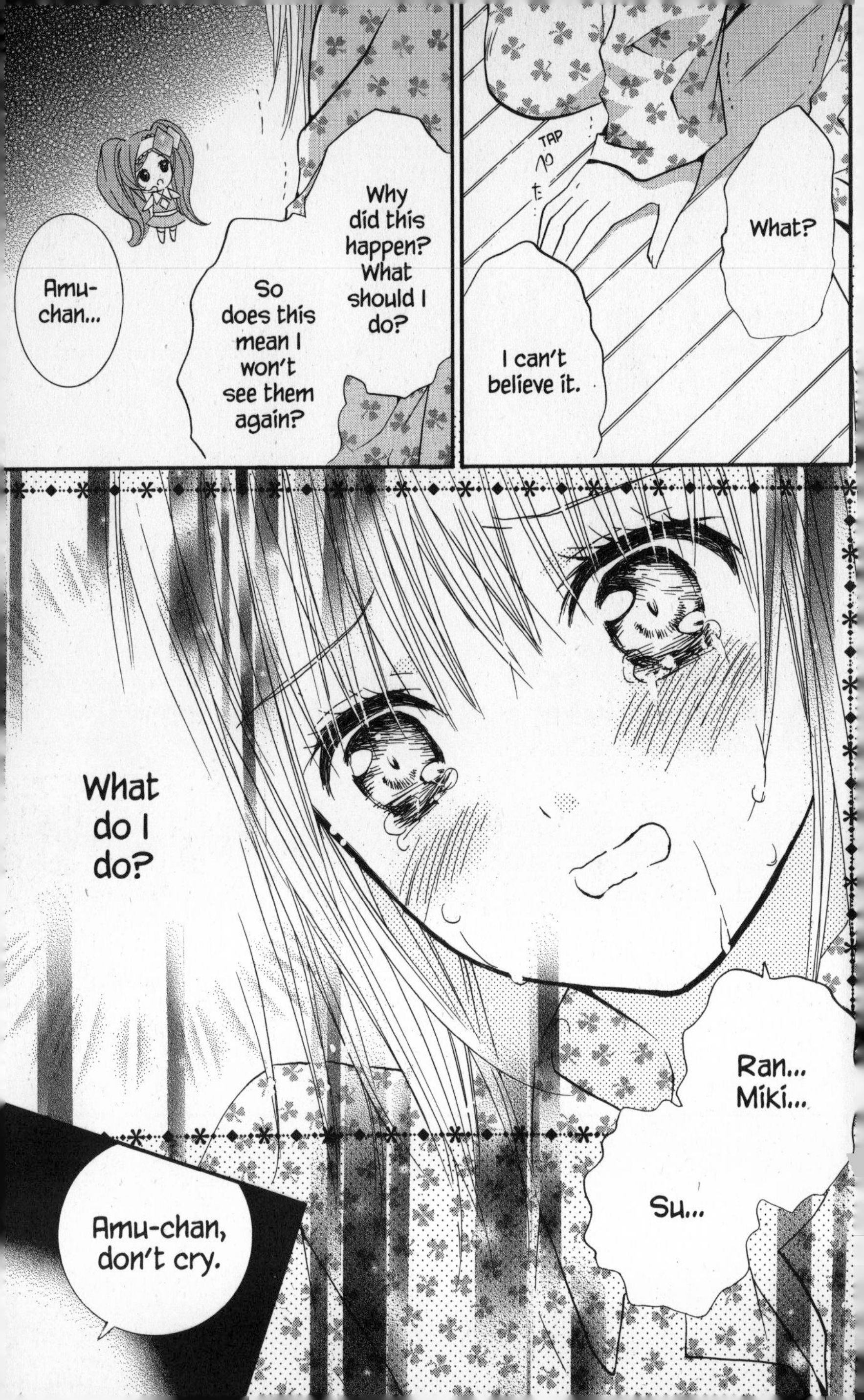
What?
TAP
I can't believe it.
Why did this happen? What should I do?
So does this mean I won't see them again?
Amu-chan...
Ran... Miki...
Su...
What do I do?
Amu-chan, don't cry.

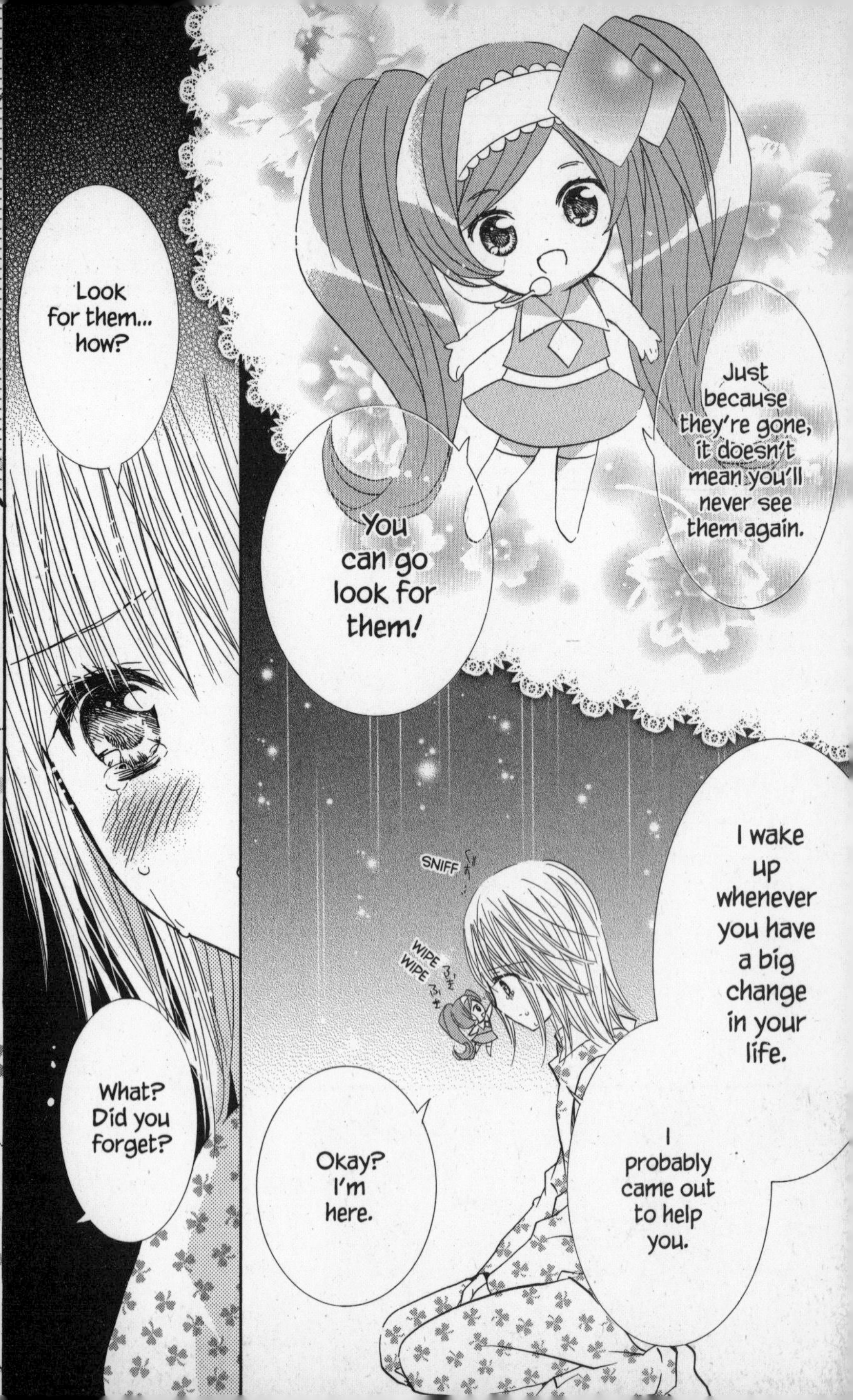
Just because they're gone, it doesn't mean you'll never see them again.
You can go look for them!
I wake up whenever you have a big change in your life.
SNIFF
WIPE WIPE
I probably came out to help you.
Okay? I'm here.
Look for them... how?
What? Did you forget?

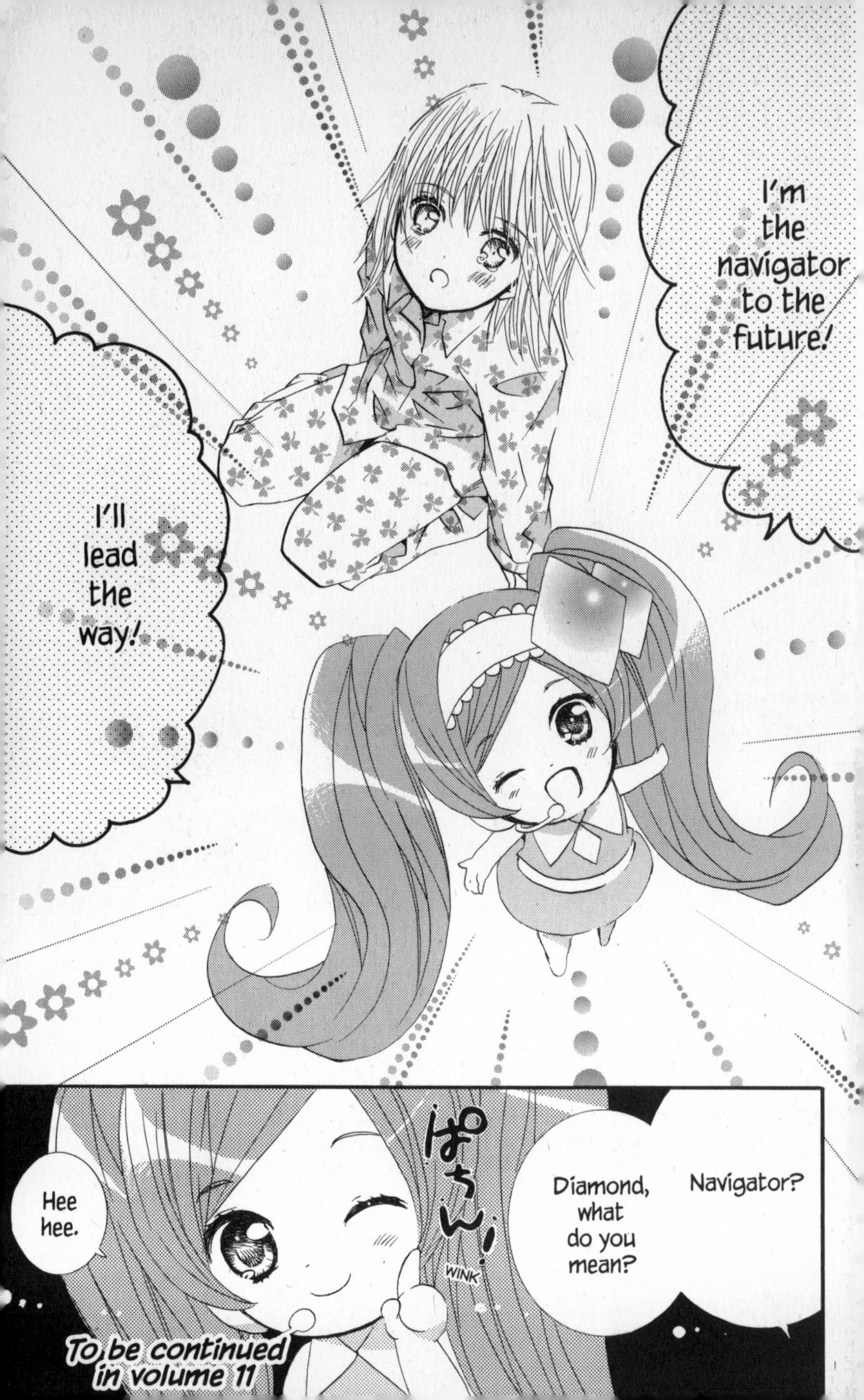
I'm the navigator to the future!
I'll lead the way!
Navigator?
Diamond, what do you mean?
ぱちん!
WINK
Hee hee.
To be continued in volume 11

About the Creators

PEACH-PIT:

Banri Sendo was born on June 7.
Shibuko Ebara was born on June 21. They are a pair of Gemini manga artists who work together. Sendo likes to eat sweets, and Ebara likes to eat spicy stuff.

Translation Notes

Japanese is a tricky language for most Westerners, and translation is often more art than science. For your edification and reading pleasure, here are notes on some of the places where we could have gone in a different direction in our translation of the work, or where a Japanese cultural reference is used.

Taiyaki, page 48

A taiyaki is a Japanese snack made with batter and filled with red beans. It is shaped like a fish. There are variations in what you can fill it with, which include cream, custard, or chocolate.

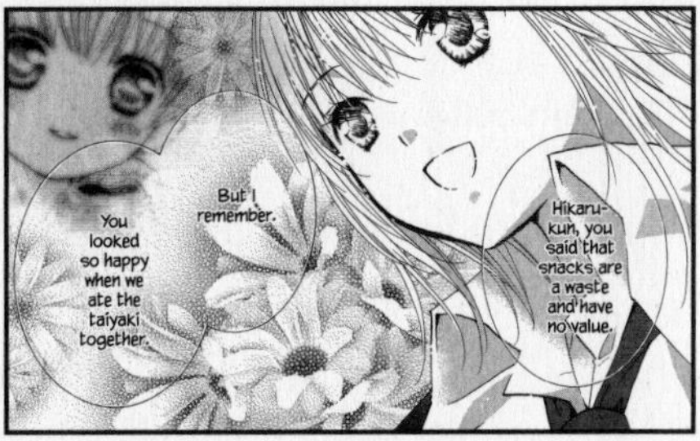
Hikaru-kun, you said that snacks are a waste and have no value.
But I remember.
You looked so happy when we ate the taiyaki together.

Ikuto, page 73

In Japanese, there are two pronunciations for numbers, one based on Chinese readings and the other based on Japanese reading. For example, the number "3" is "san" in Chinese reading and "mi" in Japanese reading.

In this case, "1" is read "i" from "ichi," the Chinese reading. The number "9" is read as "ku," the Chinese reading. The number "10" is read as "to," the Japanese reading. All of this connected reads "Ikuto."

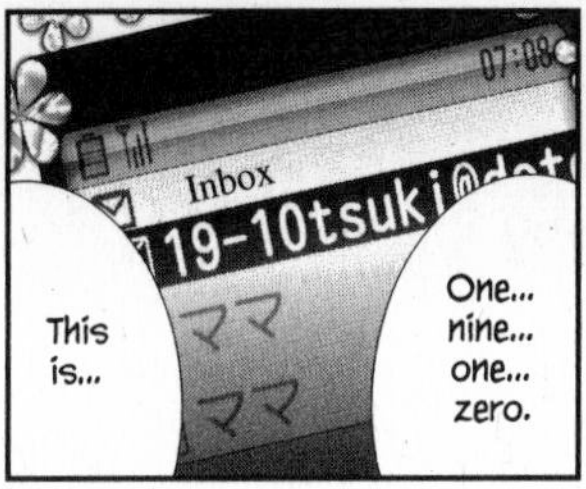
07:08
Inbox
19-10tsuki
ママ
ママ
One... nine... one... zero.
This is...

April, page 84

In Japan, the school year ends in March and the new school year begins in April. Therefore, graduations happen in March.

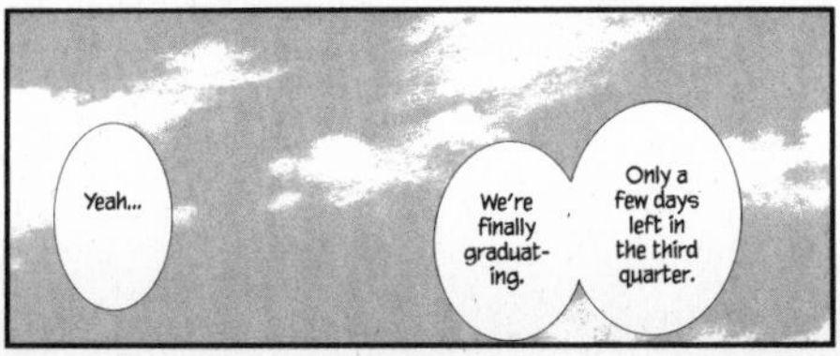
Only a few days left in the third quarter.
We're finally graduat-ing.
Yeah...

TOMARE!

[STOP!]

You're going the wrong way!

Manga is a completely
different type of reading
experience.

To start at the *beginning,*
go to the *end*!

That's right! Authentic manga is read the traditional Japanese
way—from right to left. Exactly the *opposite* of how American
books are read. It's easy to follow: Just go to the other end of the
book, and read each page—and each panel—from right side to left
side, starting at the top right. Now you're experiencing manga as it
was meant to be!